Bankruptcy in an Industrial Society

Bankruptcy in an Industrial Society

A History of the Bankruptcy Court for the Northern District of Ohio

M. Susan Murnane

University of Akron Press
Akron, Ohio

19 18 17 16 15 5 4 3 2 1

ISBN: 978-1-937378-81-3 (paper)
ISBN: 978-1-629220-15-4 (ePDF)
ISBN: 978-1-629220-16-1 (ePUB)

LIBRARY OF CONGRESS CATALOGING-IN-PUBLICATION DATA

Murnane, M. Susan, 1951– author.
Bankruptcy in an industrial society : a history of the bankruptcy court for the Northern District of Ohio / M. Susan Murnane.
p. cm.
Includes bibliographical references and index.
ISBN 978-1-937378-81-3 (pbk. : alk. paper) — ISBN 978-1-62922-015-4 (epdf) — ISBN 978-1-62922-016-1 (epub)
1. United States. District Court (Ohio : Northern District)—History. 2. Bankruptcy—Ohio—History. 3. District courts—Ohio—History. I. Title.
KF8755.O36M87 2015
346.7307'80269

2014029536

Cover: Image of the White Motor Company complex on St. Clair Avenue, June 27, 1926, from the Western Reserve Historical Society. Used with permission. Cover design by Amy Freels.

Bankruptcy in an Industrial Society was designed by Amy Freels, typeset in Minion with Helvetica Neue display type by BookComp, and printed on sixty-pound natural and bound by Bookmasters of Ashland, Ohio.

∞ The paper used in this publication meets the minimum requirements of ANSI/NISO Z39.48–1992 (Permanence of Paper).

Contents

List of Illustrations

List of Figures

Preface

Bankruptcy plays an essential role in market economies. Bankruptcy reduces the cost of credit by providing for fair and efficient debt collection. It furthers economic growth by releasing consumer demand. It facilitates entrepreneurial risk-taking by limiting the personal consequences of failure. It increases total social wealth by allowing rehabilitated debtors to resume productive activity. And, finally, it reallocates resources to more efficient uses. The development of bankruptcy law in America paralleled economic development, mirrored social change, and revealed power relations, but bankruptcy's history has received scant scholarly attention.

Despite its obvious importance, only three scholars have published book-length histories of bankruptcy in America: Noel F. Regis in 1919, Charles Warren in 1935, and David Skeel in 1995.[1] Recently, several important historical studies of specific periods in bankruptcy history have been published.[2] The Second Circuit Committee on History and Commemorative Events published a collection of essays in 1995 celebrating the Second Circuit Court's contribution to the development of bankruptcy law.[3] To date, this is the only scholarly historical investigation of a particular bankruptcy court, its relationship to the bar, and its impact on the community.

This book is a social and institutional history of the Bankruptcy Court for the Northern District of Ohio. It is not a history of bankruptcy law. I discuss bankruptcy law only to the extent necessary to understand events as they unfold in and around the bankruptcy court. Instead, I seek to explain the development of the court itself, of the people who worked there and of those who sought refuge in the bankruptcy court, within the context of northern Ohio's changing economy. In the process of narrating the story of this particular bankruptcy court, this book also describes the historical evolution of bankruptcy as an American institution.

The structure of this book is straightforward narrative history. In general, the chapters follow the development of the bankruptcy court chronologically. As the narrative moves through time, the chapters address northern Ohio's economic condition, the status of bankruptcy law and its practice in northern Ohio courts, the histories of the referees and bankruptcy judges, the development of the bankruptcy bar, and the evolution of the debtors. Because different issues become important at different times, different chapters focus on different themes. To the extent possible, the story is told from the point of view of northern Ohio's bankruptcy lawyers and referees. Much of the story is told through the eyes of long-serving Cleveland referee Carl D. Friebolin, who achieved legendary status as author of the Cleveland City Club's annual Anvil Revue from 1917 to 1965. Friebolin served as a referee in Cleveland from 1916 to 1967. His papers, which he donated to the Western Reserve Historical Society, are an invaluable resource on bankruptcy history.

This study originated as the brainchild of Randolph Baxter, then chief bankruptcy judge, who decided that the Northern District of Ohio needed a history of its bankruptcy court. He formed a historical committee, and the committee contacted the Western Reserve Historical Society for assistance. I heard about the project through historians' word of mouth, and I am deeply grateful for the opportunity to write this book.

I have acquired innumerable debts in the course of this project. First and foremost, I wish to thank the members of the historical committee for their unfailing support and encouragement. In particular, I wish to thank Judge Baxter, Judge Marilyn Shea-Stonum, and Judge Jessica Price Smith, who served on the committee as representative from the Commercial Law and Bankruptcy Section of the Cleveland Metropolitan Bar Association before her appointment to the bankruptcy court. Clerk of bankruptcy court Ken Hirz provided necessary organizational support for our meetings and uncomplainingly provided me with information, documentation, occasional office space, and access to the court's automated record system, PACER. John Grabowski at the Western Reserve Historical Society has been an invaluable resource in every possible way.

Historians always incur debts to librarians that we can never repay or even adequately acknowledge. In particular, I would like to thank Lisa Peters at the Case Western Reserve University School of Law library, Cleveland, Ohio; Jordan Steel at the National Bankruptcy Archives, Biddle Library, University of Pennsylvania School of Law, Philadelphia; Ann Sindelar at the Western Reserve Historical Society, Cleveland, Ohio; Paul Richert at the University of Akron School of Law library, Akron, Ohio; Kenneth W. Rose at the Rockefeller Archive Center, Sleepy Hollow, New York; Irene Milan, sixth circuit librarian, Cleveland, Ohio; Rita Wallace, sixth circuit librarian, Cincinnati, Ohio; archivist Robert Ellis at the National Archives and Records Administration, Washington, DC; archivist Scott Forsythe at the National Archives and Records Administration, Chicago, Illinois; Bill Rule at the Bankruptcy Judges Division, Administrative Office of the United States Courts; and Gwen Mayer at the Hudson Library and Historical Society, Hudson, Ohio.

This project involved trying to track down the names of many long-deceased lawyers who served as commissioners, registers, and referees in bankruptcy, sometimes only for short periods. I am indebted to librarians and volunteers at more local history and genealogy departments of county libraries throughout Ohio than I can possibly name. You know who you are. I wish to especially thank John Ransom at the Rutherford B. Hayes Presidential Center in Fremont, Ohio.

Many lawyers who made their careers in northern Ohio's bankruptcy courts have freely shared their memories and expertise with me. This book has been enriched immeasurably by their generosity. I wish to especially thank G. Christopher Meyer of the law firm Squire Sanders; Marvin Sicherman of the law firm Dettelbach, Sicherman & Baumgart; former bankruptcy judge Joseph Patchan, former United States trustee Saul Eisen; Case Western Reserve University professor Morris Shanker;

retired bankruptcy judges William J. Bodoh, David P. Snow, Harold F. White, and James H. Williams; and current bankruptcy judges Arthur I. Harris, Russ Kendig, Pat E. Morgenstern-Clarren, Richard L. Speer, Mary Ann Whipple, and Kay Woods.

This book has been improved immeasurably by the helpful comments of many generous readers. In particular, I wish to thank Case Western Reserve University Law School professor Kenneth F. Ledford, chief deputy clerk William A. Kurtz, Andrew L. Turscak Jr. of the law firm Thompson Hine, and his associate, James J. Henderson. Andy Turscak and Bill Kurtz proved especially valuable as readers because of the depth of their local knowledge in addition to their careful proofreading. The anonymous reviewers for the University of Akron Press offered perceptive suggestions for which I am deeply grateful. I also wish to thank Lisa Napoli for her patient editing.

No book gets written without financial support. In this case, I wish to thank the US District Court library fund, which provided most of the funds necessary to complete this project. I also wish to acknowledge the generous support from the Cleveland Metropolitan Bar Association, the Federal Bar Association, the Akron Bar Association, the Stark County Bar Association, the law firm Brouse McDowell, the law firm Squire Sanders, attorney Alan Lepene of the law firm Thompson Hine, Mary Bynum, and Ellen Toth.

One final note: I struggled with gendered pronouns and, ultimately, decided to use the old-fashioned system of male universals. Use of "he/she" proved too cumbersome, and substituting the plural "they" for the singular he or she grated on my ear. I am aware of the gendered implications of a male universal, but I know of no adequate substitute. Besides, in this story, until the 1980s almost all of the players were, in fact, men.

Chapter One
Introduction

The history of the Bankruptcy Court for the Northern District of Ohio is the history of the relationship between bankruptcy as a legal institution and the environment in which it operates. It is a complicated story, deeply influenced by the local legal culture, the careers of leading members of the bench and bar, and the economic history of the district. The economy of northern Ohio is highly representative of northern, midwestern, old-industrial America; northern Ohio pioneered modern industrial capitalism in the last quarter of the nineteenth century, and the tragedy of deindustrialization first appeared there one hundred years later. Consequently, the history of the bankruptcy court in the Northern District of Ohio offers a superb view of the relationship between law and society in modern industrial America, as both the institution of bankruptcy and the economic infrastructure of the society changed profoundly.

The Constitution authorized Congress to enact uniform bankruptcy laws, and Congress promptly did so, first in 1800 (repealed in 1803) and next in 1841 (repealed in 1842). In each case, financial panic preceded passage of bankruptcy legislation. The party in power was associated with northern commercial interests and secured passage of the bankruptcy legislation (Federalists in 1800 and Whigs in 1841), and when they lost power, the southern and western agricultural opposition (Jeffersonian Republicans in 1800 and Jacksonian Democrats in 1841) repealed the laws. Congress enacted the third federal bankruptcy law in 1867. The Panic of 1857 had returned bankruptcy to public attention, and the Civil War created financial chaos on a vast scale. The 1867 bankruptcy law was unpopular, and Congress repealed it in 1878. Immediately upon the law's repeal, commercial interests commenced lobbying for another bankruptcy law. In 1898, Congress finally enacted a bankruptcy law that, although highly contested at the time, proved to be permanent. Congress significantly revised the Bankruptcy Act of 1898 with enactment of the Chandler Act in 1938 and, again, with enactment of the Bankruptcy Code in 1978, but the basic structure of the bankruptcy law has endured.

This study follows the development of the Bankruptcy Court for the Northern District of Ohio from its prehistory in nineteenth-century Ohio insolvency law into the near present. Several interrelated threads twine together in telling this history. The bankruptcy courts changed over time from local, informal tribunals staffed by partisan political appointees paid on a fee basis to formal federal courts staffed by salaried judges with (almost) permanent tenure. The bankruptcy bar also changed as the bankruptcy courts and the bankrupts changed. The location of the story in northern Ohio furthers our understanding of the relationship between the bankruptcy courts and industrial society in America. Vitally important to the functioning of twentieth-century industrial capitalism, bankruptcy also facilitated American deindustrialization. The social and economic consequences of deindustrialization in the Midwest played out through the bankruptcy courts.

This book does not purport to expound a theory of historical development, but it informs important historiographic debates about the sources of institutional change. In particular, the history of the bankruptcy court resonates with an interdisciplinary social science theory called "American political development," which uses institutional and political history to explain the evolution of American political institutions from a decentralized "small state" governance system to the modern regulatory state.[1] Everything changed in America between 1880 and 1920. The American economy changed from a small-producer commercial economy to an urban industrial economy, and governmental institutions changed simultaneously. American political development scholars assume that economic change caused institutional change.

A related theoretical tradition called "law and society" developed after World War II at the University of Wisconsin Law School among students of legal historian J. Willard Hurst. Law and society arose in opposition to an older tradition that saw law and legal development as relatively autonomous from society. Most often, law and society adopts a functionalist view of the relationship between changes in law and changes in society that parallels American political development: legal forms change to meet changing social needs. In the 1970s, a new academic movement emerged called "critical legal studies" that critiqued functionalism and argued that the relationship between law and society is not simple or one directional. Instead, a more subtle relationship exists in which law performs an ideological function that creates the hidden infrastructure of society; it is one of the reasons why a society is the way it is. Critical legal studies acknowledges that law is not indifferent to changes in society but contends that law and society change in complicated interrelated ways. Sometimes changes in law produce changes in society, not the other way around.[2]

This study suggests that changes in bankruptcy law did not occur as simple responses to social or economic pressures but emerged as a result of multiple, sometimes inconsistent impulses and often produced unintended consequences. Congress passed significant bankruptcy legislation in 1898, 1938, and 1978, and in each case the legislation was behind the curve of history not responsive to it. In each case, the law in action created new issues that the law reformers neither anticipated nor desired. Changes in bankruptcy law changed the way industrial capitalism developed in America.

Bankruptcy and Industrialization

A dynamic national economy needs an institution like bankruptcy. Creditors need an efficient, uniform national procedure for collecting debts and resolving or reorganizing insolvent organizations, and risk-taking entrepreneurs need to be able to escape from the burden of debts resulting from economic failure in order to resume creative productive activity. Nonetheless, the American economy grew tremendously throughout the nineteenth century, even though there was no uniform national bankruptcy act except in a few short periods. After decades of lobbying, commercial business interests finally secured passage of the Bankruptcy Act of 1898. By that time, industrial capitalism was already well established and undergoing the first great merger movement.[3]

The Bankruptcy Act was enacted in the midst of the progressive state-building project at the end of the nineteenth century, and it is easy to imagine that bankruptcy evolved to meet the needs of an emerging industrial economy. But correlation is not causation, and it is not clear that the Bankruptcy Act of 1898 was enacted as a response to industrial capitalism. As enacted, the Bankruptcy Act of 1898 addressed a nineteenth-century economy that had already become a historical relic, at least in northern Ohio. The Bankruptcy Act of 1898 paralleled both the Bankruptcy Act of 1867 and the insolvency regime that Ohio had developed over the course of the nineteenth century. Most damningly, the Bankruptcy Act of 1898 made no provision for the two most important developments of the new economy: industrial corporations and consumer debtors.

Federal bankruptcy laws existed only for very limited periods before the enactment of the 1898 Bankruptcy Act, and state creditors' remedies attempted to ensure the orderly liquidation of debtors' estates for the benefit of creditors. State insolvency statutes attempted to mitigate the insolvent debtor's hardship—sometimes by freeing debtors from debtors' prison, sometimes by delaying the execution of creditors' remedies, and sometimes by preventing creditors from seizing everything in satisfaction of unpaid obligations. Typically, an insolvent debtor was able to protect from execution a minimum decent level of clothing and household furnishings and the tools necessary to pursue a living.

Only bankruptcy could discharge debtors from their debts, however, and the Constitution limited the states' ability to enact effective bankruptcy statutes. The Constitution prohibited states from passing laws impairing the obligations of contracts, and the Supreme Court ruled that such prohibition meant states could not pass laws discharging debts incurred before passage of their bankruptcy laws or discharging debts incurred in a different state.[4] Consequently, state bankruptcy laws had limited impact and were rarely enacted. Most states, including Ohio, passed insolvency statutes instead. In general, state insolvency laws adequately protected small producers who traded locally by allowing them to continue their lives in modest circumstances and reflected attitudes about the morality of debt that prevailed in many rural, interdependent communities in the nineteenth century.

Some scholars see the nineteenth-century American debate over bankruptcy as a proxy for the wider question: What kind of society would we be? Would we be a cosmopolitan commercial power on the world stage or a rural agrarian republic? The American economy grew enormously in the nineteenth century, but the growth occurred sporadically, in alternating cycles of booms and busts. Regular patterns of panic and depression produced recurring demands from commercial interests for a uniform national bankruptcy act. Less commercially oriented interests resisted, typically arguing that state insolvency laws adequately protected the legitimate concerns of honest debtors and morally condemning bankrupts as reckless and profligate. In Ohio, state court remedies remained very popular even after enactment of the Bankruptcy Act of 1898. Only after the enactment of the Chandler Act in 1938 did bankruptcy inevitably replace Ohio insolvency proceedings except in very rare, idiosyncratic circumstances.[5]

A more aggressive, long-distance, larger-scale capitalism emerged in the nineteenth century, penetrating different sections of the country and different sectors of the economy at different rates. Entrepreneurs began taking big risks in the hope of big rewards, and they needed access to the credit and capital of commercial centers. These entrepreneurs desperately needed a national bankruptcy act. In order to trade efficiently on a national scale, they needed uniform laws governing relations between creditors and debtors in which out-of-state commercial interests did not suffer undue discrimination. They also needed to be able to discharge debts in the event of failure. They could not resume their idea of a normal productive life with a small homestead and a few artisan tools. Instead, they needed renewed access to capital and credit and the ability to retain future profits for reinvestment in their enterprises. Historian Richard C. Sauer argues persuasively that the enactment of a permanent bankruptcy act in 1898 marked the final triumph of "commercial modernity" in a long-standing ideological struggle over the meaning of American freedom.[6]

The Bankruptcy Act eventually came to terms with industrial capitalism. The size and scope of industrial factories in the twentieth century changed everything. A community did not suffer greatly when a single small producer failed, but when a railroad or an industrial plant failed thousands of workers lost jobs and whole communities became endangered. Federal courts used receiverships to achieve corporate reorganizations not to save investors but to save workers' livelihoods and the viability of communities.[7] In 1938, Congress passed the Chandler Act, which brought corporate reorganization under the Bankruptcy Act. The Chandler Act also addressed consumer bankruptcies by creating wage-earner plans and other measures to enable debtors to make partial payment under the protection of the bankruptcy court.

Because passage of the Chandler Act corresponded with the Great Depression, it is tempting to think that the crisis of capitalism caused the reforms. However, the impetus for bankruptcy reform was fraud in the bankruptcy courts during the prosperous 1920s, not industrial collapse, and it is unclear what impact the reforms actually had. Corporate reorganization closely paralleled existing equity receivership practice in purpose and effect, and almost no consumer debtors used wage-earner plans, preferring simple discharge instead. Wage-earner plans benefited creditors, not debtors, and debtors generally avoided the plans. The Chandler Act's greatest impact may have occurred in the composition of the bankruptcy bar. The Chandler Act adopted a rule of economy that generated lower attorneys' fees in bankruptcy cases than in other areas of practice, and the elite corporate bar lost interest in reorganizations.

Meanwhile, a small, highly specialized, bankruptcy bar emerged in major cities that critics derisively called "bankruptcy rings."

Wage-earning consumers existed uncomfortably in the nineteenth-century social structure. Republican virtue and middle-class respectability derived from the ownership of productive property: family farms, small-scale artisanal manufacturers, and small shops.[8] Until about 1880, except for railroads and the big milling concerns of New England, most industrial production occurred in small establishments with few employees.[9]

Wage-earning became respectable at the end of the nineteenth century with the rise of large-scale enterprises. These businesses were managed in the corporate back office by a large number of educated, middle-class wage earners. An additional large number of educated, middle-class wage earners provided the enterprises with professional business services, such as law, accounting, credit reporting, sales, and advertising. By 1900, industrial manufacturing eclipsed agriculture in productivity, and by 1920, manufacturing wage-earning labor replaced small-scale farming as the typical occupation of ordinary working Americans.[10] By definition, wage earners are consumers. Instead of making the goods that sustain them, they spend their wages to buy what they need.

The Bankruptcy Act of 1898 freely allowed individuals a discharge of their debts without regard to whether the debts were incurred for business expenses or for personal consumption expenses; but the discharge was intended to benefit hard-pressed small producers like farmers, and little thought was given to the implications of freely discharging consumer debt. From the beginning, however, wage earners in financial difficulties took advantage of the discharge in large numbers. By 1920, consumer debt dominated bankruptcy, and since then consumer creditors have battled ceaselessly to place restrictions on the discharge of consumer debt. In an industrial economy such as ours, where consumer spending generates around 70 percent of total economic activity, it is tempting to conclude that allowing for the liberal discharge of consumer debt is functional, that it was intended to reduce economic friction, maintain consumer spending, and increase economic growth and stability. It is clear in retrospect, however, that it was an accident. The Bankruptcy Act of 1898 was not intended to facilitate the easy discharge of consumer debt, and ever since then, bankruptcy reformers have been diligently trying to stuff the genie back into the bottle.

Similarly, the development of corporate reorganization defies a simple causal relationship between law and society. From its invention in the nineteenth century as equity receivership to the present practice under Chapter 11, the dominant principle governing reorganization has vacillated between enforcing creditors' rights and protecting the broader community's interest in the continuation of the business. The state of the economy did not determine which of these principles was more important, but multiple factors influenced the question in complicated ways. Ultimately, the relative bargaining power among the parties to a reorganization—debtors, creditors, workers, and communities—affected the allocation of gains and losses and produced unanticipated and unintended consequences.[11]

Until passage of the Chandler Act in 1938, corporations could only liquidate in bankruptcy. Corporate reorganizations took place in federal court receiverships. Bringing corporate reorganization into bankruptcy offered significant procedural efficiencies, but Securities and Exchange Commission chair William O. Douglas had other concerns. He believed the managers of large corporations and their Wall Street lawyers manipulated the receivership process to their advantage at the expense of small shareholders and other minority interests. At Douglas's insistence, the Chandler Act created two tiers for corporate reorganization under the Bankruptcy Act: Chapter X reorganizations of large, publicly held corporations under the supervision of the SEC and Chapter XI arrangements for small, private corporations. Independent trustees replaced management in Chapter X reorganizations, and strict priority rules applied. Chapter XI arrangements presumed management would continue as debtors in possession of the corporation. Chapter XI arrangements only affected unsecured debts but allowed much more flexibility in negotiating a plan.

Douglas's reforms were so successful that Chapter X reorganization occurred infrequently, and most Wall Street law firms abandoned corporate reorganization as a practice area. Very few scholars studied Chapter X. In the 1960s, however, the Brookings Institution initiated a study of bankruptcy practices for the purpose of recommending reforms, and the study included an analysis of Chapter X. The Brookings Institution study concluded that Chapter X had been ineffective largely because management was loath to enter into reorganization until the firm had suffered such severe financial distress that it could no longer be saved. The Brookings Institution study led to the creation of a Bankruptcy Commission in 1970, and in 1978, Congress replaced the Bankruptcy Act with the Bankruptcy Code of 1978, which profoundly changed corporate reorganization law and had far-reaching consequences.

In the 1960s, bankruptcy law reform was not driven by changing economic conditions or dissatisfaction with corporate reorganization law. American industry still thrived in the 1960s, and the deterioration of the American economy lurked unforeseen in the future. Instead, a public outcry against the ease and frequency of consumer bankruptcy and corruption in its administration drove demands for bankruptcy reform, and the Brookings Institution study focused primarily on consumer bankruptcy not corporate bankruptcy. It appears that the bankruptcy policy community simply wanted to improve the social efficiency of corporate reorganization and had no appreciation of the potential for collateral damage.

The bankruptcy policy community wanted to save troubled corporations for the benefit of workers and communities, and the Brookings Institution study argued that a reorganization plan's chance for success improved significantly if the corporation filed earlier rather than later. Recognizing that management was the key to the reorganization decision, the bankruptcy policy community advocated merging the two corporate reorganization regimes into a single, flexible Chapter 11 of the Bankruptcy Code of 1978 that was mostly patterned on Chapter XI of the Bankruptcy Act.[12] Management generally fared well in Chapter 11. They retained control of the business at the commencement of reorganization and often received generous retention bonuses. If they were forced out later, they might also receive large severance payments as a reward for going quietly.[13]

In the 1970s, American industry struggled under a combination of adverse conditions: oil supply shocks, crippling inflation, global competition, and technological innovation. As corporations began reorganizing under the new Chapter 11, creative corporate reorganization lawyers quickly realized Chapter 11's strategic potential. Corporations found that they could use Chapter 11 reorganizations to unilaterally break union contracts, dump underfunded pension liabilities, avoid environmental cleanup costs, and limit mass tort liabilities. After purging their balance sheets of inconvenient liabilities, reorganized corporations enjoyed significant cost advantages over competitors that had not yet been through reorganization.

Congress had strengthened management's hand in Chapter 11 in order to rehabilitate corporations for the benefit of workers and communities and never imagined it would be used to achieve such destructive purposes. Chapter 11 has proven particularly useful at breaking labor unions. In 1979, 35 percent of manufacturing workers in the United States were union members. In 2011, 10.5 percent of manufacturing workers in the United States were union members.[14] Labor unions were unprepared for the possibility that Chapter 11 might be used to break labor contracts because National Labor Relations Board policy specifically prohibited unilaterally abrogating union contracts.

In 2005, Congress enacted business bankruptcy reforms that made Chapter 11 less advantageous to corporate management. The Bankruptcy Abuse Prevention and Consumer Protection Act encouraged the appointment of a trustee in a corporate reorganization if fraudulent financial reporting was suspected and imposed restrictions on executive compensation for corporate insiders. The Bankruptcy Abuse Prevention and Consumer Protection Act also strengthened the ability of governmental bodies to collect some debts, though it did not strengthen protections for labor-negotiated benefits.[15] Reducing management's control over reorganizations did not improve the negotiating position of workers or other community stakeholders. Changes had already occurred that decisively shifted the balance of power in favor of institutional creditors, and the number of Chapter 11 cases declined. Between 1994 and 2003, the total number of bankruptcy cases filed per year increased by an average of 8.53 percent per year, whereas the number of Chapter 11 cases filed decreased by an average of 4.13 percent per year.[16]

The debt structure of corporations changed in the 1980s, mostly because of innovations in the financial industry, and secured institutional debt became more important. Because most corporate assets secured preexisting institutional debt, debtors became dependent on their current creditors for debtor-in-possession financing. As a result, creditors could and did demand significant control over the reorganization process as a condition of continued financing. After 1991, trading distressed claims also became prevalent, allowing sophisticated investors to accumulate claims for the specific purpose of influencing Chapter 11 reorganizations. Simultaneously, organized creditor lobbies secured special exemptions for their collateral, and court decisions began moving toward narrow readings of statutory language and strict enforcement of contractual terms.[17]

All of these changes combined to alter the nature of Chapter 11 reorganization. Instead of being an institution for the rehabilitation of distressed corporations, Chapter 11 became a vehicle for selling corporate assets free and clear of claims and allocating the proceeds. Hard statistics are difficult to come by, but one widely used data set estimates that approximately 80 percent of Chapter 11 proceedings between 1980 and 1990 resulted in confirmed reorganizations, compared with 51 percent of bankruptcy proceedings between 2000 and 2002. Furthermore, 56 percent of the confirmed large business reorganizations that were completed in 2002 were asset sales, and 62 percent of the remaining cases implemented a deal that had been negotiated before the bankruptcy was filed.[18] Libertarian bankruptcy scholars argued that Chapter 11 should be abolished because the purposes of enforcing contractual claims and maximizing creditor value could be achieved more efficiently through other means.[19]

Chapter 11 did not cause the deindustrialization of the Rust Belt, but it influenced the distribution of gains and losses. In 1978, American industry was overdue for restructuring. Northern Ohio's steel mills and factories were old and technologically obsolete, and many suffered from a legacy of bad labor relations. No iron rule of history preordained the resulting devastation, however. Different legal regimes can produce different distributions of the efficiency gains accruing from economic restructuring. Chapter 11 distributed negotiating power overwhelmingly to management and institutional secured creditors. Workers and communities were reduced to the role of spectators to their own tragedy.

Institutional Change in the Bankruptcy Court

Just as substantive bankruptcy law changed over the course of the twentieth century, the institutional structure of the bankruptcy courts changed from isolated, informal proceedings funded by private fees to formal, government-funded courts fully integrated into a national judicial bureaucracy. The institutional development of the bankruptcy court and the judiciary as a whole occurred as part of a broader reconfiguration of the American state that began in the Progressive era. Often this reconfiguration is referred to as a state-building project; the transformation of the American state from a weak, decentralized state to a strong, centralized one.

In *Building a New American State*, political scientist Stephen Skowronek challenged the idea that we had a weak state in nineteenth-century America. Instead, he described American political development in the Progressive era as the change from one kind of state in the nineteenth century to a different kind of state in the twentieth century. Defining "state" as an "integrated organization of institutions, procedures, and human talents, whose specific purpose was to control the use of coercion within the national territory," Skowronek argued that the nineteenth century state achieved state-sanctioned coercion through a system of laws enforced through courts, primarily at the state and local levels.[20] Skowronek called it a state of courts and parties because political parties directed the system, not only through the election of legislators and other government officials but also through the exercise of political patronage in the courts. The state of courts and parties worked very well in nineteenth-century America. Most goods and services were produced locally by small producers. Most people lived in island communities separated from other communities by a primitive transportation and information infrastructure.[21]

The contemporary state is a very different kind of state. We live in an administrative state where most governance occurs through bureaucratic agencies staffed by politically insulated civil servants. The administrative state is situated in a highly interconnected, urban industrial economy. Most goods and services are produced in large, bureaucratically managed institutions dependent on sophisticated communication technologies over long distances and across borders. Most people earn salaries or wages and live by exchanging money for goods and services, in other words, by consuming.

The transformation from a state of courts and parties to an administrative state occurred in a rolling fashion, institution by institution. Most of the basic structure of the administrative state came into existence between 1877 and 1920. Federal courts were among the last institutions to change, and the history of the institutional development of the courts has not received much scholarly attention. Courts are unique state institutions. Even the bureaucratic, administrative state ultimately enforces its demands through courts. The history of the Bankruptcy Court for the Northern District of Ohio offers a case study of institutional change in the federal courts.

The early bankruptcy courts illustrate how the nineteenth-century system of courts and parties actually worked. Bankruptcy under the Bankruptcy Act of 1898 was very much a subsidiary function of the district court, which enjoyed almost complete administrative autonomy. Bankruptcy referees, like the registers in bankruptcy before them, were appointed and reappointed to two-year terms at the discretion of the district court. Paid out of fees from referred cases, referees worked out of their law offices scattered throughout the district, hired their own staff, and were accountable only to their referring judges. Referee in bankruptcy could be an extremely profitable office, and some of the appointees were excellent lawyers and administrators.

District court judges were (and are) the creatures of political organizations. Usually, the appointments of referees in bankruptcy were made on the basis of the referee's relationship with district court judges or their political sponsors, or with local political operatives. As the number of judges on the district court bench increased, district court judges from different political organizations needed to work out internal operating procedures for the exercise of patronage rights. Occasionally, failure to reach agreement on patronage appointments caused problems for the bankruptcy court. For example, the district court's inability to decide on the appointment of a referee for Youngstown in 1946 left the office open for several years to the great inconvenience of other referees. Eventually, the district court resolved the issue by internal agreement on the exercise of patronage rights.

Early twentieth-century progressives, intent on discrediting governance by political machine, strategically attacked partisan patronage as corrupt. The bankruptcy reform movement that ended with enactment of the Chandler Act in 1938 began with patronage scandals in the bankruptcy court for the Southern District of New York. Patronage scandals involving alleged bankruptcy rings also fueled the bankruptcy reform movement of the late 1960s. Sometimes, the scandals involved allegations that district court judges or referees received rewards for favoring certain bankruptcy professionals over others in appointing trustees, receivers, appraisers, and auctioneers. Sometimes, favored bankruptcy professionals cut deals to share bankruptcy work at the expense of the bankruptcy estate. The attempt to control patronage in bankruptcy eventually led to the creation of independent bankruptcy courts staffed by bankruptcy judges with secure tenure and the creation of the Executive Office for United States Trustees in the Department of Justice.

Among the few scholars to study institutional change in the federal courts, legal sociologists Wolf Heydebrand and Carroll Seron describe rationalization of the district courts in terms highly reminiscent of Skowronek's description of American political development: a transformation from organizations run by elite professionals that delivered adjudication services to administrative agencies efficiently moving caseloads. This transformation occurred through the development of a bureaucratic organizational structure and the introduction of business methods to case management, including the concepts of efficiency, cost effectiveness, and productivity.[22] Bankruptcy case loads were enormous from the beginning. The need for effective and efficient administration, together with periodic episodes of bankruptcy fraud, spurred the development of judicial management controls. The institutional development of bankruptcy within the judicial system accelerated rationalization of the judiciary as a whole.

The creation of a bureaucratic organizational structure for the district courts began with the Judicial Code of 1911, which separated the district courts into the trial courts of the federal system and created the circuit courts as appellate courts that reviewed district court decisions. The circuit courts had no administrative authority over the district courts, and the district courts continued to enjoy almost complete autonomy. The Department of Justice, created in 1870, submitted an annual report to Congress on the state of the judiciary, including bankruptcy, and managed the court system's appropriations requests. After 1914, Department of Justice examiners also audited court accounts. The discovery of widespread irregularities in bankruptcy accounts led to tighter administrative controls and more frequent audits.

The Department of Justice had no supervisory authority over the courts, and the court system had no internal administrative infrastructure. In 1922, Congress created the Conference of Senior Circuit Judges, later known as the Judicial Conference of the United States, to improve the administration of justice through research and recommendation, but the Judicial Conference had no administrative authority over the lower courts. One of its first actions was to create a joint committee with bar associations and other concerned professional organizations to study the need for improvements in bankruptcy administration. The bar associations complained that bankruptcy rings were looting estates, and the Supreme Court passed amendments to the general orders that were designed to prevent attorneys, receivers, and trustees from soliciting claims in bankruptcy. Investigations initiated as a result of the allegations of corruption in bankruptcy courts ultimately resulted in the enactment of the Chandler Act in 1938.

In 1939, Congress created the Administrative Office of the United States Courts as the bureaucratic infrastructure for self-governance in the judicial system. The chief justice of the United States appointed the director of the Administrative Office, and the director hired the agency's staff. The Administrative Office assumed responsibility for the functions previously performed by the Department of Justice: budgeting, procurement, auditing court accounts, examining court dockets for management and statistical purposes, and reporting to Congress. The Administrative Office also acquired administrative authority over clerical and administrative employees in the judiciary, but it lacked the authority to take any disciplinary action. The Administrative Office could only recommend appropriate action to the district court, but it reported directly to newly created circuit judicial councils that had supervisory power over the district courts in their circuits.

As the federal judiciary slowly organized itself bureaucratically, bankruptcy courts became fully integrated into the new structure. In 1942, the Judicial Conference established a Bankruptcy Division in the Administrative Office, which developed model rules and forms and worked to improve bankruptcy administration through analysis and persuasion. In 1946, Congress passed the Referees' Salary Act, which made referees full-time salaried employees with six-year terms of appointment. Although district courts still appointed referees primarily for patronage reasons, the Salary Act imposed some restrictions on the district courts' discretion. The Administrative Office recommended the number of referees that could be appointed in a district and the locations of their offices, subject to approval by the circuit judicial councils. The Salary Act also allowed circuit judicial councils to remove a referee for cause, if the district court did not do so, and to disallow the reappointment of a referee upon the recommendation of the Bankruptcy Division of the Administrative Office.[23]

Eventually, the Bankruptcy Division of the Administrative Office would become deeply involved in the supervision and management of bankruptcy courts, but it had few employees at first. The first chief of the Bankruptcy Division, Edwin L. Covey, influenced the operation of bankruptcy courts primarily through persuasion and example. Bankruptcy was not a court of record, and bankruptcy procedure varied greatly among referees. In the Northern District of Ohio, deference to long-serving referee Carl D. Friebolin created a de facto administrative infrastructure long before the creation of formal institutions. Appointed referee in 1916, Friebolin served as referee in Cleveland until 1967. He enjoyed the reputation of a scholar and an intellectual and served actively in the National Association of Referees in Bankruptcy and the National Bankruptcy Conference from their origins in the 1920s until 1965. Friebolin also trained most of the attorneys that practiced in northern Ohio's bankruptcy courts, formally through his classes at Case Western Reserve University Law School and informally through an after-hours class for practitioners known as "Friebolin College."

In 1971, Congress authorized the circuit judicial councils to appoint circuit executives to direct all nonjudicial functions of the circuit under the direction of the chief judge of the circuit. By 1978, when Congress created independent bankruptcy courts, a fully functioning federal judicial bureaucracy existed. Congress did not finally resolve the manner of appointment of bankruptcy judges to the new bankruptcy courts until 1984. The Bankruptcy Amendments and Federal Judgeship Act of 1984 profoundly changed the way bankruptcy judges were selected, their tenure, and the structure of the bankruptcy courts.[24] Instead of US district court judges making bankruptcy judge appointments, the circuit court appointed bankruptcy judges after formal screening by several tiers of committees composed of lawyers from leading big firms, bar association representatives, judges, and academics. As a result, bankruptcy judge appointments became less influenced by local partisan politics and more influenced by the candidates' status within the organized legal profession.

Although the district court lost the power to appoint bankruptcy judges after 1984, it retained significant influence over the bankruptcy court in other ways. As a unit of the district court, the bankruptcy court was bound by the district court's local rules. District court judges retained the power to appoint the chief judge of the bankruptcy court in their district, and they heard bankruptcy matters that extended beyond the jurisdiction of bankruptcy judges. They also heard bankruptcy appeals. Bankruptcy judges assumed managerial control over a separate clerk of bankruptcy court, however, and after 1994, heard appeals of bankruptcy decisions in some cases through a Bankruptcy Appellate Panel. The boundaries of power between the bankruptcy court and the district court have continued to be contested, and the United States Supreme Court decisions in *Stern v. Marshall* and *Executive Benefits Insurance Agency v. Arkinson* have reignited the debate over the limits on bankruptcy court independence.[25]

Heydebrand and Seron argue that district courts lost judicial independence as a result of their integration into larger management organizations. As caseloads increased without proportional increases in resources, Heydebrand and Seron argue that efficiently managed courts sacrificed traditional notions of due process and rule of law in favor of expedited procedures at the expense of all but the most powerful litigants.[26] The experience of the bankruptcy courts offers a different perspective. Creatures of and jurisdictionally dependent on the district courts, bankruptcy courts benefited from the bureaucratic integration of the district court. The restrictions the administrative agencies of the organized judiciary placed on the judicial independence of the district court gave bankruptcy courts functional autonomy. The independent bankruptcy courts adjudicated with more procedural formality than was possible with referee procedures under the authority of the district court.

The steady increase in bankruptcy cases, particularly consumer bankruptcy cases, has driven bankruptcy reform from the 1920s to the present. The increase became acute in the 1950s, which many commentators attributed to the rise of a decadent consumer society. The number of bankruptcy cases filed in the United States increased from 33,392 in 1950 to 110,064 in 1960, 194,399 in 1970, and 331,264 in 1980. The increase in the number of cases was not a phenomenon unique to bankruptcy. Caseloads also increased dramatically in the US district courts, although less so than in bankruptcy. In 1890, 26,244 US cases closed in the district courts, whereas approximately 20,128 bankruptcy cases were filed in 1900, the first full year of the act's operation. In 1988, 279,739 cases closed in the district courts, but 613,465 bankruptcy cases were filed. Most of the increase in district court cases occurred after 1960, and civil cases accounted for the greater portion of the increase. In 1890, 39 percent of terminated district court cases were civil; in 1988, that number increased to 85 percent. Total civil cases closed more than doubled between 1970 and 1980, from 80,435 closed civil cases in 1970 to 169,481 in 1980.[27]

Bankruptcy referees and judges, and their clerks, successfully pioneered techniques for the efficient administration of a large volume of cases by aggressively using business management techniques, computer technology, and automation. Bankruptcy courts faced an existential threat if they proved unable to efficiently administer consumer bankruptcy cases. In both of the major bankruptcy reform movements of the twentieth century—the reform movement in the 1920s that culminated in the Chandler Act and the reform movement in the 1960s that culminated in the Bankruptcy Code of 1978—reformers advocated removing consumer bankruptcy cases from the bankruptcy courts and administering them through a separate agency in the executive branch of government.

Bankruptcy referees and bankruptcy judges successfully defended against radical administrative reform by embracing more incremental changes. The Chandler Act introduced wage-earner plans as an alternative to consumer bankruptcy. The Bankruptcy Reform Act of 1978 introduced the United States Trustee Program as an agency of the Department of Justice to assume the administrative functions previously performed by referees. US trustees also policed the bankruptcy bar to prevent bankruptcy fraud. By aggressively pursuing efficient administration and cost-effective procedures, the bankruptcy courts were able to preserve consumer bankruptcy as a judicial matter.

Bankruptcy as Ideology

The Bankruptcy Act of 1898 created a nineteenth-century institution for a twentieth-century economy. Originally designed as a small-government solution to a big-government problem—the need of creditors who did business in a national market for a uniform system of collecting debts from distant business debtors—the act placed the bankruptcy function under the control of highly political, decentralized, local district courts. By the time Congress enacted the Bankruptcy Act of 1898, however, the American economy had already changed. Industrial capitalism had created a wage-based consumer economy. The bankruptcy system proved remarkably adaptive to this new economy and became one of the foundational institutions of twentieth-century industrial capitalism.

The idea of a national uniform bankruptcy act was very controversial throughout the nineteenth century. Business interests in large urban centers advocated ceaselessly for a national bankruptcy act, and rural, agrarian interests opposed it. The debate over bankruptcy paralleled a deeper debate over the meaning of America. During the nineteenth century, an ideological battle raged between those who believed expanding commerce and industry promoted a unified American nation able to hold its own on the world stage and those who grounded republican virtue in local institutions and small-scale proprietary capitalism.

Commerce and industry won the debate, and bankruptcy ceased being a political issue within a few years after enactment of the Bankruptcy Act of 1898. The Bankruptcy Act was rarely amended, and bankruptcy professionals and academics dominated bankruptcy policy making. Over the course of the twentieth century, the bankruptcy courts became deeply embedded in society and the economy. Consumer bankruptcy grew from an unintended consequence of political compromises with rural interests to the dominant function of bankruptcy courts. Consumer bankruptcy assumed the critical role of ameliorating class tensions in an industrial society. Easy consumer discharges released consumer demand and facilitated economic growth.

Toward the end of the twentieth century, the bankruptcy policy community was surprised to find that consumer bankruptcy had become controversial. The renewed controversy reflects the increasing power of a new conservative political movement rather than a fundamental alteration in the relations between debtors and creditors and the relations between capital and labor. Consumers' financial condition became more fragile after 1980, and the safety-valve function of consumer bankruptcy should have become more highly valued. Instead, a small-government vision of America gained political strength, in which liberty is defined primarily as the ability to do as one pleases with one's money with minimal government interference. One of the acceptable functions of government in this vision, however, is to make people take responsibility for paying their just debts. The new political forces self-consciously identified with an older America inhabited by self-reliant small producers. The twentieth-century bankruptcy policy consensus directly contradicted this vision of America.

Once again, bankruptcy became a proxy in a broader ideological debate over the nature of America. The bankruptcy policy community envisioned bankruptcy as a necessary mediating institution in a complicated, interdependent global economy in which individual wage earners are powerless. The new conservative movement views consumer bankruptcy as a symptom of a morally lax society and seeks to reestablish a moral economy of debt.[28] Bankruptcy redistributes resources from hard-working, self-reliant, economically productive people, and the new conservative movement considers any involuntary redistribution illegitimate unless it occurs as a result of market forces. The conservatives won a major policy victory with enactment of the Bankruptcy Abuse Prevention and Consumer Protection Act of 2005, which restricted consumer discharges, and they have so far successfully repelled any pressure to increase the scope of consumer bankruptcy in the great recession that began after the housing bubble burst in 2007.

The American economy changed profoundly in the last quarter of the twentieth century, especially in places like northern Ohio. Old factories closed, jobs moved away, and pensions and health benefits evaporated. Although new factories opened and new jobs emerged, the structure of the economy has changed. Increasingly, big, capital-intensive factories with thousands of unionized workers have been replaced by highly productive manufacturing facilities run by a few highly skilled, nonunion workers. Service industries make up an increasing proportion of American economic activity, even in Rust Belt Ohio. The industrialization of the American economy at the turn of the twentieth century changed everything. The deindustrialization of America may prove to be equally transformative.

Northern Ohio has been on the leading edge of social and economic change in America. Industrial capitalism began in northern Ohio, and the first symptoms of deindustrialization emerged there. The history of the bankruptcy court for the Northern District of Ohio provides a unique perspective on the change process. The bankruptcy court was one of the state-building institutions formed at the birth of industrial capitalism, and the institutional development of the court opens a window on the growth of bureaucratic institutions in the judiciary. Consumer bankruptcy illustrates how wage earners learned to cope with the uncertainties of industrial society, and corporate reorganization in bankruptcy facilitated deindustrialization. By illuminating the relationship between legal institutions, economic structure, and social change, the history of the bankruptcy court for the Northern District of Ohio contributes to the ongoing policy debate over the role of bankruptcy in a democratic society.

Chapter Two

Insolvency and Bankruptcy in Nineteenth-Century Ohio

Bankruptcy attempts to solve two related problems: (1) how to ensure the orderly and equitable payment to a debtor's creditors and (2) whether to treat insolvent debtors as criminals, victims, or something in the middle. Although the problems created by debts and debtors are as old as humanity, the first English bankruptcy law was not enacted until 1542, during the reign of Henry VIII. The US Constitution specifically authorized Congress to pass a uniform national bankruptcy law, and Congress periodically passed temporary bankruptcy acts: in 1800 (repealed in 1803), in 1841 (repealed in 1842), and in 1867 (repealed in 1878). Finally, in 1898 Congress enacted a permanent bankruptcy law. For most of the nineteenth century, no federal bankruptcy law existed.[1]

State laws on creditors' remedies and insolvency existed from colonial times, and in the absence of federal bankruptcy laws, state insolvency laws attempted to balance the need to collect debts for the benefit of creditors with the injustice of crushing honest debtors who failed financially through no fault of their own. As the national economy expanded, however, both creditors and debtors increasingly found insolvency laws inadequate. Although state insolvency laws attempted to ensure the orderly liquidation of debtors' estates for the benefit of creditors in accordance with the priorities established by law, in practice they favored local creditors over more distant ones. Furthermore, only bankruptcy could discharge debtors from their debts, and the Constitution limited states' ability to enact effective bankruptcy statutes.[2]

Like that of the other states and the colonies that preceded them, early Ohio law provided a comprehensive scheme regulating how creditors collected debts and what to do with insolvent debtors. From an early date, Ohio recognized the usual common-law creditors' remedies against recalcitrant or insolvent debtors and protected honest debtors from imprisonment for debt, but Ohio law did not give debtors a discharge of their debt. Subsequently acquired property in excess of very modest exemptions of household goods and tools always remained vulnerable to seizure and sale in payment of previously acquired debt.

This chapter looks at bankruptcy and insolvency law and practice in northern Ohio in the nineteenth century as a case study. It considers the role played by speculation and commercial credit in the early development of Ohio and inquires into whether the periodic availability of bankruptcy as an alternative to insolvency proceedings affected economic development. Finally, it investigates the relationship between insolvency and bankruptcy and questions whether state insolvency law influenced federal bankruptcy practice in northern Ohio.

Speculation, Insolvency, and the Settlement of Early Ohio

Ohio was conceived in the speculative fever that swept the early republic and culminated in financial panics in 1792 and 1797. In 1800, Congress passed the first national bankruptcy act, in part as a response to the imprisonment for debt of many prominent people, including Ohio territorial leaders and investors. Ohio became a state in March 1803, just months before the repeal of that short-lived bankruptcy act in December 1803. From the beginning, Ohio moved steadily to liberalize its insolvency laws.

Ohio became a territory of the United States on July 13, 1787, when the Congress of the Confederation enacted the Northwest Ordinance, and it was admitted to the union as the seventeenth state in March 1803. Initially, both Virginia and Connecticut claimed territory that later became part of Ohio. Virginia ceded its claim in 1784 in exchange for the national government's assumption of frontier military debts and title guarantees for the existing land claims of Virginians. In 1786, Connecticut ceded all but the Western Reserve, the narrow strip along the shore of Lake Erie from Sandusky Bay west of Cleveland to the Pennsylvania border, in exchange for national government assumption of Revolutionary War debts. In 1800, Connecticut also ceded its claim to the Western Reserve. Conflict between Connecticut Whigs and the second sons of Virginian patricians dominated early Ohio politics.[3]

The earliest European American settlement in Ohio occurred in 1788 when the Ohio Company established the city of Marietta in the southern portion of the state along the Ohio River; the company was motivated in part by agrarian utopianism but also by speculative interest in a potentially lucrative investment in western land financed with depreciated securities issued by the Continental Congress to fund the Revolutionary War. Frustrated former Revolutionary War officers from New England founded the Ohio Company in 1786 after unsuccessfully petitioning Congress in 1783 for a land grant on the Ohio River in lieu of back pay and pension rights. Although the Ohio Company was a joint stock company open to anyone who paid in $1,000 par value of Continental securities plus $10 specie (coin money), all but one of the early investors in the company were Revolutionary War officers, and all intended to move to the Ohio territory. The founders acted from a variety of motives. The officers resented their loss of social status and wealth in post–Revolutionary War society and feared the consequences of popular disorder and democratic excess. They hoped to establish a more just and equitable society in which their superior qualities were duly recognized and rewarded. They hoped to get rich, too. Ignoring anti-speculator provisions in the charter, the Ohio Company's founders distributed most of the stock to themselves then resold it to other investors. Divisions quickly developed between eastern and western investors and between speculators and emigrants.[4]

The Ohio Company found itself dependent on large-scale, well-connected speculators from the very beginning. Experiencing difficulty in negotiating a land purchase from Congress, the company's agent, Manasseh Cutler, became entangled with the infamous New York financier William Duer. Duer, a personal friend and sometimes business associate of Robert Morris and Alexander Hamilton, used his political connections to smooth the way for the Ohio Company's purchase of 1.5 million acres for $1 million par value of deeply depreciated Continental securities, payable in two equal installments. Duer and Cutler joined with Winthrop Sargent, who was the largest shareholder in the Ohio Company and later the first secretary of the Ohio Territory, to form a second land company, the Scioto Company, which secured from Congress an option on 3.5 million acres directly adjacent to the Ohio Company purchase. Duer brought speculators from his other ventures into the Scioto Company and the Ohio Company and acquired shares in the Ohio Company from Cutler. Cutler and Sargent's investment in the Scioto Company raised suspicions of duplicity within the Ohio Company and exacerbated existing tensions.

The Scioto Company failed spectacularly, defrauding French immigrants and ruining many investors, including Richard Platt, treasurer of the Scioto Company and the Ohio Company.[5] Meanwhile, the Ohio Company also ran into financial difficulties. Ratification of the Constitution and Alexander Hamilton's plan to fund the national debt caused the price of Continental securities to rise, increasing the cost to Ohio Company shareholders of the unpaid balance due on their stock purchases. Duer's shares had been forfeited by other investors who failed to pay for them, but Duer never paid for his shares either. The rise in the price of Continental securities also increased the cost to the Ohio Company of its second installment payment to Congress on the land purchase. After unsuccessfully attempting to negotiate for a reduced price, or more time in which to make the payment, Congress agreed to transfer the lands already paid for and canceled the remaining obligation. Ohio Company agents met in Philadelphia in April 1792 to begin the process of dissolution.

In addition to the collapse of the Ohio and Scioto companies, many large land speculations crumbled in 1792. Every major speculator in the country landed in debtors' prison, including Duer. Many credit Duer's bankruptcy with precipitating the Panic of 1792. Duer lived in debtors' prison almost continuously from 1792 until shortly before his death in 1799; he obtained a mercy release on his deathbed. The 1792 panic did not trigger a national depression because Treasury secretary Alexander Hamilton used the newly chartered First Bank of the United States to inject sufficient liquidity into the New York banks to contain the crisis. But in 1797, a severe currency contraction originating in the Bank of England produced a depression that especially afflicted merchants and artisans in the coastal cities.[6]

Throughout this period, insolvents from the business failures of 1792 remained in debtors' prison, and a campaign of pamphlets and petitions urged debtor relief while Congress considered, then tabled, bankruptcy bills.[7] Finally, in 1800 Congress enacted the first American bankruptcy act.[8] Modeled on English statutes, the 1800 Bankruptcy Act aimed primarily to benefit creditors in collecting debts. Although only creditors could invoke the law, and they could only use it against traders and merchants with significant debts, the act also greatly benefited those debtors who received discharges.[9]

The Bankruptcy Act of 1800

The US Constitution specifically granted Congress the authority to "establish uniform laws on the subject of bankruptcy throughout the United States," but Congress had hesitated to act. This provision of the Constitution excited little debate on the floor of the Constitutional Convention, and no American colony had much experience with bankruptcy laws. The mother country, England, first enacted a bankruptcy statute in the sixteenth century, primarily to help creditors collect debts by providing for an orderly and equitable procedure for locating and liquidating a debtor's assets and distributing the proceeds among his creditors. Helping creditors collect debts remained the underlying purpose of bankruptcy statutes for centuries. English law did not provide for discharge of debts until 1705, and the law permitted debt discharge only as an incentive to ensure that debtors disclosed their assets to their creditors. Between 1755 and 1770, Connecticut, Massachusetts, New York, and Rhode Island enacted short-lived bankruptcy statutes that allowed for discharge of debts under some circumstances, but none were still in effect at the time of the American Revolution.[10]

Debt drove the colonial economy, and all of the colonies had legal procedures for dealing with insolvent debtors. The shortage of specie meant that most retail transactions occurred as book accounts, and larger commercial transactions depended on the acceptance and endorsement of private bills, bonds, and notes. The social relations of debt involved performances of patronage, deference, virtue, and honor. Because the failure to pay a debt as required could have devastating social and financial consequences for both the debtor and the creditor, most creditors resorted to lawsuits reluctantly. Instead, creditors frequently renegotiated debts to give debtors the opportunity to meet their just obligations and compromised the debts of insolvent debtors through contractual arrangements called "compositions." Creditors had no choice but go to court, however, if they found debtors dissipating assets by giving preferences to other creditors or if other creditors started a lawsuit. Generally, the date of a judgment determined the order of payment on execution of a debtor's property in satisfaction of judgments. A creditor needed to get close to the head of the line to receive any payment in satisfaction of a judgment for debt.

Imprisonment for debt played an integral part in the common-law court process for debt collection. Imprisonment for debt had existed in England since the thirteenth century and continued in all of the former colonies well into the nineteenth century. In general, a common-law civil suit for debt commenced with the arrest of the debtor. The debtor secured release from jail by posting an appearance bond for the lawsuit in an amount determined by the amount of the debt alleged to be due. If the debtor could not or would not post bond, the debtor remained imprisoned until a judgment was entered in the lawsuit establishing that no debt was due or the judgment debt was satisfied. In most northern colonies, a debtor could be sold into servitude for a period of years to satisfy debts. Often, debtors who owed very little could secure their release by swearing that they owned nothing with which to pay their debts—the so-called debtor's oath.

Americans began to question the "moral economy of debt"—the ancient idea that every debtor had a moral obligation to pay just debts no matter the personal cost and no matter the misfortune that had brought about the default. By the middle of the eighteenth century, a market economy characterized by long-distance transactions among strangers emerged, at least in New England. These new opportunities carried new risks. Commerce expanded greatly in North America during the French and Indian War, but the economic contraction at the war's conclusion brought a credit contraction and many business failures. Popular attitudes toward commercial debt began to change. Because commerce depended on credit, many people considered commercial debt not sinful in the same way that debt for consumption purposes was sinful. Limited colonial experiments with debt discharge between 1755 and 1770 represented an acknowledgment that some honest bankrupts who failed through no fault of their own deserved a second chance.[11]

The American Revolution unleashed an economic maelstrom. The social relations of debt created dense interconnected webs, and many smaller merchants and traders also failed when their patrons and mentors failed. The failure of highly respected prominent people like Robert Morris and James Wilson confounded expectations and provoked social anxiety; great men should not languish in jail for debt. Morris had signed the Declaration of Independence, had attended the Constitutional Convention in Philadelphia, and was chosen to be the first senator from Pennsylvania. Known as the "Financier of the Revolution," Morris almost single-handedly marshaled the material resources that kept George Washington's army in the field. Nonetheless, Morris was confined to debtors' prison in Philadelphia from 1798 to 1801. Brilliant lawyer and Supreme Court justice James Wilson had been a conspicuous leader at the Continental Congress and the Constitutional Convention but found himself badly overextended financially. Briefly incarcerated for debt twice, he fled Philadelphia to avoid debtors' prison and died in disgrace in Edenton, North Carolina, in 1798.

Congress enacted the first bankruptcy act in 1800, prompted in part by the shocking spectacle of great men in debtors' prison but also as a result of changing ideas about moral culpability and commercial debt. Like the English statutes on which it was based, the act only applied to merchants and traders who incurred debts of a certain magnitude, and only creditors could invoke its provisions. By its terms, the act promised relief only for a limited time. Although the bankruptcy act was scheduled to expire after five years, Thomas Jefferson and his Democratic Republicans repealed it two years early, in December 1803. The Jeffersonians considered the 1800 Bankruptcy Act a Federalist benefit conferred only on commercial interests and wholly inappropriate to an agrarian society; they wanted the United States to remain an agrarian society. For the first of many times over the course of the nineteenth century, the politics of bankruptcy revealed dramatically conflicting visions of American society.

Insolvency in Early Ohio

Meanwhile, early Ohio enacted typical insolvency legislation. The first territorial government consisted of a governor and three judges, all appointed by Congress, who were to "adopt and publish . . . such laws of the original states civil and criminal as may be necessary and best suited to the circumstances of the district."[12] In 1788, the Federalist governor and Federalist judges promulgated a basic legal code for the territory based on general common-law principles, borrowing heavily from Pennsylvania statutes. Standard debt collection procedures included imprisonment for debt before and after judgment.

In 1795, the governor and judges revised and expanded the legal code, called Maxwell's Code after the publisher, to include a statute patterned after a long since repealed 1682 Pennsylvania law.[13] Unless a creditor could show cause to believe a debtor was concealing property, a judgment debtor was to be released from prison and made to satisfy his debt with personal servitude for a period to be determined by the court, not to exceed seven years if the debtor was unmarried and younger than 40 years, otherwise not to exceed five years. If the creditor refused to accept the personal service of the debtor in satisfaction of the debt, the debtor was discharged from prison and the creditor was barred from further legal action on the same debt. Ohio never passed another statute that discharged debts.

In 1798, Ohio's population reached 5,000, the threshold for establishing a territorial legislature. In December 1799, the legislature repealed the governor's statute regarding persons imprisoned for debt and enacted an insolvency statute of a sort that was common in other states at that time. After notice to creditors and a hearing before a judge at which the creditors could present evidence, judgment debtors incarcerated for debt could secure their release by swearing the following:

> I A.B. do in the presence of Almighty God, solemnly swear (or affirm as the case may be) that I have not any estate, real or personal, in possession, reversion or remainder, sufficient to support myself in prison, or to pay prison charges, and that I have not, since the commencement of this suit against me, or at any other time, directly or indirectly sold, leased, or otherwise conveyed or disposed of to, or entrusted any person or persons whatsoever, with all, or any part of the estate, real or personal, whereof I have been the lawful owner or possessor, with an intent or design to secure the same, or to receive, or to expect any profit or advantage therefore, or have caused or suffered to be done any thing else whatsoever whereof any of my creditors may be defrauded, so help me God; (or, and this as I shall answer to God at the great day).[14]

The statute only discharged the debtor from jail. A debtor liberated under this statute could not be imprisoned again on any debt incurred before his incarceration and liberation unless he procured his liberation through fraud, but the statute did not discharge the debt. A creditor could seize subsequently acquired property in satisfaction of the debt, except for property exempt from execution: necessary wearing apparel and household furniture, tools necessary to the debtor's trade or occupation, and one milk cow. However, if the debtor left the territory he lost the benefit of the statute, and his creditors could follow him and send him to jail again on the preexisting debts.

The territorial insolvency act only applied to an incarcerated debtor. In 1803, Ohio achieved statehood, and in 1805, the state legislature enacted a new insolvency statute that applied to all insolvent debtors, whether incarcerated or not, before or after judgment.[15] An insolvent person residing in the state for at least two years could file a petition for relief in the court of common pleas for the county in which he resided. If the debtor was incarcerated, the sheriff was obligated to facilitate the debtor's filing of the petition. The petition had to accurately list all of the debtor's property and assets, including debts due to him. The court had to give creditors at least sixty days' notice of the hearing, at which the debtor would be questioned under oath and evidence taken. If the court found that the debtor had honestly disclosed all assets and transferred them to a trustee appointed by the court for the benefit of creditors, the debtor received a certificate from the court that freed him from imprisonment for any debt owed at the time he filed his petition. As with the earlier statutes, the debt survived, and creditors could seize any property the debtor subsequently acquired. Although this statute has been repealed and replaced, revised, amended, and expanded many times, a statutory scheme for the assignment of property for the benefit of creditors has continued in Ohio to the present day.[16]

Imprisonment for debt appears to have been largely symbolic in early Ohio. Although, theoretically, the debtor was responsible to the jailer for the cost of his own keep—county commissioners only reimbursed sheriffs for the cost of keeping incarcerated criminals—the earliest insolvency statutes required creditors to reimburse the jailer for the cost of keeping insolvent debtors imprisoned. That requirement did not appear in the 1824 revision of the insolvency statute, and in 1834, the Ohio Supreme Court ruled that a debtor was responsible for his own keep, even if he swore an oath that he was unable to do so.[17] The change may have been caused by the expansion of "prison bounds." Traditionally, prisoners for debt with proper surety had the privilege of prison bounds, which had expanded from bounds to be determined by the local court up to 400 yards from the actual jail in 1804 to the county line in 1832.[18] Those with the privilege of prison bounds could enter private property, hold jobs, and engage in any lawful business or other activity, so long as they stayed within the boundaries that constituted prison bounds.[19] They could even sleep in their own beds, so long as the bed lay within the prison bounds.[20]

On March 18, 1838, Ohio abolished imprisonment for debt by statute, except in cases of fraud; removal, conversion, or concealment of property with intent to defraud creditors; contempt; criminal fines; misconduct in office; or breach of promise to marry.[21] The Ohio Constitution of 1851 prohibited imprisonment for debt except in cases of fraud.[22] Ohio law still allows arrest and imprisonment for debt if the debtor is attempting to remove, conceal, or convert his property with intent to defraud his creditors; if the debtor incurred the debt through fraud, wagering, contempt of court, or criminal fines; or if the debt arose from payments to public officials, misconduct in office, or breach of promise to marry.[23]

The inability to discharge debts oppressed debtors more than debtors' prison as it existed in Ohio. Without discharge, debtors could never get on their feet again. Should a debtor achieve some success, creditors always lay in wait to seize any property the debtor subsequently acquired. In many jurisdictions, including Ohio, debtors could use compositions to discharge debts remaining after insolvency proceedings. A common-law remedy, compositions were contractual in nature. Debtors promised at least two of their creditors a benefit, perhaps pro rata partial payment, in exchange for discharge of the remaining outstanding debt.[24]

Compositions proved to be of limited utility to debtors or creditors. Compositions were voluntary; neither the debtor nor other creditors could compel an obstinate creditor's agreement. Although compositions did not require the agreement of all of a debtor's creditors, only the creditors who agreed to the composition were bound by it. A nonparticipating creditor could continue any lawful collection practices to the detriment of the composition creditors. Compositions required open and fair dealing on the part of all parties, and any fraud or concealment voided the contract and left the debtor exposed to the original debt. For example, a secret composition constituted a fraud on the debtor's other creditors if the parties to the composition obtained a benefit by it that prejudiced the other creditors. Giving preferences to some creditors over other creditors invalidated a composition, but paying a creditor in full who was not a party to the composition did not defraud the debtor's other creditors.

The Bankruptcy Act of 1841

Economic conditions continued to be volatile in the early decades of the nineteenth century, but northern Ohio was too isolated from eastern markets to be much affected. Until the 1830s, most Ohioans lived along the Ohio River in the southern portion of the state, and most trade flowed south by river to New Orleans. The canals changed everything. In 1822, Ohio established a Canal Commission to identify the most feasible routes connecting the Ohio River and Lake Erie. It proposed two routes: an eastern route through the Cuyahoga River and a western route through the Maumee and Miami rivers. The legislature approved both routes in 1825. When completed, the canals opened northern Ohio for commercial agriculture. Within the lifetime of one generation, Cleveland, Akron, Youngstown, and Toledo developed into modern industrial cities.

In 1825, the Ohio legislature selected Cleveland as the northern terminus of the canal to be dug connecting the Ohio River and Lake Erie. The canal between Akron and Cleveland opened in 1827, and by 1832, had opened all the way to Portsmouth on the Ohio River. The Erie Canal, connecting Lake Erie to New York City and the world, had opened in 1825. The direction of trade changed in Ohio and began to flow north along the canal to Lake Erie and on to New York City. Cleveland became the largest port on the western end of Lake Erie, and its population and wealth increased dramatically. Because the canal provided cheap water transportation to eastern cities, inland towns and villages with access to the canal also prospered. Cleveland and its neighbor across the Cuyahoga River, Ohio City, both incorporated in 1836.

Akron began as a land speculation: early investors believed it was the best location for the proposed Ohio and Erie Canal and secured their bet with a donation of land for canal purposes.[25] Akron also connected the Pennsylvania and Ohio Canal to the Ohio and Erie Canal, opening the Mahoning Valley to development. The Mahoning Valley was among the first parts of the Western Reserve to be settled. Even though residents mined coal and produced iron for local use as early as 1826, the Mahoning Valley had remained thinly settled and isolated. A canal to the valley had been proposed as early as 1822, but the success of the Ohio and Erie Canal advanced the project. The Pennsylvania and Ohio Canal Company organized in 1835 and completed the canal to Akron in 1849. Even before the canal was completed, rolling mills opened in the vicinity of Youngstown, and the Mahoning Valley provided coal to Cleveland.

On the western side of the state, the legislature authorized the Miami and Erie Canal in stages. The northern terminus of the canal had not yet been determined in 1829 when the first section of the canal, from Cincinnati to Dayton, was completed. Toledo lay in disputed territory until after the War of 1812, contested by the British, who were supported by Native Americans. Until 1836, Michigan also claimed an eight-mile strip along the Michigan-Ohio border that included Toledo. The area around Toledo was thinly populated, cut off from the rest of Ohio by the infamous Black Swamp. Toledo emerged from the union of two other townships in 1833, in part to improve its chances of becoming the canal terminus, and incorporated as a city in 1836. Although not the designated terminus of the Miami and Erie Canal, because of the topography of the Miami River Toledo became the de facto canal terminus within a year after the completion of the canal in 1843. The Wabash and Erie Canal, which connected the Mississippi River to Lake Erie through Indiana, also reached Toledo in 1843, and Toledo rapidly developed into an important regional transportation and shipping center.

The canals made northern Ohio accessible to eastern capitalists as well as eastern markets. In 1831, the Dwight family of Massachusetts purchased and funded a dormant bank charter in Cleveland, the First

Commercial Bank of Lake Erie, the only bank in the rapidly growing region from 1831 to 1834, and one of only two banks in Cleveland into the 1840s. The Dwight family also secured control of the only other bank, the Bank of Cleveland, chartered in 1834.[26] Northern Ohio boomed between 1835 and 1837, but the economy remained overwhelmingly agricultural. Most investment in the state involved building transportation infrastructure for the transshipment of agricultural products to eastern markets.

The most severe financial panic in America up to that time commenced in the spring of 1837 and produced a depression that lasted five years. Runs on New York banks beginning on May 4, 1837, ended with all of the city's banks suspending specie payments by the morning of May 10, 1837. News of the New York banks' action caused banks in every other major city in the country, including Cleveland, to suspend specie payment within a week. Both the Commercial Bank of Lake Erie and the Bank of Cleveland suspended specie payment on May 17, 1837. The Ohio legislature enacted banking reform in 1842 that required banks that suspended specie settlement to surrender their charters, and both the Commercial Bank of Lake Erie and the Bank of Cleveland entered receivership.[27]

Economic historians contest the causes of the panic, but they agree on its consequences: assets of state-chartered banks declined by 45 percent; more than one in four of the banks operating in 1837 closed; the price of industrial, financial, and manufacturing stocks declined precipitously; and per capita investment and output fell each year for five consecutive years.[28] High wheat prices had fueled Ohio's economic growth, and the price of wheat plummeted. In Ohio, new public improvements and business incorporations nearly ceased, but Cleveland continued to grow despite the panic.[29] In 1838, nine new warehouses appeared on the Cleveland waterfront. By 1840, the canals reached the coal lands of the Mahoning Valley, and Cleveland became an important fueling stop for Great Lakes shipping. Cleveland's first blast furnace began operation in 1840.[30]

Commercial interests flooded Congress with petitions for a bankruptcy act, but there had been intermittent demands for a bankruptcy act since repeal of the previous act in 1803. Poor economic conditions following the end of the War of 1812 had turned into panic and depression in 1819, and Congress had considered and rejected bankruptcy legislation every session between 1816 and 1827. The Panic of 1837 brought renewed demands for congressional action to establish a uniform system of bankruptcy, but the Jacksonian Democrats in power resisted bankruptcy relief except as a means to discipline banks that suspended specie payment. The opposition Whigs took the Senate in 1838, and on February 2, 1840, Senator Daniel Webster of Massachusetts introduced a general bankruptcy bill in the Senate. It passed the Senate on June 25, 1840, but did not pass the House. The Whigs took the House and won the presidency in the 1840 election and reintroduced the bill in the Senate in January 1841. A Whig bill drafted in the Whig caucus was joined to a popular bill to distribute federal land to the states, and the Bankruptcy Act of 1841 passed on a strict party-line vote with no amendments allowed. It became law on August 19, 1841, effective February 1, 1842.[31] Both of Ohio's senators were Democrats and had opposed the bill. The coalition supporting the act was so unstable that a bill repealing it failed by only one vote before the act became effective.[32]

The Bankruptcy Act of 1841 constituted a profound change in national bankruptcy policy.[33] Previously, bankruptcy had been understood primarily as a creditor's remedy—a means to force the liquidation of a debtor's estate and distribute it equitably among creditors. Only creditors could initiate bankruptcy proceedings, and the benefits of debt discharge were limited to commercial traders of a certain size. The 1841 Bankruptcy Act allowed anyone except a corporation to seek a discharge of debts in voluntary bankruptcy, but only merchants, traders, bankers, and insurers who owed more than $2,000 could be forced into involuntary bankruptcy. Debtors were entitled to a discharge unless they defrauded their creditors, and although creditors could object, debtors were entitled to a jury trial on their eligibility for discharge. The legislation proved very unpopular. With Whig support, Congress repealed the 1841 Bankruptcy Act on March 3, 1843.

Some, generally Democrats, opposed a national bankruptcy bill on general principles. They saw the financial crisis as a morality play brought about by rampant speculation in land and railroads, facilitated by paper money and the credit system. People with these views tended to prefer local, community solutions and viewed bankruptcy as favoring aggressive commercial interests that threatened their way of life. Many states had changed their laws on debtor-creditor relations, making the law far less oppressive to debtors, and most states that had not yet abolished debtors' prison did so in the early years of the crisis. Many states passed stay legislation, which delayed execution on judgments for debt, and appraisal laws. Ohio enacted typical appraisal laws intended to protect farmers from the sale of land in execution of judgment at distressed prices. A jury of local land owners appraised real estate seized in execution of judgment, and no sale could occur for less than two-thirds of the appraised value.[34] Liberalized state insolvency laws encouraged many people to believe federal bankruptcy legislation was unnecessary and intrusive.

Others opposed the 1841 Bankruptcy Act as fatally flawed: expensive, inefficient, and inconvenient. More to the point, the act accomplished its principal goal of discharging a lot of debtors with very little payment to creditors. It is difficult to assess the validity of these complaints. The statistical evidence is thin, and there is no basis for comparison to state insolvency laws. In 1844, Congress asked the Judiciary Committee to inquire into the application of the repealed act. The committee solicited bankruptcy data from the district courts, but it is difficult to interpret. Officials in some judicial districts submitted no data, and the data that was submitted revealed wide discrepancies in bankruptcy filings between districts. In the aggregate, however, 98 percent of bankrupts received discharges. Bankrupts surrendered assets worth approximately 10 percent of the debts they reported, but creditors received dividends of only 0.27 percent on their debts. In Ohio, creditors fared slightly better. Of the 2,057 debtors who filed for bankruptcy, all but 112 (5 percent) received discharges. Debtors surrendered assets of $6,957,518 in connection with debts of $23,416,872, or approximately 30 percent, and creditors received a dividend of 11 percent on their debts.[35]

The administration of bankruptcy varied widely because the district courts operated independently of any supervision at this time, and the 1841 Bankruptcy Act consisted of only 15 sections, leaving the details of the act's implementation almost entirely to the discretion of the district courts. The district courts constituted the courts of bankruptcy and prescribed their own rules, regulations, forms of procedure, and fee schedules. The only official required by the 1841 Bankruptcy Act was the assignee, appointed by the district court to receive title to all of the bankrupt's property (except household necessaries not to exceed $300 in value). The assignee had full power to sue and be sued, to settle the debtor's estate, and to distribute dividends pro rata to those creditors who proved claims, after payment of fees and expenses. The 1841 Bankruptcy Act allowed but did not compel the district court to designate functions to commissioners. Appeals from decisions of assignees and commissioners were heard by the district court.

The United States District Court for the District of Ohio operated a relatively efficient bankruptcy system closely resembling the state of Ohio's insolvency system. In 1824, Ohio amended its insolvency law and created the office of the commissioner of insolvents, appointed by the court of common pleas for three-year terms. The commissioner of insolvents was responsible for receiving the debtor's property, excluding statutory exemptions, and liquidating the nonexempt property through prompt, public auction. The commissioner also approved creditors' claims; distributed the proceeds from the sale of the debtor's property pro rata among the debtor's creditors; and had broad powers to settle disputes, compromise debts, and sue on behalf of the debtor's estate. Debtors and creditors could appeal the commissioner's actions to the court of common pleas at its next session.

The commissioner of insolvents was required to maintain an office at the county seat, be available at all times, and keep books and records open for inspection by debtors and creditors. He received no salary but was paid expenses and statutory fees of 6 percent of the first $100 of the debtor's estate and 4 percent of the rest before creditors received any dividend. The debtor received a temporary certificate from the commissioner that protected him until the next session of the court of common pleas where the debtor filed his petition and received his permanent certificate under the insolvency act. The certificate freed him from the possibility of debtors' prison for all debts disclosed in his petition but did not discharge the debts. The debtor remained liable for the debts, and creditors could execute judgments on subsequently acquired assets.[36]

Approximately two thousand debtors filed for bankruptcy protection in the Judicial District of Ohio during the short time the 1841 Bankruptcy Act was in effect. The debtors came from all walks of life and all parts of the state. Even though petitions had to be filed with the district court, and in 1842 the only Ohio district court was in Cincinnati, roughly half of the petitions came from the northern counties that later formed the Northern Judicial District of Ohio. Almost all of the petitions were voluntary. The court published bankruptcy rules on February 2, 1842, and the first cases were filed on February 5, 1842.

Commentators later complained about the expense and inconvenience the 1841 Bankruptcy Act caused because of the necessity of appearing in a federal district court far from the debtor's home, but the Ohio District Court Bankruptcy Rules minimized any inconvenience. The petition had to be filed with the court if it was in session, or at the judge's residence if court was not in session, but the records reveal a frequent pattern of multiple petitions from distant counties filed simultaneously by the same attorney. The court immediately referred the petition to the bankruptcy commissioner of the county of the debtor's residence for all subsequent hearings. The rules required the court to appoint one or more commissioners for any county in which such services were required, and commissioners were appointed for almost all counties. The court appointed two commissioners forthe two most highly populated counties: Cuyahoga and Lucas. In northern Ohio, only six thinly populated counties along the Miami Erie Canal had no commissioner. Those six counties had a total population of less than 30,000, less than 2 percent of Ohio's total population of 1,519,467.[37]

In Ohio, uncontested bankruptcy cases could be resolved in the debtor's home county without the necessity of debtors or creditors ever actually appearing in federal court. Claims and debts could be proved to the commissioner by depositions. The commissioner issued a report to the court on which basis the court would grant the debtor's motion for a discharge. The debtor was entitled to notice of any objections to his discharge, and the trial could be held in his home county with the commissioner presiding. Even contested involuntary bankruptcies could be resolved by trial before a commissioner in the debtor's home county.

It is difficult to assess how well the bankruptcy process worked in practice in Ohio. Most bankruptcy commissioners left few traces. Some of the few we know something about were leaders in their communities; Daniel Chase led a company of Lucas County volunteers in the Mexican War, and John Reed Jr. was a businessman, lawyer, and newspaper editor in Maumee. Reed was also appointed commissioner in nearby Paulding and Williams counties; he was the only commissioner appointed for more than one county. However, most of the commissioners we know something about were the children of important people in their communities who had only recently been admitted to the practice of law, and they did not continue to practice law as a principal occupation in their later life. Those commissions look like patronage appointments—favors to their families designed to give the young people a good start in life. Although this sample is too small to be meaningful, those commissioners all became successful businessmen.

Lucien B. Otis, bankruptcy commissioner for Sandusky County, moved as a child with his family from Connecticut to Ohio in 1820, and his father became one of the most prominent citizens of Berlin in Erie County. Otis was admitted to the Ohio bar in 1841 and entered into practice in Sandusky County. He later served as prosecuting attorney and was elected judge of the court of common pleas in 1851. Otis moved to Chicago in 1856 and became a millionaire from real estate speculation.

John M. Edwards, commissioner for Trumbull County, was the grandson of one of the original members of the Connecticut Land

Company that purchased the Western Reserve from Connecticut in 1795. Edwards was born in New Haven, Connecticut, and educated at Yale. He practiced law there from 1826 until 1832. He moved to Trumbull County in 1832 and was admitted to the Ohio bar in 1838. After the repeal of the Bankruptcy Act of 1841, Edwards became an influential journalist and local historian.

Pitt Cooke, commissioner for Erie County, was born in Erie County, Ohio, in 1819. Cooke's father, Eleutheros Cooke, served in the state legislature in 1822, 1823, 1825, and 1840, and in 1825 he received the first charter in the United States to build a railroad. He was elected to one term in Congress, from 1831 to 1833, as an anti-Jacksonian. One of Pitt's brothers, Henry D. Cooke, was the editor of the *Sandusky Register* and the *Ohio State Journal*. Later, President Ulysses S. Grant appointed Henry Cooke governor of the District of Columbia. Pitt's other brother, Jay Cooke, founded the infamous Philadelphia banking house Jay Cooke & Company.

Pitt Cooke was appointed commissioner in bankruptcy when he was only 22 years old. He left the practice of law shortly after the repeal of the 1841 Bankruptcy Act and entered into partnership with his father-in-law in the forwarding and commission business. He took over management of the business on his father-in-law's death in 1849. When the Civil War commenced, Cooke joined his brother Jay's banking house and worked in its New York office. After the bank failed in 1873, precipitating panic and depression, he left banking and returned to Sandusky.

Historian Edward Balleisen argues that the Bankruptcy Act of 1841 facilitated the evolution of a salaried middle class and the transition to a modern industrial economy.[38] Several factors contributed to the transition. Legal work expanded dramatically, and new professional occupations emerged in the administration of the legal system, the management and sale of distressed property, credit reporting, and legal and business publishing. Vulture capitalists made fortunes speculating in the assets of bankrupt estates, and innovative entrepreneurs obtained machinery and other business assets at low cost. Without capital and disillusioned by proprietorship, many talented bankrupts migrated to urban centers where they obtained respectable high-paying salaried jobs in newly emerging large, bureaucratic business organizations. The concept of a respectable, productive citizen changed from someone who owned a farm or business to someone who was a knowledge worker with a secure and comfortable salary.

The Bankruptcy Act of 1867

The repeal of the Bankruptcy Act of 1841 corresponded with a period of rapid growth and the beginning of industrialization in northern Ohio. Railroads supplanted the canals as transportation networks in the 1850s, and northern Ohio was well situated to benefit in multiple ways. Toledo became a milling center for western grain and an important transfer center between railroad and lake transportation of goods, especially grain. Both Toledo and Cleveland developed important Great Lakes shipyards. Cleveland became a major center for construction work related to railroad expansion, including iron and steel manufacture, bridge building, finance, and banking. Cleveland entrepreneurs pioneered telegraphy, and when numerous smaller telegraph systems combined to form the Western Union Telegraph Company in 1856, the company was managed from Cleveland. John D. Rockefeller landed his first job as bookkeeper to Cleveland commission merchants in 1857.[39]

Another speculative bubble developed in western agricultural land and in the stocks and bonds of the aggressively expanding trunk railway lines that depended on western agricultural expansion for profitability. When the bubble collapsed in the summer of 1857, New York brokerage houses failed, and New York banks suspended specie payment. Banks in most of the rest of the country followed. Although the failure of the Cincinnati-based Ohio Life Insurance and Trust Company preceded the general panic, Ohio's financial system weathered the crisis well because of state banking regulations enacted after the 1837 crisis. Only one additional bank failed, the independent, uninsured Seneca County Bank. Ohio's economy did not rebound quickly, however. Ohio produced a quarter of the nation's grain at that time, and grain prices remained depressed for years.[40]

The 1857 panic renewed demands for a national bankruptcy act. Numerous memorials and petitions were sent to Congress and referred to the House Judiciary Committee, which on March 1, 1861, reported a bill very similar to the 1841 Bankruptcy Act. No action was taken on the bill, however. The onset of the Civil War produced more commercial failures, especially in New York City, where southern planters' debts to northern merchants suddenly became worthless. Another round of petitions and memorials was referred to a select committee, which reported a bill in January 1863, largely authored by Republican representative Roscoe Conkling of New York. A different bill was introduced in 1864 by Republican representative Thomas Jenckes of Rhode Island. Public opinion was deeply divided over bankruptcy. In Ohio, the legislature passed a resolution in opposition to a national bankruptcy act, while Cleveland's representative, Republican Rufus Spalding, served on the House select committee that was drafting a bankruptcy bill and strongly supported that legislation.

Congress was divided between those who opposed any bankruptcy act, or, at least, opposed a bankruptcy act that allowed creditors to file involuntary bankruptcy petitions, and those who wanted a bankruptcy act designed primarily to facilitate the collection of debts on behalf of creditors. The sectional question complicated the issue. New York merchants complained that they would not be able to collect any of the debts owed to them by southern planters without a national bankruptcy act, and Cincinnati merchants complained that their southern debtors would discharge all their debts in bankruptcy before the creditors could collect anything if an act were passed. The 1867 Bankruptcy Act threaded this needle by adopting state exemptions that protected northern debtors only (1872 amendments made the exemptions of the former confederate states equally applicable as the exemptions of states that had not seceded) and allowed a discharge only with the permission of the majority by value of the creditors if creditors received less than 50 percent in value of the debts owed them. Voluntary bankrupts had to take an oath of allegiance to the United States. Nevertheless, disproportionately large numbers of financially devastated former Confederates filed bankruptcy.[41]

Modeled on recent English bankruptcy legislation, the 1867 Bankruptcy Act specifically addressed many of the concerns creditors had under the 1841 Bankruptcy Act. Unlike the 1841 Bankruptcy Act, however, creditors chose the assignee appointed to liquidate and distribute the debtor's property. Creditors could compel a broad examination of the debtor and his wife regarding the condition and disposal of property, records and accounts, and business transactions. The debtor's discharge would be denied or revoked for any material false statement in petitions, schedules, or testimony; destruction or falsification of books and records; fraud or negligence in the care, custody, or delivery of his property; concealment of any part of his estate; removal of property from the judicial district with intent to defraud creditors; or any fraudulent conveyance, which was defined as any preference to a creditor by an insolvent person within four months of bankruptcy or any transfer within six months of bankruptcy to someone who had reason to believe the bankrupt was contemplating insolvency.

The 1867 Bankruptcy Act also addressed perceived defects in the administration of the 1841 Bankruptcy Act. Because of complaints over the expense involved in traveling to distant US district courts, the 1867 Bankruptcy Act required the district court judge to appoint a register to serve in every congressional district in the judicial district. In addition to administering bankrupt estates in the register's congressional district, a register could also prove debts of a creditor residing in his judicial district in connection with the bankruptcy of a debtor in a different judicial district. To increase the uniformity of practice between the district courts, the act directed the Supreme Court to draft general orders for use in bankruptcy.

Some congressmen reported creditor complaints that frequent appeals to the US district courts of commissioners' bankruptcy decisions had caused delay and expense in the administration of the 1841

Bankruptcy Act. To remedy this, the 1867 Bankruptcy Act enhanced and specifically defined the powers of registers. Registers could adjudicate uncontested bankruptcies, administer oaths, hold and preside at meetings of creditors, take proofs of debt, make all computations of dividends, audit and pass accounts of assignees, pass an uncontested final examination of the debtor, and do any administrative business or other tasks defined by general orders or directed by the district court. Parties had to reduce contested factual matters to writing for the register to present to the court for decision on the merits. The district court could hear certified questions at any point in the register's proceedings.

The 1867 Bankruptcy Act proved unpopular. Despite their enhanced position under the 1867 Bankruptcy Act, creditors still received low dividends, and debtors found it hard to obtain discharges. The House of Representatives voted overwhelmingly for repeal in January 1873, and many people believed the Senate would soon follow. However, Jay Cooke's brokerage house failed on September 18, 1873, throwing the country into a long and deep depression.[42] Instead of repeal, on June 22, 1874, Congress amended the 1867 Bankruptcy Act, hoping to give greater relief to debtors at a lower cost to creditors.[43]

The 1874 amendments to the 1867 Bankruptcy Act made it harder for creditors to prove involuntary bankruptcy and easier for debtors to obtain discharges. Involuntary bankrupts could receive discharges regardless of the percentage of proved debts against the estate that received any payment, and voluntary bankrupts could receive discharges if at least 30 percent of the debts proved against the estate were paid or if one-fourth in number and one-third in value of creditors agreed to the discharge. The 1874 amendments introduced compositions to bankruptcy. The court could allow debtors and creditors to enter into composition agreements, binding on all of the creditors listed on the debtor's schedules, with the agreement of a majority in number and three-fourths in value of the creditors.

The 1874 amendments to the 1867 Bankruptcy Act also attacked the perception that courthouse bankruptcy rings were milking bankruptcy estates at the expense of creditors. The act halved the fees and emoluments then being paid to registers, assignees, and others in bankruptcy cases, pending revision by the Supreme Court and publication of new fee schedules. It prohibited any clerk of court, or register, or their law partners, or any person having any interest in any fee or emolument in any bankruptcy case from taking any position in any other bankruptcy case, in or out of court, such as attorney, trustee, assignee, or of having any financial interest in any case in bankruptcy.

One very important provision of the 1874 amendments to the 1867 Bankruptcy Act required regular data collection on bankruptcy cases. Marshals, registers, clerks of court, and assignees were required to keep records and send reports to the attorney general for inclusion in his annual report to Congress. In 1870, Congress established the Department of Justice and directed the attorney general to make an annual report on its activities. The attorney general's reports reveal that the 1874 amendments did not resolve the deficiencies in the 1867 Bankruptcy Act. Dividends to creditors hovered below 10 percent of proved debts, and less than one-third of debtors obtained discharges.[44]

In 1855, Congress divided the Judicial District of Ohio into northern and southern districts, and the District Court for the Northern Judicial District of Ohio sat in Cleveland. The second district court judge, Charles T. Sherman, received his appointment on the same day the 1867 Bankruptcy Act became law, March 2, 1867. Judge Sherman's younger brothers were Ohio senator John Sherman and Civil War general William Tecumseh Sherman. By law, no bankruptcy cases could be filed before June 1, 1867. Judge Sherman appointed a list of registers on May 27, 1867, and entered brief, handwritten Rules of Procedure in Bankruptcy into the minute book on June 19, 1867. More detailed rules were printed a month later. Debtors began filing bankruptcy cases on June 1, 1867.

The Bankruptcy Act of 1867 required the district court judge to appoint registers for each congressional district from a list of candidates nominated by the chief justice of the United States, Salmon P. Chase.[45] Chief Justice Chase had deep political roots in Ohio and cared passionately about the antislavery cause. A brilliant legal scholar, Chase had defended fugitive slaves as a private lawyer in Cincinnati. In 1848, Chase was elected to the US Senate from Ohio as a member of the Free Soil Party. In 1855, he was elected governor of Ohio as a Republican. In 1860, he unsuccessfully ran for the Republican nomination for president but then joined President Abraham Lincoln's administration as secretary of the treasury. In 1864, President Lincoln appointed Chase chief justice of the United States Supreme Court.

In April 1867, Chief Justice Chase made his nominations for registers in bankruptcy while at the same time seeking the 1868 Republican Party presidential nomination. Republican Party internal politics had been contentious during and after the Civil War, which had led to the creation of factions and third parties. Chase's aspirations to the Republican presidential nomination in 1860 and 1864 were disappointed by dissension within the Ohio delegation. By April 1867, the Ohio Republican Party consisted of three factions: (1) ex-Democrats who supported Chase for the Republican presidential nomination, (2) ex-Whigs who supported Ohio senator Benjamin Wade for the Republican presidential nomination, and (3) consolidationists, led by US senator John Sherman, a long-time supporter of Chase, who wanted a strong and united Republican Party. The warring Republican factions used political patronage as a political weapon in the power struggles within the party.[46] In 1868 Chase's presidential ambitions were frustrated again. General Ulysses Grant received a unanimous nomination at the Republican convention and decisively won the presidential election.[47]

The Northern District of Ohio encompassed eight congressional districts and parts of three other districts that straddled the northern and southern judicial districts. Registers in bankruptcy were appointed for both judicial districts in those congressional districts that included counties from both judicial districts. Applicants for register in bankruptcy sent a letter of application and supporting references to the Supreme Court. If the district was represented by a Republican, the chief justice required the congressman's recommendation. The references stressed the applicants' service in the Union army and service to the Republican Party. References with personal ties to Chief Justice Chase, Senator John Sherman, or other faction leaders received the most consideration. Letters of reference typically commended the applicant as "a good radical union man."[48]

Future president James A. Garfield was the Ohio congressman from the nineteenth district, and the applications for the register in bankruptcy for that district came to the Supreme Court through his office. Garfield complained: "My only trouble is that so many good men of this district are asking me for the same place." One applicant file contained a certification that the applicant had voted "an open Democratic or Copperhead" ballot in the 1866 election. Garfield forwarded the application without recommendation, pleading ignorance of the facts, and Ohio district judge Charles Sherman vouched for the applicant's loyalty.[49]

Lucian C. Jones received the April 1867 nomination for the nineteenth congressional district. He had letters of recommendation from Congressman Garfield, Governor J. D. Cox, and Judge Charles Sherman. In 1872, Jones was elected to the Ohio Senate. He resigned and asked Judge Sherman to hold the bankruptcy register position open for him. In 1876 Jones lost his campaign for reelection to future president William McKinley and asked to be reappointed. However, Judge Sherman had died in 1873, and Martin Welker had succeeded him as district judge. Chief Justice Chase had also died in 1873, and Morrison R. Waite from Toledo, Ohio, had succeeded him as chief justice. Thus, Jones wrote to Senator Sherman asking him to mention the circumstances of his request for reappointment to Chief Justice Waite, and Jones was reappointed register.

Cleveland was located in the eighteenth congressional district, and Myron R. Keith received the chief justice's April 1867 nomination. Everyone of importance in northern Ohio recommended Myron Keith for the office of register. Keith presented petitions from members of the bar, bankers, merchants, businessmen, four members of the Ohio House of Representatives, and one Ohio state senator. Senator John Sherman, Judge Charles Sherman, and the clerk of district court, Earl Bill, were personal friends of Keith and endorsed him for the office of register. Bill specifically commended Keith as one who has "always been a most industrious hearty worker for the Republican Cause. He is one who never flags, to whose labors more than any other's is due the unbroken ascendancy of correct principles in the City & Congressional District."[50] Keith had served on the Republican Party's state central committee.

Keith had begun his legal career reading law in the office of Edward Wade, the brother of powerful Republican senator Benjamin Franklin Wade. He practiced law with Cleveland education reformer Harvey Rice from his admission to the Ohio bar in 1842 until 1847, and he served as clerk of the Court of Common Pleas of Lucas County from 1847 to 1852.[51] Registers in bankruptcy performed their official duties as part of their private law practices, and Keith represented John D. Rockefeller in commercial law matters for many years. In 1879, Keith was appointed one of the three trustees who held the stock of out-of-state subsidiaries of the Standard Oil Company on behalf of the shareholders of Standard Oil. Keith continued to represent John D. Rockefeller and the Standard Oil Company until 1897.[52]

Keith's principal competition for the register appointment was George H. Wyman, who received the recommendation of Cleveland's leading Republican, Richard Chappel Parsons, who had just been appointed marshal of the United States Supreme Court by Chief Justice Chase. Keith sent a letter to Senator Sherman advising him that Wyman was serving as the court-appointed assignee for a failed firm. The 1867 Bankruptcy Act made registers ineligible for that kind of appointment to avoid conflicts of interest, and Keith argued that the prior appointment of Wyman as assignee made him ineligible for appointment as register. Keith also sent an endorsement from a person who claimed to be a personal friend of the chief justice in the hopes of neutralizing the effect of Parsons's endorsement of Wyman.

Service to the Republican Party and the political requirements of patronage trumped other considerations in the nomination of registers. Cornelius Curry from Columbiana County received the April 1867 nomination for the seventeenth congressional district, even though he was a notorious drunkard, because he had been an active antislavery man and a Liberty Party advocate since 1844. In support of Curry, Ohio abolitionist Jacob Heaton wrote the following to Chief Justice Chase:

> Our mutual friend Judge C. Curry one of the old tried friends of freedom, in the darkest hours of peril—when you cast your lot with us, was for many years your most undeviating friend and supporter at a time when the combined political organizations were against us, and the cause we had espoused, was true and faithful, doing good service. He has never asked for the appointment of any office in the gift of the Government. He now desires the appointment of Commissioner in Bankruptcy under the late act of Congress.[53]

Many deserving "good radical union men" applied for the position of register, but Curry was the only applicant from Columbiana County. In his letter of application, Curry reminded Chief Justice Chase that Columbiana County had received no other federal patronage appointments, and Judge Sherman said that it was only fair that Columbiana County receive the office of register appointment.

Curry proved unequal to the office of register and was removed in October 1867. Joseph J. Parker from Stark County heard of the opening from district court clerk Earl Bill, and he promptly submitted his application. Parker's letters of recommendation certified that he had "always been a radical union man," and he received the appointment.[54]

Some of the nominees for register gained an advantage in their application from their service in the Union army during the Civil War, such as Frank Sawyer of Norwalk and J. R. Swigart of Napoleon. Brevet Brigadier General Moses B. Walker, "the hero of Chickamauga," received the appointment for the fifth congressional district at Findlay solely because of his war service. Walker was disabled by his war wounds and had retired on an inadequate pension. He needed the money. Walker performed poorly as register, however, and resigned in 1869. He returned to military service in the reconstruction occupation of Texas. His successor, James Irvine, prevailed over candidates with better partisan credentials for pragmatic reasons. Irvine was admitted to the Ohio bar in 1867 and entered into law partnership with Calvin S. Brice in Lima. Irvine had a good reputation for honesty and diligence, and his law office was in a convenient location for the businessmen of the district. Brice would go on to serve on the Democratic National Committee and was elected to the US Senate from Ohio as a Democrat in 1891. Irvine became a successful lawyer and businessman in Lima.[55]

Most of the registers in the Northern District of Ohio served for the eleven-year duration of the 1867 Bankruptcy Act. Most registers posted $10,000 bonds secured by sureties, but Myron Keith of Cuyahoga County was required to post a $20,000 bond and R. P. Kennedy of Logan County was allowed to post only a $5,000 bond. In most cases, the clerk accepted the sureties of three to five substantial citizens, but in some cases, eleven or twelve citizens stood as surety for a register's bond.

All bankruptcy cases were filed with the district court in Cleveland, and the district judge immediately referred them to a register in the congressional district of the debtor's residence. Most action in the case took place at the office of the register. In May 1872, Congress passed an act calling for annual terms of court for the Northern District of Ohio to be held in Toledo in addition to the terms of court held in Cleveland. The first Toledo term of district court began in December 1872, and debtors filed the first bankruptcy cases in Toledo on December 10, 1872. The clerk of court maintained a separate bankruptcy docket for Toledo. In September 1878, Congress formally divided the Northern District of Ohio into eastern and western divisions. Only eighty-four bankruptcy cases were filed in Toledo between 1872 and the repeal of the 1867 Bankruptcy Act in 1878. One judge presided over both divisions in the district until 1910.

Ohio debtors and creditors made little use of the Bankruptcy Act of 1867. In total, 2,158 bankruptcy petitions were filed in the Northern District of Ohio during the eleven years that the act was in effect, approximately the same number of cases as were filed under the 1841 Bankruptcy Act during its thirteen-month existence. In the meantime, Ohio's population had increased more than 75 percent, from 1,519,467 in 1840 to 2,665,260 in 1870. Data is scarce, but some scholars estimate the national per capita rate of bankruptcy filings at approximately twice the per capita rate of the filings in the Northern District of Ohio.[56]

Economic and Social Transformation: Prelude to Modern Bankruptcy

In 1878, when Congress repealed the 1867 Bankruptcy Act, the American economy stood on the brink of an economic transformation from a predominantly agricultural small-producer economy to an urban industrial economy. In 1880, agriculture was still the principal source of wealth in the United States, but by 1890 the value of manufactured products surpassed the value of agricultural products by a factor of three.[57]

Northern Ohio became an important driver of the new industrial economy—an early leader in such indispensable industries as iron, steel, oil, electricity, and machine tools. From 1879 to World War II, the productivity rate of northern Ohio industries grew significantly more rapidly than in the nation as a whole, and the region registered patents at a higher rate than the rest of the country. Cleveland produced more millionaires than any other city in the Great Lakes except Chicago.[58] This dramatic transformation occurred between 1878, when the Bankruptcy Act of 1867 was repealed, and enactment of the Bankruptcy Act of 1898. The economy grew very unevenly during this period. After the long recession that lasted from October 1873 to March 1879, until enactment of the Bankruptcy Act of 1898, the nation suffered five additional recessions lasting a total of 96 months.[59]

In the 1870s, Cleveland was still primarily a commercial center providing services in support of the transshipment of agricultural goods from inland Ohio to eastern cities. After the 1870s, Cleveland began refining agricultural products and other raw materials before transshipment, especially oil, iron, and steel. Cleveland became a technical leader in these industries, producing a ripple effect that encouraged the growth of additional and related industries. Cleveland's population grew rapidly: from 160,000 in 1880 to 261,000 in 1890. By 1900, with a population of 382,000, Cleveland ranked as the sixth-largest city in the country.

Cleveland's oil industry peaked early. In 1873, Cleveland led the nation in oil refining. In 1888, Standard Oil refined more than 90 percent of the nation's oil, more than 20 percent of which was refined in Cleveland. John D. Rockefeller moved Standard Oil's headquarters from Cleveland to New York City in 1885, and the principal oil fields moved south and west. By 1900, very little oil refining remained in northern Ohio, but oil refining had stimulated technical innovation in the chemical industry and provided the raw materials for paint manufacturing, still an important industry in northern Ohio.

Most of northern Ohio's industrial growth evolved out of the iron and steel industry: mining, transporting, and manufacturing iron and steel, and manufacturing things made from iron and steel, from simple commodities like nails and wires to complex machines like pumps, compressors, sewing machines, and trucks. In 1865, Cleveland supported two blast furnaces, six rolling mills, and eight foundries, all for local consumption. When Cleveland Rolling Mills started its Bessemer furnace in 1868, the Bessemer process was new and revolutionary; the first Bessemer furnace in the country opened in 1864 in Wyandotte, Michigan. Railroad tracks used Bessemer steel, but the equally innovative open-hearth process produced steel better suited for other manufacturing purposes, and Cleveland was also an early adopter of this technology. In 1875, Otis Steel installed the first successful open-hearth furnace in the country. The opening of the Mesabi iron range on Lake Superior in 1892 gave Cleveland a strategic advantage in iron and steel manufacturing by providing a plentiful source of high-quality iron ore at low transportation cost through the Great Lakes. In 1893, the Cleveland Iron Mining Company and the Iron Cliffs Company merged to form the Cleveland Cliffs Iron Company, combining mining, lake shipping, railroads, and pig iron furnaces into one business entity.[60]

Youngstown also developed into a major steel-producing region. Iron mills began to appear in Youngstown as early as the 1840s, and the population of that city reached 4,500 by 1850. The mills expanded, and the population doubled every 10 years for the next 30 years. Youngstown lay on the railway corridor between Pittsburgh and Cleveland and developed into a modern industrial city with a dozen rolling mills by 1880. Youngstown built its first modern steel mill in 1891. By 1900, the Mahoning Valley held many important steel mills, including Youngstown Iron Sheet and Tube Company, Republic Iron and Steel Company, and the Ohio Works of the Carnegie Steel Company, later part of US Steel.[61]

Toledo declined as a Great Lakes port city mostly because its harbor could not accommodate the larger ships coming into use, but it remained a transportation center with excellent railroad connections. Toledo's leading industries in the 1870s were grain milling, the manufacture of high-quality wooden wagons from local lumber sources, and bicycles. Grain milling moved west to Minneapolis after 1900, but Toledo expanded its other industries and developed new ones. By 1900, Toledo had a diversified industrial base and population of 132,000.

Toledo firms patented important innovations in bicycle design, including wire wheels and improved ball bearings, that made bicycles suitable for general use by ordinary people, and the city became the center of the national bicycle industry at the same time that bicycles became a national passion. The Maumee Rolling Mill opened in 1884, and Toledo developed a machine tool and iron products industry. The combination of bicycle technology and the iron products industry made Toledo an important early manufacturer of automobiles and automobile parts. But Toledo ultimately became famous for glass. Toledo developed nearby natural gas resources, and in 1888, Libby Glass, founded in New England in 1818, moved to Toledo in search of lower costs and superior sand and fuel. Libby made the best cut glass in the country but lost money. Michael J. Owens saved Libby by successfully mechanizing the production of light bulbs, dominating another incipient industry, and entered into a partnership with Libby in Toledo for their manufacture. In 1898, the Ford Plate Glass Company was established in Toledo, reinforcing Toledo's importance as a center for the glass industry.

Inland, both Canton and Akron had started to industrialize by the 1870s, principally manufacturing agricultural machinery. By 1900,

Canton had a population of 26,000 and had developed into a diversified manufacturer of iron products and machinery. The Hoover Vacuum Cleaner Company was founded in Canton in 1908 and continued to make vacuum cleaners there until 2007. By 1933, Hoover was the largest vacuum cleaner company in the world.

Akron became the rubber manufacturing capital of the world. Because of its location on the Ohio and Erie Canal, and its connection by railroad to Cleveland, Pittsburgh, and Columbus, Akron's earliest economic activity consisted of refining agricultural goods for transshipment; Quaker Oats started its oat mill in Akron in the 1850s. Akron experienced rapid growth, and by 1900, its population reached 42,720. In 1871, the Akron Board of Trade convinced Benjamin Franklin Goodrich to locate his new rubber factory in Akron by offering financing and other benefits. As the agricultural machinery factories in Akron failed and closed between 1900 and 1927, the rubber industry picked up the slack: The Miller Rubber Company was founded in 1892, the Goodyear Rubber Company was founded in 1898, and the General Tire and Rubber Company was founded in 1915. The rubber industry exploded with the advent of the mass market for automobiles, and Akron became a one-industry town.

Building on expertise in the manufacture of iron and steel, complex machines and machine tools, northern Ohio evolved into a manufacturing center for automobiles and automobile parts. In Toledo, the Pope Bicycle Company began producing the Pope Toledo automobile in 1900. In 1909, Pope Toledo went out of business, and John Willys moved Willys-Overland Motors from Indianapolis, Indiana, into the vacant Pope Toledo automobile factory. Successor corporations have continuously manufactured jeeps in Toledo into the twenty-first century. The Ohio Electric Company produced the Ohio Electric automobile in Toledo from 1909 until 1918. The Milburn Wagon Company of Toledo produced Milburn Electric automobiles from 1914 to 1923. Milburn Electric vehicles were very popular—President Woodrow Wilson drove one.

In Cleveland, the Baker Motor Company manufactured an electric car and White Motors, an offshoot of the White Sewing Machine

Company founded in Cleveland in 1866, manufactured a steam automobile, all before 1900. White switched to gasoline engines around 1910 and became an important manufacturer of trucks and diesel engines into the 1980s. Other important automobile companies in Cleveland included the Winton Motor Carriage Company, the Chandler Motor Car, and the Cleveland Automobile Company. Peerless Motors, founded in Cleveland in 1889, evolved from a washing machine wringer company to a bicycle manufacturer in the 1890s to a manufacturer of luxury automobiles and automobile parts in 1901. Peerless Motors, which ceased operations in 1931, was the last firm that manufactured passenger automobiles in Cleveland.

A total of eighty different kinds of automobiles were made in and around Cleveland before 1931. Although Cleveland automobile manufacturers could not compete with the mass-production efficiencies of the factories in Detroit, Cleveland became the second-largest automotive manufacturing center in the United States. In the 1920s, 70 percent of northern Ohio's steel went into the automotive industry.[62]

As northern Ohio and the nation industrialized over the twenty years between the repeal of the 1867 Bankruptcy Act in 1878 and enactment of the Bankruptcy Act of 1898, associations of businessmen and creditors' lawyers continually agitated for a new national uniform bankruptcy act. Businessmen wanted a uniform national bankruptcy act for the same reasons they had always favored national bankruptcy legislation: they wanted to be able to collect debts from their debtors everywhere in the country using a single, efficient, uniform procedure in which they would not be discriminated against in favor of local businesses.[63] By 1890, commercial interests coalesced around the Torrey Bill. Various bankruptcy bills were introduced in 1890, 1892, and 1893 but failed to secure majorities in both houses of Congress.[64]

The Cleveland Chamber of Commerce incorporated in 1892 after the merger of the Cleveland Board of Trade, founded in 1848, and the recently created Merchants and Jobbers association. It received requests from similar organizations to study and comment on the proposed bankruptcy bills. In March 1898, a committee presented a report endorsing the Torrey Bill with reservations, observing: "There is scarcely a businessman either in or out of this chamber who does not feel the urgent necessity for some adequate, fair and proper legislation on this subject." The membership adopted a resolution favoring "enactment of a national bankruptcy law of uniform operation throughout the United States" and voted to forward a copy of the committee's report to the congressional conference committee then considering the bankruptcy bills.[65]

Although creditors and the new, urban, credit-dependent businessmen wanted a national bankruptcy act, rural debtors, farmers, and small-town lawyers preferred state insolvency laws and creditors' remedies. Although the nation experienced a major depression from 1893 to 1897, the depression did not cause passage of a bankruptcy bill. The economy started expanding in June 1897, and the recent depression experience merely reinforced existing demands for bankruptcy legislation; rural people remained opposed. The principal issues in contention recapitulated old debates: how to protect creditors from preferences, fraud, and fraudulent conveyances at low administrative cost; whether to establish uniform exemptions under the bankruptcy act or to allow debtors the benefit of state law exemptions; and the circumstances under which a creditor should be permitted to force a debtor into involuntary bankruptcy, if it should be allowed at all.

Creditor compromises enabled enactment of the Bankruptcy Act of 1898. Significantly, debtors secured the benefit of state exemptions, and farmers, "wage earners" (defined as persons earning salaries or wages of less than $1,500 per year), and debtors owing less than $1,000 could not be forced into involuntary bankruptcy. The act restricted the grounds for involuntary bankruptcy to fraudulent conveyances, creditor preferences, or assignments for the benefit of creditors by an insolvent debtor, and it defined insolvency as holding assets worth less than debts—a benefit to farmers who feared being forced into bankruptcy for not meeting current bills when due because of cash-flow difficulties even though they held significant assets of sufficient value to meet their debts if given enough time to realize true value. Furthermore, involuntary bankrupts were entitled to a jury trial on the question of solvency.

The contending factions in 1898 had not changed materially since the 1867 debate over bankruptcy: some wanted no national bankruptcy, some wanted voluntary bankruptcy only, and some wanted a vigorous and comprehensive uniform national bankruptcy act. Although bills to repeal the 1898 Bankruptcy Act were introduced in 1903, 1907, and 1910, the act endured. David Skeel asks why? What made the pro-bankruptcy coalition more cohesive after 1898 than it had been between 1867 and 1878? He concludes that the emergence of organized business lobbies, such as chambers of commerce, and pro-bankruptcy lawyers' organizations, such as the Commercial Law League and the American Bar Association, created a permanent constituency for a uniform national bankruptcy act.[66] These organizations did not emerge in a vacuum. They were products of the industrial transformation that occurred toward the end of the nineteenth century; their clients were the large, bureaucratic, business organizations busily restructuring American society in every conceivable way. Commerce had won over agriculture in the century-long battle over the nature of American society.

Even though suspicions about bankruptcy declined in significance by 1898, they did not disappear. Perennial questions persisted and new problems emerged. Bankruptcy became acceptable in the nineteenth century as Americans embraced entrepreneurial enterprise as the wellspring of progress and innovation. Under these circumstances, debt discharge benefited society by freeing the talents of honest but unfortunate businessmen and giving them the opportunity for a fresh start. American businessmen could not be expected to take great risks if failure were permanent and irrevocable. However, Americans did not believe in the social utility of debt discharge under all circumstances. The discharge of debts incurred for personal consumption purposes remained suspect. In a small-producer economy it was not necessary to distinguish between consumer and business bankruptcies; most bankruptcies involved both elements. In an industrial society most people earned wages, and their debts were not incurred in unsuccessful but worthwhile business ventures. In 1898, Americans did not realize that consumer debtors would come to dominate bankruptcy in an urban, industrial economy.

The Bankruptcy Act of 1898 opened a new era in debtor-creditor relations.

Chapter Three
Implementing the Bankruptcy Act of 1898

President William McKinley signed the Bankruptcy Act of 1898 into law on July 1, 1898.[1] This act established the basic foundation of American bankruptcy law as it exists today. No significant amendments to this bankruptcy act occurred before the 1930s, and the significant changes that occurred at that time did not originate in the economic crisis of the Great Depression. Instead, scandals in the bankruptcy courts in the Southern Judicial District of New York inspired several investigations into the operation of the Bankruptcy Act in the late 1920s. In response to the problems unearthed in those investigations, and influenced by the New Deal, Congress significantly modified the Bankruptcy Act in 1938. This chapter investigates the implementation and operation of the Bankruptcy Act of 1898 in the Northern District of Ohio from its enactment to the 1920s and lays a foundation for understanding the problems that precipitated reform in the 1930s.

The period between 1898 and the Great Depression were northern Ohio's glory days. A national center of manufacturing and innovation, northern Ohio grew rapidly. In 1903, the Group Plan Commission recommended an unprecedented integrated design plan for Cleveland's center city that featured stately public buildings surrounding an extensive mall. In 1910, the first building envisioned by the Group Plan opened, the federal courthouse. Now known as the Howard M. Metzenbaum US

Courthouse in honor of the late US senator, the building is the present home of the bankruptcy court in Cleveland. Additional buildings soon followed: the Cuyahoga County Courthouse in 1911; the Cleveland City Hall in 1916; the Public Auditorium, the largest convention center in the country at the time, in 1922; the Cleveland Public Library, the third-largest research library in the nation, in 1925; and the Board of Education administration building in 1930. By 1920, Cleveland was the fifth-largest city in the United States, and the Cleveland suburb Shaker Heights had the highest per capita income in the nation.[2] Cleveland's industrial and business elite invested heavily in an infrastructure of high culture during this period. The Cleveland Orchestra, now universally acknowledged as one of the five leading orchestras in the United States, played its first concert in 1918. Leading industrialists and philanthropists incorporated the Cleveland Museum of Art in 1913 and the Cleveland Museum of Natural History in 1920.

Bankruptcy radically expanded the role of the federal courts. From inception, bankruptcy dwarfed the other business of the district and circuit courts. In fiscal year 1900, the first full year of operation, more than 20,000 bankruptcy cases were filed in the United States compared with only 10,628 other private civil suits. Nationally, in 1900, 19,540 bankruptcy cases closed reporting $265 million liabilities and $33 million assets. All private district and circuit court judgments entered that year throughout the United States totaled only $166 million. In the Northern District of Ohio, in 1900, 428 bankruptcy cases were filed compared with 195 other private civil suits. In that same year, 486 bankruptcy cases closed in northern Ohio reporting $6.13 million liabilities and $653,000 assets, whereas private district and circuit court judgments in private civil suits totaled only $159,000. Ten years later, bankruptcy court filings seemed to reach a stable plateau, but the relationship between the district courts and the bankruptcy courts in the number of cases and amount of money at stake had not materially changed. In 1910, 18,053 bankruptcy cases and 10,618 private civil lawsuits commenced in the district and circuit courts of the United States. The 15,645 bankruptcy cases closed that year

Cleveland Terminal Tower circa 1930; left to right, the Higbee Co., Terminal Tower and Union Station, Hotel Cleveland. *Courtesy of the Western Reserve Historical Society*

Aerial view of Cleveland Terminal Tower and Public Square circa 1940; the Federal Courthouse is on the lower left corner of the square. *Courtesy of the Western Reserve Historical Society*

reported liabilities of $225 million and assets of $38 million, but district and circuit court civil judgments totaled only $91 million. In the Northern District of Ohio, 511 bankruptcies and 294 private civil lawsuits were filed in 1910. The 561 bankruptcy cases closed that year reported liabilities of $8.3 million and assets of $1.025 million, whereas district and circuit court civil judgments in the district that year totaled only $1.9 million.[3]

The Referees

The Bankruptcy Act of 1898 created the federal district courts as the courts of bankruptcy. In 1898, each federal district court still operated as an autonomous institution with few restrictions other than an obligation to submit statistical data to the Department of Justice for inclusion in its annual report to Congress. The district courts appointed referees in bankruptcy, but the referees made the system work. District court judges referred bankruptcy petitions to referees for all practical purposes, and referees answered only to their referring judge.

The Bankruptcy Act of 1898 took effect with regard to voluntary petitions on August 1, 1898, and with regard to involuntary petitions on November 1, 1898. The act required the United States Supreme Court to issue general orders regulating bankruptcy procedure, but the orders did not issue until January 1899. Some jurisdictions delayed making adjudications and referring cases to referees until the general orders became available, but the Northern District of Ohio did not wait. The district court referred the first case in the western division of the Northern District of Ohio on August 1, 1898. The district court referred the first case in the eastern division on August 8, 1898.

A person could file a petition admitting bankruptcy. Such petitions were called voluntary petitions, and most petitions were voluntary. Creditors could file a petition against persons other than farmers and small wage earners, and against business corporations other than national banks, insurance companies, and railroads, alleging that the debtor had committed an enumerated act of bankruptcy within the preceding four months. The enumerated acts included concealing or conveying property in order to hinder or delay creditors or to prefer some creditors over others, including the use of state court insolvency proceedings like assignments for the benefit of creditors. Such petitions were called involuntary petitions.

A debtor could defeat an allegation of bankruptcy in an involuntary petition by proving solvency at the time that the creditors filed the petition against him, and the act adopted a novel definition of insolvency: "a person shall be deemed insolvent within the provisions of this Act whenever the aggregate of his property . . . shall not, at a fair valuation, be sufficient in amount to pay his debts."[4] Traditionally, insolvency had been defined in equity as the inability to pay debts when due. The bankruptcy definition of insolvency made involuntary bankruptcy more difficult for creditors to prove because, if contested, it required proof of the value of a debtor's assets, and a debtor could demand a jury trial before the district court judge on the issue of insolvency.

In involuntary bankruptcies, the district court adjudicated bankruptcy and could refer the case to a referee after adjudication. The district court could also choose not to refer the petition but to keep it. In voluntary bankruptcies, the debtor admitted bankruptcy in his petition. The district court judge immediately reviewed the petition and either adjudicated bankruptcy and referred the case or dismissed the petition. If the judge was out of the district, the clerk could refer a voluntary petition to a referee, and the referee could enter the formal adjudication.

The Bankruptcy Act of 1898 specifically defined "judge" as "a judge of a court of bankruptcy, not including the referee." It created the office of bankruptcy referee, and the federal district court had almost unlimited authority over bankruptcy referees. The court appointed referees for a term of two years and could remove them "because their services [we]re not needed or for other cause." The court set the boundaries of the district for which the referee would serve, and the court could change the boundaries of the referees' districts as circumstances required.[5]

The only statutory qualifications for service as a referee in bankruptcy were as follows: (1) they were competent; (2) they held no federal or state office of profit concurrent with their appointment other than commissioners of deeds, justices of the peace, masters in chancery, or notaries public; (3) they were not related by blood or affinity to any of the judges of their district court or the justices of an appellate court that reviewed the decisions of their district court; and (4) they were residents of the geographical districts for which they were appointed and maintained offices there. Referees did not need to be lawyers, although almost all of them were. Referees could not represent any party in any bankruptcy in any district and could not purchase property from a bankrupt estate. Referees did not receive salaries but received ten dollars out of the filing fee of every case referred to them and 1 percent of the dividends paid to creditors. They received their fees only when the case closed. Referees were also required to post a bond.[6]

The Bankruptcy Act empowered referees to do anything that the court of bankruptcy could do with regard to a referred case, as provided by their district court's general orders and local rules, except for those things specifically prohibited by the act. The act specifically prohibited referees from adjudicating bankruptcy; confirming or setting aside compositions; granting, denying, or revoking discharges; and punishing contempt. The act required referees to determine creditors' dividends, examine bankrupts' schedules and ensure that they were correct and filed, ensure that all required notices were sent to creditors, keep the record and make it available to all interested parties as needed, and make an evidentiary record in contested matters and transmit it to the district court. Most referees continued their private law practices after appointment. Typically, hearings in bankruptcy cases were held in referees' offices or in meeting rooms specifically rented by referees for that purpose. Referees kept the bankruptcy records in their private law offices while the case was open and filed the required case records with the clerk of the district court after the case was closed.[7]

Ambiguity immediately arose with regard to the number of referees to be appointed in a judicial district and the boundaries of the referees' bankruptcy districts. The language of the Bankruptcy Act of 1898 directed the court to appoint referees for a term of two years and to designate the limits of the bankruptcy districts for which the referees served "so that each county, where the services of a referee are needed, may constitute at least one district."[8] Despite the plain language in the statute indicating that every county should have at least one referee, as well as statements by legislators and in the congressional reports that the act intended at least one referee in every county to minimize expense and inconvenience, several judicial districts, including the Northern District of Ohio, appointed referees to districts consisting of more than one county. In 1903, Congress amended the Bankruptcy Act of 1898 to eliminate the language requiring at least one referee for every county in a judicial district. Instead, district courts were given complete discretion to appoint as many referees as they deemed necessary for the efficient administration of the Bankruptcy Act.

In 1898, the Northern District of Ohio was served by one judge: Augustus J. Ricks, a Republican, who was appointed in July 1889 by President Benjamin Harrison. Between July 29 and October 15, 1898, Judge Ricks appointed twenty-two referees to bankruptcy districts in thirty-one of the Northern District of Ohio's forty counties. After that, it appears that he appointed referees as needed. Ricks fell ill in 1900, and in January 1901, President McKinley appointed Francis J. Wing to succeed him. In May 1901, Judge Wing discovered that no referee had been appointed for Ottawa County, so he expanded the jurisdiction of Referee E. S. Stephens in neighboring Erie County to include it.

It is not possible to determine how referees received their appointments or even to construct a completely accurate list of referees appointed during this period. In 1898, district courts still operated independent of any central administration, and no list or file documenting referee appointments exists for the Northern District of Ohio for this period. Information of any kind about most of these referees is scarce. We do not have official biographies for these referees and cannot find letters requesting their appointment and singing their praises. In many cases we cannot even find obituaries. As late as 1940, no definitive national list of referees in bankruptcy existed.[9] In the Northern District of Ohio, the court frequently, but not always, entered appointments, reappointments, or resignations of referees into the bankruptcy minute book, and sometimes the district court clerk advised the Department of Justice by letter of appointments, reappointments, or resignations. Sometimes the court simply failed to formally reappoint referees, and the referees continued to serve in their bankruptcy districts nonetheless.[10]

We do know that, in general, referees in bankruptcy were political appointments, and that almost all of the referees Judge Ricks appointed were active Republicans. The Ohio secretary of state published a roster of state, federal, and local officials that included party affiliation, and until 1916 all of the referees in bankruptcy but one were listed as Republicans. The roster identified Referee Fordyce Belford of Lucas County as a Democrat, but Bedford probably received his appointment as a favor to his uncle, Circuit Court clerk Irvin Belford, a Republican. Belford was only 30 years old when first appointed referee, but his parents had been one of the pioneer families in Ohio, and his father had practiced law in Toledo for many years.[11]

United States District court judgeships were political appointments, as they still are, and Judge Ricks was no exception. Ricks came from a prominent Massillon, Ohio, family, and in 1861, he left Kenyon College in his freshman year to join the Union army. He received a commission from the Ohio governor and served with General Burnside in east Tennessee and in the Georgia campaign. After the Civil War Ricks read law in Knoxville, Tennessee, with John Baxter, a slaveholding anti-secessionist who became an ardent Republican after the war. Ricks went into law practice with Baxter and helped found the *Knoxville Daily Chronicle*, the only Republican daily newspaper in the South. In 1875, Ricks returned to Massillon to practice with Republican judge Anson Pease. In 1877, President Rutherford B. Hayes appointed Baxter to the Sixth Circuit Court. In 1878, Baxter appointed Ricks clerk of the United States Circuit Court for the Northern District of Ohio. Ricks served as standing master in chancery from 1878 until his appointment as district court judge in 1889.

Judge Ricks knew something about insolvency receiverships. As master in chancery he heard numerous foreclosure cases involving the reorganization of narrow-gauge railroads through equity receiverships in the Northern District of Ohio. By and large Ricks appears to have appointed competent lawyers to serve as referees in bankruptcy, and he appointed some extraordinary lawyers as well. Most referees served more than one two-year term. Several referees served for very long periods of time.[12]

Some referees received an appointment very early in their careers, undoubtedly because of political influence. For example, William L. Monnett was appointed referee for Crawford County on August 4, 1898, when he was twenty-eight years old and only two years out of law school. The child of one of Ohio's original pioneer families, Monnett was already a very active Republican. Before attending law school at the University of Cincinnati, Monnett read law in Judge Jacob Scroggs's office and joined the law firm as partner immediately after graduation and admission to the bar. Judge Scroggs was an important Republican activist from the party's earliest years. Scroggs attended the Springfield Convention in 1855 and was elected secretary of the first Republican national convention in Pittsburgh in 1856. Scroggs was also a delegate to the 1864 Republican convention in Chicago and chair of the Crawford County Republican executive committee from 1864 to 1870. Monnett continued the political tradition, serving as chairman of the Crawford County Republican Party Executive Committee.[13]

On July 29, 1898, Charles H. Keating was appointed referee for Richland County, where his family owned the original site of the town of Mansfield, the Richland County seat and Keating's lifelong home. Keating read law and was admitted to the bar in 1894. He had a solo law practice until he was appointed referee in bankruptcy. During this period, Keating is the only referee known to have discontinued his private law practice while serving as a referee in bankruptcy. In 1906, Keating resigned his position as referee to accept President Theodore Roosevelt's appointment as deputy auditor of the US Post Office. Keating returned to Mansfield in 1912 with the election of Democratic president Woodrow Wilson and became Mansfield's most prominent businessman. In 1913, he was appointed counsel for the Lumbermen's Mutual Insurance Co. Eventually, he became Lumbermen's general counsel and in 1933 its president. Keating was also associated with the Farmer's Savings and Trust Co., the Mansfield Savings and Loan Co., and the Richland Hotel Co.

Some referees already enjoyed high esteem as lawyers in their communities before their appointment as a referee in bankruptcy. For example, William F. Kean had been practicing law in Wooster, Ohio, since 1886 when he was appointed referee in bankruptcy for Wayne and Holmes counties in August 1898. Kean was also a Republican activist in Wooster, an incorporator of the Wooster Republican Printing Company, and an early owner of the *Daily Republican*.

Dayton A. Doyle read law for one year in Akron in the office of Republican attorney general Jacob A. Kohler before entering Cincinnati

Law School. He was admitted to the bar in 1880, and in 1885, he opened a law office in Akron. Doyle immediately ran for public office and served four years as Akron city solicitor before becoming a referee in bankruptcy. Doyle's family was among the early residents of Akron, and his father served as mayor from 1901 to 1902. Doyle resigned his referee position in 1906 when he was elected judge of the common pleas court. After retiring from the bench in 1918, Doyle entered business and was very successful. He was the first president of the Summit County Bank and incorporated Doyle Tire and Rubber Co. shortly before his untimely death from heart disease in 1920.

In Cuyahoga County, Judge Ricks appointed one of Cleveland's foremost citizens a referee in bankruptcy: seventy-two-year-old Richard Chappel Parsons. Born in New Haven, Connecticut, Parsons moved to Newark, Ohio, in 1845. He was admitted to the bar in 1851 and moved to Cleveland. Parsons's accomplishments are legendary. He was elected to Cleveland's city council in 1852,and served as its president in 1853. A Republican, Parsons represented Cleveland in the Ohio House of Representatives from 1858 to 1861, serving one term as speaker. Parsons was collector of internal revenue at Cleveland from 1862 to 1866, was marshal of the United States Supreme Court from 1867 to 1872, and represented Cleveland in Congress from 1873 to 1875. In 1876, Parsons bought an interest in the *Cleveland Herald* and became its editor.

Parsons's bankruptcy district did not include Cleveland's nineteenth ward. Judge Ricks appointed Harold Remington referee in bankruptcy for Geauga County and the nineteenth ward of the city of Cleveland. The 1898 Bankruptcy Act required a referee in bankruptcy to be resident in the bankruptcy district for which he served, and Remington lived in Cleveland's nineteenth ward. When Parsons died in January 1899, Ricks enlarged Remington's bankruptcy district to include all of Cuyahoga County. In April 1899, Ricks removed Remington as referee for Geauga County and appointed Louis J. Wood referee for a bankruptcy district that comprised Geauga, Lake, and Portage counties.

Descended from an old Puritan New England family, Remington was born in Quincy, Illinois, the son of a wealthy Baptist minister. Remington received his undergraduate education at the University of Michigan and his law degree from George Washington University in Washington, DC. He was admitted to the Ohio bar in 1892 and entered into private practice in Cleveland. Remington's family moved to Cleveland in his early childhood, and his sister Mary married future US district court judge Francis J. Wing. Nominally a Republican, Remington never actively participated in partisan politics, and it is likely that he received his appointment as a favor to his influential brother-in-law. Furthermore, the publishers of Remington's legal treatises claimed that he achieved an early reputation for excellence in Cleveland through an extensive law practice involving state insolvency litigation.[14]

Judge Wing's family was among the original settlers in Trumbull County, Ohio. Wing attended the Andover Academy and Harvard College before returning to Ohio to read law. He practiced law in Cleveland from 1874 until his death, serving as US attorney from 1880 to 1881, judge of the Cuyahoga County Court of Common Pleas from 1899 to 1901, and US district court judge from 1901 to 1905. Judge Wing resigned the federal bench in 1905, stating that he preferred the private practice of law. He died in February 1918.

Remington's appointment as a referee in bankruptcy was fortuitous. He became the first nationally recognized bankruptcy scholar when he wrote the seminal treatise *Remington on Bankruptcy*, first published in 1908.[15] *Remington on Bankruptcy* outlived Remington, continuing into a sixth edition published in 1955, and it was continuously updated until enactment of the Bankruptcy Code in 1978. Remington also published numerous magazine and law review articles on bankruptcy, a bankruptcy treatise for law students, a law school case book, and a businessmen's guide to bankruptcy.[16]

Remington helped draft the 1903 amendments to the 1898 Bankruptcy Act. Those amendments primarily involved technical corrections regarding preferences, but one amendment required dividends to be distributed to creditors in two installments separated by at least three months. This amendment sought to end a questionable practice that Remington had encountered as a referee in Cleveland. Some bankruptcy lawyers made a practice of securing the distribution of dividends as soon as their clients proved their claims in order to obtain a larger distribution from the bankrupt estate at the expense of less diligent or less knowledgeable creditors.[17]

Remington wrote an article for the *Bulletin of the Commercial Law League of America* about the 1903 amendments, and in 1909, he resigned his position as referee in bankruptcy in Cuyahoga County to direct a bankruptcy law reform project for the National Association of Credit Men.[18] Remington is credited with drafting the 1910 amendments to the 1898 Bankruptcy Act and securing their passage in Congress. The 1910 amendments principally involved technical corrections to provisions involving unfiled chattel mortgages. Remington later claimed that his Cleveland office staff typed the House and Senate committee report in 1910. President William Howard Taft presented Remington with the pen used to sign the act into law in recognition of his efforts.[19]

In 1911, Remington relocated his law practice to New York City. He specialized in bankruptcy and lectured on bankruptcy law at Brooklyn Law School. Remington remained a leader of the national bankruptcy bar for the rest of his life. He was a founding member of the National Association of Referees in Bankruptcy in 1926 and actively participated in all bankruptcy legislation that passed through Congress until his death in 1937.

In February 1910, Congress created a second federal judgeship for the Northern District of Ohio that would be located in Toledo in the western division of the Northern District of Ohio, and in June 1910, President Taft appointed Republican John M. Killits to the position. A progressive reformer by nature, Judge Killits presided over the commission that drafted Toledo's city charter between 1913 and 1914. In 1914, Killits restructured the bankruptcy court in the western division of the Northern District of Ohio. He took senior status in 1928 and died in 1938.

Killits, whose father was a dry goods merchant in Bryan, Ohio, received his undergraduate degree from Williams College in 1880 and published a newspaper in Iowa for a short time before returning to Bryan to read law with a prominent law firm. In 1884, he accepted an appointment as editor of publications for the United States Signal Bureau in Washington, DC, and at the same time served as private secretary to chief signal officer general W. B. Hazen. General Hazen grew up in Hiram, Ohio, a close childhood friend of President James A. Garfield. Hazen enjoyed a distinguished military career in the Civil War and in the Indian wars on the western frontier before President Hayes appointed him chief signal officer in 1880.

While working for the Signal Corps, Killits studied law at George Washington University in Washington, DC. He received his law degree in 1885 and was admitted to the District of Columbia bar in June 1886. Hazen died in January 1887, and Killits resigned from the Signal Corps in October 1887. In February 1888, Killits returned to Ohio and began practicing law in Bryan. He successfully ran for prosecuting attorney of Williams County in 1892 and 1895, served on the Bryan City Council in 1898 and 1899, and was elected to the Ohio court of common pleas in 1904 and reelected in 1910.

The US district court judge sitting in the eastern division of the northern district located in Cleveland, Ohio, changed frequently between 1900 and 1914. Robert Taylor succeeded Judge Wing in 1905. Judge Taylor's father was made the first comptroller of the currency by President Abraham Lincoln in 1863 and served in that capacity until his death in 1878. Taylor attended Georgetown College but graduated from Western Reserve University in 1872. He taught school while studying law and was admitted to the Ohio bar in 1877. Taylor practiced in Columbiana County and was elected county prosecutor. He lived in New York City between 1890 and 1892 but returned to Lisbon, Ohio, and successfully ran for Congress in 1894. He served in Congress until appointed US district court judge by President Theodore Roosevelt in 1905. He died in 1910.

William L. Day replaced Judge Taylor on the Cleveland bench in 1911. Thirty-five-year-old Day was the son of United States Supreme Court justice William R. Day. William L. Day was the US attorney for the

Northern District of Ohio from 1908 to 1911. He found judicial pay inadequate and resigned in May 1914 to join the Cleveland law firm of Squire, Sanders & Dempsey.

Republican presidents appointed Republican judges to the eastern division of the Northern District of Ohio until 1914, and no significant personnel changes occurred among the referees in bankruptcy. However, in 1912, Woodrow Wilson became the first Democratic president elected since enactment of the 1898 Bankruptcy Act and only the second Democratic president elected since the Civil War. Judge Day's resignation gave Wilson the opportunity to appoint John H. Clarke the first Democratic US district court judge in the history of the Northern District of Ohio. All of the referees in bankruptcy at that time were Republicans, except possibly Fordyce Belford of Toledo, and Judge Clarke wanted to appoint Democrats to the position.

Although the two judges in the Northern District of Ohio sat in different divisions of the district, one in Cleveland and one in Toledo, the two divisions constituted one judicial district. The Bankruptcy Act of 1898 called for the appointment of referees by the district court but did not specify how multiple judges within one court should make decisions about appointments. Judge Killits and Judge Clarke decided to let each determine bankruptcy court appointments in the division where he presided, and the eastern and western divisions of the Northern District of Ohio took on very different characteristics at this time.

In the western division, Judge Killits undertook a fundamental reorganization of the bankruptcy districts and referees under his jurisdiction. For many years, fifteen referees had managed bankruptcy cases in twenty-one counties. On April 24, 1914, Killits appointed Fordyce Belford referee in bankruptcy for a district in Toledo, Ohio, that comprised ten counties formerly served by six referees. Belford had been referee in bankruptcy in Toledo since 1898. His district comprised four counties immediately before the reorganization. On June 16, 1914, Killits appointed Harvey Grindel referee in bankruptcy for a district in Lima, Ohio, that comprised seven counties formerly served by four referees. Harvey Grindel was admitted to the bar in 1904 at age 38; he had studied law while working as superintendent of schools. He was first appointed referee in Lima in 1908. Before the reorganization his bankruptcy district comprised three counties. In August 1914, Judge Killits appointed George E. Crane referee in bankruptcy for a district in Kenton, Ohio, that comprised four counties formerly serviced by four referees. The child of a pioneer family, Crane had been referee in bankruptcy for Hardin County since 1898. Crane died September 16, 1916, and his bankruptcy district was reassigned; Lima absorbed three counties and Toledo absorbed one county. Since then, two referees in bankruptcy have handled all of the cases in the western division of the Northern District of Ohio most of the time.

In the eastern division of the Northern District, Judge Clarke reorganized the boundaries of the bankruptcy districts of Lake, Geauga, Portage, and Ashtabula counties without changing the total number of referees. He made few significant changes to any of the other bankruptcy districts, reducing the total number of referees by two. In the eastern division, the number of referees in bankruptcy districts would not begin to decline for many years. However, between 1914 and 1916, as their terms expired, Clarke replaced all except two of the Republican referees in the eastern district with Democratic referees. The two Republican referees Clarke retained were Harry L. Snyder in Akron for Summit and Portage counties and William G. Beer in Bucyrus for Crawford County. Snyder was admitted to the bar in 1897 and appointed referee in 1906. He served until his death in 1939. A native of Bucyrus, Beer served in the Spanish American War at Santiago de Cuba and later attended the University of Michigan Law School. Admitted to the bar in 1903, Beer was appointed referee in bankruptcy in 1912 and served until his death in 1945. We do not know why Clarke retained these two Republican referees. It may be that they enjoyed exceptional reputations and support in their communities; it may be that no deserving Democrats desired their positions.

Judge Clarke started his career as a successful lawyer and Democratic newspaper publisher in Youngstown, Ohio. He moved to

Cleveland in 1897 and became closely associated with progressive Democratic mayor Tom L. Johnson and future mayor Newton D. Baker. Clarke did not stay on the Cleveland bench very long. Baker became President Woodrow Wilson's secretary of war, and his influence helped secure Clarke's elevation to the Supreme Court in 1916. Clarke made many referee appointments from among local Democratic activists and their families. For example, he appointed Celsus Pomerene referee in bankruptcy in Canton for Stark and Carroll counties. Pomerene's brother was Atlee Pomerene, the senator from Ohio. Celsus Pomerene served as referee until his death in 1926.

Most importantly, on January 1, 1916, Judge Clarke appointed Carl D. Friebolin referee in Cleveland for Cuyahoga County. Clarke received his appointment as federal judge in the midst of campaigning for a US senate seat, and Friebolin had managed his senate campaign. Like Clarke, Friebolin was closely associated with Cleveland's progressive Democratic politicians; he was a protégé of Tom Johnson and a lifelong friend of Newton Baker. Friebolin served in the Ohio House of Representatives from 1911 to 1913 and in the Ohio Senate from 1913 to 1914, where he was elected majority floor leader. Friebolin served with progressive Democrat James M. Cox in the Ohio House, and they became lifelong friends and correspondents.

In 1912, Ohio voters approved sweeping changes to the Ohio Constitution. When James Cox was elected governor of Ohio in 1913, Friebolin was the governor's representative in the legislature. Working closely with Cox, Friebolin successfully supervised the drafting and enactment of extensive changes to Ohio law necessary to conform the general law to the new constitution and implement Cox's progressive reform agenda. Governor Cox credited Friebolin with securing legislation on workmen's compensation, the rural school code, judicial reforms, banking reforms, and more.[20] Friebolin is also credited with authoring Ohio's civil service reform act. In 1914, Cox appointed Friebolin judge of the Cuyahoga County Common Pleas Court, but Friebolin lost in the next general election and did not retain the position.

Carl D. Friebolin. *Courtesy of the Western Reserve Historical Society*

Cox remained governor of Ohio until nominated as the Democratic candidate for president in 1920. Cox's vice presidential nominee was Franklin D. Roosevelt. Friebolin campaigned extensively with Cox during his unsuccessful run for president. Cox never held another elected office but remained active and influential in Democratic Party politics through his friendships and his media empire, Cox Enterprises. Friebolin also remained actively involved in Democratic Party politics and in later years declined several opportunities for judicial appointment to higher state and federal courts.

One of the referees Judge Clark passed over for reappointment was future US district court judge Paul J. Jones, who served as referee in bankruptcy for Youngstown, Ohio, from 1912 to 1916. In 1904, Jones graduated from the University of Michigan law department, at that time an undergraduate program. He played football for the University of Michigan in 1902 on the famous "point a minute" team and was an All-American that year. Jones practiced law in his hometown of Youngstown and was an unsuccessful candidate for mayor in 1909. After Republicans reclaimed the US presidency in 1920 Jones was appointed US district court judge in 1923. Congress created a new judgeship in Cleveland for Jones, and he became the second US district court judge sitting in Cleveland, together with Judge Clarke's replacement, Democratic judge David C. Westenhaver.

Between 1923 and 1928, the district court in Cleveland was evenly divided: one Democrat and one Republican. Generally, referees continued in office, and it appears that the district court judges took turns with appointments. Four new referees were appointed during that five-year period, two Democrats and two Republicans.

Judge Westenhaver died in July 1928, and President Calvin Coolidge appointed Samuel H. West to succeed him. Once again, both district court judges serving in Cleveland were Republicans, and rumors circulated that Carl Friebolin would not be reappointed referee in bankruptcy at the conclusion of his two-year term. Friebolin kept his appointment but a second referee was appointed in the district, Republican William

B. Woods. Woods had served on the Cleveland City Council from 1912 to 1916. He ran unsuccessfully as the Republican candidate for Cuyahoga County prosecutor in 1914 and 1916. Woods was first assistant law director in Cleveland from 1917 to 1918 and Cleveland law director from 1920 to 1922. Woods continued as a referee in Cleveland until 1963 and was president of the National Association of Referees in Bankruptcy in 1948.

A referee in Cleveland for more than fifty years, Carl Friebolin dominates the history of bankruptcy in northern Ohio. A widely respected bankruptcy scholar and genuinely nice person, Friebolin served as the unofficial chief of referees in northern Ohio at a time when referees officially reported only to their referring judges. He taught bankruptcy law at Western Reserve University law school from 1934 to 1959, and he trained a generation of Cleveland's bankruptcy lawyers with his private postgraduate evening bankruptcy class. Commonly known as "Friebolin College," the class ran from at least 1947 until 1965. Friebolin College enjoyed such a wide reputation that, in 1961, newly appointed referee William B. Washabaugh of Erie, Pennsylvania, wrote Friebolin to buy a copy of the course outline.[21]

Friebolin also played important roles in every national movement involving bankruptcy law and procedure that occurred during his long lifetime. Friebolin was a founding member of the National Association of Referees in Bankruptcy, where he served at various times as president, chairman of the Legislation Committee, member of the Committee on Uniformity of Procedure and Practice, member of the editorial board of the association's journal, member of the Editorial Advisory Committee, and for many years unofficial editor of the journal's official editor, Referee Elmore Whitehurst. Friebolin was part of the committee that wrote the Chandler Act and later organized the National Bankruptcy Conference. A charter member of the National Bankruptcy Conference, Friebolin was chairman of the Committee on Definitions, the Committee on Jurisdiction and Procedure, the Nominating Committee, and the Committee on Improvements in the Bankruptcy Law; he also served continuously until his death on the all-important Drafting Committee.

At various times Friebolin also served on the Executive Committee, the Committee on Bankruptcy Administration, the Committee on Organization and Nominations, and the Consumer Bankruptcy Committee of the National Bankruptcy Conference. Edwin Covey, chief of the Division on Bankruptcy of the Administrative Office of the United States Courts, frequently consulted Friebolin, officially and unofficially. Friebolin knew everybody who was anybody in bankruptcy and sustained a lively correspondence on every topic of importance throughout his career.[22]

Friebolin's contributions to the city of Cleveland cannot be exaggerated. Born in Owatonna, Minnesota, the son of a Presbyterian minister, Friebolin moved to Cleveland when he was seven years old. He graduated from Cleveland public schools and received a law degree from Western Reserve University in 1899. In 1901, Friebolin formed a law partnership with Edgar S. Byers that lasted until 1947, when referees finally became federal court employees. Friebolin was one of the founding members of the City Club of Cleveland in 1912 and served as its president. From 1916 until 1966 he coauthored the City Club's annual satirical musical, the Anvil Revue. Friebolin involved himself meaningfully in every beneficial public cause in Cleveland, including the Red Cross, Citizen's League, Cleveland Americanization Council, Adult Education Association, Law Library League, and Chamber of Commerce. Friebolin was a trustee of Western Reserve Academy and Kent State University.

A beloved eccentric, Friebolin lived in the same house on East 69th Street in Cleveland from his marriage in 1906 until his death in 1967. He never drove a car; he took the city bus or taxis around Cleveland. He took the interurban bus to his vacation home on Lake Erie in Vermillion, Ohio; Friebolin and his brother George, an Erie County Democratic Party activist, purchased the house in 1909 for their father. A small man, Friebolin dressed well and always carried a cigar in his mouth. He did not smoke them; he chewed them. He worked voraciously. Bankruptcy lawyers complained that he was always in a hurry. He never waited for elevators, preferring to run up flights of stairs.

Friebolin was known for his wit, wisdom, knowledge, generosity, fairness, and humor. More than forty years after his death, bankruptcy lawyers who knew him still mourn.

The Rules

The Bankruptcy Act of 1898 established the district courts as the courts of bankruptcy, but circuit courts had jurisdiction of suits in law and equity between bankruptcy trustees and third parties to the extent that the suits could have been brought by the bankrupt if no petition had been filed, and circuit courts had concurrent jurisdiction with the district courts over bankruptcy fraud.[23]

Originally, district courts had exclusive jurisdiction over suits in admiralty, and circuit courts were the principal trial courts of the federal system. District courts only had jurisdiction over civil cases up to a certain dollar amount at issue and noncapital criminal cases; circuit courts heard appeals from the district courts. Circuit courts consisted of a designated Supreme Court justice and a local district court judge. Circuit riding posed practical problems for the efficient administration of the circuit courts, and jurisdictional lines blurred almost immediately. After 1802, district court judges often presided over circuit court sessions because the designated circuit justice could not appear. Circuit courts kept separate dockets at the same locations as district courts, often employing the same clerk, and both courts often sat concurrently.[24]

Federal court activity increased dramatically after the Civil War. In 1869, Congress created a circuit court judgeship for each circuit and reformed the circuit court to consist of the designated Supreme Court justice, the circuit court judge, and local district court judges, or any one of them. Supreme Court justices rarely attended circuit court after the Civil War, and district court judges acted when circuit court judges were unavailable.[25] In 1891, Congress created the circuit courts of appeal, but retained circuit trial courts in the judicial districts.[26] However, circuit judges left most trial work to district judges, and Congress finally abolished circuit trial courts with the Judicial Code of 1911.[27] After that, district courts became the trial courts of the federal system, and circuit courts became appellate courts.

Congress closely regulated federal court procedure until relatively recently, even specifying the time and place of terms of court for specific district and circuit courts. Courts did not formally control the time and place of their sessions until enactment of the Judicial Code of 1948, although the growth of court business had made the concept of court terms obsolete much earlier as the unfinished court business of one term flowed seamlessly into the next term.[28] In 1792, Congress gave the Supreme Court authority to make rules for equity and admiralty but required law cases to follow the procedure of the state in which the federal district was situated.[29] Congress did not authorize the Supreme Court to make rules governing procedure at law and equity until 1934. At that time, Congress also authorized the Supreme Court to merge law and equity through the rules of procedure, which the court promptly did when it promulgated the Federal Rules of Civil Procedure in 1938.[30]

The Bankruptcy Act of 1898 gave the Supreme Court the authority to issue general orders regulating bankruptcy practice, and the orders embodied the existing distinction between law and equity. In general, bankruptcy was considered an equitable remedy, and General Order 37 authorized the bankruptcy court to use the rules of equity practice promulgated by the Supreme Court "[i]n proceedings in equity, instituted for the purpose of carrying into effect the provisions of the act, or for enforcing the rights and remedies given by it . . . as nearly as may be." Law cases, as opposed to equity cases, involved enforcement of legal rights through money damages; for example, a suit for damages from a breach of contract is a suit at law. When proceedings at law occurred in the course of a bankruptcy, General Order 37 specified that the bankruptcy court should follow the practice and procedure for cases in law in the district courts "as nearly as may be," and the practice and procedure for cases in law in the district courts at that time was the procedure in use in the state courts.[31]

In November 1898, the Supreme Court published thirty-eight general orders and sixty-one official forms for use in bankruptcy. The general orders established the essential framework for implementing a bankruptcy court system. The general orders directed the court clerk to keep a separate bankruptcy docket and identified the information it was to contain. They defined the duties, responsibilities, and compensation of the referee, clerk, marshal, and trustees, and authorized the bankruptcy court to implement procedures to ensure the payment of fees and expenses by bankrupt estates. The general orders were published and available to the bench and bar. Modified and expanded frequently, general orders governed practice in bankruptcy until the Supreme Court promulgated the Federal Rules of Bankruptcy Procedure in 1973.[32]

Of necessity, the general orders employed broad outlines in establishing bankruptcy procedure for use by many widely divergent district courts. District courts had enjoyed local rule-making authority since 1793, and Judge Ricks established local rules in bankruptcy for the Northern District of Ohio as need arose, recording them in the court's minute book.[33] On August 18, 1898, the clerk entered in the bankruptcy minute book the first local rule for the Northern District of Ohio. That occurred only ten days after the first bankrupt filed the first bankruptcy petition under the Bankruptcy Act of 1898 and four months before the Supreme Court published the general orders. The rule required the person filing a petition in bankruptcy to deposit an additional ten dollars with the clerk to cover the cost of publication and notice to creditors and to purchase a record book for the referee. Judge Ricks promulgated only ten local rules over the course of the first three years of the Bankruptcy Act.

Most of the early local rules in bankruptcy in the Northern District of Ohio concerned expenses of administration. One rule provided that fees for appraisers be the same as under state insolvency statutes. Two rules established the referee's entitlement to fees in addition to the statutory fees, such as charges for mailing and notices, a three dollar charge per case for referee office expense, and additional charges of five dollars per day for hearings on involuntary bankruptcy or opposition to a discharge or composition. Bankruptcy Rule No. 7, dated November 13, 1899, specifically relied on the practice of the District Court for the Northern

District of New York in finding that additional fees to referees for hearings were not precluded by the provisions in the Bankruptcy Act and general orders that prohibited a referee from receiving compensation in addition to the statutory fees for performing services under the Bankruptcy Act. Fees and expenses in addition to the ten dollar deposit against fees required by the first local rule had to be paid before discharge and were assessed against the estate if in excess of the petitioner's deposit. If creditors brought an unsuccessful involuntary petition or opposed a discharge, the rules required them to post security against the referee's fees for the necessary hearings and other costs. No bankrupt could secure a discharge until the referee certified to the court that all fees and expenses had been paid and that the bankrupt otherwise qualified for the discharge.

By April 1914, the Northern District of Ohio had developed comprehensive local rules and official forms governing bankruptcy procedure from petition to discharge.[34] At the opening of the April 1914 Cleveland term, the clerk published the local rules by entering into the journal twenty-six typewritten pages setting forth thirty-three rules and eight supplementary forms. The rules incorporated the rules previously entered in the minute book on an ad hoc basis but organized them in a logical fashion and carefully revised and drafted them, explicitly incorporating statutory authority and the appropriate general orders and official forms.

In addition to establishing local procedures for implementing essential functions under the Bankruptcy Act, the local rules regulated the practice of the local bankruptcy bar to ensure against inappropriate or unethical behavior. For example, the rules enjoined attorneys from voting on a petition for a receiver without first filing a written notice of appearance specifically identifying the parties represented and the nature and amount of their claims. No one who had served as a receiver in a bankruptcy could be elected trustee in the same case, and his attorney, partner, and business associates were also barred from election as trustee in the case.[35] These rules were intended to prevent the development of so-called "bankruptcy rings": a small group of lawyers who dominated practice in the bankruptcy courts and appeared to be more interested in their own enrichment than in the distribution of dividends to creditors.

A desire to revise the general orders in order to limit opportunities for abuse of the bankruptcy process by bankruptcy rings afforded the newly created Conference of Senior Circuit Judges an opportunity to pioneer mechanisms for effective administrative reform. Chief Justice William Howard Taft and others had long advocated strongly for the creation of a formal institutional structure for administration and policy making within the federal courts, and in 1922, Congress created the Conference of Senior Circuit Judges. One of the first projects undertaken by the conference involved revising the general orders in bankruptcy. The National Association of Credit Men had requested a study of bankruptcy rules alleging abuses of the bankruptcy process by bankruptcy rings. The conference appointed a committee, and the National Association of Credit Men conducted a study and proposed changes. The committee submitted its report to the conference, and the conference referred the report to the district court judges for comment. A special conference in 1924 involving the National Association of Credit Men, the Commercial Law League, the American Bar Association, and the conference proposed extensive changes, and in April 1925, the Supreme Court promulgated the first comprehensive revision of the general orders.[36]

The Bankrupts

When Congress enacted the 1898 Bankruptcy Act, the American economy was in the midst of a fundamental restructuring that changed the kinds of debtors using the bankruptcy system in ways that the drafters had not anticipated. The 1898 Bankruptcy Act primarily addressed the needs of unincorporated entrepreneurial businesses, and before 1890, most commercial and manufacturing enterprises operated as proprietorships or partnerships. However, the corporate form offered important business advantages, and business incorporations surged in the 1880s and 1890s. Changes in state incorporation laws in the 1890s permitted corporations operating in any state to own the stock of other corporations operating in any other state. Consequently, many large industrial corporations merged, consolidating large sections of the economy between 1894 and 1905, and "corporation" became a synonym for "monopoly" in the public imagination.[37] Business establishments' increasing use of the corporate form, and the increasing scale of corporations, had the effect of decreasing the share of national income earned by unincorporated businesses and increasing the share of income earned by individuals as salaries and wages.[38]

Anyone except a corporation could file a voluntary petition in bankruptcy under the Bankruptcy Act of 1898. The act defined a corporation as any entity that enjoyed limited liability, such as a limited partnership. Most people justified bankruptcy legislation as necessary for the relief of honest businessmen who encountered financial difficulties through no fault of their own, but they believed a corporation in financial distress should liquidate and, by definition, a limited liability entity did not need a discharge of its debts. The act permitted a creditor to file an involuntary petition against a business corporation other than a railroad, bank, or insurance company in order to secure an orderly and equitable disposition of the corporation's assets through bankruptcy, and many business corporations used a friendly creditor to secure bankruptcy by admitting insolvency and consenting to an involuntary bankruptcy. Consequently, in 1910, Congress amended the 1898 Bankruptcy Act to allow business corporations other than railroads, banks, and insurance companies to file voluntary petitions in bankruptcy.[39] However, it is impossible to determine from the statistics published by the Department of Justice how often corporations used bankruptcy, because the data does not differentiate between incorporated and unincorporated business bankruptcies.[40]

Railroads, banks, and insurance companies could not use bankruptcy under any circumstances. Instead, they petitioned state or federal courts for a receiver if they needed court protection from creditors or became insolvent; receiverships vested corporate property in the receiver and prevented creditors from seizing or levying on corporate property. Large industrial corporations could file voluntary petitions in bankruptcy, but they preferred to reorganize through equity receiverships because of the flexibility inherent to an equity receivership and the bankruptcy court's inability to allow continued operation of the business for any length of time. Theoretically, three creditors could force a large industrial corporation in receivership into an involuntary bankruptcy by filing a petition within four months of the receivership—the receivership constituted a qualifying act of bankruptcy—but it did not happen very often. Even dissenting creditors could expect a greater return from an equity receivership than from liquidation in bankruptcy.[41] Equity receiverships could be filed in state or federal court, but large industrial corporations with interstate operations enjoyed significant advantages and efficiencies from federal court receiverships.

The typical federal court equity receivership involved a railroad with bond issues secured by mortgages. Typically, a bank, represented by a New York lawyer specializing in railroad reorganizations, in cooperation with the insolvent corporation, initiated the receivership by filing a creditor's bill in federal court on behalf of a creditor who was not a resident of any state in which the railroad did business. The selection of the petitioning creditor ensured federal court diversity jurisdiction in all judicial districts necessary to the reorganization's success. The bank acted before an actual default by the railroad because it wanted to be the first to secure a receivership—it did not want to risk the appointment of an unfriendly receiver. Subsequent receiverships filed in the other district courts where the corporation had property would be ancillary to the first receivership. The court would appoint two receivers, one selected by the petitioning creditor, typically an officer of the corporation in receivership, and one selected by the court. Only then would the petitioning creditor file a bill of foreclosure and have the receivers appointed under the creditor's bill also appointed receivers under the foreclosure bill. The receivers operated the corporation pending reorganization with the aid of "receiver's certificates," which gave current expenses priority over older debts.[42]

The bondholders would form a protective committee and solicit other bondholders to deposit their bonds with the committee in exchange for negotiable certificates. With the assistance of the bank's corporate reorganization lawyer, the bondholder's committee would develop a reorganization plan and solicit support for it from other creditors' committees. Eventually, a joint reorganization plan would be filed and all secured creditors given the opportunity to join in the plan or to dissent from it. Only when the plan acquired sufficient support to be operative would a foreclosure sale occur.

The plan envisioned that the joint reorganization committee would purchase the mortgaged assets of the insolvent corporation at the foreclosure sale and deposit them in a new corporation formed for the specific purpose of the reorganization. The securities of the new corporation would then be distributed to the participating creditors according to the joint reorganization plan. Nonparticipating creditors received cash on a pro rata basis with the participating creditors in exchange for their securities. The committee would take a deficiency judgment for the difference between the face value of the original securities and the sale price of the mortgaged assets. The secured creditors' deficiency judgment and the unsecured creditors shared in the sale of the unmortgaged assets, if any. Theoretically, the plan could fail if bidders at the foreclosure sale drove the price of the mortgaged assets too high, but in practice, the only bidder at the foreclosure sale was the joint reorganization committee. The court set a minimum bid for the foreclosure sale to protect nonparticipating bondholders.

In Ohio, through the 1920s, ordinary businesses, including corporations and their creditors, used Ohio receiverships extensively in preference to bankruptcy procedures. Although the reason is unclear, one investigator opined that attorneys preferred state court receiverships because they received higher compensation in state court than in bankruptcy. Ohio attorneys may also have been more familiar with the state law alternatives to bankruptcy and more comfortable with them.[43] Most commonly, secured creditors initiated an equity receivership in connection with a bill of foreclosure on a mortgage using a procedure similar to the procedure in federal court.[44] Ohio statutes also authorized the appointment of a receiver if a corporation was insolvent or in imminent danger of becoming insolvent and property was in danger of being lost, damaged, or removed. Receivers could also be appointed to preserve property pending the outcome of litigation, in aid of execution, or in connection with an assignment for the benefit of creditors.[45]

The overlap between bankruptcy and state creditors' remedies raised questions about the extent to which federal bankruptcy preempted state statutes. Early in the nineteenth century, the Supreme Court determined that the federal bankruptcy power did not preempt state insolvency statutes when no federal bankruptcy law was in effect, but that a federal bankruptcy law clearly invalidated state statutes that directly interfered with its operation.[46] The difficulty lay in determining when part of a competing state debtor/creditor regime impermissibly interfered with the federal bankruptcy law. The rule of decision in federal court complicated the question, because federal courts followed substantive state law unless the Constitution, treaties, or federal law required a different rule. An early decision from the Northern District of Ohio illustrates the problem.[47]

C. M. Zengerle was the president of the Georgian Bay Lumber Company. His wife, Margaret Zengerle, loaned the company money from her separate estate and received promissory notes from the company. Mr. Zengerle acted as Mrs. Zengerle's agent in negotiating the transaction. In February 1910, the Georgian Bay Lumber Company transferred to Mrs. Zengerle's trustee specifically identified lumber of a value equal to the amount of the debt. Mr. Zengerle again acted as Mrs. Zengerle's agent. In May 1910, the company sold Mrs. Zengerle's lumber to a third party for part cash and part notes due in installments up to October 1, 1910. The company transferred the cash and bill of account for the balance due under the sale back to Mrs. Zengerle's trustee. Mr. Zengerle again acted as Mrs. Zengerle's agent in the transaction. Shortly thereafter, the purchaser refused the remaining portion of the lumber and failed to pay the balance due on the bill of account for the lumber he had already received.

On October 31, 1910, the Georgian Bay Lumber Company made a general assignment for the benefit of its creditors. The assignment was filed on November 7, 1910, and on November 9, 1910, the company was adjudged a bankrupt.[48] At the time of the bankruptcy, the company owed Mrs. Zengerle $7,000, and her trustee was in possession of approximately $4,000 in returned lumber and the bill of account for the lumber that had been sold but not yet paid for. The bankruptcy trustee sued Mrs. Zengerle's trustee to recover the lumber and the account payable for the bankruptcy estate.

The case turned on whether certain Ohio statutes relevant to the assignment for the benefit of creditors had been superseded by the 1898 Bankruptcy Act. Under the 1898 Bankruptcy Act, the trustee could not challenge the transfer of the lumber and bill of account to Mrs. Zengerle because the transaction occurred more than four months before the filing of the petition in bankruptcy. However, Ohio statutes made a transfer of property by an insolvent debtor with intent to prefer one creditor over other creditors voidable by the other creditors, or by a receiver appointed for the benefit of the other creditors, so long as the preferred creditor was aware of the debtor's wrongful purpose. Mr. Zengerle's knowledge of the insolvency of the Georgian Bay Lumber Company was imputed to Mrs. Zengerle because Mr. Zengerle had acted as her agent in the transactions in question. Creditors or their receiver could invoke this provision to void a fraudulent transfer up to four years after it occurred. An additional wrinkle arose from different definitions of insolvency: At the time of the transfer, the Georgian Bay Lumber Company met the Ohio definition of insolvency—not able to pay its bills when due—but could not meet the definition of insolvency under the 1898 Bankruptcy Act—the company's assets, fairly priced, were not sufficient to meet the company's liabilities.

Without doubt, the bankruptcy suspended the state assignment for the benefit of creditors, but did the bankruptcy also suspend operation of all of the related Ohio statutes that governed the operation of an assignment for the benefit of creditors? If so, Mrs. Zengerle got to keep the property that secured preferential payment of her loan to her husband's company. However, if the Ohio rules on fraudulent conveyances stood despite the bankruptcy, and if the bankruptcy trustee could stand in the shoes of Georgian Bay Lumber Company's creditors for the purpose of enforcing Ohio's laws voiding fraudulent conveyances, then the bankrupt estate recovered the lumber and the bill of account and Mrs. Zengerle shared in the company's assets on a pro rata basis with all the other unsecured creditors.

The circuit court certified the question to the United States Supreme Court, and the Supreme Court ruled that the Ohio fraudulent conveyance provisions had the same purpose as bankruptcy: to require creditors to share equitably in the orderly liquidation of a debtor's assets. Therefore, the provisions did not conflict with the operation of the bankruptcy laws and were not suspended by them. Because trustees had the right under the 1898 Bankruptcy Act to recover property for the benefit of the bankrupt estate to the same extent as creditors under state law, the trustee could void the transfers to Mrs. Zengerle and recover the property without regard to the four-month limitation under the Bankruptcy Act or the inconsistent definitions of insolvency.

State law also governed the coerced collection of consumer and agricultural debts; the 1898 Bankruptcy Act prohibited creditors from filing involuntary petitions against farmers and small wage earners. Congressional debate indicated a desire to protect honest family farmers from an expanding commercial culture, but no debate occurred regarding the perceived dangers involuntary bankruptcy posed for small wage earners. In fact, bankruptcy proved a benefit to small wage earners and a problem for the consumer creditors they owed.

The 1898 Bankruptcy Act defined "small wage earners" as persons receiving less than $1,500 of wages per year, and very few wage earners received more than $1,500 per year. In 1900, nonagricultural employee annual earnings averaged less than $500, and average annual earnings did not exceed $1,000 for any category of employee.[49] Even though creditors could not bring involuntary bankruptcy proceedings against small wage earners, small wage earners threatened by garnishment of wages or other state law creditor's remedies could file voluntary petitions in bankruptcy and obtain a discharge of their debts even though they had no assets to contribute toward the payment of their debts. Many wage earners did just that.

The nation experienced a debilitating depression immediately before the enactment of the Bankruptcy Act of 1898. The economy was slowing in the spring of 1893 when a financial panic precipitated a severe credit contraction. Farmers could not obtain the credit necessary to harvest and market crops. Urban unemployment reached 17 to 19 percent the following winter. Industrial production fell precipitously, and many firms failed. Railroads and the iron industry suffered especially. By the end of 1893, 119 railroads entered receivership and thirty-two iron manufacturing companies failed. By June 1894, 154 railroads entered receivership, including the Erie Railroad.[50] This was the first depression of the industrial age, and the suffering of unemployed urban wage earners shocked middle-class sensibilities. Economic recovery began in the spring of 1896, but per capita gross domestic production did not reach 1892 levels again until 1899.[51] Urban unemployment lingered around 8 percent as late as 1899. Average nonfarm earnings did not return to their 1891 level until 1900.[52]

Distraught debtors flooded Ohio's probate courts with assignments for the benefit of creditors. Because of the high volume of insolvency cases, in May 1894, the Ohio legislature established a court of insolvency in Cincinnati to provide relief for the Hamilton County probate court. The court of insolvency consisted of one judge elected to a five-year term with original jurisdiction over all matters pertaining to assignments for the benefit of creditors and the condemnation of land for public use. The Hamilton County insolvency court worked so well that the legislature passed a similar act in March 1896, establishing a court of insolvency in Cleveland to provide relief for the Cuyahoga County probate court. Both courts remained in operation for many years after enactment of the 1898 Bankruptcy Act, and debtors continued to file assignments for the benefit of creditors in Cleveland until 1934, when the court of insolvency was dissolved. However, the number of assignments filed with the court of insolvency slowed markedly in the 1920s, and parties transferred many of the later insolvency cases to the bankruptcy court.[53]

Figure 3.1. US Bankruptcy Filings for Fiscal Years Ending 1899–1920

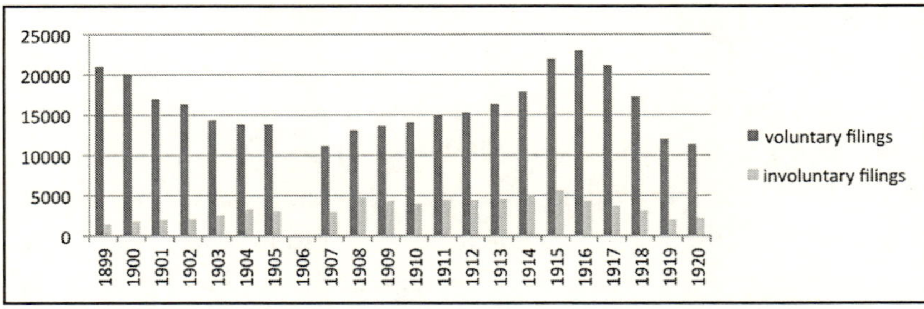

Note: This chart and the five following charts were prepared from the attorney general's reports for the years 1899 to 1920. No information is provided for 1906 because during that year the Department of Justice's fiscal year changed from September 30 to June 30 making the data incommensurate.

The insolvency courts left Ohio debtors with undischarged debts and the threat of future collection attempts; only bankruptcy could discharge debts. In 1898, many Ohio debtors took their backlog of old debts to the newly created bankruptcy courts. Debtors throughout the United States sought the discharge of old debts in the bankruptcy courts in large numbers. The number of new petitions filed began to decline almost immediately, reaching a plateau by 1903 that continued until shortly before the beginning of World War I in Europe. The number of new bankruptcy petitions filed would not return to the number filed in the first year of the 1898 Bankruptcy Act until 1915. (See Figure 3.1.)

Bankruptcy filings tended to correlate very little with the business cycle. The National Bureau of Economic Research (NBER) found business recessions between May 1907 and June 1908, January 1910 and January 1912, and January 1913 and December 1914, and bankruptcy filings increased gradually over this period. However, the NBER also found a recession between September 1902 and August 1904, and bankruptcy filings continued their decline from the initial 1899 high over this period. Also, NBER found a business expansion from December 1914 to August 1918, fueled by the production of armaments and supplies for World War I, but bankruptcy filings did not begin a precipitous drop until 1916, and they continued to drop through the recession of August 1918 to March 1919.[54]

Figure 3.2. Northern District of Ohio Bankruptcy Filings for Fiscal Years Ending 1899–1920

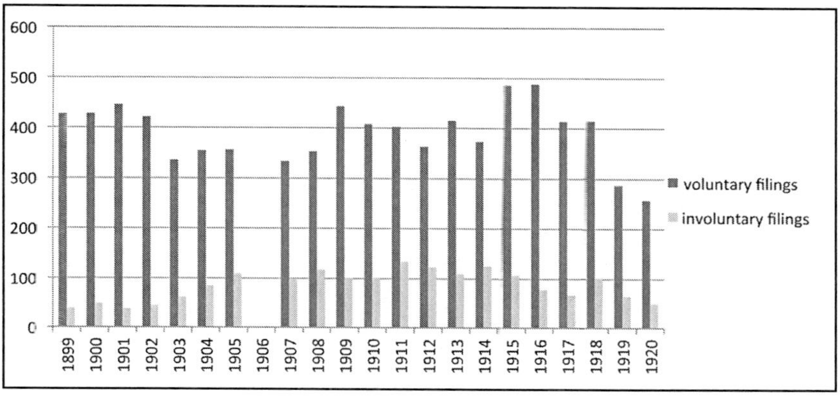

In the Northern District of Ohio, debtors filed bankruptcy at a higher overall rate than in the nation as a whole between 1907 and 1920, and total annual filings exhibited a flatter, rolling pattern, with more peaks and troughs than the national pattern exhibited. Consistent with the national pattern, bankruptcy filings in the Northern District of Ohio peaked in 1916 and then declined precipitously until 1920. (See Figure 3.2.)

The relative consistency in the rate of bankruptcy filings for the Northern District of Ohio compared with the nation as a whole may reflect northern Ohio's strong economic growth and industrial expansion during the first decades of the twentieth century, but why should a strong expanding economy experience a higher than average bankruptcy rate? A difference in the kinds of debtors who filed for bankruptcy protection in the Northern District of Ohio might suggest an explanation.

The Department of Justice collected data on the occupations of debtors in bankruptcy from 1899 to 1933 but relied for its statistics on individual referees' reports of closed cases, and the attorney general's reports complain of inconsistencies in the methodologies used by the individual referees in preparing their reports. It is difficult, therefore, to determine the occupational distribution of the bankrupts with any degree of accuracy. The problem is compounded by the large number of petitioners referees placed in the category "miscellaneous." However, rough comparisons may be made. It is clear from the data submitted to the Department of Justice that wage earners made up a very large proportion of the initial voluntary bankrupts in the Northern District of Ohio and throughout the United States. (See Figures 3.2 and 3.4.)

Figure 3.3. US Closed Cases for Fiscal Years Ending September 30, 1899–1905: Voluntary Bankruptcy Filings by Occupation

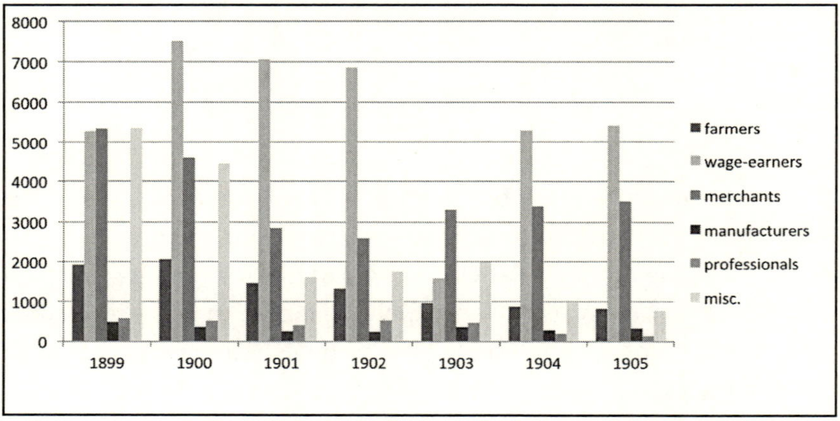

Figure 3.4. Northern District of Ohio Closed Cases for Fiscal Years Ending September 30, 1899–1905: Voluntary Bankruptcy Filings by Occupation

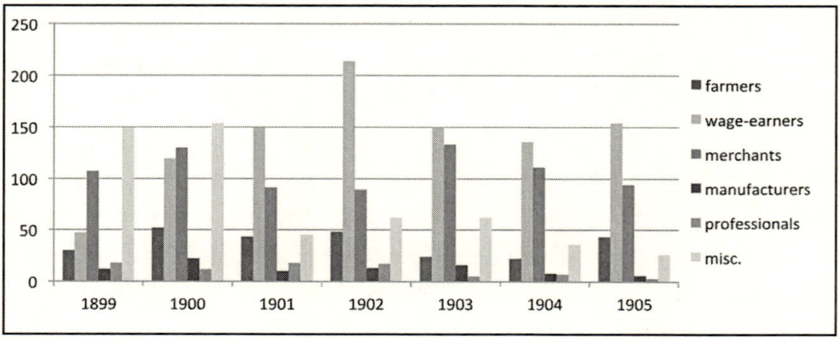

The distribution of debtors in bankruptcy between 1907 and World War I changed from the earlier period. The attorney general attributed the decline in the proportion of wage-earner bankruptcies to exhaustion of the pent-up demand for discharge from the recession that preceded the enactment of the Bankruptcy Act in 1898. Also, the data after 1907 include both voluntary and involuntary bankrupts, increasing the proportion of merchants, manufacturers, and professionals in the data. Between 1907 and 1916, merchants constituted the single largest occupation of debtors in bankruptcy in the United States, but wage earners consistently came in a close second, followed by "miscellaneous." Furthermore, both merchants and wage earners entered bankruptcy in steadily increasing numbers throughout the period regardless of the vagaries of the business cycle. (See Figure 3.5.)

The occupational distribution of debtors filing bankruptcy in the Northern District of Ohio between 1907 and World War I is more difficult to discern because of the large number of debtors characterized as miscellaneous in some but not all of the years at issue. In 1910, the single largest occupation for debtors was miscellaneous, and miscellaneous ranked second in 1907, 1908, 1909, and 1911. However, it appears that the incidence of bankruptcy may have been more sensitive to the business cycle in northern Ohio. The occupational data derive from closed bankruptcy cases, necessarily involving some lag between the filing of a bankruptcy

Figure 3.5. US Closed Cases for Fiscal Years Ending June 30, 1907–1916: Voluntary and Involuntary Bankruptcy Filings by Occupation

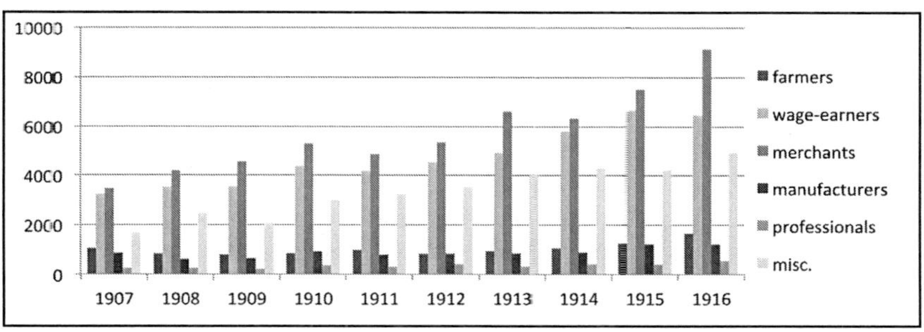

Figure 3.6. Northern District of Ohio Closed Cases for Fiscal Years Ending June 30, 1907–1916: Voluntary and Involuntary Bankruptcy Filings by Occupation

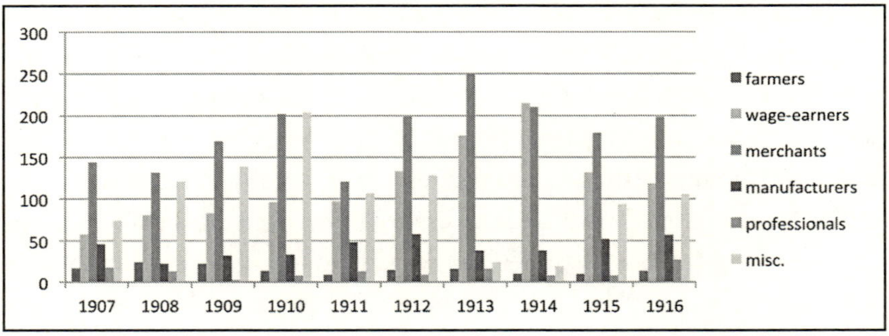

petition and documentation of the occupation of the debtor, and more merchant bankruptcies closed shortly after the end of recession years, flattening the curve and increasing total bankruptcies over the extended period. Also, wage-earner bankruptcies declined sharply at the beginning of the World War I business expansion in 1915. As in the nation as a whole, most debtors in this period were merchants, followed by wage earners. Only in fiscal year 1914 did the number of bankrupt wage earners exceed the number of bankrupt merchants. (See Figure 3.6.)

The question remains: why should northern Ohio, with an expanding industrial economy, experience greater than average bankruptcy filings? Unfortunately, no obvious rationale explains why some judicial districts experienced more bankruptcy filings than other judicial districts. The annual report of the attorney general for the year 1908 published total bankruptcy filings by district since enactment of the Bankruptcy Act in 1898. (See Figure 3.7.) The rankings changed little over the ensuing years. The Northern District of Ohio has continued to be one of the busiest bankruptcy districts in the country up to the present day.

Although a high concentration of entrepreneurial risk takers might explain a high rate of bankruptcy in commercial centers like the Southern District of New York and the Northern District of Illinois, what drove so many debtors to file bankruptcy petitions in Iowa, Minnesota,

Figure 3.7. Judicial Districts with the Most Bankruptcy Filings from Enactment in 1898 to June 30, 1908

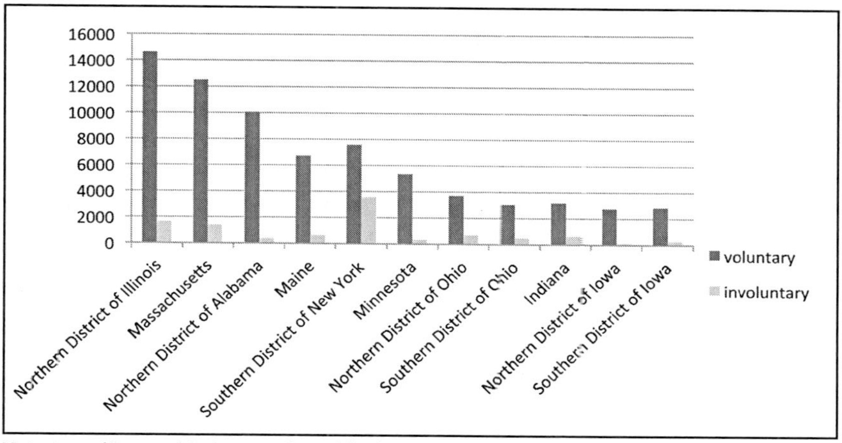

Note: *Annual Report of the Attorney General for the Year 1908* (Washington, DC: Government Printing Office, 1908), 90–95.

or Alabama? Unusually harsh state collection laws might account for a high rate of voluntary bankruptcies in districts with large rural populations like Iowa, where both the Northern District and the Southern District experienced an unusually high number of bankruptcies in roughly the same proportion, but it does not fully explain the Northern District of Alabama. Between 1898 and 1908, 10,057 debtors filed voluntary petitions in bankruptcy in the Northern District of Alabama but only 2,180 in the Middle District of Alabama and 494 in the Southern District of Alabama filed voluntary petitions during the same period. Perhaps different bankruptcy districts had distinctive legal cultures, even in the same state.[55] The annual report of the attorney general for 1905 noted criticism of Alabama wage garnishments, which drove large numbers of common laborers with few assets to file for bankruptcy. In the Northern District of Alabama, debtors had sufficient assets to pay fees in only 20 percent of the voluntary petitions filed that year. One-third of all of the voluntary bankruptcies in the country in which the bankrupt could not afford to pay fees originated in the Northern District of Alabama. Fewer than half of the voluntary petitions in bankruptcy in the Middle District of Alabama could pay their fees.[56]

Commentators noticed very early that different debtors were entering bankruptcy than the advocates of a national bankruptcy act had anticipated. Bankruptcy was intended to benefit merchants and entrepreneurs and their creditors. Legislators and advocates never considered the possibility of large numbers of consumer bankruptcies. Although the published data did not correlate estates reporting assets to the occupations of bankrupt debtors, they did reveal a significant number of "no asset" cases and cases with less than $500 in total assets. In 1905, the attorney general attributed the low average return to creditors to the large number of humble people petitioning for voluntary bankruptcy:

> The statistics with reference to the nature of the business of those who became voluntary bankrupts, disclose the interesting fact that the benefits of the law are not availed of by, or restricted to, any particular class of citizens, but that all alike take advantage of its provisions. Outside of merchants, it is to be noted that 820 were farmers and 5,426 wage-earners . . . That persons of this class take advantage of the law has been criticized in certain sources, but such criticism over looks the fact that the small liability of the wage earner, mechanic, or farmer weighs as heavily, if not more so, upon these citizens than upon the merchant with greater resources.[57]

Consumer bankruptcies became the typical bankruptcy in the 1920s, greatly exceeding all categories of business bankruptcies. Bankruptcies of all kinds increased over the course of the decade, and wage-earner bankruptcies increased as a proportion of all bankruptcies, even though the US economy experienced strong growth. Gross national product (GNP) rose 4.2 percent per year between 1920 and 1929, and real GNP grew 2.7 percent during that period.[58] By 1931, wage-earner bankruptcies accounted for nearly one-half of all bankruptcies in the United States and in the Northern District of Ohio.

Over the course of the 1920s, the economy did not grow at a consistent rate but in cycles. The end of World War I brought a sharp, short depression from January 1920 to July 1921 followed by a long, bumpy business

Figure 3.8. US Bankruptcy Filings for Fiscal Years Ending June 30, 1920–1933

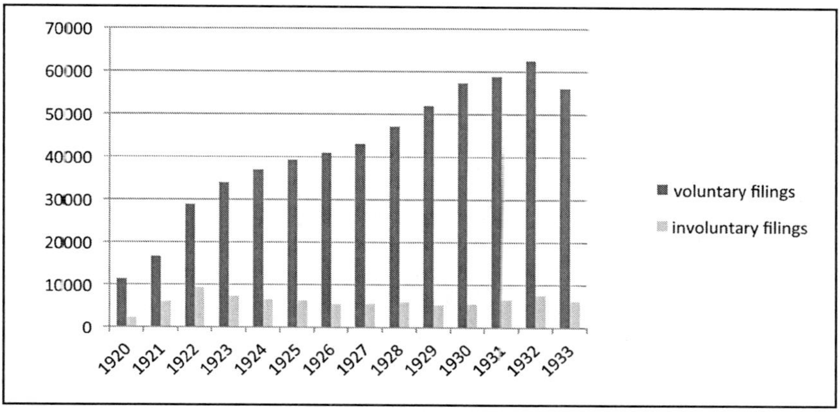

Note: This chart and the three charts that follow were prepared from the attorney general's reports for the years 1920 to 1933.

expansion through the rest of the decade.[59] However, the fluctuations of the business cycle had no effect on the aggregate rate of increase in bankruptcy filings. In the United States as a whole, bankruptcy filings increased steadily, reaching a peak in 1932. No significant change in the rate of increase in bankruptcy filings occurred after the onset of the Great Depression in 1929. (See Figure 3.8.)

In the Northern District of Ohio, bankruptcy filings also increased after 1920, but at a different pace than in the United States as a whole, perhaps reflecting northern Ohio's manufacturing role in the emerging consumer economy. The principal urban areas of northern Ohio had become leading manufacturers of durable consumer goods like bicycles, vacuum cleaners, and automobiles and their components. The rate of bankruptcy filings in the Northern District of Ohio increased rapidly after 1925, reaching a peak in 1932. As with the aggregate numbers of filings for the United States, no significant change in the rate of increase in bankruptcy filings occurred after the onset of the Great Depression. (See Figure 3.9.)

Wage-earner bankruptcies consistently accounted for the largest share of the closed bankruptcy cases in the United States from 1921 to 1931, but merchant bankruptcies increased rapidly between 1921 and 1924 and

Figure 3.9. Northern District of Ohio Bankruptcy Filings for Fiscal Years Ending June 30, 1920–1933

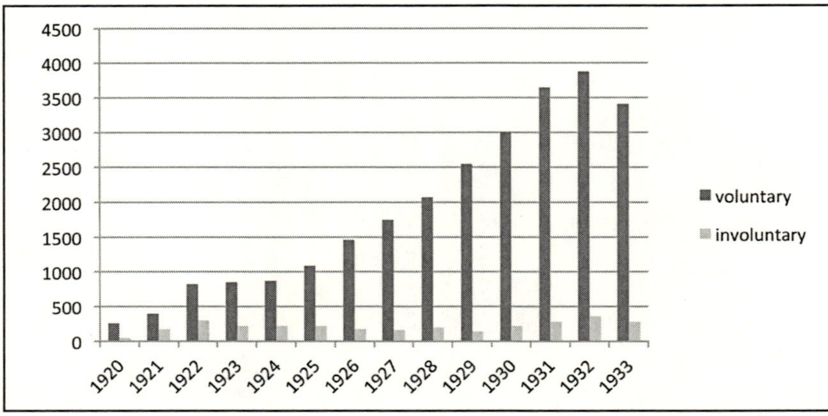

then leveled off. Farm bankruptcies also increased rapidly between 1921 and 1924. Farmers expanded production to meet wartime demand, and the end of the war precipitated a severe farm depression. Farm incomes never recovered completely before the onset of the Great Depression in 1929, but farm bankruptcies leveled off in 1924 and declined after 1926.[60] (See Figure 3.10.)

Regional differences in economic activity may have affected the rate at which debtors from different economic sectors landed in bankruptcy during this period. Wage earners did not begin to account for a significant number of closed bankruptcy cases in the Northern District of Ohio until 1926. From 1925 to 1931, wage-earner bankruptcies increased dramatically every year. Before 1926, merchant bankruptcies drove the increase in total bankruptcy cases, leading all other occupational categories until 1926, when wage-earner cases began to surge. Merchant bankruptcies leveled off after 1927 but wage-earner cases continued to increase dramatically. Farm bankruptcies accounted for an insignificant portion of the closed cases throughout the period. (See Figure 3.11.)

Consumer bankruptcy became one of the principal concerns of the bankruptcy courts in the 1920s, and consumer bankruptcy would

Figure 3.10. US Closed Cases for Fiscal Years Ending June 30, 1921–1931: Voluntary and Involuntary Bankruptcy Filings by Occupation

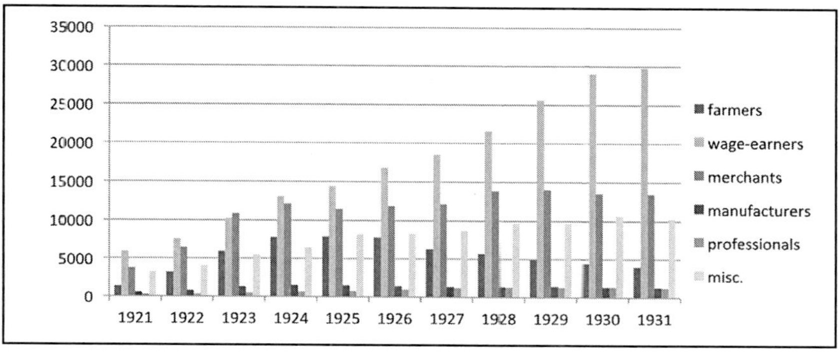

Figure 3.11. Northern District of Ohio Closed Cases for Fiscal Years Ending June 30, 1921–1931: Voluntary and Involuntary Bankruptcy Filings by Occupation

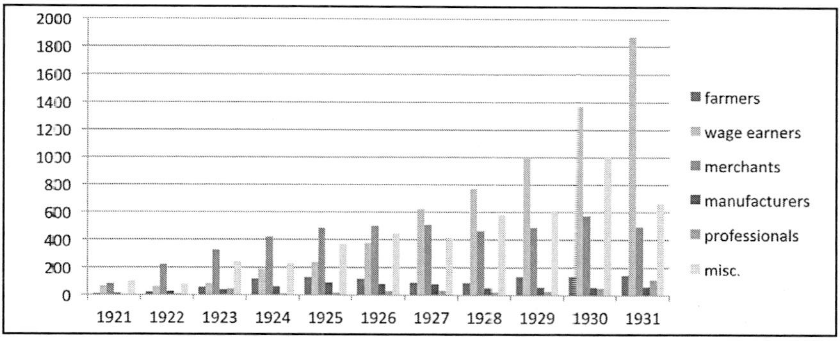

remain contentious from then on as Americans debated the meaning of virtue and the role of bankruptcy in industrial society. The United States became a modern consumer economy in the 1920s, more similar to America in the 1980s than to America in 1900. Producers and distributors of consumer goods pioneered consumer credit to facilitate the sale of their products in much larger quantities than possible on a cash basis, and consumers readily obliged. During the 1920s, large numbers of ordinary Americans acquired homes with mortgages in suburbs and commuted to work with automobiles purchased on credit. The electric grid reached all urban and suburban neighborhoods, and Americans filled their mortgaged homes with electric appliances such as washing machines, vacuum cleaners, stoves, refrigerators, and radios purchased with consumer credit. Between 1920 and 1929, consumer credit grew at the rate of 11.9 percent per year, and nonbusiness bankruptcies increased at the rate of 18.2 percent per year. For the next half century, from 1929 to 1985, consumer credit and consumer bankruptcies would increase at the same rate of 4.7 percent per year.[61]

Between 1898 and 1929, the economy of the United States completed its transition from a rural, small-producer economy to an urban, industrial economy. That transition had commenced more than a decade before enactment of the 1898 Bankruptcy Act, yet the drafters of the act had not envisioned how people would actually live in the new economy or its impact on bankruptcy. Consumer debtors represented the essential core of the new economy, but the increasing number of consumer bankruptcies shocked and dismayed many people. The most important business organizations in the new industrial economy, the large corporations, preferred federal court receivership to liquidation in bankruptcy. Small-business organizations, especially merchants, represented the kind of debtors the drafters of the Bankruptcy Act expected to see in the bankruptcy court, but they often used state insolvency courts instead of bankruptcy courts. Besides, small-business organizations constituted a declining share of total bankruptcies. By the late 1920s, there was a mismatch between the kinds of debtors who filed bankruptcy and the kinds of debtors the Bankruptcy Act had been designed to serve.

The Bankruptcy Act of 1898 structured the bankruptcy courts for a nineteenth-century world in which local debtors and creditors sought local justice from local officials using local rules. With little guidance and support, individual referees, often isolated in scattered county seats, had successfully implemented a bankruptcy system that functioned remarkably well. As the national economy expanded and became more integrated, creditors sought greater uniformity, efficiency, and convenience.

Individual district court judges and individual bankruptcy referees sometimes made changes to improve the operation of the bankruptcy courts under their control. However, without statutory reform and a centralized administrative structure, particular improvements represented the will of individual judges and referees and did not solve the need for a uniform, national bankruptcy system. As bankruptcy courts and referees gained experience with the Bankruptcy Act, they turned their attention to reforming it to meet the needs of debtors and creditors in the twentieth-century economy.

Chapter Four

The First Movement to Reform the Bankruptcy Act

The drafters of the Bankruptcy Act of 1898 crafted a bankruptcy regime for a decentralized, nineteenth-century, small-producer society, and the reality of the twentieth-century industrial economy profoundly conflicted with the nineteenth-century assumptions underlying the Bankruptcy Act. Although the fundamental problem was modernization—making the Bankruptcy Act fit the economy—scandals in the bankruptcy courts of the Southern District of New York brought the need for bankruptcy reform to the forefront of policy makers' consciousness. The impetus for bankruptcy reform derived from studies and commissions that began in the midst of the 1920s economic boom as a consequence of those scandals. Although the Great Depression intervened between the inspiration for bankruptcy reform and its implementation, most of the core concepts enacted during this period predated the Depression. Some of the early ideas that were abandoned in this round of reform would reappear decades later.

The National Bankruptcy Conference emerged during this period as a key player in bankruptcy reform. It is still the most widely respected professional organization involved in the improvement of bankruptcy law and administration. Composed of representatives from different organizations invested in bankruptcy practice, the National Bankruptcy Conference coalesced in opposition to more radical reforms proposed by commissions under the leadership of Judge Thacher of the Southern District of New York and his protégé, Lloyd K. Garrison. Northern District of Ohio referee Carl Friebolin played a very important role in forming the National Bankruptcy Conference and articulating its reform proposals.

A modernizing trend appeared in the bankruptcy courts in the early decades of the twentieth century involving professionalization through the development of bureaucratic organizations. Between 1920 and 1947, referees in bankruptcy changed from isolated political patronage appointments to participants in a system of coordinated, centralized bureaucracies. Referees in bankruptcy organized the National Association of Referees in Bankruptcy in 1926, and through that association they collaborated with bar associations and creditors' organizations to found the National Bankruptcy Conference. The National Association of Referees in Bankruptcy also played an influential role in the professionalization of the bankruptcy courts through its collaboration with the Administrative Office of the United States Courts in implementing the Salary Act. Carl Friebolin, referee in bankruptcy in Cleveland, was a charter member and early leader of the National Association of Referees in Bankruptcy, and most of the referees in the Northern District of Ohio played an active role in the organization.

The federal courts slowly accepted more centralized management. After 1922, the annual Conference of Senior Circuit Judges allowed the judiciary to confer, study, and make recommendations to the Supreme Court and to Congress. However, the circuit judges did not have the authority to criticize individual district court judges in the management of their dockets, including bankruptcy. In 1939, Congress created the Administrative Office of the United States Courts to take over budgeting and statistical analysis from the Department of Justice. In 1942, the Administrative Office created a Bankruptcy Division. Eventually, the Bankruptcy Division would supervise rules and procedures in the bankruptcy courts and limit the district courts' discretion in appointing referees by determining the number of authorized referees in any district.

This chapter explores the overlapping themes of the increasing trend toward professionalization and centralized administration and the momentum toward reforming the Bankruptcy Act to make it more responsive to changing economic and social circumstances. To the extent possible, the chapter grounds these broad themes in the actual experience of referees in the bankruptcy courts of the Northern District of Ohio.

The Referees

Republican judges reclaimed the judgeships in the Northern District of Ohio during the 1920s. As these judges eliminated offices and made new referee appointments, the partisan composition of the referees in the Northern District of Ohio also changed.

In 1923, President Warren G. Harding appointed Republican Paul J. Jones to a newly created third judgeship for the Northern District of Ohio that would be located in Cleveland, Ohio. After Judge Jones's appointment, two district court judges sat in Cleveland in the eastern division of the district and one district court judge sat in Toledo in the western division of the district. Judge Jones had been referee in bankruptcy in Youngstown between 1912 and 1916, but the first Democrat appointed to the bench since 1898, Judge (later Justice) John H. Clarke, replaced most Republican referees in the eastern division of the Northern District of Ohio with Democrats as their two-year commissions expired, including Judge Jones. After his term as referee ended, Judge Jones returned to partisan politics, receiving an appointment as Youngstown city attorney and winning election as judge of the Mahoning County Court of Common Pleas before his appointment to the federal bench in Cleveland. Judge Jones served as district court judge until his death in 1965 and became chief judge when Congress formally recognized the position in the Judicial Code of 1948.

Democratic judge David C. Westenhaver held the other district court judgeship in Cleveland at the time of Judge Jones' appointment. Appointed by President Woodrow Wilson in 1917 to replace Judge Clarke after his elevation to the Supreme Court, Judge Westenhaver died in

1928. President Calvin Coolidge appointed his replacement, Republican Samuel H. West. At age nineteen, Judge West moved to Logan County, Ohio, where he read law in the office of his uncle, William H. West, justice of the Ohio Supreme Court from 1872 to 1873. Admitted to the bar in 1893, West served as Logan County prosecutor and Ohio state senator before moving to Cleveland in 1910, where he became chief counsel for the Lake Shore and Michigan Southern Railroad. Judge West served as district court judge in the Northern District of Ohio until his death in 1938.

In Toledo, Republican judge John M. Killits took senior status in 1928 after eighteen years on the bench. President Coolidge appointed his replacement, Republican judge George P. Hahn. Judge Hahn came to the bench from private practice, but his law firm was politically connected: President Herbert Hoover had appointed Judge Hahn's law partner, Walter F. Brown, postmaster general. Judge Hahn served until his death in 1937.

In Toledo, long-standing referee Fordyce Belford fell ill in the summer of 1927 and died in July 1928. Judge Killits appointed Fred Kruse referee in bankruptcy in Toledo during Belford's illness, and Kruse served as referee in Toledo until 1947. Kruse was admitted to the bar in 1905 and had been in private practice in Toledo since then. A Republican, Kruse was not actively involved in partisan politics. In 1932, Kruse moved his office from the Nicholas Building to the newly constructed US courthouse in Toledo.

The only other bankruptcy referee in the western division of the Northern District of Ohio after 1916 was located in Lima. A Republican, Harvey Grindel, had served as referee in bankruptcy in Lima since 1908, and he would continue to serve in Lima until 1930. Grindel was sixty-four years old in 1930 but continued to practice law in Lima for the next fifteen years after his appointment as referee expired without reappointment. Judge Hahn appointed Grindel's successor, Herbert P. Eastman, who served only one two-year term as referee in Lima. Eastman was admitted to the bar in 1917 and practiced for a while with his father, Republican common pleas judge Ephraim Richard Eastman. After his term as referee, Eastman briefly practiced law in Ottawa, Wauseon, Napoleon, and Toledo, before moving to Florida, where he died of pneumonia in 1935 at age forty-two.

In 1931, Judge Hahn appointed the final referee in Lima, Republican Walter S. Jackson. A resident of Lima since childhood, Jackson graduated from Kenyon College in 1903 and from Western Reserve University in 1906. Admitted to the bar in 1906, Jackson practiced law in Lima and served as city solicitor in Lima from 1911 to 1915. Active in partisan politics, Jackson was a delegate to the National Republican Convention in 1928. Jackson served as referee until 1943, when the Lima office merged into the Toledo office.

Two district court judges sat in the eastern division of the Northern District of Ohio between 1923 and 1928: Democratic judge David Westenhaver and Republican judge Paul Jones. During those years, the court began to consolidate the offices of referees in bankruptcy, reducing the number of referee offices, which increased efficiency and reduced partisan conflict over appointments. Sometimes an office in a small town was merged into a larger office at the conclusion of a referee's term without reappointment of the referee to a new term. For example, on November 4, 1924, Referee W. W. Warren's term of office expired without reappointment, and the office of referee in bankruptcy for Columbiana County, located at Leetonia, merged into the Youngstown office, which served Mahoning and Trumbull counties. A total of four referees sitting in three different cities had served Columbiana County between 1898 and 1924. More often, the district court merged bankruptcy offices when a vacancy occurred. For example, the Mansfield office in Richland County merged into the Crawford County office at Bucyrus in 1925 when Referee Van C. Cook resigned to accept appointment as city prosecutor for Mansfield, the Richland County seat. The office for Wayne and Holmes counties in Wooster was merged into the Ashland County office at Ashland, Ohio, on January 1, 1923, when Referee Joseph O. Fritz of Wooster resigned. Fritz was fifty years old and in ill health. He had been referee in Wooster since 1918. The bankruptcy office for Ashland County was merged into the office for Stark and Carroll counties at Canton in 1931, when the referee for Ashland County, Asbury Durbin Metz, died.

By 1928, both US district court judges in Cleveland were Republicans, and referee appointments became more partisan. Democrat Carl D. Friebolin retained his appointment in Cleveland, but in 1930 the district was split with Republican William B. Woods. In 1931, sixty-seven-year-old Thomas A. Conway was not reappointed referee in bankruptcy in Elyria for Lorain and Medina counties, an office he had held since 1915, and the bankruptcy office for Lorain and Medina counties was merged into the Cleveland office. A Democratic politician, Conway was first appointed referee during then Judge (later Justice) John H. Clarke's purge of Republican referees in favor of Democrats. Before his appointment as referee in bankruptcy, Conway had been elected prosecuting attorney for Lorain County and mayor of Elyria. Conway was still active in Democratic Party politics in 1931.

In 1934, Youngstown referee Paul E. Carson's term expired without reappointment, and Judge Jones appointed Republican William J. Williams as Carson's successor. Carson was only forty-nine years old. A Democrat, Carson had been referee in Youngstown since 1916. Judge Jones preceded Carson as referee in Youngstown, but in his 1916 purge of Republican referees, Judge John H. Clarke replaced the Republican Jones with the Democrat Carson.

Williams had been active in Republican partisan politics since the beginning of the century. He was elected Ohio state representative from Youngstown in 1902 and 1904. A progressive, Williams served on the Youngstown City Charter Committee in 1923 and afterward ran unsuccessfully for mayor. Williams had some bipartisan appeal—he had read law in Judge Clarke's Youngstown law office, from which he was admitted to the bar in 1893. However, Williams had abandoned the practice of law in favor of real estate by the time President Hoover appointed Williams US marshal in Cleveland in 1930. Williams resigned near the end of his four-year term as marshal to accept appointment as referee in bankruptcy in Youngstown. United States marshal is a presidential patronage appointment, and Williams could not expect reappointment in 1934.

When the dust settled in the mid-1930s, the eastern division of the Northern District of Oho had seven referees: two in Cleveland, Carl Friebolin and William B. Woods; one in Canton, Paul D. Roach; one in Akron, Harry L. Snyder; one in Youngstown, William J. Williams; one in Bucyrus, William G. Beer; and one in Ashtabula, A. T. Ullman. Although Referee Williams, in Youngstown, had office space in the post office building, all of the other referees maintained private offices in commercial facilities. Four of the referees had been appointed since the creation of Judge Jones's judgeship in Cleveland in 1923: Ullman in 1927, Roach in 1928, Woods in 1930, and Williams in 1934. Although all four were Republicans, only Woods and Williams had been active in partisan politics before their appointments. Of the remaining referees, Snyder and Beer were the only two Republican referees in the eastern division of the Northern District of Ohio to survive Judge Clarke's partisan purge between 1914 and 1916. Friebolin, appointed by Judge Clarke in 1916, was the only remaining Democratic referee in the Northern District of Ohio.

By the end of the 1930s, the election and reelection of President Franklin D. Roosevelt had once again changed the partisan political composition of the judiciary in the Northern District of Ohio. The death of two judges allowed President Roosevelt to name Democrats to the bench. In 1941, Congress created a fourth judgeship for the Northern District Ohio, and President Roosevelt appointed the US attorney, Emerich Burt Freed, district court judge in Cleveland. No record exists of the manner in which the judges decided upon the appointment of referees, but the court continued the practice of maintaining most referees in office while the appointment of new referees split evenly between Democrats and Republicans.

In Toledo, Judge Hahn died in 1937, and President Roosevelt appointed Democratic congressman Frank Le Blond Kloeb to succeed him. Judge Kloeb served until 1964 when he took senior status. In 1939, Judge Kloeb appointed a second referee in Toledo, his colleague, Democratic congressman Frank C. Kniffin. Four years later, Republican referee Walter S. Jackson of Lima was not reappointed, and the Lima office was merged into the Toledo Office. Jackson was sixty-two years old.

In Cleveland, Judge Samuel H. West died in 1938, and President Roosevelt appointed Democrat Robert N. Wilkin to succeed him. The *Cleveland Plain Dealer* reported rumors that Roosevelt offered the appointment to Carl Friebolin but Friebolin declined the appointment because he was too old and suffered from hearing loss.[1] Judge Wilkin served with Republican judge Paul Jones and Democrat judge Emerich Burt Freed in Cleveland until Judge Wilkin took senior status in 1949. No personnel changes occurred among the referees in Cleveland or Canton. In Akron, however, long-serving Republican referee Harry Snyder died in 1939, and Democrat Everett L. Foote succeeded him. Foote had for several years served as assistant US attorney in Cleveland when he was appointed referee in bankruptcy in Akron.

In Ashtabula, in 1934, Charles J. Starkey replaced A. T. Ullman, who may have retired. Ullman had been practicing law since 1898. The principal professional accomplishment of Starkey, the son of a Republican justice of the peace, was his 1927 election to the position of Rotary Club district governor. In Youngstown, Republican William J. Williams died in 1944, and Judge Jones appointed Ross E. Diser his successor. A US commissioner in Cleveland, Diser grew up in Youngstown, the son of a prominent lawyer and local Republican politician. The long-serving Republican referee in Bucyrus, William G. Beer, died in 1945, and the bankruptcy district for Crawford County was merged into the Canton office.

Isolated in private offices scattered across judicial districts, referees in all parts of the country soon realized that they needed an organization where they could associate to share information and seek solutions to common problems. The first attempt to form an organization occurred in 1903 when between fifteen and twenty referees met in Niagara Falls, New York. The organization elected officers, and Harold Remington of Cleveland was named to the association's executive committee.

The organization soon failed, in part because of doubt whether the Bankruptcy Act would endure. In 1902, 1903, 1909, and 1910, opponents launched unsuccessful attempts to repeal the Bankruptcy Act.[2]

Other organizations interested in bankruptcy existed, including the recently created Special Committee on Bankruptcy Practice of the American Bar Association, the Commercial Law League, and the National Association of Credit Men, and many referees belonged to one or more of those organizations. In 1923, Referee Herbert M. Bierce of Winona, Minnesota, attended the annual meeting of the Commercial Law League in West Baden, Indiana, where Robert A. B. Cook of Boston, chair of the league's Standing Committee on Bankruptcy, delivered a speech commending the effectiveness of the 1898 Bankruptcy Act. Bierce had heard rumors about improprieties in the bankruptcy courts of New York City, and during the floor discussion of Cook's speech Bierce suggested that the Commercial Law League consider recommending procedural reforms to prevent abuses that might threaten bankruptcy as a permanent institution. The president of the Commercial Law League promptly appointed Bierce to the Standing Committee on Bankruptcy and suggested to Bierce that referees consider forming an organization of their own.[3]

Bierce mentioned the idea of forming an association of referees in bankruptcy to his good friend, Referee Paul H. King of Detroit. King had been thinking about forming an organization of referees and promptly surveyed referees throughout the country to gauge their interest. Shortly thereafter, Bierce and King met at a Rotary Club conference and agreed to attempt to organize the National Association of Referees in Bankruptcy. King and his Detroit colleague, Referee George Marston, invited all referees to a meeting in Detroit to be held July 9 and 10, 1926. Approximately eighty-five referees from all judicial circuits except the ninth attended the organizational meeting, including six referees from the Northern District of Ohio. By December 1926, approximately 180 referees, out of a total number of referees that varied between 530 and 540, had joined the organization. As a threshold matter, the National Association of Referees in Bankruptcy sought the cooperation of its membership in constructing and maintaining as accurate a list as possible of active referees, the first of its kind.

All referees serving in the Northern District of Ohio at that time joined the National Association of Referees in Bankruptcy except A. D. Metz of Wooster, who was seventy-six years old, and J. F. Munsell of Ashtabula, who was sixty-eight years old. Metz died five years later and his bankruptcy district was merged into the Canton district. Munsell retired within a year, and A. T. Ullman replaced him as referee. Ullman joined the National Association of Referees in Bankruptcy by 1932, making every referee in the Northern District of Ohio a member of the organization.

Referees from the Northern District of Ohio played a significant role in the leadership of the National Association of Referees in Bankruptcy.[4] Carl Friebolin, referee in Cleveland, served as president from 1931 to 1932. Fred Kruse, referee in Toledo, served as first vice president from 1945 to 1946. Kruse did not advance to president because he resigned as referee in 1946 after the reorganization of referee offices following the enactment of the Salary Act. William B. Woods served as president from 1948 to 1949, and William J. O'Neill served as president from 1970 to 1971.

Carl Friebolin, Fred Kruse, and William B. Woods actively participated in the National Association of Referees in Bankruptcy in its formative years. The infant organization was governed by three officers and a board of directors consisting of one representative from each judicial circuit. Friebolin received the first appointment as director for the Sixth Circuit. Woods served as director for the Sixth Circuit from 1942 to 1943. Kruse analyzed and reported on statistics in the *Journal of the National Association of Referees in Bankruptcy.*

The membership of the National Association of Referees in Bankruptcy elected Paul King its first president and Watson B. Adair of Pittsburgh its vice president and president-elect. Herbert Bierce was elected secretary-treasurer, and he held that position for the next twenty-three years. Bierce immediately assumed responsibility for publishing the association's journal and continued as its editor until 1950. The journal reported the proceedings of the annual conference of the association, news and information about referees and the bankruptcy courts, and scholarly articles on bankruptcy law and practice. In 1934, the journal added an editorial board, and Carl Friebolin became a charter member. He continued in that capacity until 1957, when the board disappeared. Afterward, Friebolin informally reviewed each edition of the journal for the editor. Fred Kruse joined the journal's editorial board in 1936. Over time, the *Journal of the National Association of Referees in Bankruptcy* became less of an industry newsletter and more of a scholarly journal. In 1971, the journal adopted a standard law review format.

The National Association of Referees in Bankruptcy sought the cooperation of other interested persons and organizations to improve bankruptcy practice. It recognized non-referees as honorary members, including Simon Fleischmann, chair of the American Bar Association Special Committee on Practice in Bankruptcy Matters; Robert A. B. Cook, chair of the Commercial Law League of America Committee on Bankruptcy; Harold Remington; and a few particularly useful district court judges. The National Association of Credit Men, the Merchant's Association of New York, the Association of the Bar of the City of New York, and the Cleveland Bar Association also had committees that were interested in bankruptcy law and practice. The *Journal of the National Association of Referees in Bankruptcy* reported on the activities of these organizations and invited representatives to attend the annual meeting. United States Supreme Court justice William Howard Taft expressed his hope that the new organization would encourage further improvement in the bankruptcy courts and asked to be informed of the results of the association's work.

The National Association of Referees in Bankruptcy aspired to further the professionalism of the bankruptcy courts through shared knowledge and experience, higher ethical standards, and greater uniformity of practice. To implement these goals, the association established three permanent standing committees: Legislation, Ethics, and Uniformity of Practice.

The Committee on Legislation started slowly. The 1898 Bankruptcy Act had been recently amended in 1926, and although part of the National Association of Referees in Bankruptcy's mission was to support necessary amendments to the Bankruptcy Act, particularly amendments pertaining to noncontroversial administrative and technical matters, the association did not want to become a lobbying organization for referees. A charter member of the committee, Carl Friebolin became its permanent chairman in 1927. Friebolin envisioned the committee as a vehicle for sharing the referees' collective expertise with Congress and the courts in the interest of improving bankruptcy administration. Within a few years, the Committee on Legislation was subsumed by the Special Conference Committee in the effort to influence the course of bankruptcy reform.

On the other hand, the Committee on Ethics and the Committee on Uniformity of Practice immediately began to work at implementing their missions. The Ethics Committee drafted a code of ethics, which the membership adopted at its second annual meeting, in Buffalo, New York, in August 1927. Meanwhile, between the first and second annual meetings, the Committee on Uniformity of Practice prepared and mailed to all referees a comprehensive questionnaire designed to elicit detailed descriptions of all aspects of bankruptcy practice and procedure in the bankruptcy courts of the different districts throughout the country. The committee distributed a second questionnaire in 1928 designed to determine referees' opinions as to best practices with a view to adopting a Model Code of Practice. By 1931 the committee had drafted proposed uniform rules for consideration at the 1932 annual meeting, but the National Association of Referees in Bankruptcy never adopted the rules. The accelerating movement for bankruptcy reform between 1930 and 1938 preempted the effort to adopt uniform bankruptcy rules.[5]

The Committee on Uniformity of Practice began reporting its initial survey findings in the June 1928 edition of the *Journal of the National Association of Referees in Bankruptcy*. More than 250 referees returned completed questionnaires, which disclosed a shocking lack of uniformity in practice. Although all eighty-four bankruptcy districts had local rules, they differed greatly between one district and another. Furthermore, the practices of part-time rural referees often differed radically from those of their full-time urban brethren within the same district. Of the responding referees, 32 percent devoted 90 percent or more of their time to bankruptcy matters, 29 percent devoted between one-half and three-quarters of their time to bankruptcy matters. 22 percent devoted between one-quarter and one-half of their time to bankruptcy matters, and 21 percent devoted less than one-tenth of their time to bankruptcy matters.

The questionnaire asked referees to briefly describe their manner of holding court, and the answers varied so dramatically that the committee could not classify them with any accuracy except very generally as "informal, business-like, and rapid."[6] Most referees did not have a courtroom or other special room for hearings but instead held hearings in their office, and most found the arrangement satisfactory. Most referees had no fixed days or hours for hearings, opened court without any formality, and liked it that way. Most referees' expenses were reimbursed most of the time, and although referees tried to keep an accurate account of expenses, the methods they used varied radically. In general, only the urban offices of full-time referees systematically allocated expenses among cases.

In general, referees tended to allow trustees and receivers the maximum fee allowed, unless the same person was serving as both trustee and receiver. Appraisers, auditors, and auctioneers generally received the going rate in the community or the amount allowed for similar services under state law. More than one-half of the referees stated that they had no fixed scale for attorney's fees, and the rest gave various explanations for their method of determining attorney's fees. Most referees thought attorney's fees were so low that fee splitting was not a problem.

The National Association of Referees in Bankruptcy's interest in documenting referees' actual practices in the administration of bankruptcy derived from the members' belief that it was a necessary first step toward reaching a consensus among referees on implementing improved practices. The members believed that referees understood the bankruptcy system best, and pride and professionalism argued that their association would be the most appropriate forum to articulate and advocate for effective reforms in bankruptcy administration. Public awareness of the deficiencies of the present system had been increasing, and the referees realized reform was imminent. In the preceding few years, reports critical of bankruptcy administration had been released by the Merchants Association of New York, the Association of the Bar of the City of New York, and the American Bar Association.

Referees in bankruptcy received almost no supervision. Referring district court judges generally left referees to manage their dockets as they saw fit. The Department of Justice collected a minimum of bankruptcy statistics from referees and clerks of court for inclusion in its annual report to Congress, and in 1914, the Department of Justice began sending examiners to judicial districts to audit court accounts. The examiners discovered all kinds of fraud and misbehavior, including bankruptcy fraud. The 1914 examinations resulted in twenty-three indictments and sixteen convictions, and federal investigators have attempted to police the bankruptcy courts ever since. The Department of Justice employed few examiners, however, and Internal Revenue Service income tax audits uncovered most cases of bankruptcy fraud committed by trustees. Congress passed the Income Tax Act in 1913.[7] As late as 1940, the Department of Justice employed only fourteen examiners to audit the accounts of all referees, clerks of court, US attorneys, marshals, commissioners, and probation officers throughout the United States.[8]

In 1915, the Department of Justice instituted regular biennial examinations of the district courts, including referees in bankruptcy, and in 1916 the examinations expanded to referees' methods of administration as well as their accounts. The examiners found great discrepancies with regard to referees' accounting for expenses. Some referees kept no accounts. The examiners concluded from the accounts of those referees who did keep accounts that some referees billed estates a fixed indemnity for costs that greatly exceeded the actual expenses of administering the bankruptcy estates referred to that referee. In general, referees billed estates for costs based on local rules and practices and deposited the amounts into "indemnity accounts" from which they paid their actual expenses. Referees who were lax in assessing costs could end up paying bankruptcy administration expenses from their own funds. Some referees, however, viewed indemnity funds as an additional source of income. The Department of Justice had no disciplinary authority over referees and merely reported the findings of its examinations to the district court judges with recommendations as to corrective action.[9]

Referee compensation was entirely fee based, and the examinations discovered that some referees received an extraordinarily high income from bankruptcy, often exceeding the salary received by district and circuit judges, and sometimes even exceeding the pay of Supreme Court justices. The Department of Justice particularly highlighted the incomes of referees in the Southern District of New York. In 1916 and 1917, the six referees in the Southern District of New York earned between approximately $10,250 and $33,000, and one referee earned approximately $60,000 in 1916 due to extraordinary circumstances. Excluding the outlier, the Southern District of New York bankruptcy referees earned on average approximately $15,500. For comparison, district court judges earned $6,000 per year, though their salary would increase to $7,500 in 1919. Two referees earned more than $4,400 in profit over actual expenses from their indemnity accounts, which constituted between 59 and 63 percent of total receipts for indemnity, fees, and costs.[10]

The examiners never chastised referees in the Northern District of Ohio for excessive fees or unreasonable incomes, but Carl Friebolin was one of those referees who found bankruptcy a very profitable business. Brilliant, unusually efficient, and a prodigious worker in a busy district, Friebolin consistently earned more than any other referee in the district—and more than his referring judges. From 1922 to 1930, Friebolin's bankruptcy income rose steadily from $11,750 to $25,000, averaging $19,000. For comparison, in 1926, Congress increased district court judges' salaries from $7,500 to $10,000 and Supreme Court justices' salaries from $14,500 to $20,000. Friebolin's income remained high between 1931 and 1943, ranging between $15,000 and $25,000 and averaging $17,800.[11]

Friebolin's bankruptcy income consisted of the $15 per case fee, the 1 percent commission based on the eventual distribution of dividends to creditors, and other fees fixed by local court rule. Friebolin dedicated close to 100 percent of his time to bankruptcy matters but also received regular income in lesser amounts from special master's fees and non-bankruptcy legal work. Most years Friebolin did not receive any income from a surplus in his indemnity fund over actual expenses. For the years 1920 through 1931, the only years for which we have adequate records to make a comparison, Friebolin's actual expenses exceeded the deposits to his indemnity fund by approximately 10 percent. Friebolin accounted annually to the clerk of court for his receipts and expenditures, including expenses, which he categorized as rent, publications, telephone services, clerical staff, printing, and miscellaneous.[12]

"Nothing is so helpless as an insolvent estate. It is subject to spoilation as soon as there is an adjudication."[13]

Bankruptcy filings increased steadily throughout the 1920s, and many sought to take advantage of the opportunities for profitable employment bankruptcy presented. Nationally, approximately 200,000 bankruptcy filings occurred between 1925 and 1928, twice the number of all civil cases concluded in the district courts and courts of appeal during that period. The money value of the assets in those cases exceeded the money value of all judgments rendered in all other civil cases.[14] The amount of money lying about unprotected in bankruptcy estates proved an irresistible lure. The administration of bankrupt estates needed the services of receivers, trustees, appraisers, and others, and receivers and trustees often needed to employ attorneys in connection with their bankruptcy work, all of whom needed to be paid out of the bankruptcy estate.

The 1898 Bankruptcy Act assumed that creditors would police the administration of bankruptcy out of self interest, but most bankruptcy estates had few assets in proportion to liabilities. Most creditors found that it did not pay for them to become actively involved in the administration of the bankruptcy estates of their debtors, especially as the ratio of assets to liabilities deteriorated markedly throughout the 1920s. (See Figure 4.1.)

Figure 4.1. Amount Realized by Creditors Compared with Liabilities: US Closed Cases 1921–1931

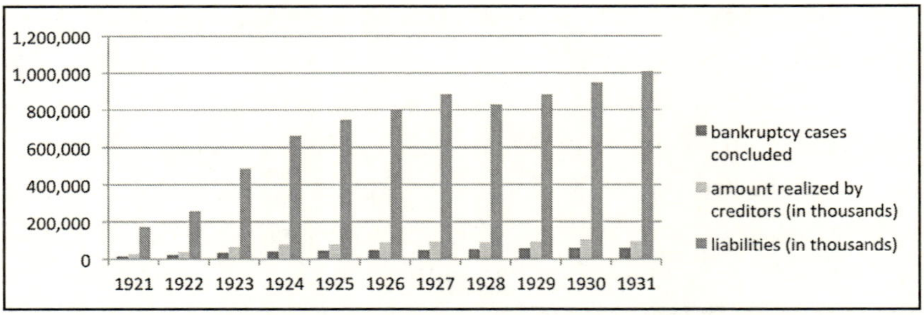

Note: Based on data in "Report to the President on the Bankruptcy Act and its Administration in the Courts of the United States," prepared by Thomas D. Thacher and Lloyd K. Garrison (Dec. 5, 1931) 3, found in US Senate Judiciary Committee, *Strengthening of Procedure in the Judicial System: Message from the President of the United States Recommending the Strengthening of Procedure in the Judicial System Together with the Report of the Attorney General on Bankruptcy Law and Practice*, 72d Cong., 1st Sess., Sen. Doc. 65 (Washington, DC: Government Printing Office, 1932).

With creditors unwilling to expend resources to ensure the honest and efficient administration of a bankruptcy estate from which they were unlikely to receive any significant dividend, the estate became very vulnerable to paying fees and expenses that primarily benefited those involved in estate administration, especially lawyers.[15]

The 1898 Bankruptcy Act did not anticipate that receivers would be employed, except in unusual circumstances. The act assumed that debtors would remain in possession of assets, in most cases until the first meeting of the creditors, and that creditors would elect the trustee who would administer the estate. Very early, however, most urban bankruptcy districts adopted the practice of appointing receivers whenever the bankruptcy petition revealed assets in excess of exemption amounts. Typically, the bankruptcy court appointed a receiver at the time of filing in an involuntary case or on the motion of a creditor in a voluntary case, and the receiver usually retained the petitioning creditor's attorney. This followed the established practice in equity receiverships, where the receiver also typically retained the attorney for petitioning creditors. By the time of the first meeting of creditors, the receiver's attorney usually obtained enough proxies from creditors unwilling to invest time in the supervision of the debtor's bankruptcy to secure the election of the receiver as trustee. Often, the attorney worked closely with credit services or collection agencies representing creditors.

The Cleveland practice followed the usual pattern. Friebolin stated in his answers to the National Association of Referees in Bankruptcy questionnaire that he usually appointed a receiver in asset cases. In any given year, he appointed many different attorneys to a few receiverships each, generally appointing younger members of the bar associated with the local branch of the National Association of Credit Men. The receivers' duties were restricted by local court rule to tasks essential to the conservation of assets, but Friebolin usually appointed the person requested and tried to appoint as receiver the person who would be elected trustee at the first meeting of the creditors.[16]

The 1898 Bankruptcy Act did not contemplate a large role for lawyers in the administration of estates. The act assumed that trustees would actually administer the estate, and it established very low statutory fees to compensate the trustees for their work. Friebolin estimated that 90 percent of the time those appointed as receivers and trustees were also attorneys. Typically, the bankruptcy court appointed new attorneys with little experience to be receivers and trustees, and they could not receive additional compensation if they performed legal work in the course of their duties as receiver or trustee. Trustees and receivers could petition the court for the assistance of attorneys, however, and attorney compensation was not set by statute. Attorneys for receivers and trustees received "reasonable" compensation for their legal work as determined by the bankruptcy court. Local lawyers with substantial experience in bankruptcy work sought appointment as attorney for the receiver and trustee, and over time those attorneys performed an increasing amount of the actual work involved in administering the estate.[17]

Bankruptcy practice in rural Ohio varied greatly, depending on the referee. Walter S. Jackson, referee in Lima, Ohio, from 1931 to 1943 covered a large rural district. Shortly after his appointment, he established a local rule that permitted no voting of any claim by an attorney, "no matter what the relationship was between the creditor and the attorney in fact who attempt[ed] to vote the claims."[18] Jackson described the situation before he established the rule:

> Before I adopted the rule, we found credit associations and so-called bankruptcy specialists from all over the state circularizing the creditors as soon as the petition was filed in the United States District Court. Frequently the result was pathetic. Some of the creditors would execute as many as five different Powers of Attorney, and then there would be a wild scramble to object to all of the claims for some minor technicality in the hope that the one which they possessed would stand up and give them the right to vote. Immediately the successful group would begin to parcel out the trusteeship, the attorney for the trustee, appraisers, etc. Skeleton organization was already adopted by promises to obtain certain claims.
>
> I have found no difficulty at all in enforcing the rule, and it has met a ready response from the bar associations. Another very commendable result has been obtained in that many reputable lawyers, both old and young, who formerly avoided bankruptcy practice as if it were tainted or soiled now engage in the practice . . . In my own practice for twenty-five years before I became a Referee I distinctly recall that it was one of the rules of our office never to handle a bankruptcy matter for the reason that the first meeting was usually a dog fight, and that the usual method to be successful in the election of a Trustee required certain things to be done which we believed were unethical, one of which was the soliciting of claims.[19]

Jackson reported that one particular attorney solicited claims and voted himself trustee in the forty-five consecutive bankruptcy proceedings before Jackson instituted his non-solicitation rule. Jackson claimed that the attorney was inefficient and unethical: "his administrations were such that reputable attorneys would have nothing to do with bankruptcy administration."[20]

Courts and commentators openly worried about the lack of independent supervision of the administration of bankruptcy estates and the opportunity for looting. By the mid-1920s, popular magazines reported on the existence of "bankruptcy rings" in large cities and claimed that they were responsible for widespread, undetected bankruptcy fraud. Most referees in bankruptcy saw the situation differently, including Carl Friebolin. To the extent that a small number of attorneys appeared before them repeatedly in bankruptcy proceedings, most referees believed it represented a laudable move toward specialization. Referees defended the efficacy of their supervision of the attorneys practicing before them and argued that the professionalization of the bankruptcy bar would inevitably improve the administration of bankruptcy estates.[21]

Creditors' organizations and bar associations formed committees, made investigations, and wrote reports highly critical of bankruptcy practice, especially in New York City. In 1922, Congress created the Conference of Senior Circuit Judges at the urging of Supreme Court chief justice William Howard Taft to be a permanent institution for advocating the improvement of the administration of the federal court system, and in 1924, a joint committee of the Conference of Senior Circuit Judges, the American Bar Association, the National Association of Credit Men, and the Commercial Law League met in Philadelphia to propose changes in the administration of bankruptcy. The Supreme Court adopted the joint committee's recommendations and, in 1925, promulgated the first extensive revisions to the general orders since enactment of the Bankruptcy Act in 1898, including rules specifically devised to limit the ability of attorneys to combine to influence the administration of bankruptcy estates.[22] In particular, the 1925 amendments to the general orders prohibited receivers or their attorneys from soliciting powers of attorney to represent claims on behalf of creditors. Attorneys, receivers, and trustees had to disclose a statement of their services and their fees to be heard at creditors' meetings. No attorney for a receiver or trustee could be appointed in a city with a population of more than 250,000 except by order of the court on a petition naming the attorney, the reasons for his employment, and a showing that the attorney had no employment or other relationship with the bankrupt or with any person whose interests may be adverse to the interests of the receiver or trustee. The rule changes proved wholly ineffective at limiting the concentration of bankruptcy work in a small number of attorneys or in preventing fraud.

In January 1929, the exposure of widespread bankruptcy fraud in the Southern District of New York precipitated a series of investigations into bankruptcy administration that resulted in concrete proposals for bankruptcy reform. A grand jury investigation into bankruptcy practices produced indictments against lawyers, receivers, trustees, and the official auctioneer for bribery, corruption, and embezzlement from bankruptcy estates. The grand jury found misconduct but did not indict two court clerks who received bribes from attorneys for advance information on bankruptcy filings. The grand jury also found that some referees failed to act when receivers and trustees were delinquent in their accounts, even though court rules demanded an inquiry.

The grand jury found serious evidence of impropriety on the part of district court judge Francis A. Winslow, especially in preferring the appointment of particular attorneys in bankruptcy matters, but suspended its inquiry so as not to interfere in ongoing impeachment proceedings in Congress. Winslow resigned to avoid impeachment. Similar accusations were also made against Judge Grover M. Moscowitz of the Eastern District of New York—Judge Moscowitz regularly appointed members of his former law firm as receivers in bankruptcy—but a congressional inquiry found insufficient improper conduct to justify impeachment. Judge Moscowitz remained a district court judge until his death in 1947.

A joint committee of New York City bar associations petitioned the District Court for the Southern District of New York for an investigation directed toward recommending changes in the bankruptcy law. Judge Thomas D. Thacher granted the petition in March 1929 and allowed the petitioning bar associations to participate in the investigation through their counsel, William J. Donovan. The bar associations funded a staff, and the US attorney made his resources available to the bar associations. Hearings were held daily between June and September 1929 before Judge Thacher and a special master, and Donovan submitted his report in

March 1930. The report relied in part on the earlier survey by the National Association of Referees in Bankruptcy on bankruptcy administration.[23]

Referees closely followed the investigation. One of the principal investigators on the staff for the committee of bar associations, Lloyd K. Garrison, attended the referees' association's annual meeting in Memphis in August 1929 and thanked the referees for their advice and assistance.[24] Garrison presented a report on the progress of the investigation and discussed the study's proposed recommendations with the association's directors, individual referees, and W. Randolph Montgomery, counsel for the National Association of Credit Men, who also attended the conference.

Referees thought their insights and interests had been largely ignored in previous reform efforts; in the past, Congress and the Supreme Court had consulted only bankruptcy lawyers and creditors. Referees believed it would be advisable for them to get involved in this reform initiative, and they thought it might be done most effectively through cooperation with other organizations interested in bankruptcy, such as the American Bar Association, the Commercial Law League, and the National Association of Credit Men. Garrison encouraged the referees to form such a committee and promised to consult with it.[25] At the Memphis meeting, the National Association of Referees in Bankruptcy adopted a resolution authorizing the appointment of a committee to confer and cooperate with similar committees of other associations interested in the improvement of bankruptcy law and administration. Other organizations soon confirmed their interest in coordinated action, and National Association of Referees in Bankruptcy president Charles T. Greve of Cincinnati appointed Referees Paul H. King, James W. Persons, Watson B. Adair, Herbert M. Bierce, George R. Beach, and Carl D. Friebolin charter members of the Special Conference Committee.

The Donovan report claimed that twenty-one law firms controlled bankruptcy practice in New York City and that competition for cases among those firms drove many of the more flagrant abuses. Attorneys filing involuntary petitions or the first petition for a receiver in a voluntary case were most likely to be appointed attorney for the receiver and trustee. Consequently, some attorneys bribed court clerks for advance information on case filings. Some creditors' attorneys also paid collection agencies and bankrupts' attorneys for advance information on insolvent debtors. Creditors' attorneys even bribed creditors to allow them to represent them at the first meeting. Sometimes attorneys worked together, one representing the bankrupt and the other representing creditors. Attorneys secured the appointment of receivers, trustees, custodians, and others for personal and patronage reasons unrelated to their competence to perform the services, and no party pursued the honest and efficient liquidation of the estate on behalf of creditors. The committee investigated practices in several other large cities and found similar abuses.

Donovan's report concluded that the problem stemmed primarily from the 1898 Bankruptcy Act's assumption that creditors would control the bankruptcy process. The Bankruptcy Act assumed that referees would be primarily concerned with adjudicative questions, but the volume of bankruptcy business, the inefficiency of trustees, and the inattention of creditors left referees mired in administrative tasks and incapable of effective oversight of the system. The report recommended the appointment of a permanent commissioner of bankruptcy in the executive branch of government to appoint and supervise the trustees and receivers as well as to engage in the ongoing study of the bankruptcy system in order to ensure its efficiency and effectiveness. Donovan's report was printed and distributed for use by the House Committee on the Judiciary.

Meanwhile, in November 1929, Professor William O. Douglas of the Yale University School of Law and the Yale University Institute on Human Relations, in collaboration with the US Department of Commerce, began a scientific study of the causes of commercial bankruptcy in New Jersey. The investigation grew from a Commerce Department survey of grocery stores in St. Louis, Missouri, that found that out of 1,200 retail groceries, one store went out of business and another opened almost every day. The St. Louis study found that consumer bankruptcy was a contributing cause of grocery store bankruptcies. The New Jersey study expanded to survey a wide variety of retail establishments in Louisville, Kansas City, Philadelphia, and Boston. The joint study confirmed Department of Justice data that most bankruptcy estates had no assets or few assets, most of the estates' assets were consumed by the costs of administration in small asset cases, and in the great majority of cases no creditors appeared at the first meeting of the creditors for the election of a trustee.[26]

The New Jersey study analyzed case files of closed cases from June 1928 to June 1929. Most of the cases involved individual business bankruptcies, and many were businesses that had started during the real estate boom of the 1920s. The study attributed the cause of most business bankruptcies to poor business methods. The investigators found that more than one-half of the businesses kept no books and records or inadequate books and records, 39 percent never took an inventory, and most made no credible credit investigations of their customers, a practice that led to bad debt losses at eight times the rate of successful businesses.[27]

The Boston study analyzed consumer bankruptcies filed between November 1930 and June 1931. Consumer bankruptcies increased more than 400 percent between 1920 and 1930. The study determined that the increase in bankruptcies during the prosperous 1920s resulted from a dramatic increase in the provision of consumer credit during that period. In 1910, only 10 percent of the total estimated retail sales in the amount of $20 billion were made on credit, whereas in 1929, 50 percent of the total estimated retail sales in the amount of $53 billion were made on credit. Additional avenues of credit had opened to consumers during that period, including installment purchase agreements, personal finance companies, credit unions, and industrial banks. The investigators concluded that the availability of consumer credit reduced buyers' resistance and increased consumer purchasing power. Consumers purchased against future income in the booming 1920s, but wage-earner incomes proved unstable. Consumers could not meet their debts when their income declined, and they filed bankruptcy. The investigators called this "extravagance," and labeled it the primary cause of consumer bankruptcy.[28]

President Hoover appointed Judge Thacher to be US solicitor general in March 1930, and in July 1930, Attorney General William D. Mitchell ordered Thacher to initiate an investigation into bankruptcy administration. Mitchell appointed Lloyd K. Garrison to be Thacher's special assistant in charge of directing the investigation. In addition to the information developed during the Donovan investigation, Garrison relied on information developed in the earlier investigations by Yale University and the Commerce Department. He also undertook on-site studies of bankruptcy administration in numerous other cities, including Toledo.

Most importantly, Garrison also sought and received significant assistance from individual referees and from the National Association of Referees in Bankruptcy through the Special Conference Committee. Garrison attended the fifth annual meeting of the National Association of Referees in Bankruptcy, held in Chicago, Illinois, on August 18 and 19, 1930, reassuring referees and seeking their cooperation in completing and returning a nationwide survey of referees, which he hoped would establish a factual foundation for assessing and comparing bankruptcy administration across the country. Garrison closely collaborated with the Special Conference Committee in the design and proposed implementation of the survey. The National Association of Credit Men also attended the Chicago meeting and participated in the design of the survey. The National Association of Credit Men promised their assistance to referees in compiling all of the necessary information.

Carl D. Friebolin was elected vice president of the National Association of Referees in Bankruptcy at the 1930 annual meeting, and this placed him in a key leadership position for the next three years. As vice president, he would ascend to president at the 1931 meeting, and then, as past president, he would continue to serve as a director through the 1932–1933 term. Friebolin also continued on the Special Conference Committee, working closely with the Department of Justice investigation and with other interested organizations.

The National Association of Referees in Bankruptcy held its sixth annual meeting in Atlantic City, New Jersey, from September 14 through

16, 1931. The Department of Justice investigation and the probability of radical bankruptcy reform dominated the discussion at the meeting. The officers invited Garrison to speak for the third consecutive year, to give him an opportunity to explain his findings and recommendations and to give the referees an opportunity to respond. The Special Conference Committee had worked closely with the Department of Justice investigation in its fact-finding mission, engaging in daily consultation and correspondence over the course of several weeks. The Special Conference Committee met with Solicitor General Thacher and Garrison in Washington, DC, the weekend before the Atlantic City meeting, where they previewed the report's conclusions and recommendations.

The Department of Justice's report on its investigation recommended several important changes to the 1898 Bankruptcy Act. Believing that many consumer debtors would pay some part of their debts if doing so were made easier and less humiliating, the report recommended the creation of a process to allow consumer creditors to amortize their debts within the bankruptcy courts, free from the threat of state law garnishment, but without calling it bankruptcy. Because debtors usually made use of state creditors' remedies earlier than they entered bankruptcy, at a point when they still had some assets available for distribution to creditors, the report also recommended amendments to make assignments for the benefit of creditors possible in a trustee-supervised bankruptcy estate and to make compositions easier to implement for consumer debtors. A new section would bring corporate reorganizations within the bankruptcy law, with procedures very similar to those of equity receivership practice. However, examiners would supervise the reorganization process to prevent abuse, and efficiencies would be achieved, such as eliminating the necessity of ancillary receiverships.

The Department of Justice report proposed appointing trustees whenever a bankrupt estate had significant assets, but it urged licensing the trustees to ensure their integrity and qualifications and raising their compensation. A cadre of civil service examiners managed by supervisors in the Department of Justice would be responsible for investigating the qualifications of the persons seeking work as trustees, inspecting and auditing the trustees, and petitioning the court for their removal when appropriate. The examiners would also be responsible for examining the debtor to ensure his eligibility for discharge. The examiners would also conduct investigations as directed by the attorney general, furnish information to the courts on administrative matters, and prepare statistics.

The Department of Justice report proposed other measures to ensure the integrity of the bankruptcy process. The report recommended giving referees the authority to suspend a bankrupt's discharge for up to two years under certain circumstances: if the bankrupt's assets were less than 50 percent of his debts at the time of his petition, unless the diminution in value were found to be beyond his control; if the bankrupt contracted a debt within four months of his petition without any probable source of repaying it; or if the bankrupt contributed to his failure through hazardous speculation, gambling, unjustifiable extravagance in living, or culpable neglect of business affairs.

The report proposed that, to the extent possible, referees be made full-time salaried employees with a six-year term of appointment. The report also recommended increasing referees' statutory powers to include discharging debtors, confirming compositions, hearing testimony in plenary matters, and holding a general power of investigation.

Solicitor General Thacher and Garrison also discussed the investigation's findings and recommendations with committees of the American Bar Association, the Commercial Law League, and the National Association of Credit Men before the September 1931 meeting of the National Association of Referees in Bankruptcy at Atlantic City. During the Atlantic City meeting Garrison held a joint meeting with members of all of the interested organizations' committees. The Conference of Senior Circuit Judges approved a tentative copy of the report at its October 1931 meeting. Solicitor General Thacher and Garrison signed off on the report and recommendations on December 5, 1931, and Attorney General Mitchell submitted them to President Hoover on December 8, 1931. President Hoover referred them to Congress on February 24, 1932.

The Hastings Bill

On March 1, 1932, Senator Daniel O. Hastings of Delaware introduced the Department of Justice bill proposing amendments to the 1898 Bankruptcy Act into the Senate, and Representative Earl C. Michener of Michigan introduced it into the House. The bill was popularly known as the Hastings Bill. Hearings commenced on April 12, 1932, before both congressional subcommittees, sitting together, and the hearings concluded on June 28, 1932. Creditors' interests strongly supported the bill. Though Congress deferred action on the bill until after the 1932 election, the momentum toward passage seemed unstoppable.

The referees hated the Hastings Bill, and many other highly respected bankruptcy lawyers also opposed it. From the lawyers' perspective, the principal problem with the Hastings Bill was the creation of a vast administrative bureaucracy outside of the judiciary to take charge of bankruptcy administration.[29] Although acknowledging problems in the administration of bankruptcy and the need for modernization, they thought the 1898 Bankruptcy Act actually worked rather well on the whole. The newly organized National Association of Federal Practitioners spearheaded opposition to the bill. Harold Remington; Robert A. B. Cook, chairman of the Committee on Bankruptcy of the Commercial Law League; and Harvard law professor James A. McLaughlin testified against the bill. Jacob M. Lashley, chairman of the Commercial Law and Bankruptcy Committee of the American Bar Association invited the Special Conference Committee of the National Association of Referees in Bankruptcy and Robert Cook to a meeting in Washington, DC, on May 3, 1932, to plot opposition strategy. Lashley testified against the Hastings Bill on May 4, 1932. Members of the Special Conference Committee attended the hearing but did not testify because of the National Association of Referees in Bankruptcy's official policy against lobbying for or against particular legislation. Instead, the National Association of Referees in Bankruptcy proffered its expertise to assist Congress, but Congress did not take advantage of the offer. Two referees testified against the bill in their individual capacities.[30]

Senator Hastings, chairman of the congressional subcommittee considering the bankruptcy bill, suggested that if bankruptcy lawyers did not like the bill before Congress, they should draft their own bill. Thus, the National Association of Federal Practitioners formed a small committee led by Philadelphia practitioner Jacob I. Weinstein to write an alternative bankruptcy reform bill and present it to the congressional subcommittees. Robert Cook convened a second meeting on June 20, 1932, in Boston. Seven people attended the meeting: Cook, Jacob Lashley, Paul King, Carl Friebolin, Harvard professor James A. McLaughlin, Boston lawyer Joseph B. Jacobs, and California lawyer Reuben G. Hunt. They formed committees and, at the end of eight days, circulated a short draft bill of changes to the Bankruptcy Act that they believed should be made immediately. They scheduled another meeting to consider their draft. By 1938 this group evolved into the National Bankruptcy Conference, and for convenience we will henceforward refer to the group as such. A charter member, Carl Friebolin remained a leader in the National Bankruptcy Conference until his death.

The National Bankruptcy Conference members met again in St. Louis on September 15 through 18, 1932, where they debated the Boston draft and approved twenty-three specific proposals for adoption. Carl Friebolin incorporated those proposals into the report of the Committee on Legislation for the National Association of Referees in Bankruptcy and presented them at the 1932 annual meeting. The National Association of Credit Men held their convention in St. Louis at the same time, and their general counsel, New York attorney W. Randolph Montgomery, joined the National Bankruptcy Conference deliberations. After careful study and sober reflection, the National Association of Credit Men had second thoughts about the wisdom of the Hastings Bill and prepared their own draft bill instead.

The 1932 annual meeting of the National Association of Referees in Bankruptcy met in Washington, DC, October 10 through 12, immediately preceding the annual meeting of the American Bar Association.

The officers invited all referees, regardless of membership in the association, in order to facilitate the broadest possible consideration of the Hastings Bill. Paul King reported on the progress of the Special Conference Committee. Professor Douglas, Garrison, Lashley, and Montgomery also addressed the meeting. The National Association of Referees in Bankruptcy continued the Special Conference Committee and approved its work with the National Bankruptcy Conference. The American Bar Association endorsed the National Bankruptcy Conference's St. Louis draft at its annual meeting the following week.

When Congress convened for a short session in December 1932, opposition to the Hastings Bill had raised sufficient questions to delay its enactment, but economic conditions following in the wake of the 1929 stock market crash had reached desperate proportions. By every measure, including bankruptcy filings, the Great Depression reached its nadir at the end of 1932. Congress felt compelled to do something, but the landslide election of Democrat Franklin D. Roosevelt over Republican Herbert Hoover and huge Democratic gains in Congress complicated action. Portions of the Hastings Bill seemed appropriate under the circumstances, and very limited bankruptcy bills were introduced into Congress. Another meeting of the National Bankruptcy Conference occurred in Washington on January 27 and 28, 1933. The conference had grown to twenty-five persons. It did not agree with much of the emergency bankruptcy legislation but tried to improve it as passing something seemed inevitable. The conference submitted its recommendations to Senator Hastings, and many were incorporated into the emergency bankruptcy legislation. The bill made it to President Hoover's desk for signature on his last day in office, March 3, 1933.[31]

The emergency bankruptcy legislation created a new Chapter VIII "for the relief of debtors" without calling it bankruptcy. Section 74 provided for compositions and extensions by individuals and partnerships (but not corporations) with the agreement of a majority of creditors in number and amount. Section 75 created special rules for compositions and extensions by farmers. Section 77 removed railroad reorganizations from district court equity receiverships to the bankruptcy courts. Advocates of the incoming administration of President Franklin D. Roosevelt appropriated the legislation, calling it a "New Deal for Bankruptcy."[32]

The provisions of section 74 overlapped in part with an un-repealed section 12 dealing with compositions applicable to individuals, partnerships, and corporations, and the coexistence of the two sections created considerable confusion. If a composition or extension agreement under section 74 could not be confirmed or completed, liquidation would follow. In June 1934, Congress revisited bankruptcy reform and amended section 74 to allow the bankruptcy court to approve a plan for the rehabilitation of the debtor over the objection of a majority in number and amount of the debtor's creditors if the court found it in the "best interest of all of the creditors . . . including an equitable liquidation for the secured creditors whose claims are affected."[33] The provision proved to be largely symbolic. Individuals petitioned for compositions or extensions infrequently, and almost all of the petitions ended in liquidation.

Section 75 of new Chapter VIII pertained only to farmer debtors and allowed for the appointment of a "conciliation commissioner" in any county where at least fifteen farmers certified their intention to file a petition for composition and extension. Section 75 charged commissioners with supervising the composition and extension and with helping farmers to comply with their obligations. The section effectively stayed state foreclosure proceedings and other collection actions so long as the farmer debtor complied with the terms of the composition and extension. The section was temporary and was scheduled to expire five years after enactment.

Few farmers took advantage of section 75 as enacted in March 1933, and in June 1934 Congress amended the section by adding new subsections that allowed farmers to significantly reduce their debts, including secured debts.[34] This act was known as the Frazier-Lemke Act, after its sponsors. If a farmer was unable to secure a composition and extension, or felt aggrieved by it, the farmer could petition to have his property appraised at fair value. The farmer retained possession of his property while he paid off the appraised value at minimal interest rates over a six-year period under the supervision of a conciliation commissioner. Almost immediately, the Supreme Court unanimously found the 1934 amendments an unconstitutional "taking" of a secured party's property, and Congress responded by quickly passing a second Frazier-Lemke Act in August 1935.[35] This act shortened the period of the stay to three years during which a farmer remained in possession of his property so long as he made rent payments to the conciliation commissioner. At the end of the three years, the farmer could buy his property at the appraised value unless a secured creditor elected to sell the property at public auction. If the secured creditor elected public sale, the debtor had the right to redeem the property within ninety days by paying the sale price plus interest. The Supreme Court found this version of Frazier-Lemke to be constitutional.[36]

Department of Justice bankruptcy statistics are incomplete and incommensurate for this period. The forms used to gather information were in the process of revision, and the revisions did not keep pace with the statutory changes. Consequently, it is difficult to determine Frazier-Lemke's impact on rural America. Nationally, closed petitions under section 75 increased dramatically from 0.5 percent of all closed bankruptcy cases in 1935 (357/67,158) to 8 percent of all petitions closed in 1936 (5,285/63,287) before returning to the previous low level. In the Northern District of Ohio, closed cases under section 75 peaked in 1935 at 3 percent of all closed cases (143/4,696) and generally constituted less than 1 percent of total cases after that. Fred Kruse became conciliation commissioner for Lucas County and a noted expert on agricultural bankruptcies for the National Bankruptcy Conference. Walter Jackson became conciliation commissioner for the counties in the Lima bankruptcy district. The Frazier-Lemke Act was scheduled to expire by its terms in March 1938; but it was periodically extended until 1949, when it was finally allowed to expire permanently.

The most important of the March 1933 bankruptcy amendments provided for the reorganization of railroads. Railroads had been specifically excluded from the 1898 Bankruptcy Act, so a railroad in financial difficulty had to resort to an equity receivership. Railroads entered the Depression badly undercapitalized and subsequently experienced a debilitating decline in revenue. Railroads avoided wholesale resort to receivership only by heavy reliance on loans from the Reconstruction Finance Corporation. By 1933, railroads faced continuing losses, but most had exhausted their lending limits. By law, the Reconstruction Finance Corporation could only lend against valuable collateral.

The new section 77 allowed a railroad to seek reorganization through the bankruptcy courts by filing a petition in the district of its principal place of business stating that it was insolvent or unable to meet its debts when due. Creditors holding at least 5 percent of outstanding debt could file an involuntary petition. After adjudication, the district court appointed a trustee from a list provided by the Interstate Commerce Commission (ICC). The ICC held hearings at which the railroad, the trustee, and creditors could submit reorganization plans and recommended a plan of reorganization to the court for its confirmation based on a determination that the plan met the public interest and that it was fair and equitable. If the court did not approve a plan, the court could dismiss the proceeding or return the case to the ICC for further consideration. If the court approved the plan, the ICC submitted the plan to shareholders and creditors for their approval.[37] Amendments enacted in 1935 allowed "cram downs." In other words, the court could confirm a plan over the objection of a class of creditors or stockholders if the court found that the plan "[was] fair and equitable, afford[ed] due recognition of the rights of each class of creditors and stockholders, [did] not discriminate unfairly in favor of any class of creditors and stockholders, and [would] conform to the law of the land regarding the participation of the various classes of creditors and stockholders."[38]

The Missouri Pacific Railroad filed the first petition for reorganization under section 77 in St. Louis, Missouri, on March 31, 1933. The

Missouri Pacific, which would not emerge from bankruptcy until 1956, was part of the railroad empire assembled by the Van Sweringen brothers of Cleveland, Ohio. Oris Paxton Van Sweringen and Mantis James Van Sweringen rose from humble beginnings to control an intricate web of corporations and holding companies worth approximately $3 billion in 1929. Best known as the developers of Cleveland suburb Shaker Heights, the Van Sweringen empire was built on leverage and railroads. As railroad revenue declined, the empire crumbled. From the Van Sweringens' point of view, Congress enacted section 77 in the nick of time.

Other railroads in the Van Sweringen system soon followed the Missouri Pacific into the bankruptcy courts. The Akron Canton and Youngstown Railroad and its lessee, the Northern Ohio Railway Company, filed for reorganization in Cleveland on April 3, 1933. The Chicago and Eastern Illinois Railway filed for reorganization in Chicago on April 18, 1933. The Nickel Plate Railroad (New York, Chicago and St. Louis Railroad) defaulted on its bonds and narrowly avoided bankruptcy several times.[39] The Erie Railroad petitioned for reorganization in Cleveland on January 18, 1938. Judge Samuel H. West appointed local corporate attorney John Hadden trustee, together with Erie Railroad's president, Charles Denny, and Hadden thoroughly enjoyed his work on the Erie reorganization. Hadden's firm eventually merged to form Arter & Hadden, one of Cleveland's earliest corporate bankruptcy law firms. The last major railroad to petition for reorganization under section 77, the Erie Railroad, was the first to emerge from it in July 1941.[40]

In June 1934, Congress amended Chapter VIII to add a new section 77B, allowing corporations to file for reorganization.[41] Patterned on railroad reorganizations under section 77, a corporation that was eligible to file for bankruptcy and that was insolvent or unable to meet its debts when due could petition for reorganization in the district where it had its principal office or assets or in any district in its state of incorporation. The bankruptcy court had the power to alter the rights of shareholders and creditors through the plan of reorganization, but two-thirds in value of each class of debt had to accept the plan. Section 77B sought to control the abuses inherent in friendly equity receiverships, where management of the debtor corporations generally controlled the reorganization process and creditors had few procedural safeguards. The section also aspired to increase the efficiency of reorganization proceedings by making ancillary proceedings unnecessary; the bankruptcy court had exclusive jurisdiction over the debtor and its property wherever located. Desperate corporations filed 1,500 cases in the first eighteen months of the act, mostly in the Southern District of New York.[42]

Under section 77B, the district court judge had discretion to appoint a trustee or continue the debtor in possession. The judge could refer matters to a special master, and the bankruptcy referee could be the special master. He usually was. Carl Friebolin explained the practice in the Northern District of Ohio:

> What the judge does is, in effect, to appoint the Referee as special master under 77B, similarly to bankruptcy petitions. In bankruptcy, after there is an adjudication, the case goes to the Referee for general administration. Our practice is that after a petition has been approved, it goes to the special master for complete administration, right up to the end. . . . We proceed very much as in bankruptcy, as soon as the petition comes over, as special master, we make an order calling the meeting within thirty days, to determine whether or not the debtor shall remain in possession, as he usually does, or whether a trustee should be appointed.[43]

Friebolin explained that the special master's order directs the debtor to file a plan for reorganization and instructs the creditors how to file their claims. Hearings are scheduled and held, and matters proceed much as they do in bankruptcy:

> When it is all done, when the plan is approved, and the master has heard the arguments against it, and for it, the hearing on the approval is held, objections are made, and the special master files his report, goes through the whole thing, attaches the orders made during the proceedings, with recommendations and that report is then sent to the District Judge, the creditors having notice of the hearing before the District Judge.[44]

Both large and small corporations filed petitions for reorganization under section 77B in the Northern District of Ohio between 1934 and 1938, but they constituted considerably less than 1 percent of the total bankruptcy filings in the district for that period. The most notorious cases came out of the collapse of the Van Sweringen empire.

In January 1929, the Van Sweringen brothers decided to organize a holding company and incorporated the Alleghany Corporation in Maryland for that purpose. The Van Sweringen brothers held most of their major railroads through the Alleghany Corporation and used Alleghany stock as collateral for their margin account at Paine Webber. In 1930, the Van Sweringens incorporated the Van Sweringen Corporation in Ohio as a holding company for some of their real estate interests, including the Cleveland Terminals Building Company and its subsidiary, the Higbee Company. The Van Sweringens had built Terminal Tower in Cleveland to support their railroad interests, and when it opened in 1930, it was the second-tallest building in the world. More than central railroad terminal facilities for a major industrial city, the Terminal Tower included an exclusive executive office tower, bank, hotel, and luxury shops. The Cleveland Terminals Building Company purchased the Higbee Company, Cleveland's premier department store, specifically to move it into the Terminal Tower complex. The Van Sweringens sold bonds to raise working capital for the Van Sweringen Corporation, and to improve the bonds' marketability, they pledged Alleghany shares as security.

Railroad revenues declined precipitously after 1929, and the value of stock in railroads and railroad holding companies declined correspondingly. The Van Sweringens kept their empire together for a while by judiciously moving money between their different corporations, and they used the new corporate reorganization statute strategically. For example, on November 28, 1934, the Alleghany Corporation filed for reorganization under section 77B in Baltimore, Maryland. The Van Sweringens sought to restructure the corporation's capital and had already secured the consent of 71 percent in value of the creditors before they filed their petition. The purpose of the petition was to force dissenting bondholders to agree to the terms of the restructuring, and it worked. The Alleghany Corporation was out of bankruptcy court by October 1936. Circumstances deteriorated rapidly, however. The Higbee Company, a subsidiary of the Cleveland Terminals Building Company, filed a petition for reorganization under section 77B in Cleveland on August 9, 1935. M. J. Van Sweringen died on December 12, 1935, and on February 3, 1936, the Van Sweringen Company and its six subsidiaries filed for reorganization in Cleveland. Higbee's parent corporation, Cleveland Terminals Building Company, and its parent corporation, the Van Sweringen Corporation, filed for reorganization in Cleveland on October 13, 1936. In January 1940, the Securities and Exchange Commission (SEC) intervened in the bankruptcy under the provisions of the Chandler Act and called the bankruptcy "the largest and most complicated in the middle west."[45]

The Van Sweringen Company was the brothers' oldest company. Incorporated on January 10, 1922, it held the brothers' east-side real estate companies, including the Shaker Company. O. P. Van Sweringen anticipated a quick resolution to the reorganization; the corporation had already secured the consent of more than two-thirds of first secured mortgage holders. Things did not turn out as he anticipated, and O. P. Van Sweringen died November 22, 1936. Judge Paul J. Jones assigned the bankruptcy to Referee William B. Woods as special master, and Woods would not close the case until June 30, 1953. Woods considered the bankruptcy successful. The proceedings allowed the company to sell off real estate lots for the benefit of bondholders. More importantly, the reorganization preserved property values in the Cleveland suburb of Shaker Heights.[46]

One more Van Sweringen bankruptcy would be filed. On February 15, 1938, employees of the brothers' country estate, Daisy Hill Farm, filed an involuntary petition against the estate's holding company for unpaid wages.

Solicitor General Thacher's drive to enact bankruptcy reform began with allegations of fraud in the administration of the 1898 Bankruptcy

Act, particularly with regard to the appointment of unscrupulous receivers, trustees, and attorneys in New York City. The District Court for the Southern District of New York attempted to police the bankruptcy bar by establishing a local rule appointing the Irving Trust Company to be the exclusive receiver in bankruptcy for the district. The Supreme Court blessed the arrangement in a 1929 amendment to the general orders.[47] Courts and creditors supported the rule and believed it increased efficiency and decreased corruption in the administration of bankruptcy estates; lawyers disliked it, however, and feared it would spread to other districts. New York bar associations sought relief from Congress, and the bankruptcy bill that Congress passed on June 7, 1934, included an anti-monopoly provision that required judges to "apportion appointments of receivers and trustees among persons, firms, or corporations, or attorneys therefore, within the district . . . so as to prevent anyone from having a monopoly of the appointments." The section also prohibited the judge from appointing a near relation as receiver or trustee and declared that the compensation allowed to a receiver, trustee, or attorney "shall in no case be excessive or exorbitant, and the court in fixing such compensation shall have in mind the conservation and preservation of the estate of the bankrupt and the interests of the creditors therein."[48] The prohibition against excessive compensation came to be known as the "principle of economy in bankruptcy administration."

The Chandler Act

Franklin D. Roosevelt was inaugurated president of the United States on March 4, 1933. The next day, Sunday, March 5, he declared a four-day bank holiday and convened the new Congress in special session for the specific purpose of passing emergency economic legislation.

Municipal bond defaults had been increasing in number since the collapse of the Florida land boom in 1926. State and local governments had engaged in an expansive debt-funded public works program throughout the 1920s, especially for road constructions, and the decline in real estate values after the October 1929 stock market crash greatly diminished revenue from real estate taxes, local government's principal source of funding. By January 1934, an estimated 1,729 municipal bonds were in default. In May 1934, Congress responded to the crisis by enacting Chapter IX governing the bankruptcy of political subdivisions of states in order to prevent dissenting minority bondholders from interfering with the orderly restructuring of municipal debt.[49] Chapter IX required municipalities to secure the consent of a majority of bondholders to a readjustment of the debt before filing a petition. Chapter IX was scheduled to expire on January 1, 1940, but Congress repeatedly extended it and, in 1946, made it permanent.[50]

In May 1936, the Supreme Court held, in a five to four decision, that Chapter IX unconstitutionally interfered with the states' sovereign rights.[51] Only eighty-nine petitions had been filed under the provision, but most of them were still pending in bankruptcy courts. Congress enacted a new Chapter IX in August 1937, different from the earlier Chapter IX primarily in the cosmetic use of language.[52] The Supreme Court found that this version of Chapter IX did not impermissibly interfere with a state's sovereign rights.[53] Between the two Supreme Court decisions, Justices Sutherland and Van Devanter had resigned from the court. Both of those justices had voted in the majority to find the original Chapter IX unconstitutional. President Franklin Roosevelt had appointed their successors, Justices Black and Reed. Both of those justices voted in the majority to find the revised Chapter IX constitutional.[54]

The 1932 election changed everything. Nationwide repudiation of the failed policies of President Herbert Hoover left the prospects of enacting the Hastings Bill very uncertain. At the first meeting of the future National Bankruptcy Conference in Boston in June 1932, the conferees rejected the idea of undertaking a complete revision of the Bankruptcy Act on the grounds of expediency; the pace at which Congress seemed determined to move on the Hastings Bill required a more focused response. Consequently, the amendments they proposed at the St. Louis meeting only covered those they deemed most immediately necessary.

The emergency legislation of March 1933 relieved enough pressure that the conferees reconsidered the idea of a comprehensive revision of the Bankruptcy Act, and they called another conference in Washington, DC, from April 29 through May 2, 1933. Twenty-one conferees attended representing the Commercial Law and Bankruptcy Committee of the American Bar Association; the Commercial Law League of America; the National Association of Credit Men; the Chamber of Commerce; the Special Conference Committee of the National Association of Referees in Bankruptcy, including Paul King and Carl Friebolin; the editor of the *American Bankruptcy Review*; and representatives of bar associations, including Harold Remington and Professor James A. McLaughlin of Harvard. The revision effort turned into a herculean task consuming years of effort. The conference formed small committees, and each committee was assigned a particular task related to the larger plan of a comprehensive review of the 1898 Bankruptcy Act. Carl Friebolin became chairman of the Committee on Administration. The reports of the committees were referred to a twelve-person Drafting Committee chaired by Jacob I. Weinstein. The committee included, among others, Paul King, Carl Friebolin, and Harold Remington.[55]

The Drafting Committee met in New York at the end of May 1933 and again in Boston in June 1933. The committee continued to meet periodically and corresponded extensively, hoping to submit a draft revision of the 1898 Bankruptcy Act at the December 1933 meeting of the National Bankruptcy Conference at Northwestern University in Evanston, Illinois, from December 7 to December 10, 1933. The Drafting Committee circulated its revision before the conference, and conferees submitted more than 400 comments and suggestions. Consequently, consideration of the draft revision was deferred to a meeting in Washington, DC, in late January 1934. The conference ordered the draft submitted to interested organizations for comment, and the Drafting Committee began writing explanatory notes. The National Bankruptcy Conference met twice more, in Chicago in September 1934 and Washington, DC, in March 1935, before it had a final product. The draft revision and explanatory notes were printed on May 15, 1935, and distributed for use by the House Judiciary Committee. The bill consisted of 125 major amendments to the 1898 Bankruptcy Act.[56]

Congressman Walter Chandler of Tennessee, chairman of the subcommittee of the House Judiciary Committee considering bankruptcy legislation, introduced the National Bankruptcy Conference draft revision into Congress on January 20, 1936. The bill became known as the Chandler Bill. Hearings commenced March 30, 1936, and numerous members of the conference testified in support of the bill. Judiciary Committee members proposed so many amendments to the bill during the committee hearings that Congressman Chandler requested a revision of the bill to incorporate the amendments. The National Bankruptcy Conference Drafting Committee met in Washington, DC, from April 17 to 19, 1936, and prepared a new draft. Chandler reintroduced the revised bill into Congress in May 1936, and members of the Drafting Committee took responsibility for explaining the revised Chandler Bill to members of Congress. Many additional amendments were proposed during the hearings, and Congress adjourned without taking action.

In the meantime, Professor William O. Douglas of Yale had been appointed chairman of the SEC, and he expressed an interest in the pending bankruptcy legislation. Douglas and his associates met with the National Bankruptcy Conference Drafting Committee in Washington, DC, and the Drafting Committee wrote Douglas's proposed changes to the corporate reorganization provisions into the Chandler Bill. This precipitated another National Bankruptcy Conference meeting in Washington, DC, at the end of March 1937 to consider the additional changes. The principal areas of discussion concerned (1) the right of the SEC to intervene in proceedings, (2) whether a trustee should be required in large corporate reorganizations instead of allowing debtors to continue in possession, and (3) whether labor unions should be heard with regard to plans of reorganization.

Congressman Chandler reintroduced his bankruptcy bill in the new Congress on April 15, 1937. Hearings resumed before the subcommittee of the House Judiciary Committee in June 1937. At the conclusion of the hearings, subcommittee members proposed so many amendments that the National Bankruptcy Conference redrafted the bill again. This bill passed the House Judiciary Committee unanimously and then passed the House of Representatives unanimously on August 10, 1937. The Senate Judiciary Committee held hearings on the bill in January 1938, and the National Bankruptcy Conference Drafting Committee helped prepare the committee report. The Senate Judiciary Committee favorably reported the bill with amendments, and the Senate approved the bill on June 10, 1938. The House concurred in the Senate's amendments on June 13, 1938. President Roosevelt signed the Chandler Act into law on June 22, 1938.[57]

The National Bankruptcy Conference met in Cleveland in July 1938 for a victory lap, and Carl Friebolin presided at the meeting. The conferees decided to become a permanent organization and formed an administrative committee. Both Friebolin and King served on the committee, and both continued to have important roles in the organization for years to come.[58]

The Chandler Act retained the basic structure, language, and procedure of the 1898 Bankruptcy Act in order to facilitate reliance on experience and precedent whenever possible.[59] After amendment by the Chandler Act, the 1898 Bankruptcy Act consisted of fourteen chapters. Chapters I through VII dealt with definitional issues, court organization, basic procedure, and liquidation: "ordinary bankruptcy" as it had existed previously. Chapter VIII still included some of the Depression-inspired emergency bankruptcy legislation, especially section 75 on compositions and extensions for farmers, a temporary provision. A new Chapter XV replaced section 77 on railroad reorganizations in July 1939.[60] Section 76 on compositions and extensions and section 12 on compositions were eliminated and replaced by new Chapters XI, XII, and XIII on arrangements. Although few aspects of bankruptcy continued unchanged, the radical changes to existing bankruptcy practice occurred in the new Chapters X through XIII.[61]

Chapter X replaced old section 77B and radically revised corporate reorganizations. Under Chapter X, whenever a debtor owed more than $250,000, the court was required to appoint a disinterested trustee and a disinterested attorney for the trustee. The trustee had a duty to file a plan for reorganization, and if the corporation's indebtedness exceeded $3 million the court was required to submit the plan to the SEC for examination and report. The court could not submit the plan to creditors for approval without giving the SEC an opportunity to file a report. The SEC had the right to intervene in the proceeding as a party in interest. The district court judge could refer the proceedings to a referee in bankruptcy or to a special master who may be a referee in bankruptcy, but only the district court judge could confirm or refuse to confirm a plan. Under the Chandler Act, this was the only major area in which final decisions had to be made by a district court judge and could not be made by a referee.

Congress expected individual debtors and small corporations to file for an arrangement under Chapter XI. The Chandler Act defined a Chapter XI arrangement as "a plan of a debtor for the settlement, satisfaction, or extension of the time for payment of his unsecured debts."[62] The court could refer the proceeding to a referee, and it usually did. The court could appoint a trustee, but the proceeding usually continued with the debtor in possession. Because Chapter XI only modified unsecured debts and individuals could not file for reorganization under Chapter X, Congress enacted Chapter XII to allow individual debtors to restructure debts secured by real property. In particular, Congress sought to provide a mechanism for the resolution of defaults on widely distributed bonds based on securitized individual real-estate debt obligations in the Chicago metropolitan area.[63] Only individual debtors could file petitions under Chapter XII, and mortgages from Federal Home Loan Banks or provided under federal home loan programs could not be modified under the chapter. Very few debtors filed petitions under Chapter XII.

Chapter XIII established the wage-earner plan, allowing consumer debtors to pay a portion of their debts out of future wages while enjoying court protection against garnishment and other state-law collection actions. Only individuals earning $3,600 or less could file a petition for an arrangement under Chapter XIII. Few did. To the general dismay of consumer creditors, most consumer debtors did not perceive any advantage in going through a Chapter XIII wage-earner plan over obtaining an immediate discharge in Chapter VII bankruptcy.

The Referees' Salary Act

Radical reform of the administrative structure of bankruptcy—and of the tenure, supervision, and authority of referees—had been the cornerstone of the movement for bankruptcy reform that began in 1929, led by Judge Thacher, William Donovan, and Lloyd Garrison. The Chandler Act made very few changes in this regard. The Chandler Act clarified that the "bankruptcy court" meant the judges or the referees of the courts of bankruptcy; it specified that a referee's bankruptcy district was not restricted to the counties where he presided but was coextensive with the judicial district of the appointing court; and it suggested that the appointment of referees be limited in order to maximize the number of full-time referees, but the appointment and supervision of referees remained entirely at the discretion of the district court. Referees' tenure remained uncertain and their compensation fee based.[64]

On April 19, 1940, Attorney General Frank Murphy appointed another committee to study bankruptcy administration. This committee used the usual sources: questionnaires to judges, court clerks, US attorneys, and referees; official reports of referees and examiners; and Department of Justice statistics. Trustees were surveyed but few responded. The committee also received input from bar associations and credit associations. It employed law students to analyze approximately 1,750 recently closed bankruptcy cases from different parts of the country. The committee submitted its report to the new attorney general, Robert H. Jackson, on December 16, 1940—Frank Murphy had resigned as attorney general after his appointment to the United States Supreme Court. The report recommended making referees full-time salaried employees with a six-year term of appointment and placing them under the supervision of a Bankruptcy Division in the Administrative Office of the United States Courts.[65] Members of the attorney general's committee began writing a bill. The National Bankruptcy Conference approved the bill at its meeting in Chicago in March 1941. The attorney general's bill was introduced in Congress in April 1941.

The Conference of Senior Circuit Judges had already decided at a special meeting in January 1940 that bankruptcy fell within the jurisdiction of the Administrative Office of the United States Courts.[66] In August 1939, Congress had established the Administrative Office of the United States Courts to manage court administration under the direction of the Conference of Senior Circuit Judges.[67] The chief justice of the United States appointed the director of the agency, and the director hired the Administrative Office's employees. The Administrative Office was responsible for budgeting, procurement, audit of court accounts, examination of court dockets for management and statistical purposes, reporting to Congress, and all administrative matters pertaining to clerical and administrative employees of the courts; however, it had no executive authority. The Administrative Office made quarterly reports to the judicial councils of the circuit courts established by the same legislation, and the circuit councils were directed to take whatever action they deemed necessary. The act that established the Administrative Office directed district court judges to "promptly carry out the directions of the circuit councils as to the administration of the business of their respective courts" but included no enforcement mechanism. Courts retained complete control over the appointment, retention, and supervision of their personnel.[68]

The Conference of Senior Circuit Judges, now known as the Judicial Conference, met in January 1941 to consider the attorney general's report and endorsed it in part.[69] The Judicial Conference approved the establishment of a Bankruptcy Division, replacing the fee system for compensating referees with salaries, employing full-time referees to the extent justified by local circumstances, and establishing a six-year term of office for referees. They agreed that referees should be allowed to retire on half pay at age seventy or if incapacitated. However, the bankruptcy courts would remain self-supporting out of fees and charges against bankruptcy estates, the amount of which would be established by the Administrative Office and approved by the Judicial Conference. The Judicial Conference authorized the Administrative Office to conduct a survey to determine the number of referees needed and their salary but retained the right to make all final decisions after consultation with the circuit councils.

The Judicial Conference disagreed with the attorney general's report to the extent that it undermined the district courts' power over referees. The Judicial Conference agreed that a district court judge's failure to remove a referee for cause, as shown by the Bankruptcy Division of the Administrative Office, should be reviewed and gave the circuit council power to remove a referee for cause if the appointing judge did not do so. However, the Judicial Conference did not agree that a referee removed for cause by the district court should have any right to a review of the court's decision. Similarly, if a referee's term expired and the Bankruptcy Division did not recommend reappointment, the referee could not be reappointed without the permission of the circuit council, but a referee who was not reappointed had no redress even if the Bankruptcy Division recommended reappointment. The Judicial Conference also disapproved of allowing the director of the Administrative Office to recommend legislative changes directly to Congress and required him to submit his recommendations to the Judicial Conference or, if it involved local matters, to the circuit councils.

The creation of a Bankruptcy Division required no legislation, but Congress appropriated funds only for a chief, one staff attorney, and a secretary. With the approval of the chief justice, in February 1942, Director Chandler appointed a seasoned referee, Edwin L. Covey from Peoria, Illinois, chief of the Bankruptcy Division. Chief Covey, who communicated with the Judicial Conference through a Committee on Bankruptcy Administration, worked to improve bankruptcy administration in the

Figure 4.2. Bankruptcy Cases Commenced in US District Courts 1905–1954

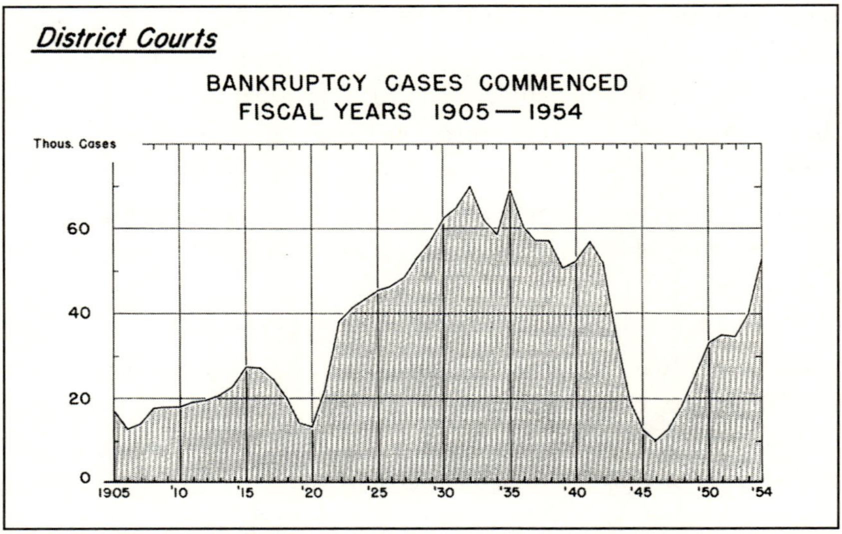

Note: Bankruptcy Division of the Administrative Office of the United States Courts, Director's Annual Report for 1956, Bankruptcy Administration, Friebolin Papers, WRHS.

field through the development of model rules and forms, advice, encouragement, and persuasion.

The salary bill proved controversial. Some part-time referees with small incomes did not support it because it made them redundant; some full-time referees with large incomes did not support it because it reduced their incomes. Some US district court judges objected to interference in their appointment power. Some federal employees objected because the referees' retirement benefits were more generous than those of other federal employees. Then World War II started. The number of bankruptcy cases declined precipitously, and referees' incomes declined correspondingly. (See Figure 4.2.) Some referees found themselves unable to pay their office expenses. Creditors worried that the bankruptcy system might collapse altogether.

In January 1945, the salary bill had been languishing in Congress for years. On January 26, 1945, the National Credit Association called a conference of all interested parties to effect a compromise. They agreed to two changes: a statement of principle that referees should be reappointed unless there was a good reason to terminate the appointment, such as incompetence or misconduct, and a change in the referees' retirement system to the less generous retirement system generally available to federal employees. With no opposition, the revised salary bill finally passed Congress and became law on June 28, 1946.[70] The Administrative Office immediately began a comprehensive national survey to implement the Salary Act and completed its report in March 1947.

The Salary Act provided that the judges of the district courts would appoint or reappoint referees in bankruptcy for that district by the agreement of a majority of all of the judges or by the senior judge if there was no agreement of a majority of the judges. Referees served a six-year term, and a full-time referee could be removed from office during his term of appointment for "incompetence, misconduct, or neglect of duty" by the agreement of a majority of the judges in the district or by the circuit council if there was no agreement by a majority of the district court judges.[71]

The director of the Administrative Office had considerable power under the Salary Act, subject to the approval of the courts. His national survey recommended the number of referees in any district, the territory each should serve, the location of their offices and other locations where they should hold court, their salaries, and the fees that should be charged to pay for the system. The director submitted his recommendations to the district court judges, the circuit council, and the Judicial Conference. The district court judges gave their recommendations to the circuit council, which in turn gave their recommendations to the Judicial Conference, which ultimately decided. Before a referee's term expired, or whenever a referee vacancy occurred for any reason, the Administrative Office recommended whether a referee be reappointed, a new referee be appointed, or the office be left vacant. The Judicial Conference could change the number of referees and the locations of their offices as circumstances required, after consultation with the Administrative Office and the circuit councils with the advice of the district court judges.[72]

The Administrative Office recommended individual referees' salaries up to a maximum of $5,000 per annum for part-time referees and a maximum of $10,000 per annum for full-time referees. The Administrative Office based its salary recommendations on the preceding ten-year average of the number of cases handled, their complexity, the amount realized by the bankrupt estates, and other material factors. The Judicial Conference determined the salaries and could increase or decrease a referee's salary once every two years if the underlying factors changed materially so long as it did not reduce the salary below the amount at which the referee was appointed. As always, the Judicial Conference made its decision after consultation with the Administrative Office and the circuit councils with the advice of the district court judges.[73]

The district court clerks collected statutory fees for the referees' salary and expense fund at the time a bankruptcy case was filed. Additional fees for the referees' salaries and expenses were collected at the time the case closed according to a schedule established by the Administrative Office and approved by the Judicial Conference. The Salary Act provided that the fees collected in bankruptcy should be set at a rate that would cover the referees' salaries and expenses. The clerk deposited those fees into a special fund for payment of referees' salaries and expenses. Even though the bankruptcy system was designed to be self-supporting, the Salary Act required an annual appropriation from Congress for the payment of salaries and expenses. At the end of fiscal year 1950, the referees' salary and expense fund had a surplus balance of $1 million.[74]

The Bankruptcy Committee of the Judicial Conference approved the Administrative Office's report in April 1947 with minor changes, and the Judicial Conference accepted the determinations on May 2, 1947. The new system went into effect two months later at the beginning of the next fiscal year, July 1, 1947.

After nearly twenty years of continuous study by various commissions and committees, the bankruptcy courts had been reshaped to reflect the realities of a modern industrial society. The Chandler Act expanded the governing law to encompass the principal economic players: consumers and large industrial corporations. It shifted the emphasis from liquidation to rehabilitation and reorganization. The Salary Act began to move the bankruptcy courts from a collection of isolated patronage offices to a coordinated system under centralized management. Although the transformation occurred during years of economic depression and world war, those forces had surprisingly little influence on the final shape the reforms took. The initial impetus for bankruptcy reform came from scandal in the administration of bankruptcy in the New York City courts. Neither the Chandler Act nor the Salary Act would eliminate the potential for scandal as bankruptcy entered the postwar era.

Chapter Five
Bankruptcy under the Bankruptcy Act: 1947 to 1978

In 1944, the Cleveland Electric Illuminating Company promoted Cleveland as "the best location in the nation." By 1980, national media derided the city as "the mistake by the lake." Cleveland's rise and fall is representative of an unfortunate trend throughout northern Ohio and other manufacturing regions bordering the Great Lakes. This chapter follows the development of the bankruptcy court in the Northern District of Ohio under the 1898 Bankruptcy Act after enactment of the Chandler Act of 1938 and the Salary Act of 1946 until the next round of bankruptcy reform in 1978. During this period, northern Ohio's economy rebounded from the devastation of the Great Depression of the 1930s, rapidly expanded in the post–World War II industrial boom, and painfully began to deindustrialize in the 1970s.

Northern Ohio suffered greatly during the Great Depression. The heavy manufacturing industries that had made the region rich between 1880 and 1930 experienced a disproportionate decline in economic activity. Scholars estimate that national unemployment in 1932 averaged 25 percent. Yet because unemployment was concentrated among nonagricultural workers, northern Ohio's highly industrialized economy fared especially poorly. Scholars estimate that 50 percent of Cleveland's industrial workers and 80 percent of Toledo's industrial workers were unemployed. Employment recovered rapidly with the onset of World War II, however, as northern

Ohio's iron and steel, automotive, and heavy machinery factories retooled for the war effort. Akron's rubber factories also produced to capacity. Toledo's Willys-Overland Motor Company, which entered federal court receivership in 1933, exemplifies northern Ohio's economic turnaround. The proceeding was converted to a reorganization under newly enacted section 77B of the amended 1898 Bankruptcy Act, and the company emerged in 1936 as Willys-Overland Motors, Inc. In 1941, Willys-Overland Motors, Inc. landed the army contract for production of the jeep.[1]

Northern Ohio's boom continued many years after the end of World War II, as its steel mills and factories supplied long-deferred domestic demand for automobiles, appliances, and other consumer durables. Northern Ohio's factories were unionized and provided workers with high wages and good benefits. In Cleveland, manufacturing employment peaked in 1967, and then began to decline. By 1980, one-third of the manufacturing jobs had left the region, and the total population declined significantly relative to the nation as a whole.[2]

Scholars debate the reasons for northern Ohio's economic decline after 1970. The completion of the St. Lawrence Seaway in the 1950s made Cleveland an international port, but it also made foreign steel imports more accessible to American factories. Similarly, the completion of the interstate highway system in the 1970s made industry less dependent on railroads and water routes, decreasing the economic value of Cleveland's strategic location. Formerly underdeveloped nations flooded world markets with steel, machine tools, automobiles, and other consumer durables that competed directly with northern Ohio's key industries. Perhaps most importantly, northern Ohio became an industrial giant between 1890 and 1930 with manufacturing productivity significantly higher than the rest of the country. After World War II, however, northern Ohio's manufacturing productivity experienced a relative decline that may have started as early as the 1930s.[3] Plants closed and jobs disappeared from old factories in urban areas, exacerbating social tensions.

Cleveland suffered a series of events in the second half of the 1960s that tarnished northern Ohio's reputation and further encouraged regional deindustrialization. Racial tensions in Cleveland exploded in riots in the Hough district over four days in July 1966. Four people died in the riots, many others were injured, and much of the neighborhood was destroyed. Almost exactly two years later, in July 1968, an exchange of gunfire between police and African Americans in the Glenville neighborhood of Cleveland left seven people dead and set off three days of rioting. On June 22, 1969, an oil slick on the surface of the heavily polluted Cuyahoga River caught fire. The fire received substantial national publicity and made Cleveland the poster child for polluted, decaying, urban industrial cities. As plants closed and the more prosperous residents moved to the suburbs, Cleveland's remaining residents had an increased need for social services at a time when the city's revenue from real property, sales, and income taxes decreased. In 1978, Cleveland became the first major city since the Great Depression to default on its bonds.

The rise and fall of northern Ohio's economy left no perceptible imprint on bankruptcy statistics. From 1947 through 1978, in good times and in bad times, consumer bankruptcies increased steadily, both regionally and nationally, in lockstep with the growth of credit in the consumer economy of the postwar era.[4] Northern Ohio was one of the busiest bankruptcy districts in the country when its economy boomed in the 1950s; it remained one of the busiest bankruptcy districts when the factories started to close. Meanwhile, the bankruptcy courts expanded steadily during this period to meet the demand from the increasing numbers of consumer bankruptcies.

This chapter describes the bankruptcy court's transition to the new bankruptcy system after the enactment of the Chandler Act of 1938 and the Salary Act of 1946. It introduces the referees in the Northern District of Ohio and discusses the circumstances of their appointments.

The discussion of referees is divided into two periods: 1947 to 1965 and 1965 to 1978. During the first period, from 1947 to 1965, the referees in bankruptcy adjusted to being salaried, full-time, district court employees with centralized management in the Administrative Office of the United States Courts. The bankruptcy court achieved its current size and configuration as new referees were appointed in northern Ohio cities to administer the increasing number of consumer bankruptcy cases. After 1965, a new generation of referees was appointed who continued the professionalization of bankruptcy practice and procedure.

The two sections on referees book-end sections that discuss the Administrative Office's advocacy for increased utilization of Chapter XIII wage-earner plans, and the growth of a specialized bankruptcy bar in Cleveland that many critics labeled a "bankruptcy ring." The question of what to do about constantly increasing consumer bankruptcies and the bankruptcy rings that fed off them had precipitated the commissions and investigations that culminated in the Chandler Act. The Chandler Act's reforms had little effect, and by the late 1960s, new allegations of misconduct by bankruptcy rings brought renewed demands for bankruptcy reform.

The Referees: 1947 to 1965

The plan that the Bankruptcy Division of the Administrative Office of the United States Courts prepared in 1947 called for three full-time referees and one part-time referee in the Northern District of Ohio: two full-time referees in Cleveland; one full-time referee in Toledo; and one part-time referee in Youngstown. The plan's implementation date was July 1, 1947, and, although the plan encouraged, to the extent possible, allowing existing referees to remain in office to retain expertise, the plan's implementation necessitated some changes in personnel. Everett L. Foote, the referee in Akron; Charles J. Starkey, the referee in Ashtabula; and Paul D. Roach, the referee in Canton, ended their service and turned their files over to Cleveland referees Carl D. Friebolin and William B. Woods on June 30, 1947. Foote and Roach inventoried their furniture, books, and other official property and sent it to Cleveland.

Two referees served Toledo immediately before June 30, 1947: Fred H. Kruse and Frank C. Kniffin. Kniffin was fifty-three years old, and Kruse was seventy years old. Kniffin, a Democrat, was appointed in 1939 by sitting Toledo district court judge Frank Le Blond Kloeb, a Democrat, and Kniffin was retained as the referee in bankruptcy in Toledo. Kniffin also traveled to Fremont, Lima, and Marion to hold bankruptcy court.

Kruse, a Republican, was popular and well respected. He was first vice president of the National Association of Referees in Bankruptcy and served the National Bankruptcy Conference as secretary, chair of the committee on farmer-debtor relief, and member of the Drafting Committee. In 1944, the chief justice appointed Kruse chair of the committee created by the Judicial Conference to study and make recommendations about the disposition and preservation of closed bankruptcy case files and to design new administrative forms for referees. As referees, both Kniffin and Kruse had maintained offices in the US courthouse in Toledo. Judge Kloeb appointed Kruse standing master of the District Court for the Western Division of the Northern District of Ohio, and Kruse kept his office in the Toledo Courthouse. In 1961, Judge Kloeb appointed a second referee for Toledo, T. Kenneth Mattimoe, who had served as Judge Kloeb's law clerk from 1944 to 1947 before entering private practice in Toledo. Judge Kloeb served as district court judge in Toledo until September 1964.

The Bankruptcy Division of the Administrative Office directed the two referees in Cleveland, Friebolin and Woods, to establish a consolidated office to serve Ashtabula, Akron, Bucyrus, Canton, and Cleveland. Friebolin had been in a law partnership with his old friend Edgar S. Byers since 1901, and the Salary Act necessitated the law partnership's dissolution. As a full-time federal employee, Friebolin could no longer engage in the private practice of law. Before the Salary Act, Friebolin had discretion to run his law firm as he pleased, but under the Salary Act the Administrative Office controlled all procurements for necessary office expenses for full-time referees. The Administrative Office surveyed all referees to determine the appropriate amounts to be allowed for hiring support personnel, travel, publications, books, supplies, communications, rent, and utilities. On July 5, 1947, Bankruptcy Division chief Edwin L. Covey sent Friebolin and Woods a budget and instructions for transitioning to the status of salaried federal employees. The budget authorized Friebolin and Woods to hire four full-time clerks. Friebolin's long-time secretary,

Elizabeth Morrison, became a federal employee and chief bankruptcy clerk for the referees in Cleveland. No separate office of clerk of bankruptcy court existed to handle bankruptcy cases, and all bankruptcy petitions continued to be filed with the clerk of district court.

The Salary Act contemplated providing referees with office space in courthouses or post offices, but no space was available in federal buildings in Cleveland in July 1947 when the act became effective. In order for government funds to be used to pay office rent, the government needed to have a lease on the premises for which it was paying rent. Friebolin and Byers occupied leased space at 2001 NBC Building, only part of which was used for bankruptcy purposes. Woods had offices at 1214 Terminal Tower Building. The commercial real estate market in Cleveland at that time did not facilitate lease-breaking, but Woods succeeded in moving into Friebolin's office. Friebolin could not, however, transfer his lease to a government entity because the Bankruptcy Division of the Administrative Office would not authorize the use of all of the leased space, and Friebolin's landlord would not let him reduce the amount of space leased. Friebolin's lease ran until December 1947, so he sought authorization to sublet the portion of the space actually used for bankruptcy purposes; in mid-October, however, the government found office space it preferred for Friebolin and Woods at 600 Marshall Building. Friebolin filed a claim with the government for rent due him at the NBC Building from August to October and remained liable on his NBC Building lease until the end of the year.[5] Friebolin and Woods would not move into the US courthouse in Cleveland until 1957.

Friebolin served as unofficial chief judge of the bankruptcy court until his retirement in June 1967 at age eighty-nine. He died two months later. As mere adjuncts of the district court, referees had no formal structure for establishing uniform practices or following precedent within their district. Referees in different cities in the same district rarely met except at conferences. Referee Doyle of Youngstown organized the first informal meeting of the referees in the Northern District of Ohio to discuss common issues and practices, which was held in Cleveland in

February 1962. Friebolin was an acknowledged expert in bankruptcy law, and the other referees sought his advice. He had taught the bankruptcy course at Western Reserve Law School from 1934 until 1959—and called the law school "Local Union No. 1."[6] His class met at 8:00 A.M. to minimize conflicts with his judicial duties. In the 1950s and 1960s, Friebolin also taught an evening class to practitioners in the National Association of Credit Management's premises in the old Arcade building on Euclid Avenue—"Friebolin College."[7] In alternating years Friebolin's class covered basic bankruptcy and recent developments.

Friebolin acquired his vast knowledge of bankruptcy law and procedure through his many years of practice as a referee and his involvement in all significant bankruptcy issues since the 1920s as a member of the National Association of Referees in Bankruptcy and the National Bankruptcy Conference. During the time in which the National Association of Referees in Bankruptcy had a formal editorial board for its journal, Friebolin served on the editorial board, and he corresponded with the journal's editor about the publication when there was no formal editorial board. The *Journal of the National Association of Referees in Bankruptcy* published digests of referee opinions and Commerce Clearing House's loose-leaf *Bankruptcy Law Reporter* contained summaries of important decisions by referees, but until enactment of the Bankruptcy Code of 1978 no reporter published full-text referee decisions after Matthew Bender discontinued *American Bankruptcy Reports* in 1945.[8] Referees kept informed on current developments in other bankruptcy courts primarily through personal relationships, and Friebolin knew everybody and corresponded extensively.

Even though the Administrative Office plan called for a part-time referee in Youngstown, no referee was serving there on July 1, 1947, the implementation date for the Salary Act. Chief Judge Paul J. Jones had appointed Ross E. Diser referee in Youngstown in 1944 after Referee William J. Williams died but Diser's term expired before the implementation date of the Salary Act, and he was not reappointed because the district court judges in Cleveland could not agree on an appointee. The appointment of referees in bankruptcy continued to be strongly influenced by partisan politics after enactment of the Salary Act, and the political affiliation of new referees reflected the partisan political composition of the district court. Toledo remained aloof from the Eastern Division of the Northern District of Ohio and was almost a district unto itself.

The two Democratic district court judges in Cleveland, Judge Robert Wilkin and Judge Emerich Freed, preferred one candidate; Judge Jones, the senior judge and a Republican, wanted to reappoint Diser. The senior judge got two votes, and Judge Kloeb in Toledo, a Democrat, refused to get involved in Cleveland matters. That left no candidate for referee with a majority of the votes of the judges of the district as required by the Salary Act. The Salary Act provided for the senior judge to make the appointment in the absence of the agreement of a majority of the judges, but none of the judges wanted to force the issue as a matter of judicial courtesy. With no Youngstown referee, Cleveland referee William Woods traveled to Youngstown as necessary to handle the bankruptcy business there, assisted by a Youngstown-based full-time deputy clerk for bankruptcy matters.[9]

Bankruptcy cases declined from their peak in 1932, forming a trough in 1947. From 1947 until 1970, however, bankruptcy filings once again began to increase steadily in the United States and in the Northern District of Ohio, regardless of economic conditions. (See Figures 5.1 and 5.2.) An investigation by the Brookings Institution between 1966 and 1970 determined that consumer debt increased steadily from a low of 14.2 percent of personal income in 1945 to a high of 56 percent of personal income in 1965, and consumer bankruptcies increased proportionally. The number of bankruptcies as a proportion of population varied greatly among states, and the Brookings Institution found that the principal determinant of a state's per capita rate of bankruptcy filings was that state's garnishment regime. High rates of bankruptcy highly correlated with oppressive garnishment statutes but not with wealth, poverty, urbanization, or other measures of the penetration of commercial culture.[10] Almost all bankruptcies were voluntary and, except for Alabama, almost

Figure 5.1. Total US Bankruptcy Filings, 1946–1970

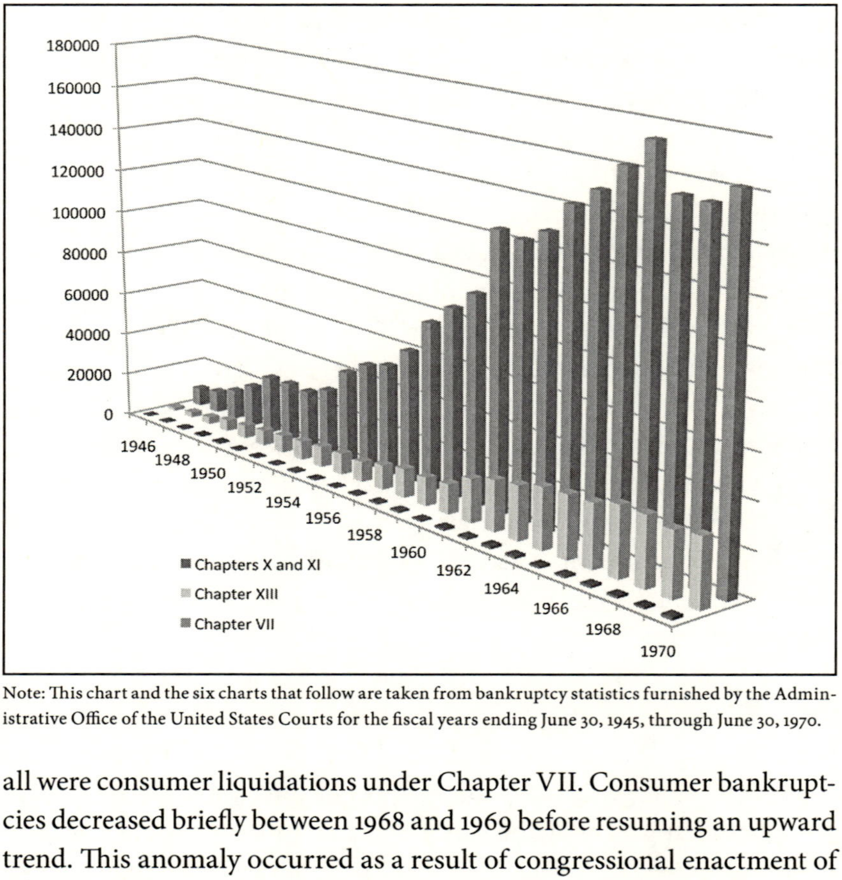

Note: This chart and the six charts that follow are taken from bankruptcy statistics furnished by the Administrative Office of the United States Courts for the fiscal years ending June 30, 1945, through June 30, 1970.

all were consumer liquidations under Chapter VII. Consumer bankruptcies decreased briefly between 1968 and 1969 before resuming an upward trend. This anomaly occurred as a result of congressional enactment of the Consumer Credit Protection Act, establishing a federal floor on creditors' ability to garnish wages under state law.[11]

Five recessions occurred between 1947 and 1970: (1) November 1948 to October 1949, (2) July 1953 to May 1954, (3) August 1957 to April 1958, (4) April 1960 to February 1961, and (5) December 1969 to November 1970.[12] Business bankruptcies increased in number around the recessions, but business bankruptcies constituted a small and decreasing proportion of total bankruptcies throughout this period. (See Figure 5.3.) Nationally, only 2,160 bankruptcies were filed under Chapter X out

Figure 5.2. Total Northern District of Ohio Bankruptcy Filings, 1946–1970

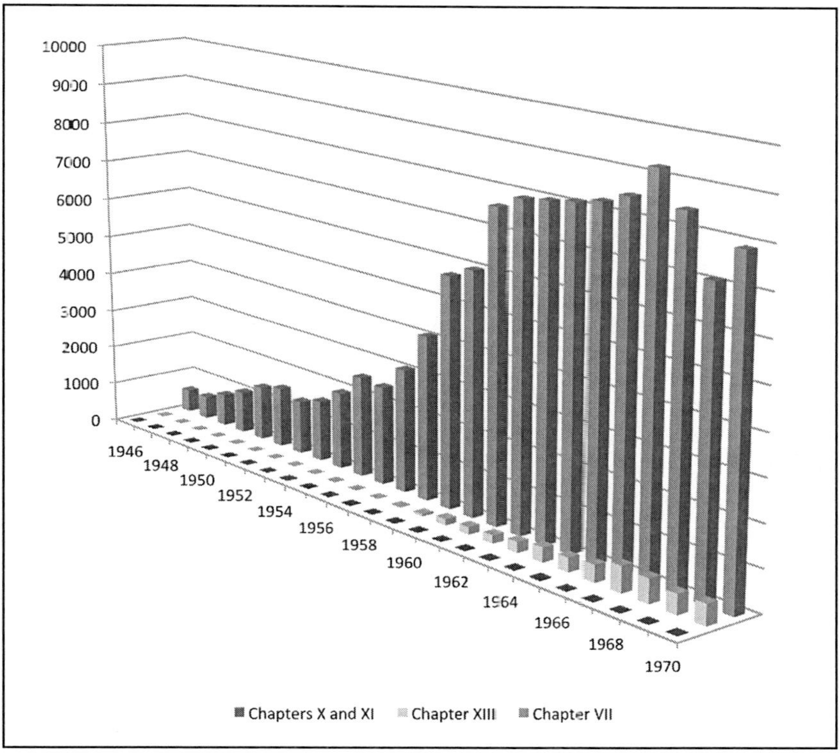

of a total of 2,518,538 bankruptcies filed between fiscal years ending June 30, 1947, and June 30, 1970, less than one in one thousand. Nationally, 17,712 Chapter XI bankruptcies were filed between fiscal years 1947 and 1970, an average of one in 142 bankruptcies. The number of Chapter XI filings peaked around recessions, and the filing rate never declined to its earlier level after the recessions ended. However, because the number of consumer bankruptcies increased at a faster rate than business bankruptcies, the ratio of Chapter XI bankruptcies to total bankruptcies declined steadily. Between fiscal years 1948 and 1950, one in forty-five bankruptcies was filed under Chapter XI. By fiscal year 1955, less than one in one hundred bankruptcies was filed under Chapter XI.

Figure 5.3. US Business Bankruptcy Filings by Chapter, 1946–1970

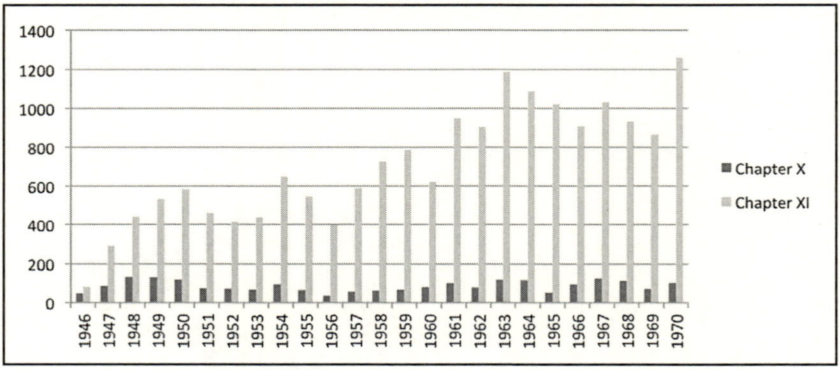

Between fiscal years 1966 and 1968, one in 212 bankruptcies was filed under Chapter XI.

In the Northern District of Ohio, business bankruptcies constituted a much smaller proportion of total bankruptcies than in the nation as a whole. As total bankruptcies increased 1,500 percent, business bankruptcies remained relatively constant. Only twenty-three bankruptcies were filed under Chapter X from the fiscal year ending June 30, 1946, through the fiscal year ending June 30, 1970, approximately one each year. Ten Chapter X bankruptcies were filed between fiscal years 1947 and 1949, but fiscal year 1955 was the only other year in which more than one Chapter X bankruptcy was filed in the Northern District of Ohio. (See Figure 5.4.) Between 1947 and 1970, 120,893 total bankruptcies were filed in the district, but fewer than one in five thousand was filed under Chapter X. Between 1947 and 1970, 272 bankruptcy cases were filed under Chapter XI, fewer than twelve per year and approximately one out of every 444 bankruptcies. A peak occurred between 1962 and 1965, when the number of Chapter XI bankruptcies filed in the Northern District of Ohio jumped from an average of twelve per year over the preceding five years to nineteen in 1962, nineteen in 1963, eighteen in 1964, and twenty-eight in 1965 before returning to twelve Chapter XI filings per year.

Figure 5.4. Northern District of Ohio Business Bankruptcy Filings by Chapter, 1946–1970

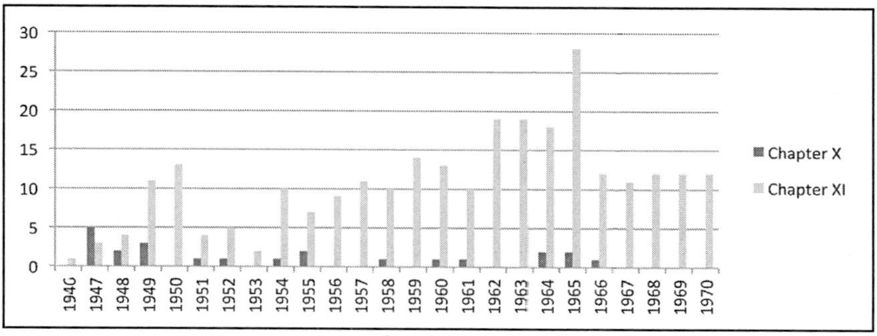

The increasing number of bankruptcy filings made it difficult for Friebolin and Woods to cover the caseload in Cleveland and the vacant Youngstown office. Friebolin and the Bankruptcy Division's chief, Edwin L. Covey, were old friends, and Friebolin wrote unofficially to Covey pleading for official intervention. Friebolin hoped that the Administrative Office had authority to press the district court judges to make an appointment, but Covey refused to get involved in the dispute; the Salary Act clearly provided that only the district court judges could make the appointment. Friebolin forwarded to Covey the suggestion of one of the three Democratic district court judges, that the matter be resolved by creating two part-time referee positions, but Covey replied that only the Judicial Conference could change the number of referees allocated to a district, the territory a referee served, or the location of referee offices. The Judicial Conference had authorized the Bankruptcy Division to resurvey a district, but the district court judges had to request the resurvey. Covey sympathized:

> It seems to me that the situation is comparable to the existence of a vacancy in a Federal Judgeship in a district where a full complement of judges is needed. We simply have to carry on as best we can until the vacancy is filled in the prescribed manner. We have been hoping that the problem in your district would work itself out in some way.[13]

Judge Wilkin assumed senior status in August 1949, and President Harry Truman nominated Charles Joseph McNamee to his seat in February 1951. Even though the partisan balance on the Northern District of Ohio had not changed—it remained one Republican to two Democrats and one Democratic abstention (Toledo)—the logjam was broken. Chief Judge Jones's choice, Ross E. Diser, was appointed referee in Youngstown in September 1951. The chief judge was from Youngstown, and the precedent was established that a judge with roots in a referee's post of duty had preference in the selection of the referee. The court's announcement stated that the appointment was the unanimous decision of the three Cleveland district court judges and that the appointment had become necessary because of the increase in the number of bankruptcy filings in the district.[14] Diser's position became full-time on January 1, 1957.

Bankruptcy filings continued to increase, and in 1958, the Sixth Circuit approved the establishment of an additional referee in bankruptcy in Akron, Ohio. The partisan political composition of the district court in the Eastern Division of the Northern District of Ohio had shifted in favor of Republicans in 1956 with President Dwight Eisenhower's appointment of Paul Weick to the bench, and on April 29, 1958, Chief Judge Jones, at Judge Weick's request, appointed Harold F. White referee in Akron. Before his appointment to the bench, Judge Weick practiced law for thirty years in Akron, where White was a loyal Republican worker.

Harold F. White was born in modest circumstances in Connecticut but entered Ohio University in 1939 because a friend said he would get a good education and have fun there, and the tuition was significantly less expensive than tuition at the University of Connecticut. White's education was interrupted by World War II—he enlisted as an infantry paratrooper but was reassigned to the coastal artillery because he had studied mathematics in college. White served in Europe under General George S. Patton and received three battle stars and the Purple Heart. White married a college classmate during the war, and both returned to Ohio University after the war. White worked for Goodyear in Akron while attending the University of Akron law school. After he graduated in 1952, he was appointed an assistant Akron prosecutor. When the Democrats won the 1954 election, White went into private practice in Akron with a law school classmate. In 1956, White worked on Republican John Ballard's campaign for Summit County prosecutor. When Ballard won, White took a position as deputy civil prosecutor in the civil division of the office of the Summit County Prosecutor.[15]

In 1954, White worked for the election of Republican George H. Bender to the United States Senate. Akron attorney Paul Weick was Bender's campaign manager, and Bender claimed credit for Weick's appointment as US district court judge in February 1956, to replace Democratic judge Emerich Freed, who had died on December 4, 1955. Previously, Congress had created a fourth district court judge position in Cleveland that President Eisenhower filled with James C. Connell, a Republican judge from the Cuyahoga County Common Pleas, in June 1954. Weick's appointment created a three-to-one Republican majority among the judges of the Eastern Division of the Northern District of Ohio. In the early spring of 1958, Judge Weick called White and asked if he would be interested in an appointment as referee in bankruptcy in Akron. White interviewed with Chief Judge Jones and received the appointment on April 29, 1958.

White received no guidance from the Bankruptcy Division of the Administrative Office in organizing his staff or setting up his office. He rented space in the Evan Savings Building at the corner of Exchange and Main Streets in downtown Akron consisting of a clerk's office with separate entrance, referee's chambers, and a courtroom with benches sent down from Cleveland. White had never practiced bankruptcy law and received no training from the Administrative Office, so he talked to Woods and Friebolin and obtained an outline of Friebolin's postgraduate course on bankruptcy.

Before White's appointment, Referee Woods came down to Akron from Cleveland once or twice a month and heard bankruptcy cases in the courtroom of the Summit County Court of Appeals. White described bankruptcy practice in Akron as "chaotic" under Woods.[16] The same small group of attorneys served as trustees and attorneys for trustees, and they sometimes became confused about which role they were playing in a particular case. White covered Canton and Bucyrus as well as Akron, and shortly after White's appointment, Referee Diser in Youngstown died of a sudden heart attack. White then covered Youngstown also, for a total of twenty-two counties.

On January 15, 1959, Chief Judge Jones appointed Harold B. Doyle referee in bankruptcy in Youngstown. A Republican, Judge Doyle had just lost his run for reelection to the Mahoning County Court of Common Pleas to future district court judge Frank J. Battisti. Doyle was seventy-one years old at the time of his appointment but had superb qualifications for the job. Doyle had been in private practice in Youngstown from 1922 to 1946 and had often served as bankruptcy trustee while in private practice. He was president of the Commercial Law League of America from 1935 to 1941. Doyle was first elected judge of the court of common pleas in 1946, and he had served as president of the Ohio State Common Pleas Court Judges Association. A leading citizen of Youngstown, Doyle had been president of the Mahoning County Bar Association. Diser's appointment had been contentious, and his office space in the Youngstown Post Office Building was inadequate and inconveniently located. Referee Doyle got bigger, more conveniently located, newly refurbished offices.[17]

Harold B. Doyle served only one term as bankruptcy referee in Youngstown. In 1961, President John Kennedy appointed Frank Battisti district court judge in Cleveland, and in January 1965, Judge Battisti appointed his old friend and political associate, Joseph T. Molitoris, bankruptcy referee in Youngstown. A Democrat, Molitoris had previously served as Newton Falls, Ohio, solicitor and Trumbull County prosecutor. Molitoris would serve as referee in Youngstown until 1983.

Bankruptcy cases continued to increase dramatically, and in 1961, the Sixth Circuit created two new referee positions in the Eastern Division of the Northern District of Ohio. On April 26, 1961, assistant US attorney William J. O'Neill joined aging Carl Friebolin and William Woods as referee in bankruptcy in Cleveland. A resident of Cleveland since early childhood, O'Neill served in the South Pacific during World War II and attended Harvard on the GI Bill after the war. He graduated in 1947. O'Neill returned to Cleveland and worked for Frank C. Sullivan, founder of Republic Powdered Metals (now RPM, Inc.) while attending Cleveland Marshall College of Law. He graduated from law school in 1952 and established a law practice in the Engineer's Building where he shared office space with legendary lawyer and Republican powerbroker George McMonagle. President and secretary of the Irish Civic Association, George McMonagle was a close associate of district court judge James C. Connell. Republican governor James A. Rhodes appointed McMonagle to the Cuyahoga County Common Pleas Court in 1964.

Republican O'Neill ran unsuccessfully for the Cleveland City Council in 1953 and 1955 and for Cuyahoga County Treasurer in 1956. O'Neill was appointed assistant US attorney on December 31, 1957, and served until appointed referee in bankruptcy by Judge Connell in April 1961, the beginning of President Kennedy's administration. At that time, the post of assistant US attorney was a political patronage appointment, and assistant US attorneys were expected to offer their resignations when administrations changed. The highly respected O'Neill was active in the National Association of Referees in Bankruptcy, and he assumed the office of president of the association at its annual meeting in September 1970, in Toronto, Canada. The Administrative Office designated O'Neill executive referee for the district after Friebolin's death in 1967. O'Neill was an advocate for reform in bankruptcy law and practice throughout his career but knew nothing about bankruptcy law when appointed referee, so he promptly enrolled in Friebolin's night classes on bankruptcy.

The other new referee position was located in Canton, Ohio, and district court judge Girard E. Kalbfleisch appointed Canton's US commissioner, James H. Emsley, to that position in May 1961. In September 1959, President Eisenhower advanced Judge Weick to the Sixth Circuit Court of Appeals and appointed Girard E. Kalbfleisch to fill Weick's seat on the Cleveland bench. Kalbfleisch was a Richland County Common Pleas Court judge at the time of his appointment to the district court.

Kalbfleisch owed his appointment to powerful Canton congressman Frank T. Bow, who also advocated for Emsley's appointment as referee in bankruptcy. Bow and Judge Kalbfleisch had been fraternity brothers at Ohio Northern University.

Born in 1902, Emsley had been a Stark County Republican activist for many years. In 1950, he managed Congressman Bow's first campaign for Ohio's sixteenth congressional district and continued as Bow's administrative assistant after his election. In 1959, Emsley managed the Republican Party's election campaign for the city of Canton and was rewarded with an appointment as US commissioner for that city.[18] With no background in bankruptcy, Emsley learned of Friebolin's bankruptcy course and asked Friebolin for a copy of his lecture notes.[19] Emsley suffered a heart attack while attending the 1971 annual meeting of the National Association of Referees in Bankruptcy in Seattle, Washington. Emsley's brother referee, William J. O'Neill, presided at the meeting as outgoing president of the association. Emsley never recovered from his heart attack and died on February 16, 1972.

Four judges sat on the district court in Cleveland in the spring of 1961 when O'Neill and Emsley were appointed referees: Republicans Paul Jones, James C. Connell, and Girard E. Kalbfleisch and Democrat Charles McNamee. By 1965, however, the partisan balance among the Cleveland district court bench had shifted back in favor of the Democrats, three to two. In September 1961, Judge Battisti was appointed to one of two newly created seats on the district court in Cleveland. Ben C. Green, a Cuyahoga County Democratic Party official and close associate of Cuyahoga County Democratic Party chairman Ray C. Miller, received the other appointment; it was a recess appointment in September 1961, followed by Senate confirmation in June 1962. Democratic judge Charles McNamee died in May 1964, and his seat was not filled. Republican Judge Paul J. Jones died in August 1965; his seat was filled by Democrat William K. Thomas in January 1966. Thomas was a highly respected Cuyahoga County Common Pleas Court judge at the time of his appointment.

The Debtors: Chapter XIII Wage-Earner Plans

The steady increase in the number of consumer bankruptcies in the 1950s and 1960s inspired many articles in newspapers and popular magazines about the moral decay of American society. The authors of those articles argued that the weight of bankruptcies brought about by irresponsible consumption would have dire consequences for the economy and society. Similar concerns had been voiced in the 1920s and had prompted the establishment of Chapter XIII arrangements for wage earners under the Chandler Act.

A voluntary alternative to Chapter VII liquidations, Chapter XIII allowed wage earners to extend their obligations, or compromise them, within the protection of the bankruptcy court. Advocates for consumer creditors argued that Chapter XIII arrangements benefited both creditors and debtors: creditors received payments on debts that would otherwise have been discharged in bankruptcy, and debtors benefited from the moral satisfaction of having met their just obligations. In general, debtors did not perceive Chapter XIII to be beneficial. Debtors sometimes preferred Chapter XIII arrangements over Chapter VII liquidations in the hope of retaining secured assets, especially a mortgaged personal residence, but on the whole, debtors overwhelmingly preferred Chapter VII liquidation over Chapter XIII arrangements. (See Figure 5.5.) Usually, a Chapter XIII arrangement merely increased a debtor's expense and aggravation before failing and converting to Chapter VII liquidation.

The use of Chapter XIII plans varied widely from district to district. The Northern District of Alabama pioneered Chapter XIII arrangements in the 1920s and accounted for almost half of the total number of Chapter XIII cases in the country in 1958. Other jurisdictions with a high proportion of Chapter XIII arrangements tended to be poor and southern: the Southern District of Alabama, the Eastern District of Arkansas, the Western District of Tennessee, and the Southern and the Middle Districts of Georgia. In contrast, the Northern District of Ohio had almost no Chapter XIII cases before 1958 and consistently handled a smaller proportion of Chapter XIII cases than the nation as a whole.[20] (See Figure 5.6.)

Figure 5.5. US Consumer Bankruptcy Filings by Chapter, 1946–1970

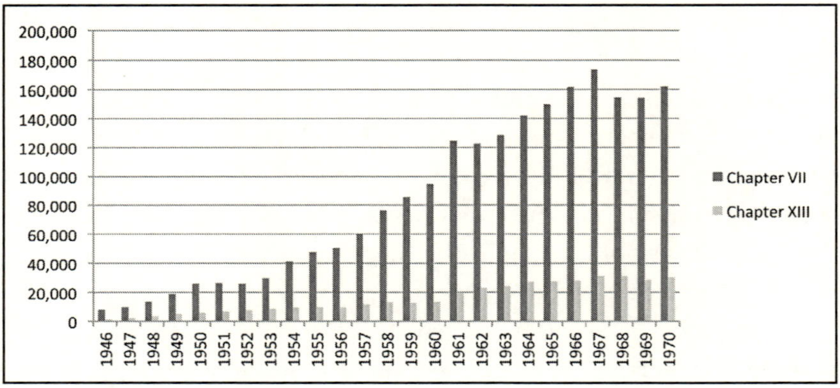

Figure 5.6. Northern District of Ohio Consumer Bankruptcy Filings by Chapter, 1946–1970

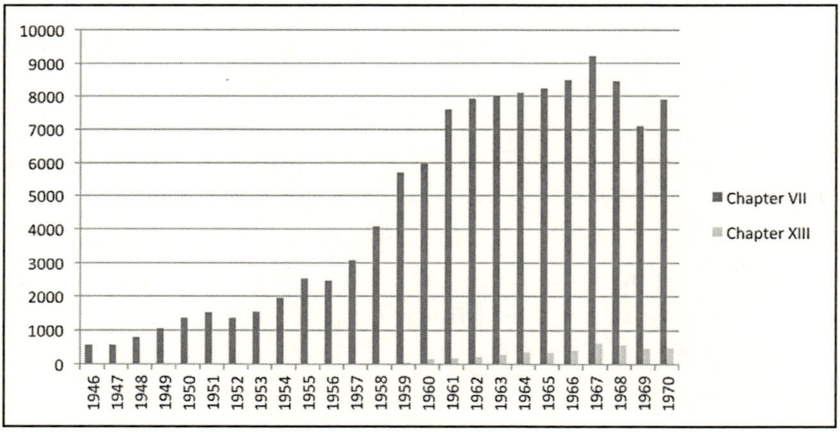

The Bankruptcy Division of the Administrative Office began encouraging greater use of Chapter XIII wage-earner plans beginning around 1956. The Administrative Office began with soft promotion, planting articles in law reviews and commercial journals, with the expectation that more debtors would use the chapter if more bankruptcy attorneys were comfortable with it. In 1958, Bankruptcy Division chief Edwin Covey addressed the annual meeting of the National Association of Credit Management in Detroit on the virtues of Chapter XIII. The association published the speech and widely distributed reprints. Covey also spoke at the annual meeting of the National Retail Association, which published his speech in its journal. Articles on Chapter XIII appeared in the *Los Angeles Times*, *Birmingham News*, *Women's Wear Daily*, and the *Wall Street Journal*. Referee George R. Kennedy of Peoria, Illinois, wrote an article on Chapter XIII for the June 1958 edition of the *Illinois Bar Journal*. The Bankruptcy Division sent a memorandum to all referees in April 1958, soliciting their attitudes toward expanded use of Chapter XIII. Friebolin responded with a detailed analysis of the chapter that exposed numerous problems, unanswered questions, and inconsistencies. A skeptic, he advocated for an immediate, in-depth study by an objective organization if extensive use were to be made of Chapter XIII.[21]

In March 1959, the Administrative Office sought more coercive measures. The Bankruptcy Division requested permission from the Judicial Conference to ask district court judges to direct referees to inquire at the first meetings of creditors whether a Chapter XIII arrangement was appropriate and to encourage the debtor and his attorney to consider one. Many bankruptcy scholars and professionals, including Friebolin, strongly opposed the suggestion that the courts should attempt to influence a debtor's decision whether to file under Chapter VII or Chapter XIII. The National Bankruptcy Conference formed a Chapter XIII Committee, with Friebolin as a member, to study the operation of the chapter and recommend improvements. In June 1962, on the recommendation of the Bankruptcy Committee of the Judicial Council of the United States, the Administrative Office gave all referees a primer on Chapter XIII excerpted from the April 1962 edition of *The Business Lawyer*.[22]

The number of Chapter XIII cases in the Northern District of Ohio increased dramatically after 1958 but remained an insignificant proportion of total consumer bankruptcy filings. (See Figures 5.6 and 5.7.) Before 1958, the district averaged one Chapter XIII case per year. Fifteen Chapter XIII cases were filed in 1958 out of a total of 4,098 voluntary bankruptcies,

Figure 5.7. Chapter XIII Cases Filed in the Northern District of Ohio, 1958–1970

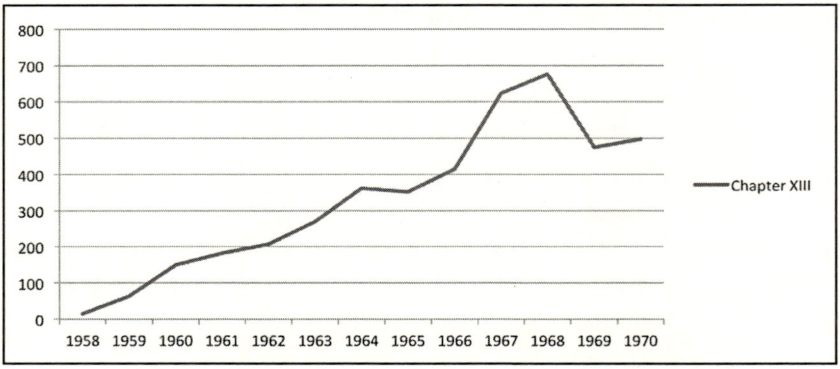

150 Chapter XIII cases were filed in 1960 out of a total of 6,148 voluntary bankruptcies, 270 Chapter XIII cases were filed in 1963 out of a total of 8,281 voluntary bankruptcies, and 676 Chapter XIII cases were filed in 1968 out of a total of 9,032 voluntary bankruptcies. Initially, almost all of the Chapter XIII cases were filed by one attorney in Toledo. By 1960, approximately two hundred Chapter XIII cases had been filed in Toledo, but only two of the cases were successfully completed. The rest of the cases were filed for the purpose of staying collection action in the local courts. A few Chapter XIII cases were filed in Akron, Ohio, between 1958 and 1960, and Referee Harold White supported their use in "appropriate cases."[23]

In Cleveland, Friebolin remained inexorably hostile to Chapter XIII arrangements. Referee William O'Neill, however, who was appointed referee in April 1961, encouraged debtors to consider them. In June 1961, *Readers' Digest* published an article on Chapter XIII that generated a lot of popular interest. In response to the article ordinary people swamped the Bankruptcy Division of the Administrative Office with requests for information, and eleven debtors filed the first Chapter XIII cases in Cleveland. The Cleveland cases were assigned to O'Neill, and he became proficient in Chapter XIII arrangements. O'Neill led the seminar on Chapter XIII litigation at the March 1966 Regional Seminar for Referees in Bankruptcy held in Cleveland. O'Neill presided over all Chapter XIII cases filed in Cleveland until the appointment of Referee Joseph ("Jerry") Patchan in 1969. Before his appointment as referee, Patchan served as the Chapter XIII standing trustee for Cleveland.[24]

By 1964, small loan companies had spearheaded a movement to authorize referees to convert a voluntary Chapter VII liquidation to a Chapter XIII arrangement without the debtor's agreement. The Chapter XIII Committee of the National Bankruptcy Conference opposed the idea. Some committee members, especially Friebolin and Referee Asa Herzog from the Southern District of New York, opposed it strongly, thinking it unjust to treat wage earners more harshly than other debtors. They believed that if businessmen could choose to discharge their debts, fairness required that wage earners should be able to do so also. A minority in the National Bankruptcy Conference supported wider use of Chapter XIII arrangements, coercively if necessary, because the rapid and unprecedented increase in consumer bankruptcies seemed to foreshadow serious economic and social consequences.[25] The Brookings Institution study found little corroboration of the corrosive effects of consumer bankruptcy. High rates of bankruptcy had no substantial negative effects on the economy. Creditors simply factored in the risk of loss as a cost of doing business. Debtors had no difficulty securing new consumer credit after bankruptcy.[26]

Friebolin and Herzog based their objection to coerced Chapter XIII cases on their observation that the districts that had large proportions of Chapter XIII cases tended to be very low income areas. They believed that Chapter XIII plans in those districts were forced on powerless people and that Chapter XIII in those circumstances did not rehabilitate debtors so much as cause unnecessary suffering. Friebolin believed most consumer bankruptcies resulted from the combination of easy credit and a cornucopia of irresistible goods. Working people with limited savings and unlimited desires could acquire the material means to a more comfortable life on credit but could not continue to make scheduled payments if anything went wrong in their lives—sickness, job loss, divorce, or any kind of unanticipated expense.[27] The moralists' claims that there was "nothing so cheap, so simple and morally revitalizing" as Chapter XIII made Friebolin suspect that "there may be reason for criticizing it as 'wage serfdom' and 'modern peonage.'" [28]

The Bar: Bankruptcy Practitioners and Bankruptcy Practice in Cleveland

Initially, elite lawyers dominated the organized bankruptcy bar in the Northern District of Ohio. The Cleveland Bar Association formed a bankruptcy committee in the 1920s to support the reform movement that began in opposition to perceived "bankruptcy rings" in the Southern District of New York and other large metropolitan areas and culminated in the Chandler Act of 1938. The bankruptcy committee included Cleveland Bar Association leader James C. Logue; corporate lawyers Frank G. Carpenter, J. Frank Pease (a Thompson, Hine & Flory partner), and Lawrence Caleb Spieth (who had joined the venerable Cleveland law firm of Spieth, Bell, McCurdy & Newell in 1919); and veteran bankruptcy lawyers Sidney N. Weitz and Charles I. Russo.

Russo enjoyed credibility with corporate lawyers and bankruptcy lawyers. Although he also served as trustee and receiver in ordinary bankruptcies, Russo became Cleveland's first high-profile big-case bankruptcy lawyer. Born in Italy, Charles I. Russo came to Cleveland as an infant. He received his law degree from Baldwin Wallace and was admitted to the bar in 1917. Russo served as assistant US attorney from 1929 to 1934 and as special counsel for the Ohio attorney general from 1945 to 1948. The United States District Court in Cleveland appointed Russo special master in many important corporate bankruptcy cases, including the reorganization of the Van Sweringen Corporation and the Cleveland Terminals Building Company. Russo taught bankruptcy law at the Cleveland Law School and served on the executive committee of the Cleveland Bar Association.

The Chandler Act profoundly changed bankruptcy law and practice. In response, the United States Supreme Court issued new general orders governing practice in bankruptcy, including a new General Order 56 specifically authorizing courts of bankruptcy to make and amend local rules governing bankruptcy practice in their courts.[29] The District Court for the Northern District of Ohio undertook a two-year project to revise its local rules under the leadership of Carl Friebolin, and the Cleveland Bar Association's Bankruptcy Committee formed a committee to assist the court. The committee completed the revision of the local rules in the autumn of 1940.

The bankruptcy rules revision committee included experienced bankruptcy lawyers Charles I. Russo and Sidney Weitz. The committee also included corporate lawyers with no particular expertise in bankruptcy, such as Harvard law school graduate John L. Yapple, a litigator for the Cleveland firm of McKeehan, Merrick, Arter and Stewart, a predecessor to the law firm of Arter & Hadden. Fellow committee member Harold H. Kahn would go on to found the Cleveland law firm Kahn, Kleinman, Yanowitz & Arnson and serve as president of the Citizens League of Greater Cleveland and trustee of the Council of Human Relations.

The Cleveland Bar Association continued the Bankruptcy Committee for a few years, but, with the exception of the year 1948, there is no record that the committee actually met from 1943 until 1958. During this period, corporate lawyers lost interest in bankruptcy practice. Instead, regular bankruptcy practitioners Ira Arnold, Charles Russo, O. O. Vrooman, Sidney Weitz, and Hugh Wells, regularly served as officers of the committee. Manager of the Cleveland chapter of the National Association of Credit Management, Hugh Wells had been a leading member of Cleveland's bankruptcy bar for many years. By 1942 he had formed the law firm of Wells and Marks and was elected to the National Bankruptcy Conference. He was vice president and a director of the Cleveland City Club.

The Cleveland Bar Association's Bankruptcy Committee became active again after 1958, but its composition changed. Most of the bankruptcy committee members now came from the small group of small-firm attorneys and solo practitioners that regularly practiced in the Cleveland bankruptcy courts and patronized Friebolin's evening bankruptcy

Friebolin College graduation dinner, 1955, (first row, seated): Harold Glickman, Allan Kleinman, Albert Sanders, Milton Sanders, unknown, Hugh Wells, Frank Mancino; (second row, seated): Henry B. Johnson, Lawrence I. Byrnes, Emory Green, unknown, Carl Friebolin, Theodore Spilka, Al Gilman, unknown, Frank Whalen, Maurice (Bud) Sayer; (third row, standing): Marvin Nebbin (seated), unknown, Maynard B. Melamed, unknown, Paul Mancino, Morris R. Blane, unknown, Leonard B. Scharfeld, Archie M. Marks; (fourth row, standing): Jerome Leiken, unknown, unknown, Howard Sokolsky, Saul Nadler, unknown, Irv Oppenheimer (auctioneer), unknown, Edward Familo, Frank Fetchet, unknown, unknown, Everett McCurdy, Ed Wallach. *Courtesy of the Western Reserve Historical Society*

course. Bankruptcy Committee members usually included Henry B. Johnson, Saul Nadler, Theodore Spilka, and Hugh Wells. Nadler had a reputation as a legal scholar. His brother and former law partner, Charles Elihu Nadler, taught bankruptcy at the Mercer University School of Law in Macon, Georgia, and had authored leading treatises on bankruptcy.[30] The group socialized in court and at bar events and held an annual banquet to commemorate the conclusion of "Friebolin College" that was attended by current students, bankruptcy court regulars, and friends of Friebolin. The evening usually included a satirical musical revue on a bankruptcy theme in the style of the Cleveland City Club's Anvil Revue. Friebolin wrote the script for the Anvil Revue every year between 1914 and 1965, in collaboration with *Cleveland Press* columnist Joe Newman.

FRIEBOLIN COLLEGE
CLASS NIGHT OF 1960
May 26, 1960

PROGRAM

Toast Master. . . . . Theodore R. Spilka

1. Welcome by Dean Spilka.

2. Introductions of Alumni.

3. In Re: DAY AND NIGHT
A Musical ? Extravaganza

Time: April 1, 1961
Place: Bar Association Committee Room

Dramatis Personae

Ben Sapp - Bar Committee Chairman

Peter Reed)
Walter Stewart) - Committee Members
John Pyke)

Ted Spilka)
Jerry Leiken) - Asspirants for
Clyde Dyson) Referee's Job
Hugh Wells)

The above characters portrayed by
Harold Glickman, Ken Snyder, Jim Fuller,
Henry Johnson, Bill Welty, Joe Coy, Nelson
Moss.

Music - Nelson Moss
Choreographer - Harold Glickman
Announcer - Bud Sayre

4. Quituation Exercises for 1960
Graduates of Friebolin College.

Diplomas Presented by Joseph Coy
Ad Infinatum

5. Presentations by Dean Spilka.

6. Acceptance by Professor Carl D. Friebolin

7. CLASS SONG:

In the Old Bankruptcy Court,
In the Old Bankruptcy Court
We're glad that you're the Referee
In the Old Bankruptcy Court,
You're a scholar and a gentleman
As well as an awful good sport
And we're glad that you're the Referee
In the Old Bankruptcy Court.

(Tune - In the Good Old Summer Time)

Friebolin College graduation program, 1960. *Courtesy of the Western Reserve Historical Society*

Bankruptcy practice was informal. Lawyers did not call referees "judge" unless, like Friebolin, they had earned the honorific in some other court. Friebolin had been appointed to the Cuyahoga County Common Pleas Court bench before becoming a referee in bankruptcy and could properly claim the title "judge" on that basis. Nationally, referees acquired the title "bankruptcy judge" with the promulgation of the Federal Rules of Bankruptcy Procedure in 1973, but referees had agitated for the title "judge" long before that. The *Cleveland Plain Dealer* had been calling referees "judge" since at least 1969. Draft bankruptcy rules using the title "bankruptcy judge" circulated in September 1971, and on April 19, 1972, Chief Judge Frank Battisti issued an order that referees in bankruptcy were to be designated "bankruptcy judges."[31]

Referees did not wear judicial robes. In part, this fact reflected referees' status as lesser judicial officers, but, in general, Americans adopted the practice of wearing judicial robes very slowly. Revolutionary America

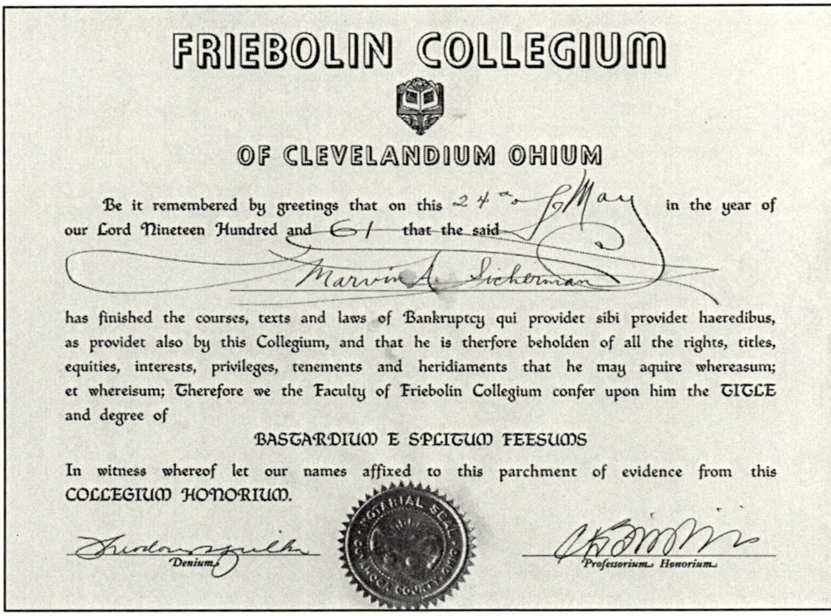

FRIEBOLIN COLLEGIUM

OF CLEVELANDIUM OHIUM

Be it remembered by greetings that on this 24th of May in the year of our Lord Nineteen Hundred and 61 that the said

Marvin A. Sicherman

has finished the courses, texts and laws of Bankruptcy qui providet sibi providet haeredibus, as providet also by this Collegium, and that he is therfore beholden of all the rights, titles, equities, interests, privileges, tenements and heridiaments that he may aquire whereasum; et whereisum; Therefore we the Faculty of Friebolin Collegium confer upon him the TITLE and degree of

BASTARDIUM E SPLITUM FEESUMS

In witness whereof let our names affixed to this parchment of evidence from this COLLEGIUM HONORIUM.

Denium

Professorium Honorium

Friebolin College diploma issued to Marvin A. Sicherman in 1961. *Courtesy of Marvin A. Sicherman*

disapproved of judicial robes as symbols of the aristocratic system they had so recently overthrown, and few judges wore robes in America throughout the nineteenth century. As recently as 1956, judges of the highest appellate courts of Arkansas, Missouri, North Dakota, Texas, and Wyoming wore no judicial robes, and US district court judges in at least three jurisdictions also wore no robes. Judges did not wear robes in all of Ohio's trial courts.[32] Cuyahoga County Common Pleas Court judges began wearing judicial robes in January 1941 after the Cleveland Bar Association waged a campaign for judicial robes to "enhance the dignity of the court."[33] The Bankruptcy Division of the Administrative Office encouraged referees to wear robes where they had access to suitable courtrooms, and referees began wearing robes in New Jersey in 1954. By 1966, referees in eighteen judicial districts, including the Northern and Southern Districts of Ohio, wore judicial robes while holding court.[34]

In 1957, Friebolin and Woods moved their chambers and hearing rooms to the fourth floor of the Federal Courthouse. The hearing rooms contained a large desk centrally located at one end of the room for the referee, two tables for lawyers, and rows of benches for all other participants and observers. Ashtrays stood on the lawyers' tables, and Friebolin's hearing room contained a spittoon. Lawyers put their feet on the desks and smoked freely until the referee entered the room. The Cleveland referees staggered docket calls for the lawyers' convenience. Friebolin held court at 10:00 A.M. and Woods held court at 2:00 P.M. When O'Neill joined Woods and Friebolin as bankruptcy referee in Cleveland, docket calls occurred exactly one hour apart beginning at 9:30 A.M.[35]

A small core of lawyers handled the vast majority of the bankruptcy business, and they all knew each other. All of the regulars were men, most of them were Jewish, and they always sat at the same seats at the lawyers' tables at the docket call. If a different lawyer tried to sit in one of the regular lawyers' seats, he would be told to move. The lawyers with reserved seats before 1960 included Morris R. Blane and one or two of Blane's associates, Lawrence I. Byrnes, Marvin L. Gardner, Albert A. Gilman, Nelson Moss, Theodore Spilka, and Maurice Weltman. Before 1960, Blane's associates Jerome (Jerry) Leiken and Myron Wasserman usually sat with Blane at the table. When Leiken left Blane's office around 1960, Saul Eisen took Leiken's place. Marvin L. Gardner died in May 1960, and Marvin Sicherman joined the table. By 1965, Morris Blane was indicted and convicted of bankruptcy fraud, so he and his associates left the lawyers' table, and Ronald Rubenstein moved in. If there were no seats at the lawyers' table, an attorney sat in the benches behind the bar. The lawyers freely joked with each other and with Friebolin during the proceedings. No court reporter transcribed proceedings at the docket call unless a party hired the reporter, and that almost never happened.

Almost all of the cases heard at the daily docket call were consumer Chapter VII liquidations. No consumer debtors could be compelled to file a Chapter XIII wage-earner arrangement instead of a "straight" bankruptcy, and few elected to do so. The debtor's lawyer filed Chapter XI arrangements with the district court clerk and took the file directly to the referee's chambers after a reference was entered by the intake clerk. The referee entered orders in chambers continuing a debtor in possession and authorizing the debtor to continue operating the business. Cleveland practice appointed different attorneys for the debtor and the debtor in possession.[36] If the referee thought a hearing was necessary in a Chapter XI case, he would set a special hearing. Chapter X corporate reorganizations were very rare in the Northern District of Ohio, and referees had very limited involvement with them.

The first half of the docket call disposed of motions. Bankruptcy practice under the 1898 Bankruptcy Act disposed of contested matters by motion. Adversary proceedings were first introduced with the Federal Rules of Bankruptcy Procedure in 1973. The motion record consisted of the written motion joined with an Order to Show Cause why the motion should not be granted, occasionally a written response, the referee's notations in the journal as to the disposition of the motion, and an order prepared for the referee's signature by the prevailing party. Lawyers made arguments informally, sometimes in ex parte communications to the referee before the docket call. The opportunity for argument in court was severely time limited. In exceptional cases a motion would be scheduled for a separate hearing.

The second half of the docket call consisted of the first meetings of creditors. Creditors filed claims and elected a trustee at the first meeting. Creditors almost never attended first meetings unless they held a secured debt and wanted to question the debtor about the location or condition of the security. However, creditors might attend through one of the attorneys in the same small group who regularly appeared in bankruptcy court. Those attorneys met before the docket call to decide who would be elected trustee in a particular case by comparing the amount and number of creditor claims each held. Sometimes deals were made so that one attorney would be trustee and another would be attorney for the trustee. If two attorneys held the same number of claims, they might agree to take turns as trustee: one attorney would be trustee in this case and the other would be trustee the next time they tied. The attorneys elected themselves trustees in this fashion in approximately half of the cases. If the creditors failed to elect a trustee, the referee would appoint a trustee. In Friebolin's courtroom, that meant his long-time secretary and chief clerk, Elizabeth Morrison, selected a trustee from a panel of approved trustees.

Most of the regular bankruptcy attorneys had connections with a creditor group that furnished them with a steady source of bankruptcy claims. For example, the law firm of Hugh Wells, Archie Marks, and Frank C. Whalen received claims from the National Association of Credit Management. The law firm of Henry B. Johnson, Claire E. Whitmer, and Maurice (Bud) Sayres had connections to the furniture industry. Saul Nadler, Marvin Neben, and Howard L. Sokolsky had a connection with the automotive credit business and a large commercial collection practice. Marvin Sicherman received claims from the Cleveland Produce Credit Association; his father had been in the produce business for many years and was still an active produce merchant. Morris Blane received claims from the Credit Security Co., Theodore Spilka received claims from the Ohio Board of Credits, and both Blane and Spilka received claims from local banks. Local court rules prohibited an attorney from soliciting claims to vote at the first meeting of creditors unless the attorney was a creditor or represented a creditor in the bankruptcy.[37] The rule was intended to limit the opportunities for attorneys to solicit claims, the kind of conduct that had produced the scandals in the Southern District of New York in the 1920s, but the rule had the unintended effect of concentrating bankruptcy practice in the hands of attorneys with ready access to claims.

After the trustee's election, the trustee would take the debtor to a corner of the courtroom or to an adjoining room for the examination of the debtor. The debtor could be examined by the referee, the trustee, or the creditors, though up to ten debtors might be scheduled for a single docket call. On average, approximately twenty-five debtors appeared weekly before each referee at the daily docket calls. The referee swore in the debtors and remained available to the examining trustee if the need arose. Examination of a debtor in a no-asset case might take twenty minutes; the examination of a debtor in an asset case might take two to three hours.[38]

Referees enjoyed great autonomy in their courtrooms, and their practices varied widely. For example, Referee William O'Neill learned shorthand in high school and kept accurate transcripts of the proceedings before him. He came to bankruptcy from a practice in federal district court and was appalled at the lack of decorum in bankruptcy court. O'Neill demanded greater formality and respect in his courtroom, and he incurred the wrath of the bankruptcy bar when he prohibited smoking. O'Neill became active in the National Association of Referees in Bankruptcy and worked diligently to improve the status and professionalism of the bankruptcy courts.

Outside of Cleveland, the smaller number of debtors allowed for more personalized attention from referees. Referee Harold White in Akron made a point of dispersing trustee appointments throughout the local bar. In Toledo, creditors rarely elected trustees. Instead, the referee usually appointed the trustee from a panel of approved trustees in the order in which they appeared on the list.[39] The practice of appointing trustees off a list did not insulate a referee from criticism, however. In 1964, the National Association of Credit Management complained to the Administrative Office of the United States Courts that Toledo referees interfered with the creditors' right to select the trustee.[40]

Reformers called the domination of the bankruptcy business by a small group of lawyers a "bankruptcy ring." The Administrative Office became concerned about potential violations of the 1934 Anti-Monopoly Act, and in April 1959, the Bankruptcy Division of the Administrative Office asked referees to audit court files for the current and two preceding fiscal years to determine whether any attorney received more than 20 percent of appointments as trustee or attorney for trustee, or more than 20 percent of fees paid. The audits revealed few referees who favored particular attorneys in enough instances to appear in possible violation of the antimonopoly rule. Nonetheless, in October 1959 the Judicial Conference announced a policy that referees should adopt procedures designed to disperse the appointments more broadly throughout the bar to ensure no violation of the antimonopoly rule, and the Bankruptcy Division ordered referees to audit appointments and payments to receivers and trustees. An analysis of the statistical reports undertaken at the same time found numerous errors in the computation of commissions and fees due attorneys and trustees and in the charges for the referees' salary and expense fund. The Judicial Conference's new policy made referees personally liable for errors in the accounts of receivers and trustees.[41]

Many referees, including Friebolin, were outraged. They thought the Judicial Conference's interference in trustee appointments was unwarranted and unwise. They argued that the 1934 statute establishing the antimonopoly rule had been superseded by the Chandler Act of 1938 and interfered with the creditors' right to appoint trustees. More fundamentally, they thought that only a small number of lawyers competed for bankruptcy appointments because the work was highly technical and poorly paid. Trustees received only five dollars per case plus a statutory maximum percent of any assets the trustee collected and paid to creditors. The trustee's fee increased to ten dollars per case in 1960.[42] Bankruptcy administration under the Bankruptcy Act functioned on the "principle of economy," and the district court approved attorney's fees in bankruptcy at significantly lower rates than prevailed in other actions or in other fields of law. Friebolin believed that, despite their meager compensation, the lawyers who regularly appeared in bankruptcy court performed competently and efficiently because of their specialization. Besides, other lawyers had no interest in competing for bankruptcy appointments. Corporate firms might represent creditors or otherwise have bankruptcy business, but big-firm lawyers generally did not appear in bankruptcy court. Instead, they usually referred their cases to one of the bankruptcy court regulars.[43]

Cleveland's bankruptcy court maintained one official monopoly. In 1938, Friebolin and Woods made Rosen & Co. the official auctioneer by Referee's Rule. The auctioneer's fee was set by district court rule. Previously, numerous auctioneers competed for work, pestering trustees and offering inappropriate incentives for appointment. Friebolin even caught an auctioneer cheating on a sale. Friebolin chose Gus Rosen to be official auctioneer as a preventive measure against corruption. Despite criticism from congressmen, competing auctioneers, and the Bankruptcy Division of the Administrative Office, Friebolin managed to keep Gus Rosen as the Cleveland bankruptcy court's official auctioneer until at least 1965.[44]

One name stood out in Friebolin's audit of prior years' appointments and payments to trustees and attorneys: Cleveland attorney Morris Blane. In 1957, no attorney received more than 20 percent of the appointments as trustee, and only Theodore Spilka, the self-proclaimed "dean of Friebolin College," received more than 20 percent of the appointments as attorney for trustee. In 1958, Morris Blane received more than 20 percent of the appointments as trustee in Cleveland, but no attorney received more than 20 percent of the appointments as trustee in the Northern District of Ohio, and no attorney received more than 20 percent of the appointments as attorney for trustee. In 1959, Morris Blane again received more than 20 percent of the appointments as trustee, and Theodore Spilka received more than 20 percent of the appointments as attorney for trustee. Regarding payments, in 1957, J. Perry Teeple from Akron, Ohio, received more than 20 percent of fees paid to attorneys of trustees. In 1958, Morris Blane and David R. Hyman from Elyria each received more than 20 percent of fees paid to attorneys of trustees.[45]

In 1962, the district court convened a grand jury investigation into Cleveland's bankruptcy ring, and Morris Blane got caught in its crosshairs. Blane had a long history of representing shady characters, including notorious Cleveland gangster Alex (Shondor) Birns. In August 1961, another one of Blane's clients, Harold I. Slote, filed bankruptcy on behalf of his company, Sterling Jewelry and Appliance Company. Analysis of the records revealed $60,000 of missing inventory. The case was referred to Referee William O'Neill, who referred the case to the US attorney for criminal investigation. Slote was indicted and pled guilty to concealing assets of the estate in bankruptcy. As part of his plea deal, Slote testified against Blane before the grand jury, and Blane was indicted. In February

1965, a jury convicted Blane of concealing $3,000 of jewelry from the Sterling Jewelry bankruptcy estate. He was sentenced to imprisonment for six years.[46]

Blane had the ill fortune to be tried and sentenced by district court judge Girard E. Kalbfleisch. New to the bench, Kalbfleisch had recent experience with Blane and the Cleveland bankruptcy ring in the administration of the bankruptcy case of the Baird-Foerst Corporation, and he felt no inclination to show mercy to Morris Blane.

The Baird-Foerst Corporation was the Cleveland distributor of General Electric heating and air conditioning equipment, and it filed bankruptcy in 1958 when it was unable to meet cash demands. During the course of the bankruptcy an audit disclosed that the company's financial statements significantly misrepresented the corporation's financial condition. Instead of a $250,000 net worth, the company had liabilities of approximately $400,000 in excess of assets. The discrepancy resulted from a systematic pattern of embezzlement and theft by false invoicing, and the company's president, Willard J. Baird, was eventually tried in state court and convicted of making false financial statements.

The bankruptcy was referred to Referee William B. Woods, who appointed Ralph H. Coleman trustee; Morris Blane and Roland Reichert attorneys for the debtor; and Hugh Wells, Marvin Neben, and Maurice (Bud) Sayre attorneys for the trustee. The attorneys requested significant fees in the case, and Woods allowed all of the fees, praising the attorneys' diligence. Local rules required the referring district court judge to certify the award of attorneys' fees. Instead, Judge Kalbfleisch slashed the fee award by two-thirds, from $53,000 to $17,000. The attorneys appealed the fee award, and Judge Kalbfleisch wrote a blistering memorandum in support of his order reducing attorneys' fees, asserting his belief that the company could have been saved by diligent action on the part of the trustee. Kalbfleisch claimed that the Baird-Foerst bankruptcy illustrated the evils of the Cleveland bankruptcy ring, especially the appointment of unnecessary and redundant attorneys, the padding of accounts, and the solicitation of bankruptcy business.[47]

As a consequence of these embarrassments, in August 1963, the District Court for the Northern District of Ohio amended its local bankruptcy court rules regarding the appointment and payment of attorneys and trustees. New Rule 4 restricted anyone from voting a claim against a bankrupt unless he owned it or had previously filed a written power of attorney with the referee. The rule permitted no solicitation of claims against a bankrupt except by a bona fide creditors' committee after approval by both the referee and the district court judge. The petition for an order approving the solicitation had to disclose the creditors and their claims against the bankrupt; when, where, and at whose instance the committee was organized; and whether any officer of the committee expected compensation, and if so, from whom the officer expected to be paid. The new rule also required all attorneys' fees in excess of $200 authorized by a referee to be submitted to the district court judge for approval. The amount of attorneys' fees that could be paid without district court approval increased to $500 in April 1964 and to $1,000 in 1965.[48]

Friebolin found the new rule unwise and insulting. He thought the new rules denied creditors the right to elect their trustee and denied referees a "general reference." Friebolin talked to two of the district court judges and learned that one had not read the revised rule before signing it, and the other did not understand the import of what he had read. The district court promulgated the rule without consulting the referees or the Bankruptcy Division of the Administrative Office of the United States Courts even though at that time changes in local bankruptcy rules needed to be cleared through the Bankruptcy Division.[49]

The Referees: 1965 to 1978

The Cleveland grand jury investigation into bankruptcy administration claimed one more victim. Judge Kalbfleisch referred the Baird-Foerst bankruptcy for criminal investigation, and the investigation disclosed that Morris Blane paid $600 to a dealer toward an automobile purchased by Referee William B. Woods. Blane had encouraged Woods to patronize a particular dealership, assuring Woods that he would get a good deal on a car. Woods claimed not to know that anyone had paid part of the cost of his car, and no allegations were made that Woods gave Blane preferential treatment. Woods promptly paid the additional $600 to the automobile dealership and resigned as referee. Woods was eighty-four years old and suffered from Parkinson's disease.[50] The district court appointed sixty-nine-year-old Republican Paul J. Gnau as Woods' replacement. Gnau practiced law in Cleveland with the firm of Benesch, Friedlander, Mendelson, Gnau, and Coplan before his appointment. He had no previous experience in bankruptcy.

As early as December 1955, Friebolin had discussed with Bankruptcy Division chief Covey the possibility of establishing a training program for newly appointed referees. Covey concurred with Friebolin that new referees seemed wholly unprepared for their duties, but Covey found that the problem of funding training seminars was insurmountable.[51] Covey continued to agitate for training seminars, and the Administrative Office finally acquiesced. In December 1963, the Administrative Office placed Referee Asa Herzog from the Southern District of New York in charge of developing a referee training seminar. The first program took place in Washington, DC, in March 1964. Approximately forty-six recently appointed referees attended, including Paul Gnau, William O'Neill, and Toledo referee T. Kenneth Mattimoe. The seminars proved a success, and by March 1968, every referee had been afforded the opportunity to attend a training seminar. The training seminars became permanent and expanded into regional refresher seminars for experienced referees. Gnau's successor, Joseph Patchan, became a regular instructor at the seminars.[52]

Carl Friebolin suffered a heart attack in late summer 1965 and subsequently reduced his committee memberships at the National Association of Referees in Bankruptcy and the National Bankruptcy Conference; however, he remained on the Cleveland bankruptcy bench. On October 22, 1965, Don C. Miller was appointed referee in Cleveland. Friebolin was not replaced after his retirement in 1967, and Miller continued in Friebolin's seat.

Between 1961 and 1965, the partisan balance on the district court changed from a three-to-one Republican majority to a three-to-two Democratic majority, and Don Miller was the brother of powerful Cuyahoga County Democratic Party chairman Ray C. Miller. In private practice at the time of his appointment as referee, Don Miller was US attorney for the Northern District of Ohio from 1941 to 1951, and he had served as president of the United States Attorneys' Association, president of the Ohio Federal Bar Association, and member of the Executive Committee of the Cleveland Bar Association. Most famously, however, Miller was one of the "Four Horsemen of Notre Dame," the backfield of the football teams Knute Rockne coached for Notre Dame from 1922 through 1924. Rockne claimed that Miller was the best open-field runner he had ever coached. Miller loved to bring his fellow referees with him to games at Notre Dame, where Miller was treated like a god. Miller was generally considered one of the nicest people in the world, and everyone who knew him loved him. He served two terms as referee, retiring in 1977, and died in June 1979.[53]

Miller received his law degree from Notre Dame in 1925. He coached football at Georgia Tech from 1925 to 1929, practicing law in Cleveland in the off-season. In 1929, Miller returned to Ohio to coach football at Ohio State. He gave up football in 1932 in favor of full-time law practice after his brother, Ray C. Miller, was elected mayor of Cleveland. Personally unassuming, Miller was a better lawyer than many people realized and a competent referee. Miller is credited with adopting the phrase "negative equity" in a 1966 bankruptcy case.[54] Before filing bankruptcy, the debtor purchased an automobile and traded in his old automobile, which had a lien on it in excess of the vehicle's fair market value. The dealer included the negative equity—the balance due on the lien of the car the debtor traded in in excess of the fair market value—in the financing for the new car. Trustee Marvin Sicherman applied for a turnover motion against the car dealer on the grounds that the financing agreement was unenforceable under then applicable Ohio law because the agreement financed an amount in excess of the purchase price of the property. In a brief,

Sicherman coined the phrase "negative equity" to express and emphasize the impropriety of the finance charges. Referee Miller concurred, and the district court affirmed.[55]

Referee Paul Gnau's appointment ended in 1969, and the district court decided not to reappoint him because of his age. Gnau was seventy-three years old and had annoyed both the district court bench and the bankruptcy bar during his term in office.[56] Six district court judges sat in Cleveland in 1969, four Democrats and two Republicans. President Lyndon Johnson replaced Judge Jones with William K. Thomas in 1966. Thomas was then serving as judge of the Cuyahoga County Common Pleas Court. Congress created a new judgeship in 1967. and President Johnson appointed Thomas D. Lambros, who was then serving as judge of the Jefferson County Common Pleas Court in Ashtabula, Ohio.

Nine attorneys applied for the referee position in 1969, and the district court had difficulty deciding whom to appoint. By this time, the judges in Cleveland had reached an agreement to take turns in judicial appointments. It was Judge Thomas's turn to name an appointment, and Thomas, strongly urged by Cuyahoga County Common Pleas judge Bernard Friedman, favored Cleveland bankruptcy lawyer Joseph Patchan. Not only was Patchan the only applicant with significant bankruptcy experience but he was also the standing Chapter XIII trustee in Cleveland and taught bankruptcy law at Cleveland Marshall Law School. Two other judges favored two of the other applicants, and United States senator Frank J. Lausche favored John F. Ray Jr. Judges Connell, Lambros, and Battisti took no position until Lambros changed his vote to support Patchan in exchange for Thomas's agreement to back Lambros's choice for an anticipated appointment for deputy clerk of court. Ray would be appointed bankruptcy judge when Patchan resigned in 1975.[57] In 1973, the Federal Rules of Bankruptcy Procedure changed referees in bankruptcy into bankruptcy judges.

Patchan was born in Brooklyn, New York, but his father moved the family to Cleveland in 1929. Patchan went to school in Cleveland and attended college at Western Reserve University. He also attended Miami

University in Oxford, Ohio, and graduated from Miami in 1943. He served in the Navy from 1943 to 1946 in Europe, Alaska, and the Pacific. Patchan returned to Cleveland after the war and took a job at the May Co., the department store where his father had been employed. Patchan started at the Cleveland Marshall Law School in 1948 and graduated in 1952. By chance, Patchan sat next to future bankruptcy referee William O'Neill at law school, and they became close, lifelong friends. Patchan began practicing law in 1955 and joined Nadler & Nadler, a collection law firm with a large bankruptcy practice and a scholarly reputation. Patchan left Nadler & Nadler in 1965 but continued to specialize in bankruptcy.

Before his appointment as referee in 1969, Patchan served as the first standing Chapter XIII trustee in Cleveland. The position of standing Chapter XIII trustee came about as a result of the Administrative Office's concern about increasing debtor utilization of Chapter XIII arrangements. In 1962, the Bankruptcy Committee of the Judicial Conference appointed a subcommittee to study the administration of Chapter XIII and recommend guidelines. The study revealed a shocking lack of conformity in administration, especially with regard to the compensation allowed to attorneys for debtors and trustees, trustee expenses and administrative costs, and record keeping. The subcommittee issued guidelines for the administration of Chapter XIII cases, which were approved by the Judicial Conference in September 1963. In addition to recommending the implementation of standard practices, the guidelines advised the appointment of a single standing Chapter XIII trustee in each "integral commercial area" to be determined by the district court judges concerned. By 1965, most districts complied with the Chapter XIII guidelines, and that year thirty-four Chapter XIII trustees organized the National Association of Chapter XIII Trustees. In the Northern District of Ohio, standing Chapter XIII trustees were appointed in Akron, Cleveland, and Toledo. A standing Chapter XIII trustee was also appointed in Warren in 1967. Patchan was the first standing Chapter XIII trustee in Cleveland, and he continued in that position until appointed referee in bankruptcy in 1969.[58]

Patchan also played an active role in establishing the Federal Rules of Bankruptcy Procedure. In 1958, Congress authorized the Judicial Conference to establish standing committees for the continuing study and revision of rules of court, including bankruptcy rules. In 1960, Chief Justice Earl Warren appointed the Advisory Committee on Bankruptcy Rules with Frank R. Kennedy as reporter. A leading bankruptcy scholar, Kennedy taught bankruptcy law at the University of Michigan Law School and was a founding member of the National Bankruptcy Conference. The Advisory Committee was charged with reviewing and revising general orders and official forms but Kennedy advocated more comprehensive reform: conforming bankruptcy rules to federal civil practice in general and to the Federal Rules of Civil Procedure in particular. In 1964, Congress gave the Supreme Court sweeping rule-making authority in bankruptcy. Kennedy continued as reporter of the Advisory Committee, and Morris Shanker of Case Western Reserve University was appointed assistant reporter.[59]

Shanker received an undergraduate degree in engineering from Purdue University in 1948. He received an MBA and his law degree from the University of Michigan in 1952. Shanker studied under Kennedy. After admission to the bar, he practiced law in Cleveland with the firm of Grossman, Schlesinger & Carter. He practiced in the bankruptcy courts and attended Friebolin College. Shanker became a full-time professor of law at Case Western Reserve University Law School in 1961, where he taught bankruptcy, taking over Friebolin's course. Shanker considered Friebolin a mentor.

The Advisory Committee followed the same working procedures that had proved so successful for the National Bankruptcy Conference in its early days. Members held meetings twice a year for three to four days where they analyzed and debated previously distributed drafts. Early in the process, Shanker sought practical input from Cleveland practitioners he respected: Referees Carl Friebolin and William O'Neill and bankruptcy lawyers Saul Nadler and Joseph Patchan. Shanker sought their "reactions to the workability and feasibility of these ideas" proposed in the new rules.[60] The Advisory Committee completed its draft rules and submitted them for comment in September 1971. The rules were accepted by the Standing Committee, the Judicial Conference, the Supreme Court, and Congress and became effective October 1, 1973. On January 1, 1979, the Bankruptcy Reform Act constituted a new Advisory Committee on Bankruptcy Rules in connection with the new Bankruptcy Code. Patchan served on that committee from its inception until 1991.

Judicial salaries lost ground in the prosperity of postwar America. However, referees anticipated a raise in 1969. The Postal Revenue and Federal Salary Act of 1967 created a commission to review and recommend salary increases for judicial employees, including referees.[61] The Bankruptcy Division of the Administrative Office expected the commission to recommend the maximum possible salary increase and expected the Judicial Conference to approve it. However, the Judicial Conference did not give referees a significant raise in 1970 and refused to authorize a salary increase again in 1972, giving as a reason that no salary increase had been authorized for magistrates. The National Conference of Bankruptcy Judges returned to Congress and secured a raise in 1976, which did not depend on the discretion of the Judicial Conference.[62]

Patchan resigned as bankruptcy judge in 1975 as he despaired of supporting a family on a bankruptcy judge's salary. Immediately after resigning, Patchan received a lucrative offer from Cleveland law firm Baker & Hostetler to lead its bankruptcy practice. Founded by Newton D. Baker, who served as mayor of Cleveland from 1912 to 1916 and secretary of war from 1916 to 1921, Baker & Hostetler was the first large firm in Cleveland to start a bankruptcy practice. The firm discovered the potential for complex litigation in bankruptcy through its involvement in a few large cases between 1969 and 1971, including the Seattle Pilots and Rolls-Royce bankruptcies. Baker & Hostetler had already recruited bankruptcy court regulars Maurice (Bud) Sayre and Henry Johnson, and it hoped to increase its influence in the field when Patchan joined the law firm.

In 1968, the American League created an expansion baseball team, the Seattle Pilots, who received financial backing from Cleveland resident

William Daley, a former owner of the Cleveland Indians. The Seattle Pilots played one season in 1969, finishing in last place. Personal problems between the team and the city management aggravated an already bad situation. Daley arranged to sell his interest in the Pilots to the Milwaukee Brewers for $10.8 million, but the Brewers needed the permission of the American League to move the team to Milwaukee. The Seattle mayor filed for an injunction prohibiting the sale of the team, and the team filed bankruptcy in order to stay the injunction proceedings and allow the sale. Baker & Hostetler represented the American League in the bankruptcy proceedings. The Pilots played in Milwaukee as the Brewers in the 1970 season.

On February 5, 1971, Rolls-Royce, Ltd. claimed the protection of a receiver under English bankruptcy law. Rolls-Royce had a division that was manufacturing jet engines for Lockheed Aircraft Corporation pursuant to a fixed-cost contract, and it was losing $264,000 on every engine it delivered. Baker & Hostetler represented Cleveland parts suppliers to Rolls-Royce in the bankruptcy. Lockheed was caught unaware by Rolls-Royce's filing, and Lockheed seemed headed for bankruptcy also. A last-minute loan guarantee program enacted by the United States Congress gave Lockheed room to recover from the economic shock.

Cleveland lawyer John F. (Jack) Ray Jr. replaced Patchan as bankruptcy judge when Patchan resigned in 1975. Ohio senator Frank Lausche advocated Ray's appointment on the recommendation of Ohio Democratic Party king-maker John E. Elder. Ray had been active in Euclid Democratic Party politics, and his law partner was former US attorney John J. Kane. Ray was known to be close with Elder, Lausche's go-to man in northeastern Ohio. Elder had been Lausche's campaign manager when he ran for Cleveland mayor in 1941, Ohio governor in 1945, and senator in 1958. Elder had allied with Ray T. Miller in defeating W. Burr Gongwer for control of the Cuyahoga County Democratic Party in 1938 and was elected treasurer of the Ohio Democratic Party Executive Committee in 1952. Rumor credited Elder with influencing the appointment of district court judge Frank J. Battisti. Ray knew little about bankruptcy when he was appointed bankruptcy judge, but he learned quickly. Judge Ray had humor, grace, intelligence, and integrity, and he was greatly mourned when he died suddenly in October 1987.

On June 30, 1976, Ray presided over what may have been the only "pre-packaged" Chapter XI bankruptcy, *In re National Mortgage Fund.* The case was filed under Chapter XI simultaneously with proofs of claim and ballots voting the creditors' acceptance of the plan for reorganization, which allowed for almost automatic acceptance of the plan. Judge Ray found the plan to be accepted by the requisite number of creditors on July 29, 1976, at the conclusion of the first meeting of creditors, and confirmed the plan on the earliest permissible date, December 14, 1976, 120 days after the first meeting of creditors.[63]

Congress created another district court judgeship for the Northern District of Ohio, and in 1971 President Richard Nixon appointed Canton native Leroy John Conti Jr. to the seat. After receiving his law degree from the University of Michigan, Conti entered law practice with his father in Canton and was elected law director of the city of Canton four times. Conti was a Republican member of the Stark County Board of Elections in 1969 when Governor James A. Rhodes appointed him a Stark County Common Pleas Court judge. Initially, US district court judge Conti sat in Cleveland, commuting daily from Canton. In 1975 Conti was designated to sit in the newly constructed federal courthouse in Akron, Ohio.

When Referee James H. Emsley died in 1972, the Cleveland district court gave Conti the choice of bankruptcy referee for his hometown. Conti knew James H. Williams from Stark County Republican Party politics. Williams was the Republican Party Chairman for Stark County, and Conti had held the position before him. Williams was born in nearby Berlin Center and had attended Kent State University for three years before enrolling in law school at Ohio State University. He earned both an undergraduate and law degree in 1957. Williams worked for the Ohio Department of Highways for a short time before receiving an appointment as assistant US attorney in Columbus, Ohio. Williams entered private practice in Canton after the 1960 election and practiced law with the firm of Blumenstiel, Williams & Blumenstiel until he was appointed referee in bankruptcy in 1972. Williams had a little experience in consumer bankruptcy before his appointment. Williams served as chief bankruptcy judge for the Northern District of Ohio from 1987 to 1997. He retired in 1999 and served on recall until 2000.

Outside of Cleveland, Toledo remained its own judicial district for all practical purposes. Judge Kloeb assumed senior status in September 1964. In June 1965, Democrat Don Young, then Huron County Common Pleas judge, was appointed US district court judge in Toledo, replacing Frank Kloeb. Don Young was the nephew of Ohio US senator Stephen Young. Judge Young appointed assistant US attorney Walter J. Krasniewski referee in bankruptcy in September 1965, replacing Frank Kniffin. Krasniewski had been an assistant US attorney since 1963, and the chief assistant US attorney in Toledo at that time was a nephew of the other referee in Toledo, T. Kenneth Mattimoe. Krasniewski would serve the bankruptcy court as referee and later as bankruptcy judge for thirty-two years. He retired in 1997.

In 1970, President Richard Nixon appointed a second US district court judge for Toledo, Nicholas Joseph Walinski. A Toledo native, Walinski graduated from the University of Toledo law school and was a Lucas County Common Pleas Court judge before his appointment to the federal bench. When Mattimoe died in April 1975, at age sixty-three, it was Walinski's turn to appoint a bankruptcy judge. Walinski chose Ottawa County attorney Richard L. Speer. Speer was born in Norwalk, Ohio, and educated at Ohio Northern University. He received his law degree in 1967 and served a short stint as an Ohio assistant attorney general before entering private practice. He was only thirty-four when appointed bankruptcy judge in Toledo, and he continued to serve until his sudden death on April 3, 2013. Judge Speer served as chief bankruptcy judge for the Northern District of Ohio from 1997 to 2001.

By the late 1960s, bankruptcy scholars and professionals were engaged in another public debate over the need for bankruptcy reform that sounded very reminiscent of the debate that preceded enactment of the Chandler Act in 1938. The Chandler Act had been in use for thirty years, but the problems that had precipitated its enactment continued unabated. Consumer bankruptcies continued to increase in number, and consumers seemed ill served by their bankruptcy attorneys and the bankruptcy process. Creditors received little from consumer bankruptcies and had almost no interest in them. Meanwhile, bankruptcy attorneys seemed to manipulate the system to their material advantage. Referees in bankruptcy performed both administrative and judicial duties, making it difficult for them to maintain a sufficient distance from bankruptcy attorneys to effectively police them.

Chapter Six
The Second Movement to Reform the Bankruptcy Act

Rapidly rising consumer bankruptcy filings and renewed scandals involving alleged "bankruptcy rings" in the 1960s caused reformers and bankruptcy professionals to form study commissions for the purpose of proposing bankruptcy reform. The study commissions approached the problem of bankruptcy reform systemically and recommended fundamental change in the institutional structure of the bankruptcy system. That effort culminated in the enactment of a bankruptcy reform act on November 6, 1978. This chapter describes the content of the reform proposals and the struggle between referees, the Administrative Office of the US Courts, Article III judges, and others to shape those proposals into legislation that served their institutional interests.

The Bankruptcy Reform Act of 1978 profoundly changed the relationship between the bankruptcy court and the US district court. This chapter narrates the convoluted history between the Supreme Court decision in *Northern Pipeline Construction Co. v. Marathon Pipe Line Co.*, which found the new bankruptcy courts unconstitutional, and the resolution of the jurisdictional crisis in 1984.[1] The chapter reveals the practical consequences of the new institutional structure by following its implementation in the new bankruptcy courts of the Northern District of Ohio.

The Bankruptcy Reform Act of 1978 brought comprehensive change to bankruptcy law and practice. Furthermore, the 1898 Bankruptcy Act included numerous substantive rules of bankruptcy procedure that the 1973 Federal Rules of Bankruptcy Procedure had already superseded. Even though Congress did not adopt the more radical reform proposals, the Bankruptcy Reform Act of 1978 did not attempt to merely reform the 1898 Bankruptcy Act but instead created a new Bankruptcy Code in place of the 1898 Bankruptcy Act. To minimize confusion between the Bankruptcy Code and the Bankruptcy Act, the Bankruptcy Code used Arabic numerals for numbering code chapters, whereas the old Bankruptcy Act used Roman numerals. For example, both Bankruptcy Act Chapter XIII and Bankruptcy Code Chapter 13 govern wage-earner arrangements. In this book, "Bankruptcy Act" refers solely to bankruptcy law before the bankruptcy reforms of 1978. The 1978 bankruptcy reform legislation included extensive changes to the administrative structure and function of the bankruptcy courts in addition to the enactment of the Bankruptcy Code of 1978. The term "Bankruptcy Code" refers solely to the new bankruptcy law enacted in the Bankruptcy Reform Act of 1978 and codified at Title 11, United States Code.

The reorganization of the bankruptcy courts and bankruptcy practice under the new Bankruptcy Code took place against the backdrop of profound economic change, especially in the industrial manufacturing cities of the Great Lakes region. Long protected from foreign competition by the devastation of World War II, corporate management initially failed to appreciate the danger posed by new technologies and new products coming from Europe and Asia. The factories, factory workers, and labor agreements of the industrial cities of northern Ohio were old. Changing the way things were made would be painful and expensive. Initially, corporate management simply closed old plants and opened new plants in greener pastures with no prior industrial history, mostly in the nonunionized south, and the old plants and old workers were left behind. Eventually, however, old resources were put to new uses, and the industrial cities of the Great Lakes region began to recover. But the new jobs were different from the old jobs; they required different skills and, mostly, paid less. And there were fewer of them in the aggregate.

Most of the corporate restructuring took place outside of the bankruptcy courts, through corporate mergers and takeovers, plant closings, and downsizing. Some of it was facilitated by Chapter 11 bankruptcy reorganizations initiated in other jurisdictions. Significant bankruptcy reorganizations in the Northern District of Ohio from this period are discussed more fully in the next chapter. Because anxiety over the causes and consequences of industrial restructuring permeated the environment as the new bankruptcy regime took shape, this chapter begins with an overview of deindustrialization in the Northern District of Ohio.

Economic Decline in Northern Ohio

The 1970s and 1980s brought difficult economic times to northern Ohio. After a long expansion through most of the 1960s, the United States suffered a shallow recession from December 1969 through November 1970, followed by rising inflation. The Oil Producing Exporting Countries proclaimed an oil embargo in October 1973 to punish the United States and Europe for supporting Israel in the Yom Kippur War, and the oil embargo threw the economy into another recession lasting from November 1973 through March 1975. This was the most severe recession since World War II, and it affected the automobile-based industrial economy of the Great Lakes region particularly severely. The recovery was marred by persistent and increasing inflation, and then the price of oil spiked again after the Iranian Revolution disrupted oil supplies in 1979. Inflation reached 13.5 percent in 1980, and the new chairman of the Federal Reserve, Paul Volcker, raised interest rates to unimaginable heights to bring inflation down. A brief recession from January 1979 to July 1980 was followed by a severe recession from July 1981 to November 1982. Private employment in the Cleveland Primary Metropolitan Statistical Area peaked in 1979 then declined 13 percent by 1983 before beginning to improve.

The recessions of the 1970s and 1980s heralded the restructuring of the American economy away from manufacturing toward services, especially financial services. Employment in the Cleveland area substantially recovered, but the new jobs were different from the old jobs; service industry jobs replaced manufacturing jobs. Between 1970 and 1990, Cleveland lost more than one-third of its manufacturing jobs while jobs in service industries increased by 80 percent. Service jobs resulted in an income distribution that was more unequal than the income distribution in manufacturing jobs, and service jobs also paid less than manufacturing jobs in the aggregate. By the early 1990s, Cleveland manufacturing output had rebounded but with many fewer workers. Despite the increase in manufacturing, more than three times as many people worked in services as in manufacturing. In the 1990s, Cleveland became a leading provider in health services, insurance, and finance.[2]

Many of Cleveland's iconic corporations disappeared during this period. One such company, Standard Oil Co., illustrates the change. John D. Rockefeller started the Standard Oil Co. in Cleveland in 1870. He expanded nationwide by forming corporations in other states and moved his national headquarters to New York to be close to the big banks, but there always remained an Ohio Standard Oil in Cleveland. In 1882, Rockefeller formed the Standard Oil Trust to hold the stock of corporations doing business in different states, and in 1899 he reorganized the trust as a New Jersey holding company. In 1911, the United States Supreme Court found the holding company a combination in restraint of trade in violation of the Sherman Anti-trust Act.[3] The holding company was broken up into its constituent corporations, including Standard Oil of Ohio (Sohio). The corporation became immense. In 1983, Sohio was the twenty-fifth largest American company by sales and the tenth largest by net income.[4]

In 1969, Sohio exchanged stock for BP Oil Corp., the US subsidiary of the British Petroleum Co., in order to acquire BP's Alaskan oil leases. In 1987, BP acquired all of the stock in Sohio and merged it into a new subsidiary, BP America, Inc., headquartered in Cleveland. In 1998, BP America purchased Chicago-based Amoco, and the corporation's headquarters moved to Chicago.

Another example is the George Worthington Company, which was Cleveland's oldest firm when it filed a petition for reorganization under Chapter 11 in 1986. The company started in 1829 when young George

Worthington came to Cleveland from Utica, New York, and noticed the shortage of picks, shovels, and wheelbarrows among the men building the Ohio and Erie Canal. Worthington went to Cooperstown, New York, to borrow money from his brother and returned to Cleveland with tools to sell. Worthington used the profits to open a hardware store. The store prospered and grew with the city and incorporated in 1887. The company became a wholesale supplier to hardware stores nationwide and a founding member of Sentry Hardware Corporation, a national association of hardware wholesalers. In 1984, the company incurred heavy debt at high interest rates to move its headquarters from Cleveland to suburban Mentor. The wholesale hardware business began to sour, but the George Worthington Company pursued expansion anyway. The company filed a Chapter 11 petition in September 1986 and emerged from bankruptcy in January 1988. Unfortunately, the wholesale hardware business came under severe pricing pressure from foreign competition, and the George Worthington Company filed a second Chapter 11 petition in February 1991. The company liquidated a few months later.

The oil price shocks of the 1970s and the recessions that followed disproportionately affected the rubber, steel, and automotive industries on which northern Ohio had depended since the beginning of the region's industrialization in the late nineteenth century. Sudden and severe increases in the price of gasoline made Americans turn to fuel-efficient imported automobiles that rode on European designed and built radial tires. American consumers liked the imports, and American automobile and tire manufacturers have been playing catch-up ever since. American steel and rubber manufacturers met the challenges of foreign competition by abandoning antiquated plants in Ohio, Indiana, Pennsylvania, and elsewhere, the plants on which the industry had been built, and building new plants to meet the new technological challenges in southern, non-union states with low labor costs. Most of this restructuring took place outside the bankruptcy courts.

The reorganization of the rubber industry in Akron illustrates the deindustrialization of the old manufacturing establishment and its replacement with a new, smaller, knowledge-based white-collar economy. Between 1970 and 1990 all manufacturing of passenger automobile tires left Akron. Tire industry jobs in Akron declined from 37,000 in 1964 to 6,000 in 1997. Although Akron retained some corporate headquarters, research and development, and the manufacture of specialized racing tires, almost all of the good, unionized manufacturing jobs in tire plants left northern Ohio. Only Cooper Tire and Rubber Company, a niche manufacturer in Findlay, Ohio, still manufactures ordinary passenger automobile tires in northern Ohio.[5]

B. F. Goodrich quit making tires in Akron in 1975, and it was the first company to go out of the tire business altogether. B. F. Goodrich's tire operations formed a joint venture with Uniroyal in 1986, and in 1989, the Michelin Corporation's North American division purchased the combined business and moved it to Greenville, South Carolina, near Michelin's newest and most productive radial tire factory in North America. Goodrich continues as a Fortune 500 aerospace company headquartered in Charlotte, North Carolina, with operations around the globe, including northern Ohio.

Poor labor relations aggravated the difficult economic climate for tire manufacturers in the 1970s. The United Rubber Workers negotiated industry master contracts on three-year cycles. In 1976, the union aggressively sought big wage gains with cost-of-living clauses to make up for punishing inflation. Facing cutthroat foreign competition and deteriorating domestic sales, negotiations broke down, and the United Rubber Workers struck at Firestone, Uniroyal, Goodyear, and Goodrich. The strike lasted 130 days and marked a tipping point in Akron's tire industry. Goodyear, Firestone, Mansfield Tire and Rubber, Mohawk Rubber, and General Tire all closed plants in Akron in 1978.

Goodyear had been making tires in Akron since 1898 and embraced radial tires. By 1976, Goodyear was the world's largest producer of radial tires and was considering expanding radial tire production in Akron, but the company wanted union concessions. After the acrimonious 1976 strike, Goodyear built a new plant in Lawson, Oklahoma, instead. In 1978,

Goodyear built another plant in Gadsden, Alabama. Goodyear closed its last plant in Akron in 1978 but turned it into the Goodyear Technical Center. Research and development takes place at the Tech Center, and Goodyear designs and builds its racing tires there. In 1986, Goodyear survived an attempted hostile takeover by British financier Sir James Goldsmith by selling off all non-tire operations. Goodyear is the only remaining tire company with its headquarters in Akron.

Firestone's early radials failed after use, and by 1978 Firestone faced the largest tire recall in American history. Deeply in debt, in 1980 Firestone closed seven of its seventeen plants, including one in Barberton, Ohio. A few months later Firestone closed its last plant in Akron; the plant had been in operation since 1915. In 1988, Japan's oldest tire company, Bridgestone, purchased Firestone. In 1992, the headquarters of Bridgestone/Firestone moved to Nashville, Tennessee, but the company retained a technical center in Akron. By 1992, Akron had developed a reputation as a center for polymer research.

General Tire closed the last tire plant left in Akron in 1983. The company had diversified into many fields after World War II, including aeronautics, defense industries, automotive products, and media. It changed its name to GenCorp in 1984 and moved its corporate headquarters to the Akron suburb of Fairlawn. GenCorp successfully defended against a hostile takeover attempt in 1987 by selling its tire business to the German tire company Continental AG. The new company, Continental General Tire Corporation, moved its headquarters to Charlotte, North Carolina, in 1993. In 1999, GenCorp spun off its polymer business into a new company, Omnova, located in GenCorp's old headquarters in the Akron suburbs. Omnova maintains a technical center in Akron and a latex plant in the Akron suburb of Mogadore. GenCorp's aeronautic and defense industries relocated to California.

Alone among industrialized nations, the American steel industry emerged unscathed from the devastation of World War II. Even after reconstruction in Europe and Japan, nearly half of the world's steel was still produced in the United States in 1950. By 1969, however, foreign imports began to penetrate the American steel market. American steel manufacturers sought, and obtained, protection from imports in the form of two voluntary restraint agreements limiting imports from Europe and Asia between 1969 and 1974. Instead of using the breathing space to modernize manufacturing facilities, however, American steel manufacturers began a program of disinvesting in domestic integrated steel mills and using the savings to diversify out of steel.

Between 1968 and 1971, a merger mania afflicted American steel manufacturers. Four intra-industry mergers involving nine firms further concentrated an already highly concentrated industry. Ten inter-industry mergers involving ten steel manufacturers revealed a strategy of embedding low return-on-equity steel operations in conglomerates. In northern Ohio, Lykes Corporation, a New Orleans–based shipping company, bought Youngstown Sheet & Tube in 1969. Youngstown Sheet & Tube was founded in 1901 and headquartered in suburban Youngstown. Texas-based conglomerate Ling-Temco-Vought acquired Jones & Laughlin Steel Corp. in 1968. The corporation changed its name to LTV in 1971. Headquartered in Pittsburgh, Jones & Laughlin had been making steel in the Monongahela Valley since the late nineteenth century. In 1978, LTV acquired Lykes and merged Youngstown Sheet & Tube into Jones & Laughlin.[6]

In 1977, steel was the third-largest industry in the United States, behind automobiles and oil. Between 1978 and 1982, nearly half of all steel mills closed. Nationally, steel employment fell from 449,000 to 289,000. Northern Ohio suffered plant closings in Cleveland, Youngstown, Massillon, and Lorain. Some plants changed ownership but continued to make steel. For example, in 1981, Armco sold its mill in Marion, Ohio, to Steel Bar Products. Today, Nucor owns and operates the mill.[7]

In 1979, US Steel determined that only half of its plants could be modernized cost effectively and formally adopted a policy of "capital starvation" for the rest. The doomed plants included all the US Steel plants in Cleveland and Youngstown. Management resolved to deploy resources into more profitable investments, and in 1982, US Steel purchased the

Marathon Oil Corporation. Marathon provided the steel manufacturer a hedge against energy costs, but more importantly, oil was profitable. In 1982 and 1983, Marathon earned $2.348 billion in operating profits compared with $1.486 billion in operating losses from steel manufacturing. US Steel changed its name to USX in 1986, and US Steel became the name of a division of USX.[8]

In 1978, US Steel closed the Ohio Works in Youngstown and the nearby plant in McDonald. Private investors purchased the McDonald plant and reopened part of it in 1981. The McDonald plant was built in 1918, and the town grew up around the plant. McDonald Steel Co. survives as a specialty steel manufacturer. US Steel razed the Ohio Works in 1980 after Youngstown activists sued unsuccessfully to force US Steel to let an employee- and community-owned cooperative purchase the plant. US Steel closed the Cuyahoga Works, the last US Steel plant in Cleveland, in May 1984. In 1986, US Steel sold the Cuyahoga Works to American Steel & Wire Corp., a private equity venture, which reopened and operated the facilities. The plant has continued operating under changed ownership.

Youngstown suffered disproportionately from the integrated steel manufacturers' disinvestment. Youngstown, once the second-largest steel-making city in the nation next to Pittsburgh, saw most of its mills close between 1977 and 1982. In September 1977, Youngstown Sheet & Tube announced that it was closing its largest plant in the region, the Campbell Works, and moving corporate headquarters to Chicago. Five thousand workers lost their jobs. After the merger of Lykes and LTV, Jones & Laughlin announced the closing of Youngstown Sheet & Tube's Brier Hill Works, idling 1,500 more workers. In November 1979, US Steel announced the closing of the Ohio Works and the McDonald finishing mill, idling 3,500 more workers. Republic Steel began layoffs at its Youngstown pipe mill and blast furnace in 1978, eliminating another 2,600 jobs. The plant closings proved catastrophic for the local business community. Employment fell more than 26 percent in the Youngstown-Warren metropolitan area between 1976 and 1982.[9]

Cleveland industrialist Cyrus Eaton created Republic Steel in 1930 from the merger of Youngstown's Republic Iron and Steel Company and several smaller steel companies. At the time of its creation, Republic Steel was the third-largest steel manufacturer in the country. In October 1983, LTV's Jones & Laughlin Steel Co. merged with Republic Steel to form LTV Steel Co., the third-largest steel manufacturer in the country at that time, behind US Steel and Bethlehem Steel. LTV Steel established its headquarters in Cleveland.

In July 1986, LTV Steel petitioned for reorganization under Chapter 11 of the new Bankruptcy Code in the Southern District of New York. LTV's petition listed more than $4 billion in liabilities, more than half associated with underfunded union pension plans. Immediately after filing its petition, LTV stopped paying medical and life insurance benefits to 78,000 retired employees, 11,000 of them in the Youngstown area. LTV closed its last steel plant in the Youngstown area in August 1986. In 1988, Ira Rennert's family holding company, Renco, purchased the mill and reopened it as Warren Consolidated Steel, Inc. LTV had been the lowest-unit-cost integrated steel manufacturer in the country, and it enjoyed one of the lowest labor cost structures in the industry. It succumbed to bankruptcy because the smaller steel manufacturing entity created from the merger of the three old integrated steel corporations could not support the legacy costs of its constituent corporations. The three constituent corporations had operated sixteen plants employing 85,000 workers in 1971. By 1987, LTV Steel was operating six plants and employing 20,000 workers. Employment in the steel industry had declined 40 percent between 1979 and 1988; LTV's employment in the steel industry had declined 60 percent over the same period.[10]

LTV Steel was headquartered in Cleveland, and the LTV bankruptcy stunned the Cleveland business community. Nearly every business in the Cleveland metropolitan area did business with LTV or sold goods and services to its employees and retirees. LTV owed the Cleveland electric utility $4.1 million; the electric company was LTV's seventh-largest unsecured creditor.[11] In northern Ohio, the economic fallout from LTV's bankruptcy truncated the economic expansion enjoyed in the rest of the country between 1983 and 1990.

Disinvestment in integrated steel mills in the United States corresponded with the rise of mini-mills. In general, mini-mills are small producers of low-value steel made from scrap that is processed in electric arc furnaces. Integrated steel mills produce higher-quality steel from ore that is processed in large blast furnaces, refining the ore in multiple steps with great precision. Relatively inexpensive to build, geographically flexible, and employing fewer people with lower skills than integrated ore-based steel mills, mini-mills expanded dramatically in the 1970s and 1980s. Initially, most mini-mills were located in the South, where nonunion labor and new manufacturing customers could be found. Mini-mills posed a formidable challenge to integrated steel mills in the markets where they competed. They enjoyed significant cost advantages over integrated mills and averaged a return on assets twice that of integrated steel mills. By the 1980s, however, depressed conditions in the former steel manufacturing districts of the North made them desirable locations for new mini-mill construction.[12]

Youngstown aggressively confronted the collapse of the steel industry, creating the Youngstown Industrial Corporation (YIC) to purchase and redevelop abandoned steel mills. The city cleaned up abandoned mills, relieved new users of environmental liability from prior users, and gave ten-year tax abatements. By 1995, the Youngstown-Warren metropolitan area had regained more than three-quarters of the 40,000 steel jobs lost in the 1970s and 1980s.[13]

Youngstown's first attempt at brownfield redevelopment proved a huge success. YIC purchased the old Brier Hill mill and open-hearth furnace from Jones & Laughlin in 1980 and resold 70 percent of the abandoned plant to Hunt Energy Corporation in 1981 for use in the construction of a new mini-mill. Hunt Energy was a successor corporation to the Hunt Valve Corporation of Salem, Ohio, which produced hydraulic components for industrial use. Hunt Steel Co. began producing steel in the new facilities in 1983. Undercapitalized and unable to meet its electric bill,

Hunt Energy petitioned for reorganization under Chapter 11 in Cleveland in February 1984.

Hunt Energy sold its Youngstown mini-mill to North Star Steel, a subsidiary of the privately owned grain giant Cargill Inc. in 1985. North Star built a new seamless pipe mill and began producing pipe in 1988. The mill expanded in 1990. In 1995, North Star began construction on a new mini-mill in rural Delta, Ohio, near Toledo, operated as a joint venture with Australian BlueScope Steel Corp., formerly BHP. North Star's Toledo mill has been very successful.

In 2002, the French steel-tubing producer, Vallourec S.A., bought the North Star Steel mill in Youngstown through a limited partnership, V & M Star, which has become the leading producer of steel tubing for the oil and gas industry in the United States. Hoping to profit from the natural-gas boom resulting from new techniques in extracting gas from the Marcellus shale formation underlying eastern Ohio and western Pennsylvania, V & M committed to a significant expansion in Youngstown in 2008.

Toledo's economic decline followed the rise of vulture capitalism as well as the decline of the American automotive industry. In 1980, Toledo was in the midst of a major urban redevelopment effort. It boasted six Fortune 500 company headquarters: glass manufacturers Owens-Corning, Owens-Illinois, and Libby-Owens-Ford; and automotive suppliers Champion, Dana, and Sheller-Globe. During the course of the next decade, half of these corporations disappeared along with significant losses in employment and corporate commitment to the community. None of Toledo's six Fortune 500 companies escaped unscathed. Manufacturing employment in Toledo fell from 58,000 jobs to 45,000 jobs between 1977 and 1988, and more than 9,000 of the lost jobs came from Toledo's six Fortune 500 companies. Toledo lost an additional 9,000 manufacturing jobs between 1988 and 1992.[14]

Michael Owens perfected the automatic glass bottle machine in 1913. Owens-Illinois was created in 1929 from the merger of Toledo's Owens Bottle Company and Illinois Glass. In 1979, Owens-Illinois committed to building its new corporate headquarters in downtown Toledo to anchor an ambitious urban redevelopment program. The timing could not have been worse. The corporation downsized in response to the 1980s recession, closing production facilities and eliminating employees. In 1987, the takeover firm Kohlberg Kravits Roberts & Company acquired Owens-Illinois in a leveraged buyout and took it private. The new corporate owners sold many assets to raise cash, and the company went public again in 1991. In 1993, Owens-Illinois sold Libby Glass to raise more cash. In 2006, Owens-Illinois moved its corporate headquarters to suburban Perrysburg, Ohio.[15]

Libby-Owens-Ford, the product of a 1930s merger between Toledo's two principal plate glass manufacturers, sold its name and glass operations to British manufacturer Pilkington Group in 1986. The new corporate owner sold or spun off other corporate divisions, but the US office for Pilkington's operations remained in Toledo.

Owens-Corning was created from a 1937 joint venture between Owens-Illinois and Corning Glass to develop products using fiberglass. The phenomenal success of fiberglass encouraged Owens-Corning to develop a research-based business strategy. In 1986, Owens-Corning suffered a hostile takeover attempt by Wickes Companies, a California building materials retailer. Owens-Corning defended with a leveraged buyout financed by Drexel Burnham Lambert. In order to retire the debt incurred to defend against the takeover, Owens-Corning laid off employees, closed plants, gutted research and development, and sold subsidiaries. The surviving corporation was lean and profitable and expanded in a disciplined fashion. However, in October 2000, Owens-Corning filed for bankruptcy reorganization under Chapter 11 in Delaware in response to a $6 billion judgment in an asbestos litigation class-action lawsuit.

Sheller-Globe, created in 1966 from the merger of two older companies, expanded aggressively by acquiring other companies, and in 1986, the conglomerate Knoll International Holdings acquired Sheller-Globe. In 1988, the investment banking firm Gibbons Green arranged an ill-conceived purchase of Sheller-Globe in partnership with the conglomerate United Technologies Corporation. Immediately after the deal closed, Sheller-Globe ran out of cash. The unsatisfactory transaction caused the dissolution of Gibbons Green. United Technologies purchased Gibbons Green's interest in Sheller-Globe, turning it into a corporate division.[16] Lear Corporation purchased the division from United Technologies in 1991.

Champion Corporation had been making spark plugs in Toledo since 1910. The company struggled in the late 1980s as the American automotive industry faced severe pricing pressure and stiff foreign competition. Members of the founding Stranahan family still controlled the company, but many younger family members wanted to sell the business. In January 1989, Champion agreed to merge with Dana Corporation, but in February 1989, Cooper Industries, an Irish company with its US headquarters in Texas, made a better offer. In October 1998, Cooper Industries sold its automotive division, which included Champion spark plugs, to Federal Mogul Corporation. Champion now survives as a brand of Federal Mogul.

Dana Corporation began in 1904 in Plainfield, New Jersey, as the Spicer Company, producing the Spicer encased universal joint. Charles Dana invested heavily in the firm in 1914, and it became successful during World War I as a major contributor to the production of the Liberty Truck. Spicer grew by acquisition, and the company moved to Toledo in 1928. In 1946, the company changed its name to the Dana Corporation. Dana prospered in the postwar economy as a leading producer of axles, drive-shafts, and transmissions and grew by acquisition within the automotive industry. In the 1970s, Dana adopted progressive personnel policies and was considered one of the best-run companies in the nation. The decline of the American automotive industry in the 1980s and 1990s radically reduced Dana's sales and profitability, however, and the company filed for reorganization under Chapter 11 in the Southern District of New York in March 2006. A streamlined Dana emerged in February 2008, supported by private equity funding and union concessions. Dana shed legacy costs for retiree health benefits through the creation of a Voluntary Employee Benefit Association.

The industrial infrastructure of northern Ohio, which had been remarkably stable since the 1890s, changed profoundly over the course of the 1980s. Seminal corporations that had defined industries for decades suddenly diversified out of their traditional lines of business, abandoning long-standing manufacturing facilities and the cities that had grown up around them. Mergers and takeovers cut the bonds of loyalty between corporations and the people and places that had nurtured them. By the 1990s, most of the structural damage had been done in northern Ohio, but the region would continue to decline relative to the rest of the nation in terms of income and population growth.

Many factors contributed to the rapid and devastating restructuring of northern Ohio's economy in the 1980s, including changes in federal income tax rules; the development of private equity and junk bond financing; and the relaxation of federal regulation in the fields of labor relations, antitrust, and trade. The new Bankruptcy Code also contributed to the deindustrialization of northern Ohio, as creative bankruptcy lawyers deployed Chapter 11 in ways the code's drafters had not anticipated. Enacted in 1978 with a transition that lasted into the 1980s, the new bankruptcy system evolved simultaneously with economic and institutional changes, influencing each other in subtle ways.[17]

The Bankruptcy Reform Act of 1978

Bankruptcy scholars and professionals began laying the groundwork for another round of bankruptcy reform in the 1960s. Under the auspices of the Brookings Institution, David T. Stanley and Marjorie Girth began a comprehensive study of the bankruptcy system in 1965 for the purpose of making recommendations for reform. This first serious study of the bankruptcy system since the Chandler Act in 1938 found problems with bankruptcy administration that were remarkably similar to those reported by William J. Donovan and Lloyd K. Garrison in their reports in the early 1930s. The Brookings Institution published its bankruptcy study in 1971.[18]

After brief hearings in 1968 and 1969, Congress created a Bankruptcy Commission on July 26, 1970. Tasked to study the operation of the bankruptcy courts and recommend legislative changes, the commission began its work in June 1971 and issued its report in 1973. The commission's work was deeply informed by the findings and conclusions of the Brookings Institution's bankruptcy study.

The Brookings Institution study focused primarily on consumer bankruptcies because they made up the vast majority of bankruptcy cases; the study concluded that the existing system served neither debtors nor creditors well. The Chandler Act's attempt to address the evils of rising consumer bankruptcies—Chapter XIII arrangements for wage earners—had proved ineffective. Despite the Administrative Office's best efforts, the proportion of consumer debtors filing under Chapter XIII remained small and constant. Consumer debtors received little guidance from their attorneys and no credit counseling to prepare them to avoid bankruptcy in the future. Creditors received little return on their claims and had no incentive to get involved in the administration of bankruptcy, leaving the field open for exploitation by so-called bankruptcy rings.

The Brookings Institution report also recommended bankruptcy reforms that were remarkably similar to the reforms recommended by earlier reports. The Brookings Institution report recommended fundamental structural reform: small business and consumer bankruptcies should be removed from the courts and administered by an independent administrative agency in a non-adversarial setting; only corporate reorganizations would remain under the jurisdiction of the district court.

Although Congress clearly expected referees to be part of the Bankruptcy Commission, the judiciary systematically excluded them. Referees in bankruptcy also had no voice at that time on the Bankruptcy Committee of the Judicial Conference of the United States, and relations with the staff of the Bankruptcy Division of the Administrative Office had deteriorated markedly since the days when referee Carl Friebolin and Bankruptcy Division chief Edwin Covey conferred confidentially based on their long friendship and a shared worldview. The referees' grievances extended beyond their exclusion from the policy discussion to the organized judiciary's indifference to the stagnation in referees' pay and the deterioration in their working conditions. Adding insult to injury, several district courts had recently consolidated bankruptcy clerks into the office of the clerk of district court and usurped other resources intended for the operation of the bankruptcy courts.[19]

Cleveland referee William O'Neill was president of the renamed National Conference of Referees in Bankruptcy in 1970. He tried unsuccessfully to establish better relations with the Bankruptcy Division and to secure its support for referee representation on the Bankruptcy Committee of the Judicial Conference. When Chief Justice Warren Burger appointed no referees to the Bankruptcy Commission, O'Neill wrote the chief justice requesting that the National Conference of Referees in Bankruptcy be allowed to appear before the commission. When that failed, he appointed an ad hoc committee to advise him on strategies to ensure that referees' expertise and interests were communicated to the commission. In November 1971, Professor Frank R. Kennedy, executive director of the commission, invited the National Conference of Referees in Bankruptcy to submit information to the commission, and the National Conference of Referees in Bankruptcy created a liaison committee to work with the commission. Kennedy valued the referees' input and invited representatives to testify before the commission at the public hearings scheduled to begin in March 1972. Several referees testified at the hearings.[20]

The Bankruptcy Commission was charged with drafting a bankruptcy reform bill to accompany its report, and the outlines of the commission's bill were known to the referees. The commission's bill adopted the Brookings Institution's recommendation of a bankruptcy agency in the executive branch of government to handle the administrative functions formerly handled by referees. The commission's bill also expanded the bankruptcy court's subject matter jurisdiction. Bankruptcy courts would hear all actions concerning debtors' property, which was broadly defined to include rights and interests that could have been recovered only through litigation in state or US district courts under the 1898 Bankruptcy Act. The commission's bill also defined creditors' claims against the estate broadly to include un-matured and potential claims.

To correspond with the greater power and status of bankruptcy judges, the commission's bill recommended that they be appointed by the president to fifteen-year terms, as was done in Tax Court. The sitting referees would not continue in office under the new bill.[21]

The commission's bankruptcy reform bill threatened existing referees' livelihoods. Far fewer referees would be required if consumer bankruptcies were administered by a new executive agency, and presidential appointment ensured that only lawyers with strong, current political connections could expect an appointment as referee in bankruptcy. Existing referees who had been out of politics for years could not hope to compete for appointment with lawyers who had been politically active more recently. Substantively, referees also believed the proposed structure would not serve the interests of debtors and creditors better than a modified version of the existing bankruptcy system. Referees and many bankruptcy lawyers argued that the employees of an administrative agency would not be more efficient or economical than fee-based trustees and that an administrative agency would find itself facing the same kinds of conflicts of interest that bedeviled referees and attorneys in the existing system.

Referees testified against the proposals contained in the Bankruptcy Commission's anticipated bill at the March 1972 hearings, and the commission suggested that the National Conference of Referees in Bankruptcy prepare its own draft bill. In June 1972, Referee Saul Seidman, then president of the National Conference of Referees in Bankruptcy, wrote to the Bankruptcy Division of the Administrative Office advising it that the National Conference of Referees in Bankruptcy had been asked to draft a bill and suggesting the formation of a liaison committee within the Bankruptcy Committee of the Judicial Conference to study and prepare a unified response to the commission's report and recommendations. The Bankruptcy Division opposed the creation of a liaison committee because Judicial Conference policy opposed commenting on legislation unless specifically requested by Congress or the legislation was initiated by the Judicial Conference. Furthermore, influential district court judges opposed appointing referees to any Judicial Conference committee. Frustrated, the referees began drafting their own bankruptcy reform bill under the leadership of Kentucky referee Joe Lee. The referees' bill adopted the commission's recommendation that the jurisdiction of the bankruptcy court be expanded but did not endorse the creation of a new administrative agency for bankruptcy.

The Commission Bill was introduced into both houses of Congress in October 1973, but the Watergate impeachment hearings sidelined its immediate consideration. Referee Joe Lee assumed the presidency of the National Conference of Referees in Bankruptcy in 1973, and in November 1973, Lee wrote Southern District of New York judge Edward Weinfeld seeking a meeting to discuss policy issues regarding the pending Commission Bill. Judge Weinfeld, who chaired the Bankruptcy Committee of the Judicial Conference and sat on the Bankruptcy Commission, had strenuously opposed direct referee participation on the committee and the commission. Weinfeld rebuffed Lee and suggested that Lee direct his concerns directly to the congressional committees considering the bill. The referees successfully used Weinfeld's rebuff to defend against accusations of insubordination when the referees completed drafting their bill and submitted it to Congress as the Judges' Bill. The recently promulgated Federal Rules of Bankruptcy Procedure made referees "bankruptcy judges," and their organization had changed its name to the National Conference of Bankruptcy Judges.

Representative Don Edwards of Kentucky had been a member of the commission and had introduced the Commission Bill into Congress. However, Edwards also represented Joe Lee in Congress, so he introduced the Judges' Bill into Congress, too. Edwards agreed to consider both bills together in committee, ensuring that the bankruptcy judges would be deeply involved in the committee's consideration of all major decisions affecting bankruptcy reform. Hearings on the bills occurred in 1975 and 1976. In December 1976, Edwards told supporters of both bills to compromise on a single bill or no bankruptcy reform would be enacted. Representatives of the National Conference of Bankruptcy Judges and the Bankruptcy Commission met in an Atlanta, Georgia, hotel room to reach agreement on a compromise bill. Congressional staffers Ken Klee and Richard Levin worried that giving bankruptcy judges less than lifetime appointment under Article III would not pass constitutional muster. After consulting constitutional scholars, the compromise committee concurred with Klee and Levin and changed the bill to provide for the lifetime appointment of bankruptcy judges. On January 6, 1977, the opening day of the new Congress, Representative Edwards introduced the Compromise Bill.[22]

The Judges' Bill had advocated that referees be appointed by the judicial councils of the circuit courts to fifteen-year terms, but the Compromise Bill called for presidential appointment of bankruptcy judges to a lifetime term under Article III of the Constitution. The Judicial Conference and the Bankruptcy Committee had not participated in the hearings on the bills, and they had voiced no objection to presidential appointment of bankruptcy judges in the four years since the Bankruptcy Commission issued its report making that recommendation. However, the Judicial Conference now objected strenuously to making bankruptcy judges either Article I (term) or Article III (lifetime) federal judges, and Chief Justice Burger formed an Ad Hoc Committee on the Bankruptcy System (which the bankruptcy judges called the "gang of fifteen") in March 1977 to oppose the creation of an independent bankruptcy court. The bankruptcy judges had made a very favorable impression in Congress through their testimony and committee work, and many in Congress thought they had been treated unfairly by the district courts and the Judicial Conference. Congressional staff had been frustrated by the Judicial Conference's failure to participate in the legislative process, and they viewed the organized judiciary as elitist. Congress did not respond sympathetically to the Judicial Conference's belated opposition to an independent bankruptcy court.[23]

The Compromise Bill cleared the House Judiciary Committee in September 1977. Floor amendments designed to replace an independent bankruptcy court with a bankruptcy court much like the existing one but with bankruptcy judges appointed by the circuit judicial council to fifteen-year terms gained sufficient traction on the floor that the bill's managers pulled it in order to plan a counter attack. The strategic retreat worked, and despite intense lobbying by the Ad Hoc Committee, the Compromise Bill passed the House, un-amended, on February 1, 1978.[24] Meanwhile, a bill similar to the House bill but without Article III (lifetime) status for bankruptcy judges progressed in the Senate. That bill cleared committee without significant amendment in July 1978. Almost immediately, staff began discussing how to compromise the House and Senate bills. As the congressional session neared adjournment, the Senate amended the House bill and passed it on September 7, 1978. After some parliamentary maneuvering, the House concurred in the Senate amendment with another amendment on September 28, 1978. Senator Strom Thurmond of South Carolina placed a hold on the bill but agreed to release it if Attorney General Griffin Bell negotiated a compromise. Bell had been a judge on the Fifth Circuit Court of Appeals, and Senator Thurmond knew him personally and trusted him.

Bell's compromise retained the bankruptcy court as an adjunct of the district court but with practical independence. Bankruptcy judges would be appointed to fourteen-year terms by the president, with due consideration for the recommendations of the circuit judicial council, and confirmed by the Senate. No bankruptcy judges had to be admitted to the Judicial Conference until the end of the transition period on March 31, 1984. Bell's compromise passed the Senate on October 5, 1978, and the House on October 6, 1978. Despite an extensive lobbying effort by Chief Justice Burger, President Jimmy Carter signed it into law on November 6, 1978, the last day before the bill expired.

The Bankruptcy Reform Act of 1978 established a freestanding Bankruptcy Code at Title 11 of the United States Code. The district court retained original and exclusive jurisdiction of all cases under Title 11 and original, but not exclusive, jurisdiction of all civil proceedings arising in or related to cases under Title 11; however, the bankruptcy court exercised the district court's jurisdiction. The bankruptcy court consisted of bankruptcy judges, appointed by the president to a fourteen-year term and confirmed by the Senate. A bankruptcy judge could be removed from office during his term only for incompetence, misconduct, neglect of duty, or disability by majority vote of the judges of the judicial council of his judicial circuit. The most senior bankruptcy judge younger than seventy years became chief bankruptcy judge and was responsible for assigning work among the judges of the bankruptcy court.

The Bankruptcy Reform Act of 1978 established functionally independent bankruptcy courts with the power to appoint their own employees, including law clerks, subject only to budgetary restrictions, without interference from the district court. If the judges of the bankruptcy court could not agree on an appointment, the chief bankruptcy judge could make the appointment. The bankruptcy court would appoint its own clerk of court subject to certification by the district court that the volume of bankruptcy cases in the district necessitated one, and only the bankruptcy court could remove the clerk of bankruptcy court. The clerk of bankruptcy court had authority to hire deputies, assistants, and employees, as determined by the Administrative Office, subject only to approval by the bankruptcy court. Bankruptcy became a court of record, and case reporters began publishing bankruptcy judges' opinions.[25]

The federal judiciary initially resisted recognizing the bankruptcy judges' enhanced status under the Bankruptcy Code. Although the bankruptcy reform act amended the Judicial Code and required that bankruptcy judges be invited to the circuit judicial conferences, fewer than half of the circuits did so without demeaning reservations. In the Sixth Circuit, for example, which includes the Northern District of Ohio, bankruptcy judges were not listed in the directory among the judiciary but listed separately after the circuit executive and clerk. The bankruptcy judges sometimes resorted to organizing separate bankruptcy programs immediately before the judicial conference because the conference planners neither consulted the bankruptcy judges nor included bankruptcy issues in the program.[26]

The Bankruptcy Code became effective October 1, 1979, with a transition period until March 31, 1984. Cases filed before the effective date were adjudicated under the 1898 Bankruptcy Act as amended, and cases filed after the effective date were adjudicated under the Bankruptcy Code. The Bankruptcy Reform Act of 1978 directed the Administrative Office to conduct studies during the transition period to determine the number of bankruptcy judges needed under the Bankruptcy Code. During the transition period the reform act also directed the Administrative Office to create a committee of at least seven bankruptcy judges to advise the director regarding issues that occurred during the transition.

Existing bankruptcy judges whose terms expired during the transition period had their terms extended without appointment until March 31, 1984, unless the chief judge of the circuit court found them unqualified after consulting a merit screening committee consisting of representatives of the state bar association, a law school located within the state, and a local bar association. If a vacancy occurred, the district court appointed a new bankruptcy judge as under the 1898 Bankruptcy Act, unless the circuit merit screening committee found the applicant unqualified. The term of office of an interim appointee expired at the end of the transition period. The Bankruptcy Reform Act of 1978 anticipated that by the end of the transition period all bankruptcy judges would be appointed by the president and confirmed by the Senate.

The Supreme Court decision in *Northern Pipeline Construction Co. v. Marathon Pipe Line Co.* abruptly halted the orderly transition to the new bankruptcy system.[27] In January 1980, Northern Pipeline Construction Co. filed a petition for reorganization under the new Bankruptcy Code. In March, Northern Pipeline filed a civil action for breach of contract against Marathon Pipe Line Co. in the bankruptcy court pursuant to the enlarged jurisdiction that the court enjoyed under the Bankruptcy Code. In *Marathon,* the Supreme Court held that the broad jurisdiction to determine claims granted under the new Bankruptcy Code, including claims originating under state law such as those in *Marathon*, could only be exercised by judges created under Article III of the United States Constitution, and bankruptcy judges did not qualify as Article III judges because they did not have lifetime tenure. Many years later, Akron bankruptcy judge Harold F. White found himself alone in an elevator with Justice Sandra Day O'Connor at a judicial conference, and he took advantage of the opportunity to ask her whether the Supreme Court had any idea of the consequences that its decision in *Marathon* would generate. Justice O'Connor confirmed that they had not a clue.[28]

The Supreme Court decided *Marathon* in June 1982 and stayed the decision until October 4, 1982, to give Congress an opportunity to fix the jurisdictional defect in the new law. The Supreme Court extended the stay to December 24, 1982. Congress did not act, and the Supreme Court refused any further stay. The Judicial Conference leapt into the breach and directed the Administrative Office to draft a proposed emergency rule for each district to adopt in order to keep the bankruptcy system operating through the transition period in the absence of congressional action. The rule was fashioned to meet the explicit defects identified in the Supreme Court's decision in *Marathon,* and all circuits adopted the rule. The legal authority for the courts to fix a jurisdictional defect by rule was, and remains, controversial.[29]

The district court judges of the Northern District of Ohio unanimously adopted the emergency rule, and on December 21, 1982, Chief Judge Frank J. Battisti issued General Order No. 61 promulgating it. The rule deemed all bankruptcy cases in the district to be referred to the bankruptcy judges. It separated matters into those arising under the Bankruptcy Code, and matters related to bankruptcy proceedings. Matters related to bankruptcy proceedings included civil matters that could be heard by a district court or a state court in the absence of a bankruptcy petition. Bankruptcy judges held hearings, made findings, drafted proposed judgments but entered no final orders in matters related to a bankruptcy proceeding without the consent of the parties. District court judges entered final orders in matters related to a bankruptcy proceeding and reviewed the final orders of bankruptcy judges. Bankruptcy court clerks continued to receive and maintain all records relating to bankruptcy proceedings under the emergency rule.

Marathon caused surprisingly little disruption in the day-to-day operation of the bankruptcy courts. Some cautious bankruptcy lawyers sought "comfort orders" signed by the district court judge instead of accepting a final order from the bankruptcy judge, but most district court judges simply reiterated the bankruptcy judge's findings. In general, bankruptcy judges administered bankruptcy cases without challenge because bankruptcy lawyers were comfortable with bankruptcy courts, and district courts did not want to hear bankruptcy cases.[30]

The decision in *Marathon* opened the door for all sides to reargue in Congress the appropriate status of bankruptcy judges in a newly heightened partisan environment. Since enactment of the Bankruptcy Reform Act of 1978, Republicans had taken control of the presidency and the Senate. Article III status for bankruptcy judges would give President Ronald Reagan and the Republican Senate an extraordinary patronage opportunity in the appointment of 227 new bankruptcy judges with lifetime tenure. The federal judiciary remained steadfastly opposed to Article III status for bankruptcy judges, and some reinforced their opposition to giving bankruptcy judges lifetime appointment by reciting recent scandals involving abuse of office by three bankruptcy judges: Harry Hackett of Detroit, J. Douglas Williams of Anchorage, and Mark Schlachet of Cleveland. On the other hand, it was not clear how the bankruptcy judges could constitutionally exercise an expanded jurisdiction in independent courts without Article III status. Crafting a legislative solution to the problem was complicated by renewed demands from creditors emboldened by the recent Republican election victories to amend the new Bankruptcy Code to curtail consumer bankruptcies. Further complicating matters, in February 1984, the Supreme Court held that labor agreements were "executory contracts" that a corporation in reorganization could unilaterally reject, subject to the approval of the bankruptcy court. A US Senator from Ohio, Howard Metzenbaum, spearheaded Democratic demands to include in any bankruptcy bill rigorous standards designed to protect labor agreements.[31]

On June 29, 1984, Congress finally passed a compromise bill. The legislation created bankruptcy judges as "units of the district court" to serve as "judicial officers of the United States District Court established under Article III." Bankruptcy judges would be appointed by the circuit court of appeals to fourteen-year terms, and they could be removed by a majority vote of the circuit council for incompetence, misconduct, neglect of duty, or disability. The legislation delineated the bankruptcy court's jurisdiction as "core" and "non-core" in terms that mirrored the resolution crafted by the Judicial Conference in the emergency rule. The transition period and the emergency rules expired on March 31, 1984, so Congress extended the terms of the bankruptcy judges to June 27, 1984, but that deadline passed, too. The legislation that Congress passed on June 29 purported to extend the bankruptcy judges' terms until final enactment of the legislation by making the legislation effective June 27, 1984. President Reagan signed the new bankruptcy law on July 10, 1984. The Bankruptcy Amendments and Federal Judgeship Act of 1984 provided for those bankruptcy judges serving at the time of enactment to continue in office until four years after the date of their last appointment or October 1, 1986, whichever was later.[32]

On June 29, 1984, the director of the Administrative Office, William E. Foley, sent a memorandum to all circuit and district court judges advising them that because the bankruptcy judges' appointments had expired on June 27, 1984, the Executive Committee of the Judicial Conference had authorized an increase in the number of temporary magistrate positions equal to the number of existing bankruptcy judges. Foley encouraged the bankruptcy judges to apply for those positions so that they could continue to administer the bankruptcy laws. In the Northern District of Ohio, Chief Judge Frank J. Battisti issued General Order No. 83, modifying the emergency rule for the administration of bankruptcy after *Marathon* by substituting the term "magistrates" for "bankruptcy judges." Foley also authorized court clerks to appoint temporary bankruptcy consultants, in the number of the existing bankruptcy judges, in order to bridge the gap until the magistrate appointments could be completed.

Foley's suggestion that bankruptcy judges continue their duties as magistrates infuriated most bankruptcy judges. In 1968, US commissioners became salaried US magistrates. District court judges worked closely with magistrates and identified with them, and the Judicial Conference had held authorized pay raises for bankruptcy judges hostage to Congress's failure to simultaneously raise magistrates' pay. The Judicial Conference had openly aspired to combine the offices of referee in bankruptcy and magistrate since at least 1970, and they had attempted to achieve that end during the negotiations in Congress over bankruptcy judges' status under the Bankruptcy Code.[33]

On July 11, 1984, the day after President Reagan signed the Bankruptcy Amendments and Federal Judgeship Act, Foley sent the infamous "no pay" memorandum to all circuit and district court judges and to all "former bankruptcy judges." Foley said that because of the probable unconstitutionality of Congress's attempt to retroactively extend bankruptcy judges' appointments, he could not approve the payment of any "former bankruptcy judge's" salary. He suggested that magistrates handle bankruptcy cases until the courts of appeals could appoint bankruptcy judges as provided in the new act. Foley acted without the benefit of experienced leadership in the Bankruptcy Division of the Administrative Office. Berkeley Wright, chief of the Bankruptcy Division, and his assistant chief, Kent Presson, both retired on December 31, 1983. Wright had been with the Bankruptcy Division since 1964; he became assistant chief in 1964 and chief in 1972. Presson had transferred from the General Accounting Office to the Bankruptcy Division in 1965 and became assistant chief in 1972. Replacements would not be appointed until 1986.[34]

Foley's memorandum produced chaos in the bankruptcy courts; almost no work was accomplished while different courts devised different approaches to continue functioning. The Sixth Circuit reassured bankruptcy judges that they would be paid somehow. On July 15, 1984, Chief Judge Frank Battisti issued General Order No. 84 ordering the bankruptcy judges of the district "to accept the jurisdiction conferred upon them by the Bankruptcy Amendments and Federal Judgeship Act of 1984 and to function thereunder." Bankruptcy judges in the Northern District of Ohio returned to work as though circumstances were normal.

Foley's memorandum received almost universal condemnation. On July 12, 1984, New Jersey congressman Peter W. Rodino, chairman of the House Judiciary Committee, wrote the chief justice of the United States demanding assurances that all documents relating to Foley's "no pay" memorandum would be retained for use in future hearings. Rodino questioned the authority for an administrator working under the supervision of the chief justice to decide that legislation was unconstitutional, a question that undoubtedly would come before the Supreme Court. On July 20, 1984, several bankruptcy judges brought suit against Foley to compel the payment of their salaries, and Foley rescinded his memorandum the same day. Foley retired in 1985. He had been with the Administrative Office since 1964 and director since 1977.

Foley's ill-advised memorandum rallied the district court judges behind the bankruptcy judges against the Administrative Office. Although many questioned whether the 1984 amendments to the Bankruptcy Reform Act of 1978 meaningfully addressed the constitutional issues raised in *Marathon,* the bankruptcy courts operated under the revised regime without serious challenge until 2011, when the Supreme Court's decision in *Stern v. Marshall* revived the issue of the extent of a bankruptcy court's constitutional authority to finally adjudicate certain types of claims. In 2014, the Supreme Court faced the question again in *Executive Benefits Insurance Agency v. Arkinson* and, in a unanimous decision, refused to give a definitive answer.[35]

The Transition to the Bankruptcy Code in the Northern District of Ohio

The Bankruptcy Reform Act of 1978 profoundly diminished district court influence over the bankruptcy courts, and many district court judges found it difficult to accept the change. The tension between the district court and the bankruptcy court during this transition found expression in the evolution of the role of independent clerk of bankruptcy court in the Northern District of Ohio.

Historically, the bankruptcy court in the Northern District of Ohio had always exercised managerial control over its clerks. Before the Salary Act of 1946, bankruptcy referees were self-employed attorneys receiving bankruptcy referrals from the district court, and their clerks were their law office employees. Bankruptcy petitions were filed with the district court clerk, but referees kept the bankruptcy files in their law offices. The Bankruptcy Act required referees to make the records available to the public at all times, and referees certified a record to the district court when necessary. Referees returned the bankruptcy files to the clerk of the district court with a final accounting at the conclusion of a bankruptcy case.

Referees became judicial employees under the Salary Act, but they received a budget from the Administrative Office for the payment of necessary clerical staff whom they hired and supervised. In Cleveland, Referees Carl Friebolin and William Woods brought their law office staff with them when they came under the Salary Act, and record keeping continued much as it had before. Debtors filed petitions with the clerk of district court and referees closed bankruptcy cases through the clerk's office, but while the cases were open the bankruptcy court's clerks continued to maintain bankruptcy files in bankruptcy court office space under the supervision of the bankruptcy judges. The Salary Act did not directly address the question of who really employed the clerical personnel in bankruptcy court, but it established a fee structure to ensure that the bankruptcy courts paid the salaries and expenses of personnel performing necessary bankruptcy court functions out of bankruptcy fees.

Beginning in 1963 in the Northern District of Illinois, numerous district courts moved to consolidate bankruptcy court clerks with the clerk of district court. By 1978, at least fifteen district courts had done so. The consolidations occurred for a variety of reasons, sometimes admirable and sometimes not, but consolidation inevitably caused bankruptcy judges to lose control over the resources and support staff necessary for the efficient administration of the bankruptcy courts. Bankruptcy judges were not consulted about the wisdom of consolidation and felt demeaned by it, but bankruptcy judges had little power to object. They had no independent voice at the Judicial Conference or the Administrative Office, and the district courts that ordered consolidation appointed, or declined to reappoint, the bankruptcy judges.[36]

On January 17, 1974, Chief Judge Frank J. Battisti consolidated the bankruptcy clerks located in Cleveland into the office of the clerk of district court but made an exception for the personal secretaries of the bankruptcy judges. On October 7, 1974, Battisti ordered the bankruptcy clerks located in Akron and Youngstown consolidated into the offices of the clerk of district court located in those cities, again making an exception for the personal secretaries of the bankruptcy judges. Consolidation meant that bankruptcy clerks were hired, fired, managed, and supervised by the clerk of district court rather than the bankruptcy court. As in other matters, the Western Division of the Northern District of Ohio at Toledo remained a separate world, and the bankruptcy clerks in Toledo remained under the supervision of the bankruptcy court.[37]

The clerk of district court always enjoys a close relationship with the district court; the clerk is appointed by the district court and is responsible to it. In 1973, Chief Judge Battisti appointed Mark Schlachet clerk of district court. Schlachet was twenty-seven years old at the time of his appointment and only a few years out of law school. He served as clerk of district court until 1977, when Battisti appointed him bankruptcy judge to fill the vacancy created by Don Miller's retirement at the conclusion of his second six-year term. Rumors circulated that Battisti traded appointments with Judge John M. Manos: if Manos supported Schlachet's promotion from clerk of district court to bankruptcy judge, Battisti would support Manos's choice of James S. Gallas for clerk of district court. Once he was appointed bankruptcy judge, Schlachet hired Battisti's niece, Linda Battisti, as his law clerk.[38]

Mark Schlachet owed his appointment as clerk of court and later as bankruptcy judge to the close personal relationship between Schlachet's father-in-law, Les Brown, and Chief Judge Battisti. Brown owned an unpretentious furniture store on the edge of downtown Cleveland where for many years Battisti maintained a private hideaway in a back room. Brown had an unsavory business history, making him an unusual intimate for Chief Judge Battisti, reputedly the most powerful man in Cleveland. An eccentric self-made man from rough-and-tumble Youngstown, Battisti inspired deep loyalty from his admirers for his courage and social conscience, most famously in his management of the Cleveland school desegregation case, *Reed v. Rhodes*.[39] Even Battisti's critics generally did not question his personal integrity, attributing his dubious associations and apparent favoritism to an authoritarian management style and misplaced loyalty.

Eventually, the close relationship between Battisti and Schlachet, and a series of scandals involving bankruptcy court appointments to people associated with them, raised embarrassing questions. Around March 1982, a federal grand jury opened an investigation into allegations that Battisti and Schlachet ran a patronage ring through the bankruptcy courts, though no charges were brought against either judge. Schlachet resigned his appointment as bankruptcy judge in October 1982, after the circuit court issued a highly critical report threatening disciplinary action against him for misbehavior in connection with appointments in bankruptcy cases. In May 1985, the district court judges of the Northern District of Ohio staged a revolt against Battisti's chief judgeship, voting in favor of changing the court rules to set district court policy by majority vote of all of the judges through four standing committees. Battisti fought unsuccessfully through 1989 to retain his power as chief judge, resigning in January 1990; however, he continued to serve as a district court judge until his death in 1994. Battisti had been chief judge of the district court for the Northern District of Ohio since August 1969.[40]

Battisti attempted to retain control over the clerks of the newly established bankruptcy court by making strategic appointments. The Bankruptcy Reform Act of 1978 de-consolidated the bankruptcy clerks and the clerks of district court, but the new bankruptcy courts with their independent clerks of court would not come into existence until the end of the transition period on March 31, 1984. During the transition, the bankruptcy courts continued under the 1898 Bankruptcy Act but with additional powers conferred by the Bankruptcy Reform Act of 1978. For example, the 1978 Bankruptcy Reform Act specifically gave bankruptcy judges the same authority to hire clerks and employees during the transition period that they would enjoy after March 31, 1984. During the course of the congressional hearings on bankruptcy reform, congressmen heard testimony from bankruptcy judges underscoring the inefficiencies of the consolidated clerks' offices. Favorably impressed by bankruptcy judges, and perceiving district court judges as overly interested in preserving their own power and patronage opportunities, on September 22, 1978, Congress enacted separate legislation to amend the 1898 Bankruptcy Act and ensure that bankruptcy judges secured immediate managerial and financial control over their clerks and employees.[41]

On September 27, 1978, Chief Judge Battisti issued an order implementing the de-consolidation of the clerk of district court and the clerk of bankruptcy court without completely relinquishing his influence. Battisti's order made Schlachet: "the bankruptcy judge to sign appointments of all employees appointed pursuant to Section 62(a) (2) and (3) of the Bankruptcy Act, to serve as the principal payroll certifying officer for such employees, and to execute all administrative duties, responsibilities and functions expressly and impliedly devolving upon him pursuant to the letter and spirit of the Bankruptcy Act."[42] On June 8, 1979, the bankruptcy court announced the selection of Joseph Benik to be clerk of bankruptcy court, and his formal appointment followed on October 1, 1979. Benik had been with the district court clerk's office since 1952, and he was chief deputy clerk of court at the time of his appointment.

Benik and Battisti were close; Battisti had engineered Benik's appointment as chief deputy clerk in April 1970. When the newly appointed clerk of district court, Dominic J. Cimino, fell ill before the appointment of a chief deputy clerk, Battisti unilaterally appointed Benik to fill the position temporarily, incurring the public anger of several of his colleagues for not consulting them. When the district court judges voted on the appointment of the chief deputy clerk a few months later, Benik won only because Battisti engaged in unprecedented voting procedures, simultaneously disallowing a telephone vote against Benik and allowing a Toledo judge to vote for him. By tradition, Toledo judges did not get involved in Eastern Division affairs and in return were granted independence in their own operations. Because Battisti had two votes as chief judge and only two Cleveland district court judges supported Benik's promotion, the four Cleveland judges who opposed it asked the judicial council of the circuit to review the appointment. The judicial council declined to get involved in a purely local dispute.[43]

Despite Chief Judge Battisti's attempts to retain influence over the clerk of bankruptcy court, relations between the bankruptcy court and the district court remained cordial. Akron bankruptcy judge Harold F. White was the senior bankruptcy judge in 1978 and became chief bankruptcy court judge under the 1978 Bankruptcy Reform Act. White, who served as chief bankruptcy judge from November 1978 to October 1984, defended the independence of the bankruptcy court but respected Battisti. Both judges were alumni of Ohio University in Athens, and both judges had served in the Army Corps of Engineers during World War II. On July 10, 1984, the Bankruptcy Amendments and Federal Judgeship Act transferred the authority to certify the need for a clerk from the district court to the bankruptcy court, and on August 22, 1984, Chief Judge White did so, formally reappointing Joseph Benik to the position.[44] Benik proved to be loyal to the bankruptcy court. He took early retirement in 1987 because of ill health and died in 1990.

Director William Foley of the Administrative Office made one final attempt to undermine the independence of the new bankruptcy court. On October 11, 1984, only a few months after his unsuccessful July 11, 1984 "no pay" memorandum declaring the retroactive extension of bankruptcy judges' appointment likely to be unconstitutional, Foley issued a memorandum opining that the language of the legislation that transferred the party responsible for making the certification of need for a bankruptcy clerk did not explicitly identify the clerk of bankruptcy court as the accountable officer for bankruptcy fees and costs; therefore, the clerk of district court rather than the clerk of bankruptcy court remained the accountable officer for maintaining the registry of funds. The comptroller general of the United States disagreed in a decision dated May 22, 1985, ruling that Congress clearly did not intend to remove the clerk of bankruptcy court as the accountable fiscal officer of the bankruptcy court by giving the bankruptcy court the ability to certify the district's need for a clerk of bankruptcy court.[45]

Litigation already pending in Cleveland would conclusively establish the independence of the clerk of bankruptcy court from the district court. In February 1984, bankruptcy clerks in the Northern District of Ohio underwent training for electronic noticing in bankruptcy cases. In the course of practicing with the system, several clerks unintentionally sent offensive messages to debtors and bankruptcy lawyers. In May 1984, the clerk of bankruptcy court, Joseph Benik, with the approval of the bankruptcy court, fired the offending employees. Three employees were offered an appeal to the bankruptcy court; instead, they appealed their dismissal to the district court under a grievance system established for district court employees. On June 18, 1984, Benik filed a motion in district court to dismiss the employees' grievance for lack of jurisdiction, arguing that the district court had no jurisdiction over bankruptcy court personnel matters; his motion was denied.

By the time the district court heard the employees' grievance, President Reagan had signed the Bankruptcy Amendments and Federal Judgeship Act into law, thereby reestablishing the bankruptcy court. The district court ordered the employees of the clerk of bankruptcy court reinstated nonetheless, and Benik appealed. The Sixth Circuit Court of Appeals reversed the order of the district court finding that the 1984 bankruptcy amendments "divested the district court of any supervisory authority it may have had over the hiring and firing of deputy clerks." Benik had requested representation by the US attorney for the Northern District of Ohio but was refused. Former bankruptcy judge Joseph Patchan represented the bankruptcy court in the litigation pro bono.[46]

The appointment of a new director of the Administrative Office in July 1985, L. Ralph Mecham, and the long-deferred appointment of a chief of the Bankruptcy Division, Francis F. Szczebak, helped to mend relationships between the Administrative Office and the bankruptcy judges. Mecham served as director until 2006, and Szczebak served as chief until 2010, bringing much needed continuity to institutions under stress. Most importantly, Mecham and Szczebak appreciated the professionalism of bankruptcy judges and advocated relentlessly for the judges and the staff under their jurisdiction.[47]

Judge Schlachet's resignation in October 1982 opened a vacancy on the bankruptcy court, and on April 1, 1983, the district court appointed Medina attorney Alice M. Batchelder to be the first woman bankruptcy judge in the Northern District of Ohio. A 1971 graduate of the University of Akron Law School, Alice Batchelder practiced law in a small firm with her husband, William G. Batchelder, a rising Republican star in the Ohio legislature. William G. Batchelder graduated from the Ohio State University School of Law in 1967 and won his first election to the Ohio House of Representatives in 1968. He served continuously until term limits forced him to forgo reelection in 1998, achieving the post of speaker pro tempore in his last term. William Batchelder served briefly on the Medina County Court of Common Pleas before his appointment and subsequent election to the Ohio Ninth District Court of Appeals. He returned to the legislature in 2006. In 2010 he became Speaker when Republicans regained majority status.

An early and ardent supporter of President Reagan, Alice M. Batchelder unsuccessfully sought appointment to the district court judgeship created when President Reagan elevated Judge Robert B. Krupansky to the Sixth Circuit Court of Appeals in 1982, but she accepted appointment to the bankruptcy court instead.[48] In February 1985, Judge Batchelder was nominated to a new district court judgeship created by the Bankruptcy

Amendments and Federal Judgeship Act of 1984; the Senate confirmed her on April 3, 1985. In December 1991, she was appointed to the Sixth Circuit Court of Appeals. Judge Batchelder became chief judge of the Sixth Circuit on August 14, 2009.

A second bankruptcy court vacancy during the transition opened in 1983 when Judge Joseph T. Molitoris in Youngstown retired, and the district court in Cleveland nominated Mansfield Republican Vickie L. Jackson in January 1983. Jackson graduated from Indiana University School of Law in 1976 and worked as a staff attorney for the East Ohio Gas Co. before opening her own law practice in Mansfield, where she was the first woman and the first African American to hold the position of service-safety director. She and her physician husband intended to move to Youngstown after her appointment.[49]

During the interim between enactment of the Bankruptcy Reform Act of 1978 and the April 1, 1984, effective date for the new bankruptcy courts, district court nominees for bankruptcy judge received the same merit screening committee review that existing bankruptcy judges received before the automatic extension of their terms. The merit screening committee assembled to review Jackson's appointment consisted of lawyers designated by the Ohio State Bar Association and the Mahoning County Bar Association, both of whom came from Mahoning County. The third member of the merit screening committee was Ernest Gelhorn, dean of the Case Western Reserve School of Law. The merit screening committee found Jackson not qualified because she had no trial experience, thus killing her appointment. Some believed her nomination was a deliberate snub to Chief Judge Battisti as Battisti came from Youngstown and had backed a Mahoning County candidate.[50]

The merit screening committee's rejection of Jackson's nomination set off accusations of racial bias, but the principal objection to her appointment was parochial: she did not come from Youngstown. Cuyahoga County Republican Party chairman Robert E. Hughes called Jackson's rejection "a political lynching" and vowed that President Reagan would appoint her when the new courts came into existence on April 1, 1984. Approximately fifty attorneys had applied for the bankruptcy judge position, including many from Youngstown, and Youngstown congressman Lyle Williams pledged his support to any candidate from his congressional district. Williams dragged two leading candidates to Washington in an attempt to influence President Reagan's choice of nominee: Warren municipal judge Charles A. Young and Youngstown attorney William T. Bodoh.[51]

The merit screening committee insisted that its decision to reject Jackson's nomination was unanimous and made on the merits. Jackson unsuccessfully sought review by a new merit screening committee. The district court unsuccessfully sought circuit judicial council review of the decision of the merit screening committee; however, the circuit judicial council declined on February 20, 1983, stating it had no authority to review the committee's findings. On March 6, 1984, the district court decided not to appoint anyone. Its appointment authority expired April 1, 1984, and Congress had not completed legislation necessary to establish new bankruptcy courts in compliance with the Supreme Court decision in *Marathon*. Under the Bankruptcy Reform Act of 1978, President Reagan would make the appointment, and the Ohio Republican congressional delegation announced that it would back Judge Charles Young for the appointment.[52]

The Bankruptcy Amendments and Federal Judgeship Act, enacted on July 10, 1984, changed the manner in which bankruptcy judges would be appointed; the circuit court of appeals would appoint bankruptcy judges from a short list of candidates selected by the circuit judicial council. All vacancies were to be advertised, and a merit selection panel consisting of local judges and attorneys would evaluate the applications before submitting a list to the judicial council of those it considered most qualified. An Ad Hoc Committee on Appointment of Bankruptcy Judges reviewed the evaluations and made a recommendation to the judicial council, and the judicial council submitted to the circuit court the three candidates it considered best qualified.

On June 10, 1985, the Sixth Circuit Court of Appeals appointed Republican William T. Bodoh bankruptcy judge in Youngstown, the first appointment in the Northern District of Ohio under the new rules. Judge Bodoh had maintained a low profile in the controversy over the Youngstown appointment, but he had support on the circuit court. Born in Newark, Ohio, Bodoh was a self-made man. His father died at age 56, leaving his family dependent on Social Security survivor's benefits, and his mother worked cleaning office buildings. Bodoh received his undergraduate degree from Ohio University in 1961 and his law degree from the Ohio State University College of Law in 1964. After law school, he served as an Ohio assistant attorney general from 1964 to 1967. Bodoh worked as a staff attorney for the East Ohio Gas Co. in Cleveland before entering private practice. He was a partner in the Youngstown law firm Manchester, Bennett, Powers & Ullman at the time of his appointment. Judge Bodoh served in Youngstown until his retirement on January 1, 2004.[53]

Judge Batchelder's appointment to the district court bench in April 1985 created a bankruptcy court vacancy in Cleveland, and the circuit court appointed Republican Randolph Baxter in October 1985. Baxter had been an assistant US attorney since 1978, and, as chief of the Appellate Section at the time of his appointment, he was well known to the circuit court bench. He was the first African American to serve as bankruptcy judge in the Northern District of Ohio.

Born in segregated Columbia, Tennessee, six months after the first race riot following the end of World War II, Baxter was the ninth of eleven children born to a custodian and a domestic worker. He first visited northern Ohio as an undergraduate at the Tuskegee Institute when he played trumpet in the ensemble accompanying the Tuskegee choir on tour.

Baxter returned to northern Ohio to attend the University of Akron School of Law, but his law studies were interrupted by the escalating war in Vietnam. Baxter had joined the Reserve Officer Training Corps at Tuskegee, and at the end of his first year at the Akron School of Law he was commissioned a second lieutenant in the armored division of the Army and sent to Vietnam. Baxter served as a platoon tank commander in Vietnam from July 1969 to July 1970, participating in the invasion of

Cambodia in May 1970. Baxter resigned his commission in July 1971 at the rank of captain and returned to law school. He graduated in 1974.

Baxter held various jobs during and after law school. During law school he worked for the City of Akron Department of Planning and Urban Development. His boss there, James R. Williams, became US attorney for the Northern District of Ohio in 1978, and he hired Baxter as an assistant US attorney in the Civil Division in 1978. In 1982, Baxter was made chief of the Appellate Division of the Office of the United States Attorney, a position he held at the time of his appointment to the bankruptcy court.[54]

The Bankruptcy Amendments and Federal Judgeship Act of 1984 also changed the manner of selecting the chief bankruptcy judge. The Bankruptcy Reform Act of 1978 made the senior bankruptcy judge by tenure chief; the Bankruptcy Amendments of 1984 gave the district court the power to appoint the chief bankruptcy judge. The district court appointed John F. Ray Jr. chief bankruptcy judge on October 4, 1984. Chief Judge Ray died unexpectedly in October 1987, and the district court appointed James H. Williams to succeed him as chief bankruptcy judge.

Chief Judge Ray's death created another vacancy on the bankruptcy court, and the circuit court appointed David P. Snow to fill it. A native of Boston, Massachusetts, Snow graduated from Dartmouth College and Harvard Law School and practiced law with the Cleveland law firm Jones, Day, Reavis & Pogue from 1960 until his appointment. Snow headed Jones Day's Commercial Law Department, which handled the firm's bankruptcy litigation starting in 1980. Snow recruited an associate for his department, Marilyn Shea-Stonum. A graduate of the Case Western Reserve University School of Law, Shea-Stonum had clerked for Chief Judge Battisti.

The Bankruptcy Amendments and Federal Judgeship Act of 1984 extended the term of bankruptcy judges serving at the time of its enactment until four years after their last appointment or October 1, 1986, whichever was later. The act also created a presumption in favor of reappointment of any bankruptcy judge serving at the time of its enactment

Bankruptcy Judges in the Northern Judicial District of Ohio, 1986; front row, left to right: Judge Richard L. Speer, Judge William J. O'Neill, Judge Harold F. White, Judge Walter J. Krasniewski, Judge Randolph Baxter; back row, left to right: Judge James H. Williams, Chief Judge John F. Ray Jr., Judge William T. Bodoh. *Courtesy of the US Bankruptcy Court, Northern District of Ohio*

who desired reappointment, unless the merit screening committee found the judge unqualified. All of the bankruptcy judges serving in the Northern District of Ohio at the time of the legislation's enactment sought initial reappointment. Consequently, no further vacancies occurred until the retirement of Judge Harold F. White in 1994. Marilyn Shea-Stonum, by then a partner in the bankruptcy division at Jones Day, received the appointment to fill Judge White's seat on the bankruptcy court in Akron.

Slowly, the Article III judiciary came to accept bankruptcy judges as judicial officers. In 1990, Chief Judge Gilbert S. Merritt of the Sixth Circuit appointed bankruptcy judge William Bodoh a nonvoting member of the circuit judicial council. By statute, only Article III judges could be voting members of the judicial council. Although the Bankruptcy Reform Act of 1978 required the inclusion of bankruptcy judges at circuit conferences, only the Ninth Circuit had appointed bankruptcy judges to be nonvoting members of the circuit judicial council. Chief Judge Merritt announced that he expected the bankruptcy representative to participate fully and to actively represent the interests of the circuit's bankruptcy judges. Merritt chose Bodoh as the first bankruptcy judge to serve on the council because Bodoh had recently been elected circuit representative to the National Conference of Bankruptcy Judge's board, and the Sixth Circuit representative to the board has continued to serve on the circuit judicial council.[55] Soon, bankruptcy judges would also sit on committees of the Judicial Conference of the United States.

United States Trustee

Reformers initiated the investigations and produced the reports that resulted in enactment of the Bankruptcy Reform Act of 1978 out of concern over the steadily rising rate of consumer bankruptcies and allegations of corruption associated with control of the process by so-called bankruptcy rings. Yet the new Bankruptcy Code did not reduce the number of consumer bankruptcies. As before, consumer bankruptcies closely followed consumer indebtedness. Consumer household indebtedness continued to increase steadily on a per capita basis after enactment of the Bankruptcy Code, and the proportion of household debt attributable to revolving balance credit cards also increased substantially. Consumer bankruptcy filings increased correspondingly.[56]

Most scholars attribute the explosion in the availability of revolving balance credit cards to the 1979 Supreme Court decision in *Marquette National Bank of Minneapolis v. First of Omaha Service Corporation*.[57] Before *Marquette*, many states had usury laws that restricted the rate of interest on consumer credit. With interest rates capped, only very creditworthy customers could get credit cards. In *Marquette*, the Supreme Court ruled that nationally chartered banks in one state could issue credit cards in another state, and the credit card issuer would be governed by the banking laws of the state where it was located rather than the state where the customer resided. In other words, a credit card company located in a state like Nebraska, which had high maximum interest rates on personal loans under state usury laws, could issue a credit card to a resident of Minnesota, which had low maximum interest rates on personal loans under state usury laws, and the Nebraska interest rates would apply. The higher interest rates available under the Nebraska credit cards made it profitable to issue credit cards to persons with imperfect credit, and widespread deregulation of the credit card industry resulted. As credit cards became more widely available, more consumers took on household debt, and per capita bankruptcies increased in direct proportion.

The Bankruptcy Reform Act of 1978 addressed the problem of corruption in consumer bankruptcies through the creation of the Office of the United States Trustee within the Department of Justice. The Bankruptcy Reform Act of 1978 created a pilot program involving eighteen judicial districts. The Northern District of Ohio was not one of the districts included in the pilot program. In October 1986, Congress extended the program to all districts except Alabama and North Carolina and made the program permanent with a two-year transition.[58]

Congress envisioned the US trustee as a representative of the public interest with a duty to ensure the efficiency and integrity of the bankruptcy system, and US trustees assumed administrative duties formerly exercised by bankruptcy judges. Congress believed that US trustees could perform administrative duties more effectively than bankruptcy judges and that bankruptcy judges would benefit from being able to concentrate on judicial duties. Congress also wanted to remove the appearance of impropriety that followed bankruptcy judges' involvement with and appointment of administrative officials like trustees and receivers. The US trustees operated independently of the bankruptcy courts. As salaried employees of the Department of Justice, US trustees were covered by civil service ethics rules that prohibited them from receiving anything of value from any party or engaging in private employment. Aloof from all the interests swirling around a bankruptcy, Congress intended the US trustees to police the public interest in the fair and efficient administration of the bankruptcy laws.

The Office of the United States Trustee consists of twenty-one regions with a regional office headed by a US trustee and an executive office in Washington, DC, headed by a director. Ohio and Michigan constitute Region 9, and the regional headquarters is located in Cleveland. Region 9 has five field offices in major cities, each headed by an assistant US trustee. Cleveland is the only city in the Northern District of Ohio with an office of the US trustee. A large staff of assistant US trustees, trial attorneys, bankruptcy analysts, and support staff fulfills the mission of the US trustee.

Congress intended the Office of the United States Trustee to fill the role that reformers in the 1930s and 1970s had envisioned for an independent bankruptcy agency. Thus, US trustees were charged with the supervision of bankruptcy proceedings to ensure both debtor compliance with the Bankruptcy Code and honest and faithful performance by bankruptcy attorneys and other professionals. In Chapter 11 reorganizations, where the debtor typically remains in possession of the business, US trustees appoint creditor committees, review applications for professional fees and expenses, and monitor reorganization plans and disclosure statements. In consumer bankruptcies, US trustees supervise standing Chapter 13 trustees and the private trustees appointed under Chapter 7.

The appointment of standing Chapter 13 trustees is subject to the approval of the attorney general. The Executive Office of US Trustees announces all openings and publishes uniform application forms. In the Northern District of Ohio, a standing Chapter 13 trustee is appointed in every city where the bankruptcy court sits. Standing Chapter 13 trustees administer Chapter 13 arrangements on behalf of debtors by receiving debtors' payments and distributing them to creditors according to the terms of the confirmed plan. Standing Chapter 13 trustees retain a percentage of all payments distributed to creditors and deposit it to a fund for compensation and reimbursement of expenses; the director of the Executive Office of US Trustees determines the percentage withheld. Standing Chapter 13 trustees receive compensation based on a percentage of funds administered up to a maximum compensation determined by the attorney general. Standing Chapter 13 trustees maintain their own offices; pay their own expenses, including insurance and employee fidelity bonds; and are subject to stringent ethical, auditing, and financial reporting standards. The US trustee appointed long-time Cleveland bankruptcy lawyer Myron E. Wasserman the first standing Chapter 13 trustee in Cleveland under the United States Trustee Program. One of Carl Friebolin's bankruptcy court regulars, Wasserman attended Friebolin College and appeared on Friebolin's list of "Trustees, Receivers, and Distributing Agents" in the 1960s.

Most bankruptcies were Chapter 7 liquidations, and accusations of improper influence by bankruptcy rings occurred most frequently in that context. Many observers credited the trustee program with effectively eliminating bankruptcy rings by appointing and supervising private trustees in Chapter 7 cases.[59] In all likelihood, however, bankruptcy rings disappeared because innovations such as conforming bankruptcy practice to federal civil practice through the Federal Rules of Bankruptcy Procedure, as well as the publication of bankruptcy court decisions in bankruptcy reporters, made it easier for nonspecialized lawyers to practice in the field of consumer bankruptcy.[60]

The US trustee appoints qualifying attorneys to a panel of Chapter 7 trustees. In most cases, the bankruptcy court clerks appoint an interim trustee in Chapter 7 cases from the panel immediately after a petition is filed, usually by simple rotation, and the interim trustee presides over the first meeting of creditors. Although creditors retain theoretical power under the Bankruptcy Code to elect a different trustee, it almost never happens. The Chapter 7 trustee discovers the debtor's nonexempt assets, if any, and converts them to cash for distribution to creditors. The trustee also moves to dismiss any defective bankruptcy petition. As under the 1898 Bankruptcy Act, panel trustees are not government employees and receive as compensation a small fee per case paid out of the debtor's filing fee and a commission based on distributions, if any, to creditors. Panel trustees maintain their own offices and pay their own expenses.

The 1986 enabling legislation left it unclear whether the US trustee was a partisan appointment, but it quickly became one. Nonetheless, the office has functioned without serious allegations of favoritism or impropriety. The US trustee's staff have always been career Department of Justice appointments with civil service protections, and both standing trustees and panel trustees have generally served competently and professionally.

In October 1987, President Reagan's attorney general appointed longtime Cleveland lawyer Conrad J. Morgenstern the first US trustee for Region 9. Morgenstern received his law degree from Western Reserve University in 1949 and was a solo law practitioner specializing in commercial litigation and corporate law. Although Morgenstern occasionally appeared in bankruptcy court, he had minimal knowledge of consumer bankruptcy. Morgenstern reputedly knew a senior appointee in the Reagan Department of Justice. He resigned in 1993 and became an investment banker with Brown, Gibbons, Lang & Co.[61]

President Bill Clinton's attorney general appointed Cleveland lawyer Donald M. Robiner to be US trustee for Region 9. Robiner knew nothing about bankruptcy law, but he knew Ohio senator Howard M. Metzenbaum. Robiner resigned in September 2001 and returned to private practice in Beachwood, Ohio. Robiner died in 2004 at age 68.

After the election of President George W. Bush, Cleveland bankruptcy lawyer Saul Eisen was appointed US trustee for Region 9 in August 2002. One of the regulars in Carl Friebolin's bankruptcy court, Eisen started practicing law in Morris Blane's law firm and attended Friebolin College. Eisen had represented all kinds of parties in all kinds of bankruptcies over the course of his career and had served continuously as a Chapter 7 trustee from 1960 until his appointment as US trustee. Eisen was respected professionally and had served as president of the Cuyahoga County Bar Association, the Bankruptcy Section of the Cleveland Bar Association, and the National Association of Bankruptcy Trustees, which is the professional association for Chapter 7 trustees. A Republican active in Beachwood, Ohio, city politics, Eisen told political associates that he wanted the job of US trustee, and he received the appointment. Eisen retired in September 2007.[62]

In July 2008, President George W. Bush's attorney general, Michael B. Mukasey, promoted career staff attorney Daniel M. McDermott to US trustee for Region 9. McDermott had been with the Office of the US Trustee since inception and had served as an assistant US trustee since 1991. Despite established precedent that US trustee was a partisan appointment, incoming President Barack Obama chose not to disturb McDermott's appointment, and McDermott still serves as US trustee for Region 9.

An Executive Office for US Trustees in Washington, DC, supervises the United States Trustee Program and is responsible for legal guidance and policy direction. The attorney general appointed the first director of the Executive Office, former bankruptcy judge Joseph Patchan, in 1995. Patchan served until 2000. Patchan left his law firm, Baker & Hostetler, in 1991 to serve as assistant general counsel and deputy general counsel of the Resolution Trust Corporation, which was created in 1989 to liquidate insolvent savings and loan associations in the aftermath of the savings and loan crisis between 1986 and 1989.

If the bankruptcy reforms of 1978 did not succeed in reducing the incidence of consumer bankruptcy, the United States Trustees Program greatly increased the ability of the bankruptcy courts to fairly and efficiently administer them. Unlike the earlier reforms of the 1898 Bankruptcy Act, however, no quiet period followed enactment of the Bankruptcy Code as bankruptcy judges and lawyers worked out the practical implications of the new law. Instead, almost immediately, a newly invigorated conservative movement questioned whether the Bankruptcy Code coddled debtors, undermined American values, and threatened American prosperity. Ideological arguments about the meaning of consumer bankruptcy in American society would make renewed demands for bankruptcy reform a partisan political issue into the twenty-first century.

Chapter Seven
Case Studies under Chapter 11

Chapter 11 of the Bankruptcy Code governed all corporate reorganizations formerly governed by Chapter X and Chapter XI of the 1898 Bankruptcy Act as amended by the Chandler Act in 1938. Chapter 11 allowed all corporations the benefit of flexible rules and a presumption in favor of retaining the debtor in possession, which was intended only for small, private corporations under Chapter XI. Chapter 11 gave all corporations the ability to negotiate with all classes of creditors, which was formerly allowed only under Chapter X. Chapter 11 proved extremely useful to large public corporations, which used it to solve new and different kinds of problems in difficult economic times.

Large corporate law firms had largely abandoned corporate reorganizations after enactment of the Chandler Act, which brought corporate reorganizations under the jurisdiction of the bankruptcy court and significantly reduced corporate counsel's attorneys' fees because of the Bankruptcy Act's "principle of economy." The Bankruptcy Code abandoned the principle of economy and adopted in its place a market approach to attorneys' fees, authorizing fees based on the customary attorney's fees for similar services in other fields of law.[1] Corporate reorganization became a profitable practice area, and large corporate law firms found bankruptcy to be an essential component of a full-service corporate law practice. Increasingly, corporate reorganization attorneys used Chapter 11 strategically as part of the restructuring of American industry that occurred in the last third of the twentieth century. This chapter discusses the development of the corporate bankruptcy bar in the Northern District of Ohio.

The movement for bankruptcy reform in the 1960s and 1970s originated with concern over the increase in the rate of consumer bankruptcies and the perception of corruption through domination of the consumer bankruptcy process by so-called "bankruptcy rings." Almost none of the criticism of the bankruptcy process or recommendations for reform involved corporate reorganizations. Nonetheless, the most profound and long-lasting substantive changes in bankruptcy law under the 1978 Bankruptcy Code came from the consolidation of corporate reorganization in Chapter 11.

After the enactment of the Chandler Act of 1938, large public corporations could reorganize under Chapter X of the Bankruptcy Act, whereas small private corporations and unincorporated businesses could enter into arrangements with their unsecured creditors under Chapter XI. In Chapter X reorganizations, the bankruptcy court appointed an independent trustee to operate the business and prepare the reorganization plan. Chapter X directed the trustee to make a thorough investigation into the financial condition of the business and the reasons for the business's financial difficulties. Afterward, the Securities and Exchange Commission (SEC) reviewed the plan, and the bankruptcy court held a hearing to approve it. Chapter XI offered debtors more flexibility by allowing the debtor's management to continue operating the corporation in most circumstances, and the debtor devised the plan of arrangement. Chapter XI arrangements only affected unsecured debt, and the bankruptcy court could approve a plan provided it was also approved by a majority in number and a majority in value of each class of creditors affected by the plan.[2]

The Bankruptcy Code of 1978 combined provisions from Chapter X and Chapter XI into a single Chapter 11, which presumed that the debtor would remain in possession and operate the corporation and gave the debtor in possession the initial exclusive opportunity to propose a plan of reorganization. The bankruptcy court could appoint a trustee if necessary, and the court could appoint an examiner at the request of a creditor or the US trustee if no trustee was appointed.

Originally, Chapter 11 directed the bankruptcy court to appoint an unsecured creditors' committee and other committees of creditors and equity security interests as the court deemed necessary; it also gave the committees broad authority to act in the interests of their constituents. When Congress expanded the United States Trustee Program, the US trustee became responsible for appointing the unsecured creditors' committees and any other committees it found to be necessary. Creditors' committees assumed responsibility for supervising the reorganization process on behalf of the creditors. Creditors' committees could conduct wide-ranging investigations of the debtor in possession; advise the creditors it represents with regard to plans for reorganization; appear and be heard on any issue in the case; and hire professionals, including attorneys, accountants, business consultants, or other agents, as approved by the court.

A Chapter 11 plan of reorganization could impair secured and unsecured claims and could accept or reject executory contracts. A plan could be confirmed even if a class of impaired creditors did not accept the plan if the court found the plan to be "fair and equitable." A secured creditor could have a plan "crammed down" so long as the creditor received the "indubitable equivalent" of the value of its security.[3]

In 1938, then SEC chairman William O. Douglas intended Chapter X as a device to break the elite New York law firms' domination of corporate reorganization through federal court equity receiverships. Chapter X did that, and big corporate law firms disdained bankruptcy practice after enactment of the Chandler Act. By the 1960s, however, clever bankruptcy lawyers at boutique firms discovered that they could avoid the constraints of Chapter X and use Chapter XI in reorganizing middle-sized publicly held corporations. The more sophisticated bankruptcy lawyers formed the nucleus of a new, more dispersed, elite bankruptcy bar.[4]

As the American economy began painful restructuring in the 1970s, a few large corporate law firms began to hire high-quality, high-visibility bankruptcy lawyers away from boutique firms. The combination of years of economic turmoil and the more accommodating reorganization provisions in Chapter 11 made big corporate reorganizations far more useful and far more common. By the middle of the 1980s, all of the big corporate law firms had in-house bankruptcy practices.[5] Eventually, a disproportionate share of the large corporate bankruptcy work migrated to firms located in New York City or Delaware.[6] However, some of the oldest and largest industrial manufacturing companies in the country were still located in northern Ohio, and many of these companies suffered greatly in the volatile economy of the 1970s and 1980s. Consequently, the Northern District of Ohio received some of the important, early Chapter 11 cases.

This chapter describes from different perspectives a few of the influential Chapter 11 bankruptcy reorganizations in the Northern District of Ohio. Some cases illuminate the evolution of the bench and bar in northern Ohio. Some cases are important in the development of bankruptcy law and practice and revelatory of emerging patterns in corporate finance and governance. The cases offer partial explanations for many of the changes in American society during the 1980s and illustrate in painful detail the process of deindustrialization and economic decline in northern Ohio.

Mansfield Tire and Rubber Company

The Cleveland law firm Baker & Hostetler, one of the nation's largest and most respected law firms, established the first big corporate firm bankruptcy section in Cleveland in 1975, when it recruited former bankruptcy judge Joseph ("Jerry") Patchan. Patchan filed the first petition for corporate reorganization under Chapter 11 of the new Bankruptcy Code, *In re Mansfield Tire and Rubber Company,* the instant the bankruptcy clerk's office opened on the morning the Bankruptcy Code of 1978 became effective, October 1, 1979. The case was heard by bankruptcy judge James H. Williams in Canton, Ohio.

Patchan and Williams confronted numerous issues of first impression in the case. For example, Chapter 11 imposed an automatic stay of proceedings involving the debtor with some exceptions. One of the exceptions allowed actions to enforce the police and regulatory powers of a state to continue. Mansfield Tire and Rubber Company (Mansfield) had been self-insured under Ohio's workmen's compensation laws until 1978, when the company began purchasing insurance. Did the Chapter 11 filing stay administrative proceedings to adjudicate Mansfield's self-insured workmen's compensation liability? (No) One of the first responsibilities of the bankruptcy judge was appointment of an unsecured creditors' committee. The unsecured creditors' committee is usually composed of between five and seven of the largest creditors willing to serve, and the Pension Benefit Guaranty Corporation (PBGC) was one of Mansfield's largest creditors. Was it ineligible to serve on the unsecured creditors' committee because it was a governmental unit? (Yes) Mansfield had significantly underfunded its pension liabilities, and therefore owed federal pension excise taxes. Was this liability a tax entitled to priority over general unsecured creditors or was it a penalty entitled to no priority? (The pension excise tax was a tax entitled to priority.)[7]

Mansfield's bankruptcy filing was expected. The old rubber industry centered in Akron had been crushed by the combination of the oil crises, foreign competition, new technology, obsolete facilities, and union troubles. Mansfield fell into default with its lenders in June 1978 and closed its last two manufacturing plants in Ohio in August 1978. One of the tire plants was built in 1912, the year Mansfield commenced business. Mansfield's tire plants in Ohio made old-fashioned bias tires, but Mansfield had built a modern plant in Tupelo, Mississippi, that made both bias and radial tires. Mansfield hoped to sell the Tupelo tire plant and reorganize around its manufactured wood products business in Springfield, Tennessee. The reorganization failed, and Mansfield ceased all tire operations in October 1980. Eventually, Mansfield liquidated all assets through a liquidation trust formed as part of a reorganization plan that was confirmed on December 30, 1985. The plan called for payment in full of administrative expenses and secured claims and anticipated a 33 percent pro rata payment to creditors holding unsecured claims.

White Motor Company

On September 4, 1980, the White Motor Company and five affiliated corporations filed petitions for reorganization under Chapter 11. The White Motor bankruptcy cases included the parent corporation, White Motor Company; its financing subsidiary, White Motor Credit Corporation; Gemini Corporation, a subsidiary that manufactured truck cabs for White Motor and other customers; White Farm Equipment Company; and Canadian subsidiaries White Motor Corporation of Canada, Ltd., and White Motor Credit Corporation of Canada, Ltd. The petitions were jointly administered for procedural purposes only and assigned to bankruptcy judge Mark Schlachet.

G. Christopher Meyer, a young attorney at the venerable Cleveland law firm Squire, Sanders & Dempsey, filed the petition on behalf of the debtors. Squire Sanders had been White Motor Company's corporate counsel for years, but it had no significant experience in representing debtors in bankruptcy at the time White Motor and its affiliates filed their Chapter 11 petitions. Few of Cleveland's corporate law firms had yet acquired any significant bankruptcy experience. To provide the needed expertise, Squire Sanders contacted the leading New York bankruptcy firm of Levin & Weintraub to associate as cocounsel to the debtor in possession. Meyer dubbed the association "the best bankruptcy school in the world," and it helped Meyer became one of Cleveland's leading bankruptcy lawyers.[8]

With approximately $1 billion in unsecured debt, the White Motor case was up to that time the largest and most complex bankruptcy filed under the 1978 Bankruptcy Code.[9] The consolidated enterprise had sales of $1.2 billion in the year preceding the bankruptcy filing and more than ten thousand employees. More than forty thousand entities filed claims in the consolidated cases.[10] The bankruptcy court and bankruptcy counsel found themselves struggling to construct workable procedures out of untested provisions in the new Bankruptcy Code.

Many of Cleveland's corporate bankruptcy lawyers got their start in the White Motor bankruptcy, learning the ropes from nationally prominent New York bankruptcy lawyers involved in the case. Harvey Miller, bankruptcy star at Weil, Gotshal & Manges represented Prudential Insurance Company. Leonard M. Rosen from Wachtell, Lipton, Rosen & Katz represented the John Hancock Mutual Life Insurance Company and the Mutual Life Insurance Company of New York. Joel B. Zweibel from Kramer, Kamin & Frankel represented the New York Life Insurance Company. John Jerome from Milbank, Tweed, Hadley & McCloy represented the Chase Manhattan Bank. Herb Minkel from Fried, Frank, Harris, Shriver & Jacobson represented Bank of America. Richard Lieb from Kronish, Lieb, Shainswit, Weiner & Hellman represented Dana Corporation. Atlanta bankruptcy pioneer Morris Macey from Macey, Zipson, Zusman & Sikes represented an outside lender providing floor-plan financing to White Motor dealers.

Before their involvement with the White Motor bankruptcy case, among Cleveland's next generation of big corporate bankruptcy lawyers, only former bankruptcy judge Joseph Patchan and Edward R. (Ted) Brown had meaningful bankruptcy experience. Patchan led a small bankruptcy division at Baker & Hostetler, and Brown had started doing bankruptcy cases in the early 1970s at Cleveland's Arter & Hadden. In the White Motor bankruptcy, Patchan represented Citibank and the bank creditors group; Brown and New York counsel Shearman & Sterling represented the unsecured creditors' committee.

Other important Cleveland bankruptcy lawyers in the case included Forrest B. Weinberg at Hahn, Loeser & Parks, who represented the creditors' committee in the affiliated White Motor Credit Corporation bankruptcy. Future bankruptcy judge Pat E. Morgenstern-Clarren worked with Weinberg on the White Motor Credit case as a young associate at Hahn Loeser. Weinberg subsequently taught bankruptcy law at Cleveland Marshall College of Law from 1985 until his untimely death in 1988 at age sixty-one. He brought a younger partner into the case, David Heiman. In 1984, David Heiman left Hahn Loeser to found a bankruptcy practice at Cleveland's Jones Day Reavis & Pogue, one of the top corporate law firms in the United States. Heiman was the only Cleveland lawyer mentioned in a 1990 *National Law Journal* article on bankruptcy superstars.[11] Future bankruptcy judge David Snow, then leading the commercial law practice at Jones Day, and his young associate, future bankruptcy judge Marilyn Shea-Stonum, represented creditor Eaton Corporation in the White Motor bankruptcy.

The Cleveland bankruptcy lawyers who appeared in White Motor represented a new generation. The only bankruptcy regulars in the case who carried over from the old days in Carl Friebolin's courtroom were Joseph Patchan and Marvin Sicherman. Sicherman represented creditor Rockwell International Corporation. Soon, bankruptcy practice became an essential function in any corporate law firm, and explosive growth occurred in big law firm bankruptcy departments in the late 1980s. Jones Day, one of the first large law firms to expand nationally, had only two full-time bankruptcy lawyers in 1985; in 1991 it had fifty-five bankruptcy lawyers, eight of them stationed in Cleveland. Baker & Hostetler increased its bankruptcy department from three lawyers in 1988 to twenty in 1991. Squire, Sanders had seventeen bankruptcy lawyers by 1991. Calfee Halter & Griswold employed three lawyers doing only bankruptcy work in 1991.[12]

The White Motor Company was founded by inventor Thomas H. White in Cleveland in 1866 as the White Manufacturing Company and quickly became a major manufacturer of sewing machines. The company soon diversified into bicycles, automatic lathes, and automobiles. It produced the steam-powered White Steamer automobile from 1901 to 1909. In 1906, the White Manufacturing Company split into two companies, the White Sewing Machine Company and the White Motor Company. In 1910, White Motor began manufacturing gasoline-powered trucks. It developed a reputation for quality trucks, and in its East 79th Street plant it made almost all of the trucks used by the United States Army in World War I.

White Motor expanded by acquisition after World War II, purchasing the Oliver Farm Equipment Company in 1960, the Canadian firm Cockshutt Farm Equipment Company of Canada in 1962, and farm equipment manufacturer Minnesota Moline in 1963. In 1969, the three

The White Motor Company complex on St. Clair Avenue, June 27, 1926. *Courtesy of the Western Reserve Historical Society*

firms merged to form White Farm Equipment Company (White Farm). White Motor also purchased the Euclid Road Machinery Company from General Motors in 1968. Euclid manufactured heavy-duty trucks and construction machinery. A disastrous farm economy in the 1970s generated serious losses in White Farm's business. To strengthen the company, White Motor attempted to merge with White Consolidated, the successor to the old sewing machine company. In the 1950s, White Sewing Machine had evolved into a highly leveraged conglomerate. The Department of Justice Antitrust Division and outside investors successfully opposed the merger.

The farm machinery business improved, and in 1973 White Motor formed a wholly owned subsidiary, White Motor Credit Corporation, to facilitate sales through subsidized lending to dealers. White Motor began a historic expansion, but the recession of 1974 left it effectively insolvent and dependent on bank credit. White Consolidated and White Motor attempted to merge again, relying on the "failing business" antitrust exception, but the merger failed. White Motor limped along until the recession of 1980. The farm sector suffered disproportionately in the 1980 recession, and White Motor Credit Corporation found itself financing an insupportable inventory of farm equipment at dealers' showrooms while interest rates skyrocketed. White Farm ceased manufacturing in April 1980. In September 1980, White Motor Credit Corporation's banks refused to extend additional credit, and White Motor and its affiliated corporations filed Chapter 11 petitions for reorganization.

Approximately 250 creditors appeared at the first meeting of creditors, which was held on October 14, 1980, at a major downtown Cleveland hotel. White Motor had closed the East 79th Street plant in June 1980, and many current and retired employees who had worked at the plant appeared at the meeting. The attorney for the creditors' committee chaired the meeting, but bankruptcy judge Mark Schlachet attended it and invited a group of employees to return with him to his courtroom after the meeting concluded. On October 17, Judge Schlachet entered an order appointing an examiner in the case pursuant to Bankruptcy Code Section 1104(b), which authorized the appointment of an examiner at the request of a party in interest when no trustee is appointed. Judge Schlachet's order stated that White Motor employees moved orally for an examiner at the meeting in his courtroom after the first meeting of the creditors.

The appointment of the examiner broke new ground in bankruptcy procedure. The provision entered bankruptcy practice in the 1978 Bankruptcy Code, and no one had any experience with it. Judge Schlachet ordered a wide-ranging investigation into allegations of corporate mismanagement and abuse of the reorganization process to the detriment of the employees. For examiner, Schlachet appointed the law firm of Climaco, Seminatore, Lefkowitz & Kaplan, a politically connected labor law firm with no prior bankruptcy experience. The appointment raised serious ethical questions. Shortly after the firm's appointment, Climaco hired a lawyer who had just passed the bar exam, Gino Battisti, the nephew of chief US district court judge Frank J. Battisti. At a 1981 Christmas party, Gino Battisti bragged to US district court judge Ann Aldrich that he was hired as part of a deal and would receive as compensation 10 percent of the fees paid the Climaco firm for its work on the White Motor examiner engagement.[13]

Climaco, Seminatore, Lefkowitz & Kaplan perceived its role as that of an advocate for White Motor employees and retirees and a counterweight to the big New York and corporate law firms. As a result, many of the creditors' lawyers involved in the White Motor bankruptcy opposed the Climaco firms' participation in the case. They viewed the examination as an expensive witch hunt and were troubled by the close connection between the examiner and Judge Battisti. Many of the corporate lawyers questioned whether the Climaco firm had the necessary expertise to serve as examiner in a complicated case like White Motor.

When Judge Schlachet resigned in October 1982, the White Motor bankruptcy was assigned to bankruptcy judge William O'Neill. He ordered Climaco, Seminatore, Lefkowitz & Kaplan to wind up its examination, and it filed its report on November 2, 1982. As anticipated, the report found that the New York banks had violated their fiduciary duties to White Motor and faced possible equitable subordination of their claims. The report also found that the estate had potential preference recoveries against the banks. The examiner concluded, however, that the debtor's plan for reorganization compromised those potential claims, and, therefore, the debtor in possession had no obligation to pursue the claims. The banks filed a rebuttal. White Motor's new chief executive officer, Wallace B. Askins, found the examiner's report useful in negotiating with the banks, and Judge O'Neill granted the examiner's fee request of $1,125,256 in full.[14]

An initial question in the White Motor bankruptcy concerned the composition of creditor committees. The bankruptcy court consolidated, for procedural purposes only, the bankruptcy cases of six related corporations. White Motor management wanted one consolidated creditors' committee, fearing that a proliferation of creditors' committees would multiply expenses and eat up the time and attention of debtor's management and counsel. Under the Bankruptcy Code, creditors' committees enjoyed extensive investigative powers in order to discharge their responsibility to monitor the reorganization process.

Most of the corporations in the White Motor bankruptcy had both institutional and unsecured debt. White Motor Credit had institutional debt only, however, and White Motor and White Motor Credit owed hundreds of millions of dollars to twenty-one overlapping banks. White Farm had extensive unsecured debt, mostly to trade creditors. Both White Motor and White Farm had unsecured debt to tort victims. The bankruptcy court sent notice of a hearing on the composition of creditors' committees to the largest creditors of each debtor and to any creditor who had requested notice. All of the creditors who responded sought separate committees for each debtor, and the bankruptcy court complied.[15]

On January 8, 1981, the SEC moved for the appointment of an equity security holders committee. Counsel for White Motor and the SEC developed a plan for locating potential members of an equity committee, but after five months only one significant shareholder had been located who was willing to serve on the committee. That shareholder and the only other nonemployee shareholder who agreed to serve on the committee both purchased stock in White Motor after the petition for reorganization had been filed. Four small shareholders applied to be appointed to the committee, all of whom had larger stakes as employee creditors than as shareholders. One of the small shareholders, George Basen, was one of the employees who orally asked Judge Schlachet to appoint the examiner. Basen believed the bankruptcy was the result of corporate mismanagement, and he solicited the participation of the other three small shareholders. Judge Schlachet appointed all six applicants to the equity security holders committee over the objection of the institutional creditors, reasoning that the institutional creditors had not objected to forming an equity security holders' committee in principle, and no one else applied to serve on the committee.[16]

Judge Schlachet appointed a lawyer for the equity security holders committee and granted leave for the committee to participate in a joint investigation with the examiner into antitrust claims. Under the strict application of the absolute priority rules under old Chapter X, equity security holders had no interest in the bankruptcy of an insolvent debtor because they could receive no distribution from the estate. New Chapter 11 loosened the application of priority rules and encouraged bargaining among different interests in the estate in the interest of efficiency. Kenneth Seminatore for the examiner, the SEC, and some bankruptcy lawyers hoped that equity security holders committees would become common and provide important protections for independent small investors in corporate reorganizations. However, the White Motor equity security holders committee proved ineffectual. The joint investigation with the examiner discovered no actionable wrongdoing, and the committee secured no distribution for shareholders.[17]

In December 1980, the bankruptcy court authorized the sale of all of the stock of White Motor's wholly owned subsidiary, White Farm Corporation, to TIC Investment Company, owned by Dallas entrepreneur Stratton J. Georgoulis. The sale occurred under section 363 of the Bankruptcy Code, which authorized the sale of assets "not in the ordinary course of business." The sale also took place before confirmation of a plan of reorganization. TIC Investment Company paid almost no cash consideration for White Farm but promised to expend the necessary tens of millions of dollars to reopen and operate the plants, and it assumed all obligations to White Farm's employees and former employees under the company's employee welfare benefit plan. Most importantly, if TIC continued to operate White Farm for at least three years, the sale would permit White Motor and its affiliates to escape a $250 million potential liability to the PBGC for underfunded pensions.[18] The sale was successful from that perspective. TIC operated White Farm until 1985, when Allied Products Corporation purchased all of White Farm's assets. In 1993, AGCO purchased the White tractor brand from Allied Products.

White Motor continued operating under Chapter 11, but it was losing money. In June 1981, Swedish corporation AB Volvo offered to purchase substantially all of the assets of White Motor and Gemini so long as the sale could be authorized and completed by August 1981. Volvo's purchase would reduce White Motor's manufacturing business to a "pot of cash." No other serious purchaser for White Motor's manufacturing business or assets had come forward. No plan of reorganization had been filed or confirmed. The proposed sale raised the question for the first time whether a Bankruptcy Code section 363 sale of assets not in the ordinary course of business could be used to dispose of substantially all of a debtor's assets without the procedural protections of a confirmed plan of reorganization. After reviewing the legislative history of section 363, Judge Schlachet found that Congress did not intend that substantially all of a debtor's assets be sold through section 363 except in an emergency, but that White Motor would lose significant value if the sale were not consummated, and a plan of reorganization could not be confirmed within the time constraints of the sale agreement.[19]

On August 20, 1981, Judge Schlachet held a hearing on the proposed sale to Volvo and approved it. The sale required the closure of manufacturing facilities and the rejection of union contracts. White Motor terminated employee pension and welfare plans effective November 21, 1981, pursuant to agreement. The PBGC became the trustee for White Motor's pension plans and filed claims for unpaid pension fund contributions and other employer obligations.[20] White Motor also provided health insurance to its employees and retirees through a welfare benefit plan. By agreement, White Motor continued health insurance to its active, laid-off, and retired union and nonunion employees while White Motor negotiated a permanent resolution.

Congress created the PBGC with enactment of the Employee Retirement Income Security Act of 1974 (ERISA),[21] which required corporations to fund defined benefit pension plans and established stringent vesting rules for pensions; however, ERISA allowed unfunded pay-as-you-go employee welfare benefit plans and excluded them from the vesting rules.

Case law left retired employees' entitlement to welfare benefits unclear; each case depended on the terms of the particular agreements and the facts of the case. The Sixth Circuit eventually held that the purchaser of White Farm could terminate its welfare plan for retired nonunion employees under the terms of their welfare plan agreement.[22]

Eventually, Congress passed legislation to protect retiree welfare benefit plans in the case of bankruptcies pending on the date of the initial temporary legislation so long as benefits were still being paid. In 1986, LTV Steel filed a Chapter 11 petition for reorganization in the Southern District of New York and promptly terminated 78,000 former employees' health insurance under welfare benefit plans. In October 1986, Congress responded with temporary legislation to prevent the plan terminations, and in June 1988, Congress passed legislation creating section 1114 of the Bankruptcy Code. Section 1114 requires debtors in Chapter 11 reorganizations to continue a welfare benefit plan until the plan is modified by agreement or by a court order finding that the modification is necessary to permit reorganization and treats all creditors fairly and equitably.[23] Unfortunately, however, section 1114 did not address the fundamental problems underlying welfare plan terminations. Escalating health costs and the absence of an obligation for employers to pre-fund plans made it unlikely that any welfare plan would be adequately funded. The zero-sum nature of bargaining among creditors over inadequate assets in a bankruptcy made it unlikely that any plan for reorganization could be confirmed if it required funding a welfare benefit plan for retirees.[24]

White Motor wanted to protect retired employees, and it had a negotiating partner in the Employees Creditor Committee. In anticipation of the hearing on the section 363 sale of White Motor's manufacturing assets, Judge Schlachet had appointed an Employees Creditor Committee on August 8, 1981. The United Auto Workers served on the committee. Brian Bash, then a young lawyer with Cleveland law firm Kahn, Kleinman, Yanowitz & Arnson, represented the committee. Currently, Bash practices law in the bankruptcy group at Baker & Hostetler. White Motor negotiated with the Employees Creditor Committee for the establishment of a Voluntary Employee Benefits Plan to assume all liability for payment of health and survivor benefits to White Motor retired employees and those employees who were eligible to retire on the previous welfare plan's termination date, November 21, 1981. The Voluntary Employee Benefits Plan qualified under ERISA and Internal Revenue Code section 501(c)(9). The plan was funded through a trust established upon confirmation of White Motor's plan for reorganization on November 18, 1983. White Motor contributed $60 million to the trust and participating employees also contributed monthly. The White Motor Voluntary Employee Benefits Plan has been very satisfactory and has been able to increase benefits over time. It is still in operation and is expected to pay benefits to participants for decades to come.

The White Motor Voluntary Employee Benefits Plan was innovative and unprecedented. Although Internal Revenue Code section 501(c)(9), which gives tax-exempt status to voluntary employee benefit associations, had been in the Internal Revenue Code since 1928, final regulations under the section did not issue until December 1980. Since the 1990s, voluntary employee benefit associations established for the purpose of providing health benefits to retired employees of distressed or bankrupt companies have become more common, the most famous being the voluntary employee benefit associations established in 2007 for retired employees of Ford, General Motors, and Chrysler. The White Motor Voluntary Employee Benefit Plan is the oldest of this type and stands out as an example of best practices in a difficult environment.[25]

White Farm manufactured tractors, corn pickers, and combines, and White Motor manufactured heavy trucks. From time to time, both product lines had been involved in accidents causing serious injury or death. By the time White Motor and White Farm filed their bankruptcy petitions, injured parties had filed numerous product liability cases against the debtors in state and federal courts throughout the United States. Many of the lawsuits involved multiple defendants, and White Motor and White Farm were insured under complicated layers of liability insurance. The petitions for reorganization stayed the product liability lawsuits, but the question remained: how would the product liability claims against the debtors be handled? White Motor would have difficulty formulating a plan for reorganization unless it knew the amount it owed on the product liability claims.

Under the 1898 Bankruptcy Act, tort victims whose claims against a debtor had not been reduced to judgment could not participate in bankruptcy because their claims were contingent and unliquidated. Instead, tort victims could file or continue lawsuits against the debtor despite the bankruptcy, and the bankruptcy did not discharge the claims. The Chandler Act of 1938 allowed contingent and unliquidated debts to participate in bankruptcy, so long as the debt could be liquidated or reasonably estimated without undue delay under the direction of the bankruptcy court. This almost never happened, and case law providing guidance on how to reasonably estimate lawsuits never developed. The Bankruptcy Code of 1978 reversed the policy regarding contingent and unliquidated claims and made all obligations of the debtor provable, without regard for the difficulty involved in liquidating or estimating the claim; however, neither the code nor the Bankruptcy Rules suggested appropriate procedures bankruptcy courts could use in estimating unliquidated claims.[26]

White Motor proposed that the bankruptcy judge appoint a special master to create a program to hear and decide all of the product liability claims, and White Farm filed a companion motion in its bankruptcy case. Because of the sale of White Farm to TIC in December 1980, the White Farm bankruptcy and the White Motor bankruptcy cases continued separately.

On April 11, 1981, the bankruptcy court appointed former Cuyahoga County Common Pleas judge Sam A. Zingale special master for White Farm's product liability program. On June 30, 1981, White Farm filed its Plan of Reorganization. On August 20, 1981, White Farm filed its First Amended Plan of Reorganization, and the disclosure statement for the amended plan included a description of the product liability program, which proposed to attempt to settle as many claims as possible by agreement. Claims that could not be settled by agreement would be referred to the special master for hearing without a jury in accordance with the law of the state where the action had originally been filed. Product liability claims constituted $76 million out of $96.6 million total in the class of non-priority unsecured claims, and more than two-thirds of the class by value and one-half in number voted to confirm the plan. The bankruptcy court confirmed the plan on October 30, 1981, and approved the product liability program included in the plan at a hearing on May 3, 1982. Some product liability plaintiffs objected to the special master's product liability program, but none of them filed an appeal of the order confirming the plan for reorganization or the approval of the product liability program.[27]

A hearing on the product liability problem in White Motor was held on April 22, 1981. The bankruptcy court again appointed Judge Zingale special master, but the bank creditors appealed the appointment of a special master. US district court judge Ann Aldrich denied a motion for a stay, and the special master formulated the product liability program for White Motor on the same terms as the product liability program for White Farm. The bankruptcy court approved the program on July 7, 1982, and the bank creditors appealed. On September 13, 1982, Judge Aldrich stayed the White Motor product liability program pending appeal. Then, on September 20, 1982, the Supreme Court found the jurisdictional provisions in the 1978 Bankruptcy Reform Act unconstitutional in *Northern Pipeline Construction Co. v. Marathon Pipe Line Co.*[28]

Judge Aldrich ruled that *Marathon* meant that the bankruptcy court did not have the power to hear the product liability cases and, therefore, could not delegate that power to a special master. She vacated the appointment of the special master in White Motor.[29] White Motor appealed, and the Sixth Circuit Court of Appeals reversed Judge Aldrich's decision. The court of appeals held that the Supreme Court had ruled that its decision only applied prospectively, and the emergency rule promulgated after *Marathon* automatically referred the case to the bankruptcy court with authority to do all necessary acts to determine the product liability cases, including appoint a special master. The court of appeals also ruled, however, that the district court had the authority to withdraw a bankruptcy referral in whole or in part and to vacate or modify the orders of the bankruptcy court. The court of appeals remanded the case to the district court, advising Judge Aldrich that she had four alternatives: the product liability cases could be heard by the district court, the bankruptcy court, or a magistrate judge sitting as special master, or they could be returned to the courts where they originated.[30]

On June 1, 1983, Judge Aldrich held another hearing on the product liability problem. White Motor sent notice to hundreds of product liability plaintiffs and dozens appeared through counsel. The product liability cases had been stayed since White Motor filed its bankruptcy petitions in September 1980. Judge Aldrich ruled that the special master's determinations of product liability claims made under the product liability program while it lasted and which had not been appealed were valid and could not be attacked. However, product liabilities claims that had not been determined by the special master should be returned to the courts where they originated.

On September 8, 1983, White Motor filed a Second Modified Plan of Reorganization, which set aside a reserve fund for payment of successful product liability plaintiffs. The bankruptcy court confirmed the plan on November 18, 1983. White Motor's reorganization proceeded while the product liability cases were determined in the courts where the cases originated.[31]

On April 1, 1983, Judge Aldrich also vacated the appointment of the special master in the White Farm bankruptcy reorganization and called a hearing on June 29, 1983, to decide what to do with the product liability cases. By that time, all but eighteen of forty-five original claims had already been settled by the special master's product liability program. Most of the product liability plaintiffs who appeared at the hearing preferred to return to the courts where their cases originated, but White Farm and the official creditors' committee strongly argued for the continuation of the special master's product liability program in order to facilitate timely distribution of funds. In White Farm, Judge Aldrich remanded the product liability cases to the bankruptcy court for determination through the special master's product liability program, relying on the success of the plan up to that time and the failure of dissatisfied product liability plaintiffs to object to it in a timely manner.[32]

The White Motor bankruptcy reorganization was deemed a great success. The implementation of innovative procedures secured far more for all stakeholders, including employees, than would have been achieved by liquidation.

White Motor Credit Corporation paid all its creditors in full. White Motor Credit's plan for reorganization contemplated the company's sale, and the bankruptcy court approved the plan in December 1981. Forklift company Clark Equipment bought White Motor Credit Corporation and entered into an agreement with Volvo to finance Volvo White trucks and truck dealers.

White Farm continued in business under new ownership and paid 65 percent of the unsecured non-priority claims, including the product liability settlements under the product liability program. White Motor Canada paid 85 percent of its creditors' claims, and Gemini Corporation paid 70 percent of its creditors' claims.

Creditors of White Motor received approximately 50 percent of their allowed claims. The pieces of White Motor left after the sale of assets to Volvo reorganized as Northeast Ohio Axle Company and White Motor Financial, which owned 26 percent of Northeast Ohio Axle and a $300 million tax loss carry forward from White Motor Corporation. Promising shelter from future corporate income taxes, the tax loss carry forward proved a valuable asset. Northeast Ohio Axle expanded by purchasing niche corporations. The corporations got bigger, and Northeast Ohio Axle changed its name to Neoax. In 1987 Neoax moved to Connecticut.[33]

Terex

Terex Corporation made giant earth-moving equipment. The name, "Terex," was a combination of "terra" (earth) and "rex" (king). In 1973, Terex built the biggest truck in the world, the Terex 33-19 Titan, though Caterpillar eventually built a bigger truck in 1998. Terex began in 1897 in

Cleveland as G. A. Armington & Company, engineers and manufacturers of hoisting equipment. A talented engineer, George Armington had previously chaired the mechanical engineering department at the Case School of Applied Science. G. A. Armington & Company moved to Euclid in 1909 and became the Euclid Crane & Hoist Company. Armington's sons were also imaginative engineers, and Armington and his son Arthur developed early crawler tractors and rotary scrapers. In 1926, they established a Road Machinery Division of Euclid Crane & Hoist, and in 1931, they incorporated the Euclid Road Machinery Company, which developed the first off-road dump trucks. By 1940, Euclid Road Machinery equipment dominated the Pennsylvania anthracite coal mines and the Minnesota iron mines. Euclid Road Machinery expanded to take advantage of the post–World War II construction boom, opening a factory in Scotland and expanding its facilities in Euclid. General Motors Corporation (GM) purchased the corporation in 1953 and operated it as the Euclid Division of GM.[34]

The post–World War II housing boom and interstate highway construction drove demand for Euclid products in the 1950s. GM expanded existing facilities and looked for appropriate locations for new facilities. The rural corridor between Cleveland and Akron anticipated rapid growth from industrial expansion and housing developments. Local governments formed development committees to manage growth and solicit new business development. In 1957, Chrysler opened a new, state-of-the-art stamping plant in Twinsburg, Ohio. In 1957, GM broke ground on a new plant for the Euclid division located on a 423-acre tract outside of Hudson, Ohio. Production commenced at the new plant in 1959. GM's Euclid trucks enjoyed an international reputation for high quality, and the Euclid plant and its big trucks and earth-moving equipment became central to Hudson's economy and identity.[35]

On October 15, 1959, the Department of Justice filed an antitrust suit against GM claiming that GM threatened to monopolize the off-road hauler market. GM entered into a consent decree in 1968 pursuant to which it agreed to sell the Euclid Division's off-road truck lines to White Motor Company and refrain from manufacturing or distributing

The groundbreaking ceremony for the new GM Terex plant in Hudson, Ohio, March 27, 1957; Ohio Governor C. William O'Neill is on the earthmover. *Courtesy of the Hudson Library and Historical Society*

haulers in the US market for four years. GM retained the right to make and market off-road haulers in Canada and Scotland and to make scrapers and loaders in Hudson in an Earthmoving Equipment Division. GM reentered the hauler business in the United States in 1972 as the Terex Division of GM. In addition to the Hudson plant, GM remodeled facilities in Brooklyn, Ohio, for use by Terex, which had other manufacturing facilities in North America, Scotland, and Brazil.[36]

In January 1981, GM sold its Terex Division to German holding company IBH. Upstart Horst-Dieter Esch started IBH in 1975 at age thirty-one. By 1981, IBH consisted of ten corporations primarily engaged in the manufacture of construction equipment. Esch built his empire by purchasing distressed companies at deep discounts, and he had difficulty securing financing from the conservative German banking establishment. In 1980, the small German private bank Schröder, Münchmeyer, Hengst & Company began financing IBH after IBH purchased 50 percent of a failing construction company from it in exchange for stock in IBH. IBH suffered losses as the market for construction equipment declined,

Terex GM 33-19 Titan hauler, October 8, 1974. *Courtesy of the Hudson Library and Historical Society*

and Schröder, Münchmeyer, Hengst collapsed on November 3, 1983. The bank still held an equity interest in IBH, however, and it had lent money to IBH greatly in excess of its legal lending limit under German banking law through its Luxembourg office and off–balance sheet entities. Eventually. Esch and Ferdinand Graf von Galen, Schröder, Münchmeyer, Hengst's head, were convicted of fraud by German courts as a result of their relationship, and both served time in prison.[37]

On November 4, 1983, IBH entered receivership under German law, and Esch instructed Terex and other subsidiaries to commence insolvency proceedings immediately. Terex did its corporate and financial legal work through New York counsel but used Cleveland's Squire, Sanders & Dempsey for legal work in labor and other areas of law. At 7:30 A.M. on November 4, 1983, Terex contacted Cleveland lawyer G.

Christopher Meyer at Squire, Sanders & Dempsey. Terex had an immediate cash problem. Terex's bank, First Milwaukee, had seized all of Terex's cash on deposit as a set-off in connection with an agreement for financing foreign receivables. A Chapter 11 petition needed to be filed immediately to enable Terex to receive the maximum benefit from bankruptcy law provisions regarding set-offs of funds on deposit in the interval before filing a petition. Terex filed a petition for reorganization under Chapter 11 of the Bankruptcy Code in the Northern District of Ohio at 4:47 P.M. that afternoon. The case was assigned to Judge Harold F. White in Akron, Ohio. Future bankruptcy judges David P. Snow and Marilyn Shea-Stonum represented creditors in the Terex bankruptcy.

Terex's bankruptcy stunned the Hudson community. Production was down at the plant, but Terex management had assured Hudson leaders in June 1983 that the plant would stay open. The United States was the single-largest market for construction and mining machinery in the world, and Terex was committed to keeping manufacturing facilities in the country. Terex management and local officials unsuccessfully solicited public funds for Terex's reorganization. Ohio governor Richard F. Celeste and US representative John Seiberling assigned teams to work with the company to no avail. Ultimately, Terex would cease all operations in northern Ohio.[38]

The Terex bankruptcy confirmed a bankrupt company's ability to unilaterally reduce negotiated wages and benefits. Labor relations with Terex under IBH ownership had begun inauspiciously. The union contract with GM expired in January 1981, concurrent with the change in ownership, and the new management demanded immediate wage concessions. Off-road construction equipment sales were down and competition from Japanese manufacturers was intense. Management sought additional concessions in the new union contract under negotiation. Furthermore, Terex's hourly workers considered themselves to be elite workers and were accustomed to considerable shop-floor autonomy. The new management created ill feeling among workers by imposing demeaning work rules, such as dress codes and bathroom passes.[39]

Two years later Terex was losing money, and union workers accepted an additional 3 percent wage cut with their March 1983 contract. After filing its Chapter 11 petition for reorganization in November 1983, however, Terex determined that it needed still more wage concessions. Unable to achieve concessions through negotiation, Terex unilaterally reduced wages by 31 percent to union-represented hourly workers. The United Auto Workers filed an application for payment of the additional wages due under the union contract, but in *NLRB v. Bildisco & Bildisco* the Supreme Court decided the question against the union on February 22, 1984. The court held that labor contracts were executory agreements that a debtor in possession could reject unilaterally if the agreement burdened the estate and the equities favored rejection.[40] In April 1984, Terex also reduced employees' health benefits, and eliminated benefits for laid-off employees. By April 1984, most of Terex's 2,700 workers had been laid off.

GM was Terex's largest unsecured creditor, and many employees hoped GM would take Terex back. IBH still owed GM for Terex's purchase, and GM held a security interest in IBH's Terex stock. Terex also guaranteed IBH's notes to GM and leased its Ohio manufacturing facilities from GM. Worldwide construction activity had slumped, however, and unfavorable currency exchange rates burdened American exporters of manufactured goods.

GM showed no interest in retaking control of Terex but agreed to facilitate Terex's reorganization. IBH had separately incorporated Terex's national operations in Scotland, Brazil, and the United States but had vested all Terex intellectual property in the Scottish subsidiary. GM purchased the Scottish subsidiary, now Terex Equipment Ltd., from the IBH receivership, securing control of Terex's rights in the intellectual property. GM licensed the intellectual property back to Terex, but Terex could not produce trucks as cost effectively as the Scottish subsidiary. Consequently, business consultants recommended that a business partner be located and Terex and Terex Equipment be sold as a package. Terex would finish work in progress, but Terex Equipment would be the principal manufacturing entity of construction machinery under the Terex brand. Terex would continue to distribute and service Terex machinery in North America and Asia.[41]

A plan for reorganization was approved on September 2, 1986. The plan created a New Terex and a Reorganization Trust that held all of the common stock of New Terex. New Terex had agreements with GM and Terex Equipment that would allow a combined Terex and Terex Equipment to be sold to a business partner. Terex agreed to deposit funds aggregating $8 million into the Reorganization Trust to pay unsecured creditors, including Terex employees. GM received special preferred stock in New Terex. GM still owned the land and buildings at the Brooklyn and Hudson plants, and although the Brooklyn plant closed in 1985, GM leased the Hudson property back to New Terex.

In October 1986, Northwest Engineering, Inc., of Green Bay, Wisconsin, purchased Terex and Terex Equipment. Northwest kept its corporate headquarters in Green Bay and moved most manufacturing to Scotland. Terex's distribution warehouse moved to suburban Memphis, Tennessee. On September 30, 1988, the Hudson plant closed; only a skeleton crew of one hundred employees still worked there. The 432-acre site was then sold to a Chantilly, Virginia, real estate developer.[42]

Local development officials were already working on creating an enterprise zone to facilitate the redevelopment of the 432-acre Terex facility in Hudson. In 1982, the Ohio legislature passed legislation enabling the designation of urban enterprise zones designed to encourage urban renewal by allowing cities to offer tax abatements in exchange for economic development in blighted areas. In 1987, the legislature renewed the enterprise zone program and expanded its provisions so that rural counties could also take advantage of it. The program allowed communities to designate an area an enterprise zone if it met certain criteria, including declining population, below-average income, high unemployment, and vacant or undeveloped industrial property. Once an area was designated an enterprise zone, a community could negotiate with businesses considering relocating to the zone for the abatement of up to 75 percent of real and personal property taxes for ten years.

In March 1988, Mark Hansel of the Summit County Development Office explained to the Hudson Area Chamber of Commerce that it was possible to qualify much of the area proposed for the Western Reserve Enterprise Zone, which included the former Terex plant, despite the community's affluence and growing population by careful gerrymandering and averaging in area that recently became part of the Cuyahoga Valley National Recreation Area. Designation of the Western Reserve Enterprise Zone occurred in April 1988. In September 1989, Fabri-Centers, Inc., which owned the popular Jo-Ann Fabric stores, moved its corporate headquarters into the redeveloped former Terex facilities after receiving generous tax abatements.[43]

Revco

In July 1988, Revco D.S., Inc., filed a Chapter 11 petition for reorganization as a result of a leveraged buyout from two years earlier. Revco was the first billion-dollar, complex leveraged buyout to end up in bankruptcy court, and it quickly degenerated into an unseemly brawl. Bankruptcy judge Harold F. White's unpretentious Akron, Ohio, courtroom hosted some of the most important bankruptcy lawyers in the country and changed the course of the law. In many respects, Revco's experience illustrated the rise and fall of the leveraged buyout phenomenon.

In the 1950s, W. Braddock Hickman investigated the rate of return on corporate bonds between 1900 and 1943 for the National Bureau of Economic Research. He found that investing in a diversified portfolio of low-quality high-yield corporate bonds, also known as "junk bonds," produced better yields than investing in a portfolio of investment-grade bonds. T. R. Atkinson confirmed the finding for the years between 1944 and 1965.[44] In the 1970s, brilliant misfit Michael Milken developed a niche clientele based on a junk-bond investment strategy at the Wall Street investment firm of Drexel Burnham Lambert. In 1985, Milken began using his network of junk-bond investors to finance leveraged buyouts, and Drexel became the epicenter of the leveraged buyout frenzy of the late 1980s. Between 1986 and 1988, specialized investment firms put together

232 leveraged buyouts involving at least $100 million each and worth $150 billion in the aggregate. In contrast, only ninety-two deals worth $47 billion in the aggregate were completed between 1980 and 1985.[45] In the 1980s, leveraged buyouts typically involved the purchase of a large manufacturing or retail public corporation by a private corporation formed specifically for that purpose in which the funds used to pay the old corporation's shareholders came from high-yield junk bonds issued by the new private corporation.

The leveraged buyout boom did not last long, and it ended badly for Drexel. The SEC investigated everyone involved. The first indictment of a Drexel insider, Dennis Levine, came down in May 1986, and Levine gave the SEC numerous defendants from various Wall Street investment banking houses. On November 14, 1986, Ivan Boesky was indicted, and he agreed to cooperate with the government. Boesky had been one of Milken's clients since 1983. Now both the SEC and a federal grand jury were investigating Drexel. In 1988, the SEC filed civil charges against Drexel. Threatened with criminal charges under the Racketeer Influenced and Corrupt Organizations Act, Drexel plead nolo contendere to criminal securities charges in December 1988. In March 1989, Milken was indicted on securities charges. In February 1990, Drexel filed bankruptcy under Chapter 11. Under pressure, Milken eventually pled guilty to questionable securities offenses and served two years in prison. He was released in March 1993.

Revco started in 1945 as the Regal Drug Store in Detroit. Future Revco chief executive officer and board chairman Sidney Dworkin started as an accountant in the drug store. Regal Drugs owned a subsidiary, the Registered Vitamin Company, which sold vitamins door-to-door. In 1956, the Registered Vitamin Company became Revco D.S., Inc., and Revco became a pioneering discount drug operation. Revco expanded rapidly. In 1961 it purchased a Cleveland drug store chain. In 1964, Revco went public and moved its headquarters to Cleveland. In 1966, Revco's founder retired, and Sidney Dworkin became Revco's president. Eventually Dworkin's sons also entered Revco's management.

Revco aggressively pursued national expansion. By 1973, Revco ranked second nationally in the number of stores operated and third in sales. Revco continued to expand and moved its headquarters to Twinsburg, Ohio, in 1975. Revco manufactured private-label vitamins and generic drugs for sale in its stores. In 1984, the Food and Drug Administration investigated a Revco product associated with infant deaths, E-Ferrol, and Revco's stock suffered a sharp decline from which it never recovered. Dworkin feared a takeover. Dworkin had become chief executive officer and chairman of the board of directors in 1983, but he and his sons owned little stock. To strengthen his influence on the board of directors, Dworkin engineered the Revco stock-for-stock purchase of Odd Lott Trading Company, a retail closeout chain owned by some friends that Dworkin believed would be his allies on the board. The transaction proved to be a disaster for Dworkin. Within a few months of the transaction, Odd Lott's former owners had accused Dworkin's son of financial impropriety and threatened a takeover. Revco bought out the Odd Lott interest for $98 million in cash and took a $35 million write-off on Odd Lott merchandise. Revco's commercial paper rating was downgraded, and Dworkin was forced to resign as president of Revco.[46]

Dworkin remained chief executive officer and chairman, however, and in September 1985, Dworkin, William B. Edwards, Revco's new president, and Glenn Golenberg, a Cleveland merchant banker, began discussing the possibility of a management leveraged buyout. Golenberg contacted the Wall Street firm Salomon Brothers to arrange the deal, and Salomon brought in Transcontinental Services Group, N.V., a Netherland Antilles corporation. This would be Salomon's first leveraged buyout. In March 1986, an investor group consisting of thirty-eight members of current Revco management (including Dworkin and Edwards) offered to purchase 100 percent of Revco stock for $33 per share in cash and preferred stock in the new company. Salomon contacted Wells Fargo Bank to arrange a syndicate to provide senior financing for the deal. The first attempt at a deal failed. Wells Fargo could not get a syndicate together, and an independent committee formed to advise Revco shareholders on the buyout recommended against accepting the deal. In August 1986, the investor group offered $38.50 per share cash, and this time the independent committee recommended accepting the offer.

The deal closed in December 1986 in a series of transactions that left Anac, a new corporation formed for the specific purpose, owning Revco at a cost of about $1.2 billion in new debt. Transcontinental owned 51.0 percent of Anac's common stock, Revco management owned 28.9 percent, Salomon owned 13.1 percent, Golenberg owned 1.4 percent, and 5.6 percent was offered to the public. Management paid cash for half of the value of its stock and paid for the rest of the stock in notes and old Revco stock. Preferred stock was held by New York Life and Transcontinental, and a small amount was sold to the public. The election of the board of directors was predetermined by a stockholders' agreement that was part of the leveraged buyout, and the board of directors of Anac and Revco after the buyout was the same as the board of directors of Revco before the buyout.[47]

New Revco assumed new debt in the leveraged buyout consisting of $700 million in three series of 13.125 percent to 13.3 percent subordinated bonds with junk ratings, and a $455 million five-year term loan from a syndicate of banks arranged by Wells Fargo and Marine Midland. New Revco also assumed $175 million of old Revco debt. In 1985, Revco had only $48 million long-term debt, but that amount increased to $309 million shortly before the leveraged buyout. Revco paid nearly $80 million in fees in connection with the deal: Salomon received $38.8 million; Wells Fargo received $17 million; Golenberg & Company received $6 million; Goldman Sachs received $4.3 million; Revco's Cleveland corporate law firm, Benesch Friedlander, received $2 million; New York Life received $1.76 million; New York law firm Cleary Gottlieb received $1.6 million; Transcontinental Services Group received $0.6 million; and various other financial service and law firms received smaller sums.[48]

Repayment of new Revco's new debt depended on rosy assumptions about the profitability of Revco's future performance, but Revco's operations fell far short of expectations the autumn before the leveraged buyout closed. On January 2, 1987, four days after the deal closed, Revco's treasurer warned management that Revco's cash flows in the preceding six weeks were $30 million less than expected. Revco had committed to use half of "annual consolidated cash flow" to pay down principal on the bank loans. Revco also committed to sell assets worth $255 million by November 12, 1988, and apply the proceeds to the principal on the bank term loans, but progress on the sales was disappointing. In March 1987, Edwards replaced Dworkin as chief executive officer, and Dworkin received a generous severance package and other benefits. In September 1987, Dworkin agreed to a repurchase of his stock in Revco at the price at which he had invested in the leveraged buyout. Edwards moved from chief executive officer to chief operating officer. Boake Sells, former chief executive officer of Dayton Hudson Corporation, came into Revco as chief executive officer and chairman.

Revco's deteriorating financial condition left it unable to stock stores adequately for the 1987 Christmas season, and Revco suffered poor sales. Salomon stopped pushing Revco junk bonds and proposed a restructuring plan. Revco rejected Salomon's plan and retained Drexel for help in restructuring. Banks began meeting regularly with management and the board. Edwards resigned as chief operating officer in March 1988 and received a generous severance package and other benefits. Revco defaulted on an interest payment on June 16, 1988, and filed a Chapter 11 petition for reorganization in the Northern District of Ohio on July 28, 1988.

The Revco leveraged buyout was the biggest deal of Glenn Golenberg's career. He told three people about the deal before it was publicly announced: his friend Bernard Shavitz, New Jersey businessman Steve Saltzman, and Memphis clothing store owner Van Weinberg. Golenberg did not trade on his information but his friends did, and the SEC charged them with insider trading in May 1989. Weinberg had tipped off four golf buddies: Carl Reiter, Stephen Lightman, Ray Dan, and Lawrence Adler, a broker at E. F. Hutton. They traded on the information and were also charged with insider trading in May 1989. Adler also placed twenty-five clients in Revco common stock and options, but they were not charged with any securities violations. All eight who were charged settled their cases without admitting guilt and paid large fines. Golenberg was not barred from the Revco board of directors but was fined and banned from the securities business for four years. He moved to Los Angeles, California.

Sidney Dworkin told a business partner, Howard Passov, that there might be a Revco leveraged buyout. Passov told his father; his broker, J. Christopher Rodeno; and a business associate, Vincent Giorgi. Rodeno told a client, Marvin Block. Vincent Giorgi told his brother, Carmen Giorgi. Dworkin did not trade on the information and was not charged with any wrongdoing, but the others bought and sold Revco options and stock and were charged with insider trading in July 1989. They settled their cases without admitting guilt and paid fines. Passov went to trial but settled his case before verdict. Shirley Shiffman, an administrative assistant at Golenberg & Company, and her husband, George, were also charged with insider trading. They settled the case without admitting guilt but paid no fines. By the time they settled they were divorced, George Shiffman was in bankruptcy, and Shirley Shiffman had no money.[49]

The Revco bankruptcy was assigned to Judge Harold F. White in Akron, and it overwhelmed the available facilities at the modern Seiberling Federal Courthouse, which had opened in 1975. Beth A. Dick, recently appointed clerk of bankruptcy court in June 1987, scrambled for resources. The clerk's office anticipated hiring two additional staff people and installing two additional computer terminals just to accommodate the Revco workload. Eventually, a room in the courthouse would be set aside to hold Revco's pleadings and transcripts. The Akron clerk's office could only generate 7,500 notices at a time in a case, but for the Revco case it would need to generate notices for forty thousand creditors and twenty-eight thousand employees. Revco retained Baker & Hostetler as bankruptcy counsel, and the law firm provided the bankruptcy clerk with sophisticated computer software to facilitate noticing. Judge White, like all other bankruptcy judges in the district at that time, had a staff of one secretary and one law clerk. Between 1989 and 1991, Judge White's staff doubled. He hired an additional secretary and law clerk to work solely on Revco matters.[50]

The Bankruptcy Reform Act of 1978 had created the United States Trustee Program, and in October 1987, Cleveland lawyer Conrad J. Morgenstern was appointed the first US trustee for the region covering the Northern District of Ohio.[51] On August 9, 1988, Morgenstern presided over the first meeting of Revco's creditors in a rented auditorium at the University of Akron. Revco was a big case, and Morgenstern played an active role in it.

On September 28, 1988, Morgenstern filed a motion to appoint an examiner under Bankruptcy Code section 1104(b)(2) to investigate the Revco leveraged buyout. All parties, including the debtor, opposed the motion as not being in the best interests of the parties. Judge White denied the motion as premature; the trustee could file a motion later in the case if appropriate. Morgenstern appealed, and the district court dismissed the appeal on the grounds that the trustee lacked standing because he had no pecuniary interest in the bankruptcy, and, therefore, he was not "an aggrieved party." The trustee appealed both questions to the Sixth Circuit Court of Appeals, which held that the US trustee, as representative of the public interest, had standing to appeal the bankruptcy court's order. Furthermore, the court of appeals found that appointment of an examiner was mandatory under section 1104(b)(2) on request of the US trustee whenever "the debtor's fixed, liquidated, unsecured debts exceed $5,000,000."[52]

On June 14, 1990, Judge White approved the appointment of Brooklyn Law School professor Barry Lewis Zaretsky as examiner to investigate possible causes of action resulting from Revco's leveraged buyout. The examination focused on this question: Was Revco's leveraged buyout a fraudulent conveyance under state law? The leveraged buyout could not be challenged as a fraudulent conveyance under the Bankruptcy Code because it occurred more than a year before Revco filed its petition for reorganization. Judge White ordered Zaretsky to file a report by July 17, 1990, because the statute of limitations on potential causes of action in

Michigan (a state with a relatively short statute of limitations) expired on July 25, 1990.[53] Zaretsky submitted a preliminary report on July 16, 1990, and a final report on December 27, 1990.

In general, a fraudulent conveyance is a transaction without fair consideration if the transaction leaves the debtor insolvent or with an unreasonably small capital. Zaretsky concluded that Revco did not receive fair consideration for the bank term loans and indentures it entered into in the leveraged buyout because they did not benefit the corporation in any meaningful way. The proceeds merely served to buy out one set of shareholders for the benefit of another set of shareholders. Whether the transaction left Revco insolvent or with inadequate capital remained a contested question, but the examiner found it likely.

Zaretsky recommended against seeking disgorgement of the proceeds of any fraudulent conveyances because of the expense and delay involved. Instead, he favored requiring participants in the fraudulent transactions to fund payments to victims in a consensual plan of reorganization. Zaretsky recommended against filing suit in Michigan by July 25, 1990, but he recommended filing other lawsuits by the end of 1990 to protect other fraudulent conveyance claims and other possible civil actions, unless a consensual plan for reorganization was confirmed earlier.[54] The examiner concluded that fraudulent conveyance claims might also lie against the professionals who received fees in connection with Revco's leveraged buyout and against the shareholders in Anac (the corporation formed to facilitate the leveraged buyout) in connection with the Dworkin and Edwards buyouts.

Revco had not proposed a plan of reorganization in the nearly two years since filing bankruptcy, and its fourth extension of time to file a disclosure statement and plan of reorganization would expire on July 31, 1990. Revco had been unable to devise a consensual plan of reorganization because the parties could not determine their risks or strategies in the uncertain state of the law. Trade creditors had unsecured claims of $195 million that would not be paid in full unless creditors involved in the leveraged buyout gave them something to avoid fraudulent conveyance litigation, and trade creditors were the only creditors not involved in the leveraged buyout. The only creditors lower in priority than trade creditors were shareholders. They controlled the board of directors and wanted something in exchange for their cooperation. The junk bondholders opposed concessions as they would likely come out of their share.

National bankruptcy stars from New York, Los Angeles, and Chicago traveled to Akron to represent parties to the Revco bankruptcy. By July 1990, negotiations were deadlocked and the lawyers had run up fee requests of $35 million, much of it involving legal research into fraudulent conveyance law and leveraged buyouts. In frustration, Judge White put the out-of-town lawyers on an "expense account budget."[55] A year later, Revco's bankruptcy still languished, and Judge White ordered 25 percent of fees withheld until the reorganization was completed.[56]

Revco's examiner's report directly confronted the threshold question: Does fraudulent conveyance doctrine apply in the leveraged buyout context in the absence of extraordinary fraud? Two US circuit courts had ruled on the question: the Third Circuit had ruled that it did, and the Ninth Circuit had ruled that it did not.[57] Those who argued against applying fraudulent conveyance law to leveraged buyouts believed they were beneficial engines for the efficient allocation of capital and should not be discouraged. Besides, fraudulent conveyance law originated in sixteenth-century creditors' remedies, and "a firm that incurs obligations in the course of a buyout does not seem at all like the Elizabethan deadbeat who sells his sheep to his brother for a pittance."[58] The examiner's report and Revco's experience strengthened the argument that fraudulent conveyance law remained relevant in the evolving context of complex financial engineering.

Judge White extended Revco's exclusive time to file a reorganization plan until October 31, 1990. In early October, Revco's creditors presented a plan of reorganization and asked for a hearing on their motion to end Revco's exclusive time to file a reorganization plan. The creditors' plan had the support of Revco's chief executive officer, Boake Sells, but it did not have the support of the corporation's board of directors or the pre–leveraged buyout note holders. As Zaretsky had recommended, the plan offered compensation to trade creditors for forgoing filing fraudulent conveyance lawsuits, other than suits to recover $7 million in severance pay to ousted executives Sidney Dworkin and William Edwards.

Judge White heard the creditors' motion on October 23, 1990. He ended Revco's exclusive time to file a plan after October 31, 1990, and authorized the filing of a fraudulent conveyance lawsuit to protect against the expiration of statutes of limitations. On November 5, 1990, the trade creditors filed a lawsuit against seven thousand participants in the leveraged buyout. On November 15, 1990, the creditors formally presented their plan for reorganization but withdrew it in January 1991 after another slow Christmas season doomed the financial projections on which the plan depended.[59]

On April 2, 1991, bondholders filed a motion asking for liquidation unless Revco confirmed a reorganization plan by August 2, 1991. Judge White denied the motion, with leave to file again, but ordered Revco to file a plan of reorganization by August 2, 1991. On June 8, 1991, Revco finally submitted its first reorganization plan. The plan called for trade creditors and junk bondholders to accept stock and left Revco with $431 million in long-term debt. Litigation would be dismissed against everyone except Salomon Brothers, Sidney Dworkin, and William Edwards.

Negotiations began in earnest. Revco still operated 1,150 stores in ten states with sales of $1.9 billion. In September 1991, Eckerd drug stores submitted a plan to buy Revco. A privately held national chain, Eckerd would go public and use the proceeds of stock sales to pay off some of Revco's debt from the leveraged buyout. Eckerd's plan would not pay the banks in full, and bondholders and trade creditors would receive stock in the new public corporation. In September 1991, the creditors submitted another plan in which they would reduce Revco's debt below Revco's plan and end up owning 100 percent of Revco. Salomon Brothers agreed to pay $9.5 million into the kitty in exchange for dismissing a lawsuit against it. Salomon later upped its ante to $14 million. In October 1991, Revco rejected Eckerd's plan but agreed to withdraw its own reorganization plan in favor of the creditors' plan. Everything fell apart in November 1991. Wells Fargo, the principal bank creditor, sold its debt to an investor group organized by Bear Stearns & Company. No one knew the new creditor's bargaining position. Then Rite Aid submitted a plan to buy Revco in exchange for cash, the assumption of some liabilities, and publicly traded stock.

Judge White scheduled a vote among all the plans for early January 1992. Rite Aid campaigned aggressively for its plan, running advertisements soliciting votes. At the last minute, Rite Aid increased its offer by another $35 million. The creditors' plan was considered most likely to win, but junk bondholders did not support it. Eckerd won the vote. Negotiations continued because Judge White still had to decide whether to confirm the plan. The infamous "grave dancer" Sam Zell's Chicago-based Zell/Chillmark Fund, L.P. had been advising the official creditors' committee since 1988.[60] On January 8, 1992, Zell/Chillmark offered to give the creditors' plan an additional $160 million in exchange for stock and two seats on the board of directors.

Rite Aid bowed out; the deal had become too expensive. Creditors united behind the Eckerd plan. Revco submitted a competing plan. Eckerd's plan became a political issue; it would close Revco's Twinsburg headquarters and cost Ohio seven hundred jobs. Employees organized a letter-writing campaign urging Judge White not to confirm Eckerd's plan, and Ohio senator Metzenbaum joined the campaign. On January 30, 1992, Zell/Chillmark sweetened Revco's offer with an additional $250 million in cash for junk bondholders and creditors in exchange for increased stock ownership. Zell/Chillmark also promised to pay $7.5 million toward Eckerd's expenses in unsuccessfully pursuing Revco. The expense money would come from stock subscription rights offered to junk bondholders and trade creditors. If they didn't buy enough rights to make the promised payment to Eckerd, Zell/Chillmark promised to make up the difference in exchange for more stock.[61]

On February 14, 1992, Eckerd dropped its offer to buy Revco. Judge White confirmed Revco's plan of reorganization on March 12, 1992. In

April 1992, Dworkin and Edwards dropped their appeal of the order of confirmation in exchange for dismissal of the fraudulent conveyance lawsuit the trade creditors brought against them. The trade creditors agreed to drop their lawsuit in exchange for $3.5 million; Revco raised the $3.5 million by selling additional stock to junk bondholders and Zell/Chillmark. Salomon paid $30 million to settle a class-action lawsuit brought by creditors claiming failure of due diligence in the leveraged buyout. Revco's prospects looked promising. According to Wall Street rumors, Goldman Sachs & Company was buying lots of Revco junk bonds. Zell fired Revco's chief executive officer and president, Boake Sells, in June 1992. In 1997, drug store chain CVS bought Revco and closed the Twinsburg headquarters.

Revco was the first of the large, complex leveraged buyouts to result in bankruptcy, but it wasn't the last. The junk bond market collapsed after 1989, and the number of deals declined by 90 percent between 1988 and 1991. By 1991, more than 30 percent of the large leveraged buyouts had defaulted, and most of them resulted in Chapter 11 reorganization. The total value of leveraged buyout deals increased modestly in the late 1990s before crashing again, and it would not reach the 1989 peak until 2003. Leveraged buyouts returned stronger than ever after 2001, rebranded as private equity deals. The new private equity deals substituted securitized collateralized debt obligations for the junk bonds of the 1980s deals.[62]

Edgell Communications

The Chapter 11 reorganization of Edgell Communications presented an attractive alternative model for the reorganization of a failed leveraged buyout. Edgell reorganized through a "pre-packaged" bankruptcy and spent only thirty-one days under the supervision of the bankruptcy court. A pre-packaged bankruptcy occurs when the creditors have accepted a plan for reorganization in a binding vote before the debtor files the petition. Edgell was the first and may be the only true pre-packaged bankruptcy reorganization filed under the Bankruptcy Code in the Northern District of Ohio.

Robert L. Edgell had been in the publishing business his whole life. Just out of college, he founded his own trade company, Edgell & Associates, in 1945. In 1961 he founded Ojibway Press to acquire Davidson Press, a trade magazine publisher located in Duluth, Minnesota. In 1968, Harcourt, Brace & World (later known as Harcourt Brace Jovanovich) purchased Ojibway Press and several other smaller publishing houses to form a trade magazine division. In 1970, Harcourt Brace hired Robert Edgell to head the division. The division prospered and diversified into school supplies and trade shows.[63]

In 1987, Harcourt Brace successfully beat back a hostile takeover attempt by British publisher Robert Maxwell, and it sold assets, including the trade magazine division, to pay for the takeover defense. A management investor group headed by Edgell purchased the division in a leveraged buyout arranged by Kidder, Peabody & Company. A new holding company, New Century Communications, bought the division for $334 million. The investor group named the new corporation Edgell Communications and headquartered it in Middleburg Heights, Ohio.

New Century Communications financed the leveraged buyout with secured loans from General Electric Credit Corporation, Kidder's parent corporation; $100 million in debentures sold by Kidder in a private placement; $45 million in preferred stock and warrants; and common stock purchased by Kidder and affiliated corporations, Robert Edgell, and other management investors. GE Credit's secured loans consisted of a senior term loan in the amount of $110 million, a $75 million secured fixed rate note, and a $20 million revolving loan for working capital. Kidder received fees in excess of $15 million plus expenses in connection with the transaction: a $3.341 million advisory fee, a $3.4 million commitment fee and a $1.6 million funding fee in connection with bridge financing, $1.4 million for locating permanent funding, $3.5 million for the sale of debentures, and $1.8 million for the sale of preferred stock. GE Credit received $2.245 million in loan commitment fees.

The timing of Edgell Communications' leveraged buyout could not have been worse. The deal was struck in September 1987, at the end of a historic bull run on Wall Street, and the parties consummated the deal in December 1987, becoming the first leveraged buyout consummated after the stock market crash on October 19, 1987. Edgell Communications had been growing rapidly before the leveraged buyout and announced its intention to expand aggressively. The interest payments Edgell Communications committed to in the leveraged buyout depended on the continuation of rapid growth. Unfortunately for Edgell, advertising revenues fell and a period of cautious growth followed. Edgell Communications had insufficient cash flow to service its debt.[64]

Robert Edgell resigned as chief executive officer in March 1990, and retired Dun & Bradstreet executive Richard Swank replaced him in May 1990. On January 1, 1991, Robert Edgell leapt to his death from the balcony of his seventh-floor Florida condominium. New Century Communications stopped paying interest on its junk bonds, and Water Street Corporate Recovery Fund, a Goldman, Sachs & Company vulture capital venture, went on an Edgell Communications junk bond buying spree, eventually securing 54 percent of the junk bonds. In June 1990, the long, drawn-out process of negotiating the restructuring of Edgell Communications' debt began. By the spring of 1991, Goldman Sachs had made a deal with Kidder and GE Credit to exchange securities for securities, but minority junk bondholders held out. Bankruptcy could force the minority junk bondholders to accept a deal.

Meanwhile, Edgell Communications' management, working with its counsel Skadden, Arps, Slate, Meagher & Flom, contacted Christopher Meyer at the Cleveland law firm of Squire, Sanders & Dempsey to act as bankruptcy counsel for a potential filing. A solid company with too much debt, Edgell seemed a good candidate for successful reorganization, but rumors of impending bankruptcy would devastate Edgell's revenue streams and doom the company. The leveraged buyout left Edgell with a concentration of interested creditors who could confidentially negotiate a pre-packaged bankruptcy. Only impaired creditors could vote on a plan for reorganization, and Edgell's largest creditors, Kidder and GE Credit, had possible civil liability for breach of fiduciary duty, fraudulent conveyance, or equitable subordination because of their involvement in Edgell's leveraged buyout. A proposed plan for reorganization would have to give Kidder and GE Credit releases from any potential liability.

Edgell Communications' attorneys reached agreement after months of negotiation with the principal creditors for a joint plan of reorganization of both Edgell Communications and New Century Communications. GE Credit was the only secured creditor, and it would amend and restate its loan agreements. The secured loans were not impaired. Trade creditors would be paid in full and were also not impaired, thereby avoiding the need to solicit agreement from a continuously changing body of creditors. Debentures were impaired: GE Credit held about 22.6 percent of the debentures, Goldman's Water Street held 54 percent, and unrelated creditors held the rest. The debenture holders other than GE Credit received pro rata shares in a beneficial trust that held all of the common stock of Edgell and its holding company. GE Credit received less than a pro rata interest in the beneficial trust in order to provide something to equity interests to encourage acceptance of the plan. Equity interests were impaired, but they would likely receive nothing except through the plan. Preferred stockholders received a 5 percent interest in the beneficial trust and an option to purchase an additional 3.5 percent. Common stockholders received a 3.5 percent interest in the beneficial trust and an option to purchase an additional 1.5 percent. Warrants attributable to Kidder's stock ownership were redistributed among the other stockholders. Preferred and common shareholders received additional warrants for executing releases of Kidder, GE Credit, and affiliated corporations.[65]

Edgell Communications sent creditors a confidential reorganization memorandum on November 20, 1991. All impaired classes of creditors approved the plan of reorganization before the due date of December 23, 1991. On December 23, 1991, Edgell Communications and New Century Communications filed for Chapter 11 reorganization in the Northern District of Ohio and were assigned to Judge William O'Neill. Instead of the usual negative news reports of a bankruptcy filing, the companies were able to describe the filings as the means to implement a restructuring already successfully approved by creditors. On January 23, 1992, thirty-one days later, the corporations emerged from Chapter 11 under the name Advanstar. At the time, the case was the fastest Chapter 11 reorganization in US history. Advanstar continues in operation today; it has since been sold twice to private equity groups and is currently headquartered in Boston.

LTV: Liquidate, Terminate, Vacate[66]

The steel industry in northeastern Ohio underwent a major restructuring in the 1980s that continued into the new millennium. Steel companies that had been mainstays of communities for decades failed. New corporations reshuffled the bits and pieces of the old steel companies to form new, often transitory, entities. Although some new mills were built, and other plants were modernized and kept in use, each reconfiguration resulted in closed mills, fewer workers in the remaining mills, and reduced pay and benefits for the remaining workers and retirees. Northern Ohio's old steel companies carried huge unfunded liabilities for worker pension and benefit plans that could be eliminated through Chapter 11 reorganization, and most of the steel industry's restructuring occurred through bankruptcy courts for that reason. The damage to the economy and the community from the steel crisis was cumulative, but the LTV Corporation's bankruptcy filed in Youngstown in 2000 dealt the final blow. It is impossible to tell the story of the LTV bankruptcy in isolation from the broader collapse of the steel industry in northern Ohio. Moreover, at one time or another, most of the steel companies that passed through northern Ohio's bankruptcy courts had been a part of LTV Steel.

The fundamental problem the steel industry faced was that steel was a global commodity, and the steel market had suffered from persistent overcapacity since the 1960s. With razor-thin profit margins under the best conditions, any disruption in global demand for steel threw the industry into crisis. Furthermore, dramatic growth in steel productivity resulted in a steady decline in steel employment worldwide, and governments everywhere felt intense political pressure to support their domestic steel industries. Steel employment worldwide decreased from 2,357,000 steelworkers in 1974, to 1,388,000 in 1990 and 836,000 in 1999. In the United States, steel employment decreased from 521,000 in 1974 to 204,000 in 1990 and 153,000 in 1999. Foreign steel-producing countries' attempts to protect their domestic producers resulted in dumping and export subsidies. American steel makers could not make steel at the prices set by foreign imports.[67]

Founded by Oklahoma native James J. Ling, LTV began in 1947 as Ling Electrical Construction and Engineering Company. LTV entered the steel business in 1968 when it purchased a controlling interest in Jones & Laughlin Steel Company. In 1975, LTV acquired 100 percent of the stock of Jones & Laughlin and made it a wholly owned subsidiary. In 1978, LTV merged with Lykes Corporation, the parent corporation of Youngstown Sheet & Tube Company, and Youngstown Sheet & Tube also became a wholly owned subsidiary of LTV. In 1981, LTV merged Youngstown Sheet & Tube into Jones & Laughlin Steel, creating the nation's third-largest steel company. In 1983, LTV acquired Republic Steel Corporation, and in 1984 Republic Steel merged with Jones & Laughlin to form LTV Steel Company, a subsidiary of LTV.

In approving the merger of Jones & Laughlin and Republic Steel, the Department of Justice required LTV to divest itself of a stainless steel mill in Massillon, Ohio, because of antitrust concerns. That mill became Enduro Stainless, Inc. In November 1985, the Enduro plant shut down over a dispute with its supplier, LTV, and in February 1986, Enduro Stainless filed a Chapter 11 petition for reorganization in Canton, Ohio. The two largest creditors in the bankruptcy were LTV and the United Auto Workers. In April 1986, bankruptcy judge James H. Williams appointed a trustee to manage the company, and Enduro's chief executive officer, Robert E. Newstat, and chief counsel, Lawrence D. Greenberg, resigned. Subsequently, they were convicted of bankruptcy fraud. In October 1986, Mercury Stainless Corp. of Wheeling, Illinois, bought Enduro and restarted the mill. The mill passed through several other owners before closing in 2002.[68]

In July 1986, precipitated by punishing foreign competition and a $2 billion underfunded pension plan liability, LTV Steel filed its first Chapter 11 petition for reorganization in the Southern District of New York. The Bankruptcy Code gave corporations some flexibility in selecting a venue for filing petitions. Taking advantage of that flexibility, LTV filed in New York based on the location of a relatively minor affiliate, Chateaugay Corporation, which became the name of the resulting reorganization case.

Shortly after LTV Steel filed its petition, the PBGC terminated LTV's pension plans. Assuming LTV's pension fund liability tripled the PBGC's accumulated deficit, raising it to nearly $4 billion. Because the PBGC did not pay all benefits promised under LTV's negotiated pension plans, the United Steelworkers sued LTV Steel in the Southern District of New York to compel LTV to make up the lost benefits. LTV settled the lawsuit, agreeing to create a "follow-on" pension plan to make employees' benefits equal to the promised benefits under the terminated plans.[69]

The PBGC objected to bankruptcy court approval of a new union agreement that included the follow-on plan, arguing that the follow-on plan was abusive. The PBGC feared that allowing follow-on plans after involuntary terminations in bankruptcy would enable corporations with significantly underfunded pension plans to shift the cost of the plans without any opposition from unions because the employees would receive the same benefits in either case. The PBGC lost its argument before the bankruptcy court, and in August 1987, it began the administrative process to restore LTV's terminated pension plans. The PBGC ordered the plans restored in September 1987, and when LTV did not comply, the PBGC brought an enforcement action against LTV in the district court. The PBGC lost in the district court and the court of appeals, but prevailed in the United States Supreme Court. LTV exited Chapter 11 in June 1993 with more than $3 billion in underfunded pension liabilities, but the PBGC gave LTV a thirty-year payment plan.[70]

LTV emerged from Chapter 11 protection with a smaller and more focused organization; it had sold or closed more than thirty plants and had reduced its workforce by 30,000 employees. In June 1988, LTV sold its

Warren steel works to Warren Consolidated Industries Inc., a division of private equity investor Ira Rennert's holding company, Renco Group. An integrated mill previously owned by Republic Steel, Warren Consolidated changed its name to WCI in 1991. LTV also decided to divest its special bar steel division, also previously part of Republic Steel. In November 1989, the steelworkers union purchased the special bar steel division in a leveraged buyout using an employee stock option plan. The new corporation was called Republic Engineered Steels, Inc. Both Republic Engineered Steels and WCI would land in Chapter 11 reorganization again.[71]

The New York investment banking firm of Lazard Frères & Company put the Republic Engineered Steels deal together. This was not the first leveraged buyout of a steel company that Lazard Frères had arranged using an employee stock option plan for the purpose. In 1984, Lazard Frères had organized Weirton Steel's leveraged buyout by an employee stock option plan. Weirton began making steel on the West Virginia side of the Ohio River in 1909. In 1929, it merged with Great Lakes Steel Corporation and the Hanna Iron Ore Company to create National Steel. Weirton continued to operate independently as a division of National Steel. In 1982, National Steel wanted to divest itself of Weirton, but the unfunded pension liabilities made sale to an outside investor unlikely. Facing the certainty of the mill closing, the nonunion steelworkers in the company town bought the mill with borrowed money through an employee stock option plan. At the time, Weirton was the largest employee-owned company in the nation.[72] Weirton sold shares of stock to the public in 1989 and remained profitable into the 1990s, but Weirton succumbed to the steel glut of the late 1990s. The recession that began in 2001 sealed Weirton's fate. Weirton filed a Chapter 11 petition for reorganization in the Northern District of West Virginia in 2003, and the PBGC took over its pension plans.

In order to buy Republic Engineered Steels, the employee stock option plan borrowed $70 million from LTV and $190 million from banks. Employees invested $4,000 cash each for a total of $20 million, and LTV funded the employee cash contributions with severance payments. The financial press praised Republic Engineered Steels' leveraged buyout as a bold experiment in attempting to create a new cooperative corporate culture. Republic Engineered Steels reported losses for several years while experiencing a significant positive cash flow because of special tax accounting rules available to stock option plans. This enabled the company to pay off its debt, modernize facilities, and expand with pretax money.[73] Republic Engineered Steels went public in 1995, and the employee stock option plan tax benefits ended in 1997. In September 1998, the private equity firms Blackstone Management Associates and Veritas Capital Management purchased Republic Engineered Steels in another leveraged buyout. Republic Engineered Steels merged into another bar steel company Blackstone owned, Bar Technologies International, to create Republic Technologies International. The merged company would become the nation's largest high-quality special bar steel producer, but it carried $1.7 billion in debt.

Blackstone bought Republic Technologies just before special bar steel prices collapsed. The global steel market is highly competitive and volatile. The special bar steel market suffered from overcapacity throughout the 1980s, and many mills closed. However, special bar steel was essential for automobile production. The sport-utility vehicle boom in the 1990s increased demand for special bar steel, and closed special bar steel mills reopened. In the summer of 1997, the currency markets in several rapidly industrializing Asian nations crashed, and a recession in those countries followed, depressing steel demand. With local steel demand low, the "Asian tigers" pushed cheap exports to America to keep their steel mills open. A glut in the American steel market depressed domestic steel prices again.

Except for steel, the American economy expanded in the late 1990s, fueled by a bubble in technology stocks and Internet start-ups. The dot-com bubble burst in the spring of 2000 with a precipitous stock market crash. Economic activity slowed rapidly; steel capacity utilization fell from 91 percent in May 2000 to 64 percent in December 2000. The economy entered recession in March 2001, and Republic Technologies filed a Chapter 11 petition for reorganization in Akron in April 2001. Between December 1997 and April 2001, nineteen American steel companies filed Chapter 11 petitions for reorganization in bankruptcy court.[74] The economy deteriorated further after September 11, 2001. The economy stopped shrinking in November 2001, but economic recovery was slow and weak.

Copperweld Steel, located in Warren, Ohio, competed with Republic Engineered Steels in the special bar steel market. Copperweld Steel began as a division of Pittsburgh-based Copperweld Corporation, which began in 1915 as a manufacturer of bonded bimetallic wire for conductive use, like telephone lines. In 1939, Copperweld built a new mill in Warren, Ohio, to make high-quality special bar steel. The Warren plant was very profitable until the early 1980s, and in January 1987, Copperweld Corporation spun the struggling Warren special bar steel plant off as Copperweld Steel, a wholly owned subsidiary of CSC Industries. Daido Steel of Japan invested heavily in CSC and acquired a majority interest.

Copperweld Steel continued to lose money. As the Japanese asset bubble unwound in 1990 and 1991, Daido stopped supporting Copperweld Steel financially. Copperweld Steel failed to meet minimum payments for its pension plans in July 1993, and both CSC and Copperweld Steel filed Chapter 11 petitions for reorganization in Youngstown on November 23, 1993. The PBGC assumed responsibility for Copperweld Steel's employee pension plans in December 1994. In October 1995, Reserve Group, an Akron-based private investment company, purchased Copperweld Steel through a parent corporation, CSC Ltd.

In 1998, Copperweld Steel completed an expensive modernization just as steel prices collapsed again. CSC filed another Chapter 11 petition in Youngstown on January 12, 2001. In February 2001, the bankruptcy converted to a Chapter 7 liquidation. The steel mill closed on April 13, 2001. In August 2001, a Pittsburgh buyout firm, Renaissance Partners, investigated the possibility of restarting the Copperweld Steel plant, but investors abandoned the project after the September 11, 2001, terrorist attacks. CSC had been the fourth-largest employer in Trumbull, Mahoning, and

Columbiana counties, but most of the plant was sold at an auction in October 2001.[75]

The bankruptcy court in Youngstown, Ohio became a center for steel company bankruptcies. Wheeling-Pittsburgh filed its second bankruptcy in Youngstown in November 2000, and LTV Steel filed its second bankruptcy there in December 2000. Wheeling-Pittsburgh was headquartered in Pittsburgh, and in 1985, it filed its first bankruptcy petition there. LTV Steel was headquartered in Cleveland, where most of its facilities were located. Both corporations had subsidiaries near Youngstown, and by filing those petitions in Youngstown first, subsequent petitions of related corporations would be consolidated and heard in Youngstown.

Judge William T. Bodoh presided in bankruptcy court in Youngstown. LTV claimed to file in Youngstown because Judge Bodoh had experience with steel cases. Labor supporters suggested that steel companies filed petitions in Youngstown because Judge Bodoh was unsympathetic to unions. Bodoh had been a management-side labor lawyer in private practice, and he had a lot of experience negotiating labor contracts for steel companies. He described himself as an "economic high priest . . . People come to me and they confess their financial sins and I give them absolution."[76]

Judge Bodoh also had experience with very big bankruptcies. One of the biggest, Phar-Mor, was filed in Youngstown in August 1992, after auditors Coopers & Lybrand disclosed that founder and president Michael I. (Mickey) Monus, chief financial officer Patrick B. Finn, and other executives had embezzled at least $350 million over several years. Later, the total loss would be valued at $1.1 billion. Monus, a hero in Youngstown, had founded the World Basketball League, and some of the embezzled funds went to support the league. He had started Phar-Mor in 1982 with one store and had grown it to more than 300 stores by 1992. He headquartered Phar-Mor in decaying downtown Youngstown, bringing badly needed business back to the struggling city in the grim days following the steel mill closings of the 1980s. Phar-Mor fired Monus and Finn and sued Coopers & Lybrand for failing to detect the fraud earlier.[77]

The Phar-Mor case did not end well. A much smaller drug store chain emerged from bankruptcy under new management in 1995 but did not survive. Phar-Mor filed a second petition for reorganization in September 2001 that ended in liquidation. In 2002, a joint venture headed by Pittsburgh-based grocery store chain Giant Eagle, an early investor in Phar-Mor, purchased the assets at auction. Finn pled guilty to fraud and embezzlement charges and testified against Monus at his trials. Monus's first trial ended in a hung jury but his second trial ended in conviction. Monus was also prosecuted for bribing a juror at his first trial, and that trial ended in acquittal. Both Finn and Monus served substantial jail time.

In November 2000, Wheeling-Pittsburgh filed its second bankruptcy in Youngstown because Judge Bodoh was there. Wheeling-Pittsburgh emerged from bankruptcy in August 2003 by securing a $250 million government loan guaranty made available through the Emergency Steel Loan Guarantee Act of 1999. The US senator from West Virginia, Robert Byrd, was instrumental in securing Wheeling-Pittsburgh's loan guarantee. West Virginia's other US senator, Jay Rockefeller; West Virginia governor Bob Wise; and Ohio governor Robert Taft also advocated for Wheeling-Pittsburgh's loan guarantee.[78]

LTV Steel ran out of cash in December 2000 when the Chase Manhattan Bank refused additional financing. LTV's chief executive officer, William H. Bricker, sent a letter to seventy-five state, local, and national political leaders begging them to pressure Chase to make new loans to LTV because 18,000 LTV employees would lose their jobs if LTV shut down.[79] No deal was made, and on December 29, 2000, the LTV Corporation, LTV Steel, and LTV's subsidiary, Copperweld Corporation, filed Chapter 11 petitions for reorganization in Youngstown, Ohio. LTV had purchased Pittsburgh-based Copperweld Corporation in 1999. Copperweld Corporation had been Copperweld Steel's parent corporation from 1939 to 1987 when Copperweld Corporation spun off Copperweld Steel as a separate company. The bankruptcy court jointly administered all the cases.

LTV Steel needed to secure immediate control over its working capital or it would have to close down all operations. Consequently, LTV

Steel filed a motion for an interim order permitting LTV to use cash collateral, which Chase and British financial institution Abbey National Treasury Services, PLC, claimed to own pursuant to a structured finance agreement. The cash collateral consisted of the proceeds from accounts receivable and inventory pledged to secure loans to LTV Steel. Chase and Abbey National claimed that the finance agreement constituted a true sale, and therefore, the cash collateral was not part of LTV's estate in bankruptcy. LTV argued that the agreement was in fact a secured loan and subject to the ordinary Chapter 11 rules governing secured loans. In that case, the collateral was protected by the automatic stay. Although the Bankruptcy Code exempted certain kinds of financial securities from the automatic stay in bankruptcy, the status under the Bankruptcy Code of the kind of structured finance agreement at stake in LTV was untested and uncertain.[80]

LTV entered into the first structured finance agreement at issue in October 1994. The banks believed they got "bankruptcy isolated" collateral, that is, collateral that would not be part of LTV's estate if it filed bankruptcy, and LTV got cheaper access to credit. To facilitate the transaction, LTV created a wholly owned subsidiary, LTV Sales Finance Company, and LTV purported to sell all of its accounts receivable to LTV Sales on an ongoing basis for $270 million. LTV Sales borrowed $270 million from Abbey National and gave a security interest in the accounts receivable acquired from LTV Steel as collateral for the loan. Chase served as Abbey National's agent in the transaction. LTV Steel entered into a second, similar transaction with Chase in 1998. LTV created a wholly owned subsidiary, LTV Steel Products, LLC, and purported to sell all of its interest in inventory to Steel Products on an ongoing basis for $30 million. Steel Products borrowed $30 million from Chase, posting the inventory as collateral for the loan.

Judge Bodoh heard LTV's motion for an interim order to use cash collateral on December 29, 2000, as part of the first-day hearings. Three buses carried about 150 steelworkers from Cleveland to Youngstown to demonstrate on behalf of LTV. Politicians accompanied the demonstrators, including Congress members Dennis Kucinich and Stephanie Tubbs Jones, six Cleveland City Council members, and representatives of Cleveland mayor Michael R. White. Chase reached a compromise with LTV: It would not object to LTV's use of cash collateral and, in return, would receive regular ongoing interest payments and priority in the bankruptcy for the indebtedness. Judge Bodoh entered the agreed interim order, finding that Chase and Abbey National's interest in the collateral was adequately protected and that the order was in the best interests of the estate and creditors. LTV continued to operate for the time being.

Abbey National did not appear at the hearing and objected to the order on the basis that LTV did not own the collateral and the bankruptcy court lacked jurisdiction over it. On February 5, 2001, Judge Bodoh heard and denied Abbey National's motion for modification of the interim order, finding that the bankruptcy court had jurisdiction over the collateral under the broad definition of property of the estate in bankruptcy under the Bankruptcy Code. Under the Bankruptcy Code, an estate in bankruptcy includes "all legal or equitable interests of the debtor in property as of the commencement of the case," and Judge Bodoh ruled: "To suggest that Debtor lacks some ownership interest in products that it creates with its own labor, as well as the proceeds to be derived from that labor, is difficult." Furthermore, bankruptcy is a proceeding in equity, and Judge Bodoh found that the equities favored LTV: "Allowing Abbey National to modify the order would allow Abbey National to enforce its state law rights as a secured lender to look to the collateral in satisfaction of this debt. This circumstance would put an immediate end to Debtor's business, would put thousands of people out of work, would deprive 100,000 retirees of medical benefits, and would have more far reaching economic effects on the geographic areas where Debtor does business."[81] Chase and Abbey National reached agreement with LTV over debtor in possession financing, obviating any further litigation.

Judge Bodoh's decision was the first and for a long time the only published decision to question whether structured finance agreements using special-purpose entities may be challenged in bankruptcy court as not true sales but secured loans. It caused considerable consternation on Wall Street.[82] Companies had used special-purpose entities in structured finance agreements since at least the 1980s, but their status as true sales was rarely litigated. Financial institutions unsuccessfully sought to include provisions protecting special-purpose entities with the expansion of special treatment for derivatives enacted in the Bankruptcy Abuse and Consumer Protection Act of 2005. Over the same period, several states, including Ohio and Delaware, passed laws seeking to prevent the recharacterization of sales of property to a special-purpose entity as a secured loan. State laws do not necessarily bind bankruptcy courts, but structured finance arrangements were not challenged. Consequently, the use of special-purpose entities in structured finance agreements dramatically increased based on the unwarranted assumption of "bankruptcy isolation." After the 2008 financial crisis, challenges occurred more frequently and sometimes succeeded.[83]

LTV Steel and its supporters hoped for a successful reorganization, but LTV did not secure an emergency steel loan guarantee, and negotiations with the steelworkers' union stalled. In June 2001, General Motors, LTV Steel's largest customer, announced that it would not renew its contract at year end. LTV finally reached an agreement with the steelworkers in August 2001, but the terrorist attacks on September 11, 2001, would change the situation. The economy was still in recession, and business conditions entered a freefall. Steel demand declined further. Bethlehem Steel filed a Chapter 11 petition for reorganization in bankruptcy on October 15, 2001, in the Southern District of New York. Bethlehem Steel had historically been the second largest steel company in the United States behind only US Steel and was number eight on the original Fortune 500 in the 1950s. (US Steel was number two.)[84]

In November 2001, LTV Steel gave up and sought authorization from the bankruptcy court to shut down. Judge Bodoh commenced hearings on December 4, 2001, on LTV's petition to shut down and auction off all of its integrated steel plants. The hearings continued for three days. Workers and retirees came from Cleveland to Youngstown by the busload

JOURNEY INTO JUDAISM
Effects of the Holocaust on a family, **E1**

SANTIAGO WARRANT
Browns tight end cited in marijuana case, **D1**

CAVS	84
NETS	96

CLEVELAND.COM
Plain Dealer news online

THE PLAIN DEALER

METROPOLITAN 35¢

SATURDAY, DECEMBER 8, 2001

'They're walking around with a shopping cart full of termination notices'

LTV SHUTDOWN BEGINS

Blast furnace first to go

JENNIFER SCOTT CIMPERMAN
Plain Dealer Reporter

LTV Corp. will stop making steel within 48 hours.

A U.S. Bankruptcy Court judge granted the Cleveland steel maker permission to do so at about 4 p.m. yesterday. By then, it was no surprise to workers.

"They're walking around with a shopping cart full of termination notices, one of those big pushcarts," said a salaried worker who didn't want to use his name. "It's like being in a morgue."

To many Clevelanders, LTV's smokestacks were part industrial icon, part eyesore. But to thousands of LTV workers, the maze of ductwork, railroad tracks and corrugated buildings along the east bank of the Cuyahoga River was a second home, albeit a sweaty, backbreaking one.

For decades the mill churned out steel for electric generators, station wagons, refrigerators.

SEE LTV | A8

JOHN KUNTZ | THE PLAIN DEALER

EDITORIAL: Life after LTV. **B8**
AID CALL: Protect steel, ITC urges. **C1**
TOMORROW: How an LTV minimill failed. And, a look at Nucor Corp., an LTV competitor that makes money.

'Where do I go from here?'

SANDRA LIVINGSTON
Plain Dealer Reporter

Reality began setting in for Jim Matt after Thanksgiving as his LTV Corp. maintenance crew shrank and he was left to take a solitary lunch in the shanty.

Headaches, once rare, had become frequent.

He and co-workers had taken their spouses on group cruises and a trip to Walt Disney World. Now his work family was breaking up.

"I sit there and wonder, where do I go from here," Matt said Tuesday as the first day of court hearings on the company's fate ended.

"It's similar to going to a morgue to identify a body and you hope it's not a loved one," he said. "I hope the corporation stays afloat."

Yesterday, the bad news became official.

A judge approved a plan that allows the company to stop making steel and sends thousands off the job.

SEE WORKERS | A9

Taliban give up

Kandahar in chaos; Omar's escape angers White House

KIM MURPHY
AND JOHN HENDREN
Los Angeles Times

QUETTA, PAKISTAN — Taliban soldiers fled the southern Afghan city of Kandahar yesterday as the formal ground war against the fundamentalist regime drew to an end.

But the surrender left what had been the last Taliban stronghold in chaos and the whereabouts of

STALLED: Anti-Taliban

are no longer a part of Afghanistan."

Yet Bush administration officials who had repeatedly voiced their insistence to Karzai that Omar be "brought to justice" voiced anger that the surrender of the Taliban's birthplace occurred without his capture.

Pentagon and White House officials said that they believed the one-eyed Taliban chief remained in Kandahar but that they could not be certain.

An intelligence source said the

Front page of the Cleveland Plain Dealer, December 8, 2001. *Courtesy of the Cleveland Plain Dealer*

to demonstrate outside the courthouse, chanting, "Let's make steel." At its peak, LTV had employed 15,000 steelworkers in Cleveland, and 3,000 steelworkers still worked in LTV mills there. Politicians scrambled to put together a rescue program. Cleveland mayor-elect Jane Campbell and Congress members Dennis Kucinich, Stephanie Tubbs Jones, and Steve LaTourette all made a pilgrimage to Youngstown. Creditors, banks, and steelworkers negotiated a compromise: LTV could close the mills and sell its steel assets, but the mills would stay on hot idle a little while longer to give the steelworkers additional time to find a buyer. The mills closed on December 8, 2001. In March 2002, the PBGC took over LTV's pension plans covering approximately 82,000 workers and retirees. The financial impact on Cuyahoga County would be devastating.[85]

The auction of LTV's assets occurred on February 27, 2002. New York investment banker W. L. Ross won the auction. He formed International Steel Group and reopened many of the facilities, including LTV's East Side plant in Cleveland. Ross assumed environmental responsibilities and recognized the union. The new steel company produced half the steel that LTV had produced before its reorganization and employed half of LTV's previous workforce, but it made steel in northern Ohio. In December 2002, LTV sold its tubular steel business and continued to seek a buyer for Copperweld Corporation, which LTV had purchased in a highly leveraged transaction. Despite an extensive search, no buyers materialized that were willing to pay more than Copperweld Corporation owed for debtor-in-possession financing. In November 2003, a reorganized Copperweld Corporation emerged from Chapter 11, owned by its debtor-in-possession lenders. The PBGC terminated old Copperweld Corporation's pension plans. In 2005, a Canadian firm, Dofasco, purchased most of Copperweld Corporation assets and kept the tubular products and automotive divisions. The bimetallic division was sold to its management, and in September 2007, a Chinese firm, Fushi International, purchased Copperweld Bimetallics, LLC, and changed its name to Fushi Copperweld.

Meanwhile, Republic Technologies had filed a Chapter 11 petition for reorganization on April 2, 2001, in Akron, before Judge Marilyn Shea-Stonum. The PBGC terminated Republic Technologies' pension plans in June 2002. In July 2002, private equity investors KPS Special Situations Fund and Hunt Investment Group purchased six Republic Technologies plants and formed a new company, Republic Engineered

Products. Republic Engineered Products suffered from deferred maintenance issues under the previous ownership, and it never recovered from unanticipated damage resulting from the East Coast power blackout in August 2003. In October 2003, Republic Engineered Products was back in Chapter 11 before Judge Shea-Stonum. Republic Engineered Products was the forty-first American steel company to file Chapter 11 since December 1997, half of which had gone out of business.[86] In December 2003, private equity investor Perry Strategic Capital bought Republic Engineered Products in an asset auction. In July 2005, Mexican corporation Industrias CH, S.A. de C.V. purchased Republic Engineered Products from Perry, and Republic became a wholly owned subsidiary of Industrias CH's Grupo Simec. It remains North America's leading producer of special bar steel.

The American steel industry was in chaos. In December 2001, US Steel argued that the solution was a US government–facilitated consolidation of American steel firms, preferably by merger with US Steel. Recently divested of its earlier acquisition of Marathon Oil, US Steel suggested that the US government pick up the legacy costs of merger candidates, financing them with tariffs on imported steel. The US government had no interest in US Steel's grandiose plans, however, and free traders and new entrants to the steel industry also objected. But consolidation of the American steel industry proceeded nonetheless, led by new entrants and foreign steel companies.[87]

Investor Wilbur L. Ross created ISG from the remnants of LTV Steel in February 2002. ISG purchased Bethlehem Steel out of bankruptcy in April 2003. When ISG purchased Weirton out of bankruptcy in February 2004, it surpassed US Steel as the largest unionized integrated steel company in the United States. In April 2005, Netherlands-based Mittal Steel merged with ISG to form the world's largest steel company. In 2006, Mittal merged with Luxembourg-based Acelor Steel, then the world's second-largest steel company. Both Mittal and Acelor were new entrants to the steel industry. Indian billionaire Lakshimi N. Mittal founded Mittal

Steel in 1989 and grew the company by acquisition and consolidation. Three older steel companies merged in February 2002 to form Acelor.

Renco purchased WCI in 1988 out of LTV's first Chapter 11. In September 2003, WCI filed a Chapter 11 petition in Youngstown before Judge Bodoh. On December 31, 2003, Bodoh resigned and joined the Columbus, Ohio, law firm of Frost Brown Todd LLC, and the case was reassigned to Judge Shea-Stonum. The WCI case became a battle between Renco and the distressed purchasers of WCI bonds. Initially, the steelworkers' union backed Renco. WCI, supported by Renco, and the bondholders each filed competing plans for reorganization, but Judge Shea-Stonum refused to confirm either plan. Subsequently, the union decided to support the bondholders' plan and Renco's plan evaporated. WCI emerged from Chapter 11 in March 2006 owned by the bondholders, but Renco remained liable for the old pension plan. The Russian steel company OAO Severstal purchased WCI in July 2008. Severstal expanded internationally by aggressively purchasing steel companies. In May 2008, Severstal purchased Bethlehem Steel's old mill at Sparrow's Point, Maryland, from Mittal and sold it to Renco in March 2011. Severstal acquired Wheeling-Pittsburgh when it purchased the private equity firm Esmark in August 2008. Former US Steel executive James P. Bouchard founded Esmark in 2003. Esmark began buying steel distribution centers and acquired Wheeling-Pittsburgh Steel in a proxy fight in 2007.

The industrial landscape of northern Ohio had changed almost beyond recognition in the thirty years after passage of the Bankruptcy Code in 1978. Many factors contributed to the failures of nearly all of the region's old industrial institutions, but it is unquestionable that the availability of Chapter 11 reorganization profoundly shaped the process. Old entrenched management gave way to new private equity and foreign interests, but the losers usually received generous severance packages. Big corporate law firm lawyers, investment bankers, and financial engineers discovered an unimaginably lucrative income stream in implementing the transactions. Workers in the old industrial industries, however, ended up with broken union agreements, lost or diminished pension and welfare benefits, and fewer jobs at lower wages. Communities were left with abandoned factories, environmental clean-ups, and a declining tax base.

In enacting Chapter 11, Congress specifically aspired to protect ongoing businesses for the benefit of workers and communities. The extent to which Chapter 11 achieved this objective remains a contested question.

Chapter Eight
The Political Economy of Bankruptcy

The Bankruptcy Reform Act of 1978 marked the end of an era. From enactment of the Bankruptcy Act of 1898 until 1978, bankruptcy policy carried almost no partisan political baggage. Before the Bankruptcy Act of 1898, bankruptcy had been highly partisan, a contentious proxy for regional, economic, and ideological interests throughout the nineteenth century. The controversy surrounding bankruptcy vanished with passage of the act, however, and by the 1920s, bankruptcy professionals had formed nonpartisan professional associations where a nonpartisan policy community reached consensus about technical changes to bankruptcy law and practice through deliberative processes. Classic organizations of this type included the National Conference of Bankruptcy Judges and the National Bankruptcy Conference. Both of these organizations had been instrumental in the bankruptcy reform movements that culminated in the Chandler Act in 1938 and the Bankruptcy Reform Act of 1978, the only major reforms made to the Bankruptcy Act before 1978. After 1978, however, bankruptcy policy devolved into a partisan political wedge issue, and the bankruptcy policy community found its voice drowned out by special-interest lobbyists and corporate propaganda campaigns. This chapter describes the successful political campaign waged by the consumer credit industry through partisan politics to reform consumer bankruptcy.

This chapter also describes the institutional changes in the bankruptcy court of the Northern District of Ohio during this same period.

Although bankruptcy policy making became partisan, bankruptcy institutions professionalized, and partisan politics almost disappeared from the selection of bankruptcy judges. The Bankruptcy Amendments and Federal Judgeship Act of 1984, the act that resolved the jurisdictional problem revealed in 1982 in *Northern Pipeline Construction Co. v. Marathon Pipe Line Co.*, changed the way bankruptcy judges were selected.[1] Before 1984, district court judges made bankruptcy judge appointments that were profoundly influenced by local partisan patronage networks. Indeed, bankruptcy appointments in the Northern District of Ohio had been made principally for partisan patronage reasons since at least the Bankruptcy Act of 1867. After the bankruptcy amendments of 1984, however, the circuit courts appointed bankruptcy judges after formal screening by committees composed of big firm lawyers, bar association leaders, judges, and academics. As a result, bankruptcy judge appointments became less influenced by partisan politics and more influenced by the candidates' status within the organized legal profession. Also, as the bankruptcy court became more independent of the district court and partisan politics, it became more closely integrated into the centralized administrative agencies of the organized judiciary.

Although the professionalization of the bankruptcy court after 1984 seemed to promise a nonpartisan technocratic meritocracy, Supreme Court decisions in 2011 and 2014 have left the future development of the bankruptcy court uncertain.[2] In 2011, the Supreme Court held in *Stern v. Marshall* that Congress cannot withdraw the power of Article III judges to decide matters that would traditionally constitute a suit at common law, thus limiting the ability of bankruptcy judges to decide certain kinds of claims. Two important questions emerged as a result of this decision. The first question was whether a bankruptcy court possessed statutory authority to submit proposed findings of fact and conclusions of law on matters identified by the bankruptcy statute as "core" but that it lacked constitutional authority to adjudicate through entry of a final order. Core proceedings are matters that involve substantive bankruptcy rights or that only arise in the bankruptcy context. "Non-core" proceedings are actions that do not arise due to the filing of a bankruptcy but that may affect or be affected by the bankruptcy. The other question, which created a split in circuit court decisions, was whether a party could consent to a bankruptcy judge entering a final order on a matter that, absent such consent, would require final disposition by a federal district court judge.

In 2014, the court answered the first question in *Executive Benefits Insurance Agency v. Arkinson,* holding that the statute creating the constitutional issue also contains a curing mechanism that allows "Stern Claims" (claims identified in the statute as core claims but that the Constitution prohibits bankruptcy courts from finally adjudicating) to be ruled upon by a bankruptcy court through proposed findings of fact and conclusions of law, subject to *de novo* review by the district court. However, the court declined to answer the second, bigger question, leaving the circuit split unresolved.

Consumer Bankruptcy in the Northern District of Ohio

The Bankruptcy Reform Act of 1978 left public opinion about consumer bankruptcy unsettled and politically volatile. Consumer bankruptcy had increased dramatically since the 1960s, alarming many in the bankruptcy policy community as well as the consumer credit industry. Since the 1920s, many had argued that consumer debtors should be required to pay some of their debts as a condition of discharge, and the Chandler Act of 1938 introduced Chapter XIII wage-earner plans as a way for consumer debtors to voluntarily make partial payment to their creditors. In the Bankruptcy Code of 1978, the bankruptcy policy community addressed the failure of a significant number of consumer debtors to use Chapter 13 by making Chapter 13 easier for debtors to use and more beneficial to them, especially if they had debts secured by property that they wished to retain. The consumer credit industry opposed this approach and advocated instead for means testing consumer debtors to make Chapter 13 mandatory except when the bankruptcy judge found hardship. Consumer credit industry lobbyists continued unrelentingly to push their agenda until they finally succeeded with the enactment of the Bankruptcy Abuse Prevention and Consumer Protection Act of 2005.[3]

Between 1920 and 1984, the number of consumer bankruptcies followed the amount of real consumer credit in a stable relationship with infrequent minor variations. In general, between 1920 and 1984, the total number of consumer bankruptcies, the number of consumer bankruptcies as a percent of the population, and the proportion of consumer bankruptcies to total bankruptcies increased in direct relationship to the increase in consumer credit. Between 1920 and 1984, the number of consumer bankruptcies per $1 billion in constant dollars of consumer credit (the consumer bankruptcy multiplier) averaged 1,735. After 1985, however, the rate of consumer bankruptcies in relation to the amount of consumer credit began to accelerate. By 1997, the consumer bankruptcy multiplier had increased to 2,009.[4]

Different explanations for the increase in the number of consumer bankruptcies suggested different policy responses. The consumer credit industry argued that the increase was the result of moral laxness caused by the ease with which consumers could file bankruptcy and the lack of any stigma associated with it. Consumer bankruptcy reformers had been making the same claim since the 1920s. The proposed policy solution to this explanation for the rise in consumer bankruptcy, restricting consumer debtors' access to Chapter 7 bankruptcy, gained favor among conservative politicians and the public in the 1980s.

Another possible explanation for the increase in consumer bankruptcies argued that changes in the credit industry itself had produced changes in the composition of the households receiving consumer credit. As a result, households with lower annual incomes received an increasingly larger share of consumer credit, and those households were more likely to end up in bankruptcy than households with higher annual incomes.[5] The policy solution suggested by this explanation, limiting the provision of consumer credit to low-income households, did not receive support from either consumer advocates or the consumer credit industry. Consequently, this explanation argued in effect for tolerating a high rate of consumer bankruptcy as a cost of business in the consumer credit industry.

Big differences existed among states in the per capita incidence of consumer bankruptcy cases and in the distribution of the cases between Chapter 7 and Chapter 13, which were determined by both state law and demographic criteria. In general, states with high non-homestead exemptions tended to have more Chapter 7 bankruptcies per capita, whereas states with high income amounts exempt from garnishment tended to have fewer Chapter 7 bankruptcies per capita. High rates of unemployment and divorce also correlated with more per capita Chapter 7 bankruptcies. States with higher homestead exemptions tended to have fewer Chapter 13 cases, whereas high divorce rates correlated with more Chapter 13 cases. Higher educational attainment also correlated with fewer Chapter 13 cases, and the higher the state's educational level, the more likely it was that a consumer bankruptcy in that state would be filed under Chapter 7 rather than Chapter 13.[6]

The Northern District of Ohio had always been one of the busiest bankruptcy districts in the nation, but the total number of bankruptcy cases per capita filed in the Northern District of Ohio did not significantly deviate from the national per capita filing rate between 1984 and 2000. After 2001, however, the total number of bankruptcy cases filed in the Northern District of Ohio increased dramatically over the number of bankruptcy cases filed in the nation as a whole on a per capita basis. (See Figure 8.1.) The excess consisted almost entirely of consumer Chapter 7 bankruptcies. Northern District of Ohio debtors filed significantly fewer Chapter 13 wage-earner plans on a per capita basis than the nation as a whole between 1984 and 2004. (See Figures 8.2 and 8.3.)

Most commentators attribute the 2005 spike in consumer bankruptcies to the acceleration of bankruptcies that otherwise would have been filed in 2006 to avoid the more restrictive rules under Bankruptcy Abuse Prevention and Consumer Protection Act of 2005. That legislation only produced a temporary decline in the number of consumer bankruptcies,

Figure 8.1. Total Bankruptcy Filings per Capita, United States, Ohio, and Northern District of Ohio, 1980–2007

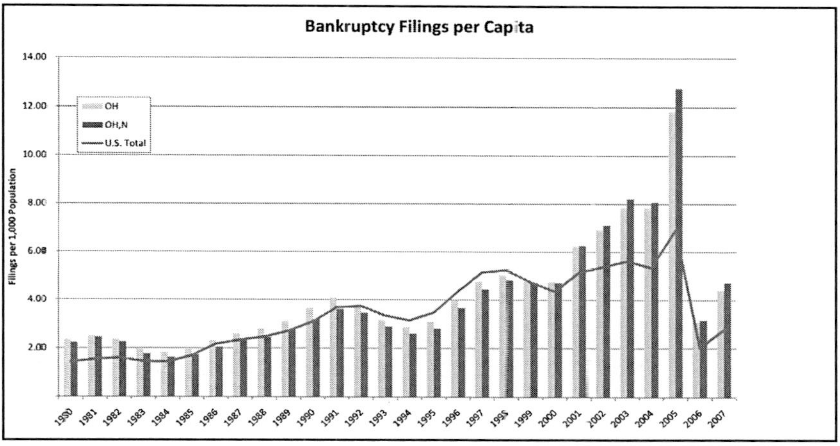

Note: This chart and the two following charts were prepared by the Bankruptcy Judges Division of the Administrative Office of the United States Courts based on published bankruptcy filing statistics and internal population estimates from Bureau of the Census statistics.

Figure 8.2. Chapter 7 Bankruptcy Filings per Capita, United States, Ohio, and Northern District of Ohio, 1980–2007

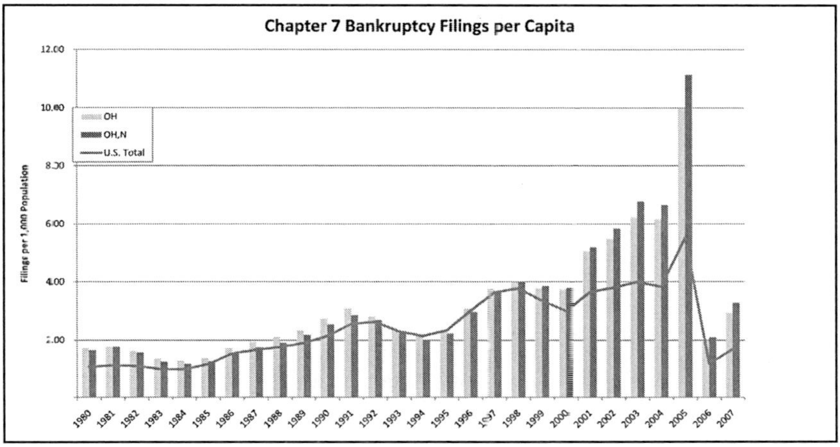

Figure 8.3. Chapter 13 Bankruptcy Filings per Capita, United States, Ohio, and Northern District of Ohio, 1980–2007

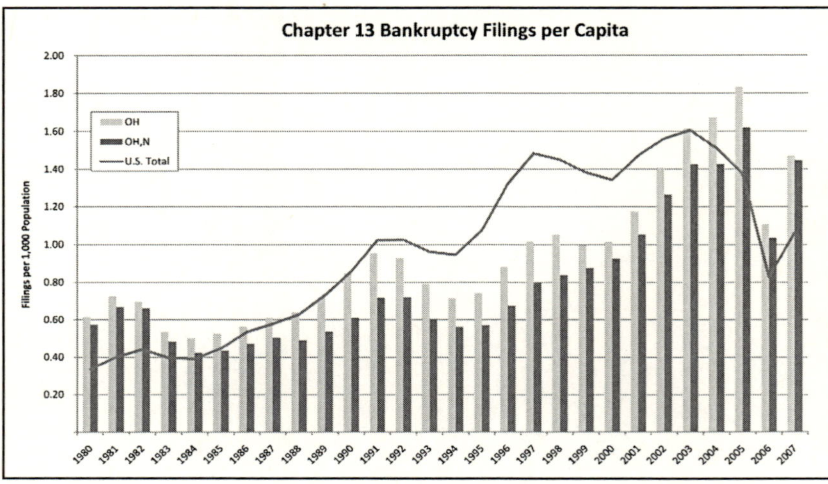

however. The number of consumer bankruptcies resumed its increase after 2006, nearly returning to 2004 levels by 2010. Nationally, 1,563,145 debtors filed for Chapter 7 bankruptcy in 2004, and 1,536,799 debtors filed in 2010. In the Northern District of Ohio, 39,092 debtors filed for Chapter 7 bankruptcy in 2004, and 31,342 debtors filed for Chapter 7 bankruptcy in 2010.[7]

The excess of per capita bankruptcy filings in the Northern District of Ohio over the national average after 2000 is remarkable because, for decades, northern Ohio had been depressed economically compared with the rest of the nation without deviating significantly from average per capita bankruptcy filing rates. Since the 1970s, all of the industrial Great Lakes rust belt had suffered from the decline of the American automotive and steel industries. By 2005, however, Ohio ranked second in the number of households per consumer bankruptcy cases filed, at 37.19. Indiana ranked first at 34.41. The national average was 60.16.[8]

One possible explanation for the discrepancy is that the Cleveland metropolitan statistical area never experienced the business cycle

Figure 8.4. Cleveland Metropolitan Statistical Area Payroll Employment since March 2001

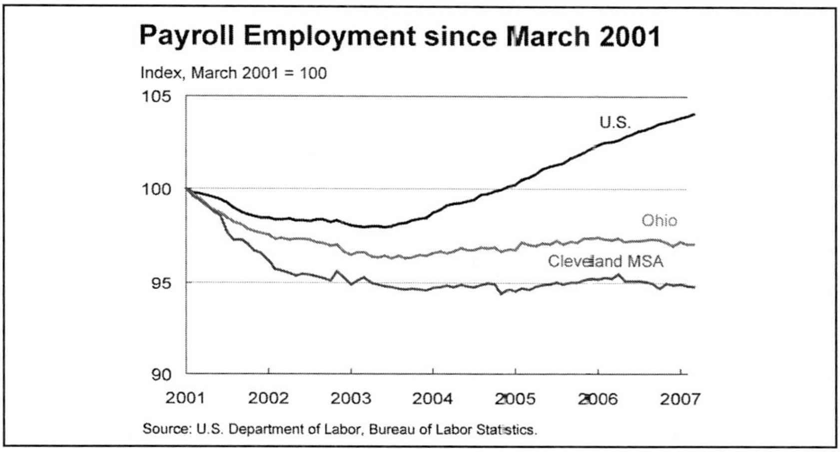

recovery that most of the rest of the nation enjoyed after the 2001 recession. Cleveland remained a manufacturing center with a significantly higher proportion of manufacturing employment than the nation as a whole, but that proved a mixed blessing. The manufacturing sector shed 16.6 percent of its jobs from the peak of the previous business cycle in 2001 to 2006, but Cleveland lost 23.4 percent of its manufacturing jobs. Employment in all non-manufacturing jobs in the United States increased 6.6 percent over that time period, but Cleveland lost 1.4 percent of its nonmanufacturing jobs. As Figure 8.4 illustrates, total national nonfarm employment increased by 6 percent between 2001 and 2007, but no employment growth occurred after the steep initial decline in the Cleveland metropolitan statistical area.[9]

In addition to continuing industrial decline, northern Ohio was one of the first regions to suffer the destabilizing repercussions of predatory lending on a large scale. Ohio lacked adequate regulatory means to police the home mortgage industry, and Cuyahoga County treasurer Jim Rokakis had been battling predatory lending since the 1990s. By 2002, Ohio began to experience a significant increase in mortgage delinquencies and foreclosures. By 2004, Ohio's rate of mortgage delinquency was 35 percent higher than the national average, and Ohio's foreclosure rate was 300 percent higher than the national average. The leading edge of the 2008 financial crisis struck northern Ohio.[10]

The dramatic increase in the number of consumer bankruptcy cases was not accompanied by an increase in the number of bankruptcy judges, however. The district coped by aggressively adopting computer technology and Internet-based communication to increase productivity in case management. The effort has been successful. The Administrative Office consistently evaluates the Northern District of Ohio as one of the more effective and efficient bankruptcy districts.

The Politics of Consumer Bankruptcy Reform

Before 1978, bankruptcy had been relatively uncontroversial for many years. Bankruptcy professionals dominated the policy discussion, and reform legislation occurred infrequently. Generally, Congress allowed changes in the law to function for a while to see how they worked before it entertained additional changes. No period of policy peace followed the 1978 Bankruptcy Code, however. Before Congress settled the new bankruptcy court's jurisdictional issues raised by *Northern Pipeline Construction Co. v. Marathon Pipe Line Co.*, a political revolution occurred that radically changed the policy landscape.[11] Lobbyists for consumer creditors waged an unending war from 1980 until 2005 to means test consumer access to Chapter 7 liquidations.

The extraordinary rise in consumer bankruptcies raised alarms as early as the 1960s, when the ratio of consumer bankruptcies to total bankruptcies first reached approximately 90 percent. Concern about a consumer bankruptcy crisis had been one of the issues that prompted the Brookings Institution to investigate bankruptcy in the 1960s and caused Congress to create the Bankruptcy Commission in 1971. The reports issued by those investigations initiated the legislative process that culminated in the Bankruptcy Code of 1978. Armed with creditor-financed studies, lobbyists for the consumer credit industry argued that many more consumer bankrupts could pay a significant portion of their debts through Chapter 13 wage-earner arrangements. They tried to get Congress to enact provisions in the Bankruptcy Code that compelled wage earners with above average incomes to file Chapter 13 arrangements instead of Chapter 7 liquidations. Bankruptcy lawyers, professors, and consumer advocates in the policy community argued instead to encourage debtors to use Chapter 13 by making it easier to use and more beneficial to debtors. The traditional policy community prevailed, and the Bankruptcy Code retained Chapter 13 as a voluntary alternative to Chapter 7 bankruptcy.

Republican Ronald Reagan won the presidential election in 1980, and the Republicans reclaimed the Senate for the first time since 1954. Consumer credit industry lobbyists renewed their effort to amend the Bankruptcy Code and coerce more consumer debtors to file Chapter 13 arrangements. A consortium of consumer creditor organizations wrote a proposed bill and convinced sponsors to introduce it in both houses of Congress in autumn 1981. The Senate Judiciary Committee reported the bill to the floor in May 1982, but the House bill stalled in Committee.

In June 1982, the Supreme Court decided *Northern Pipeline Construction Co. v. Marathon Pipe Line Co.* In *Marathon,* the Supreme Court held that bankruptcy judges did not have constitutional authority to exercise the expanded jurisdiction granted by the Bankruptcy Code. Congressional attempts to cure the issue of bankruptcy judge jurisdiction raised by *Marathon* became entangled in the consumer bankruptcy controversy. A 1984 Supreme Court decision that allowed debtors in possession to reject labor agreements as executory contracts further complicated matters.[12] Labor unions, a core Democratic Party constituency, wanted provisions reversing the decision written into the bill resolving the bankruptcy judges' jurisdiction. Competing bankruptcy bills languished in committee in both houses of Congress.

In March 1984, Republican backers of the consumer bankruptcy reforms held the bankruptcy judge jurisdiction bill hostage in the House of Representatives while Ohio's Democratic senator, Howard M. Metzenbaum, threatened to filibuster the bill in the Senate. A compromise brokered between Metzenbaum and Republican senator Strom Thurmond of South Carolina allowed the bankruptcy judges' bill to go forward with amendments addressing the two collateral issues. Under certain circumstances, debtors in possession could reject labor agreements as executory contracts if the bankruptcy judge found it was necessary to the success of the plan of reorganization, and bankruptcy judges could dismiss a Chapter 7 petition if the court found that it constituted a "substantial abuse."[13]

Republicans lost control of the Senate in 1986 and the presidency in 1992, but the political climate had shifted in favor of conservatives. In 1991, the consumer credit industry renewed its campaign to coerce more consumer debtors into filing Chapter 13 arrangements. Credit card issuers and industry associations had formed the National Consumer Bankruptcy Coalition to lobby Congress and mount a media campaign against permissive consumer bankruptcy, and in November 1991, the National Consumer Bankruptcy Coalition drafted a bill that was introduced into the Senate with bipartisan support. The bill included the recommendation for a bankruptcy review commission. The bankruptcy policy community did not see the need for another bankruptcy commission so soon after the 1978 Bankruptcy Reform Act, but the consumer credit industry believed it could use a commission to change attitudes about the causes of, and appropriate policy responses to, consumer bankruptcy. The bill passed the Senate but died in the House.[14]

Similar legislation was introduced in the Senate in March 1993. That legislation passed the Senate unanimously but died in the House. Other bankruptcy reform legislation was introduced in the House in September 1994, however, and it included a provision for a bankruptcy review commission. That legislation passed the House on October 5, 1994, and the Senate passed the House bill on October 6, 1994. President Bill Clinton signed the Bankruptcy Reform Act of 1994 on October 22, 1994.[15]

The Bankruptcy Reform Act of 1994 made Chapter 13 more beneficial for debtors, and it made numerous other narrow changes to the Bankruptcy Code. Most importantly, however, the 1994 act created the

National Bankruptcy Review Commission to "investigate and study issues relating to the operation of . . . the Bankruptcy Code . . . [and to] solicit divergent views of all parties concerned with the operation of the bankruptcy system."[16] The 1994 act directed the Bankruptcy Commission to submit a report within two years of its first meeting stating its factual findings and conclusions and recommending appropriate legislative or administrative action.

The Bankruptcy Commission received a narrow mandate. Congress specifically stated: "the Commission should be aware that Congress is generally satisfied with the basic framework established in the current Bankruptcy Code. Therefore, the work of the Commission should be based upon reviewing, improving, and updating the Code in ways which do not disturb the fundamental tenets of current law."[17] The Bankruptcy Commission retained staff that included leading members of the national bankruptcy policy community. Professor Elizabeth Warren of Harvard was appointed reporter, and Professor Lawrence P. King of New York University served as adviser. In the 1994 election, the Republicans regained the Senate and took the House of Representatives for the first time since 1954. Lobbyists for the consumer credit industry saw their opportunity, and the Bankruptcy Commission disintegrated along ideological lines.

Consumer bankruptcy proved to be the most contentious issue considered by the Bankruptcy Commission. Consumer bankruptcies had increased dramatically since enactment of the Bankruptcy Code in 1978, and the consumer credit industry lobbied hard to enact restrictions that would prevent debtors who were less destitute from filing for liquidation under Chapter 7. Instead, debtors who had some means to repay creditors would be required to enter into Chapter 13 plans. Most of the bankruptcy policy community opposed the consumer credit industry's proposed reforms, including most bankruptcy judges and the National Bankruptcy Conference, but they were outmaneuvered. The consumer credit industry lobby had the resources to outspend all critics.

The Bankruptcy Commission submitted its report in October 1997. By a vote of five to four the report did not recommend fundamental changes in consumer bankruptcy. The four dissenting commissioners argued that the commission's recommendations ignored the costs of consumer bankruptcy and favored Chapter 7 liquidations over Chapter 13 arrangements. The dissidents argued for means testing debtors' access to Chapter 7. The consumer credit industry financed studies claiming that the abuse of Chapter 7 bankruptcy imposed high costs on all consumers.[18]

The idea that consumer debtors should be treated differently from business bankrupts had a long history. Bankruptcy had been intended for small business entrepreneurs from its inception. Nonetheless, consumer bankrupts met the eligibility criteria for discharge of debts and took advantage of it. Consumer bankruptcy made up a large part of total bankruptcies from the beginning. Commentators expressed discomfort with the idea of consumers discharging debts incurred for personal living expenses; it seemed so unvirtuous. The increasing rate of consumer bankruptcy in the 1920s had been one of the principal concerns (along with corruption in the bankruptcy courts) behind the bankruptcy commissions that culminated with passage of the Chandler Act in 1938. Chapter XIII wage-earner plans were introduced into bankruptcy law at that time. In the 1960s, the Administrative Office had pressured referees into strong-arming consumer debtors' lawyers into considering Chapter XIII more often. The consumer credit industry had pushed legislation to compel debtors to file under Chapter XIII unless they could show hardship.[19]

Congressional conservatives did not wait for the Bankruptcy Commission report before making their move. One month before the Bankruptcy Commission report appeared, they introduced into the House of Representatives legislation adopting the consumer credit industry's position on means testing eligibility for Chapter 7. The day after the report was submitted, Republican senator Chuck Grassley of Iowa filed similar legislation in the Senate. Hearings were held in 1997 and 1998, and both houses passed legislation in 1998. The leadership agreed on a conference report in October 1998, but the legislative session ended before the Senate acted on it. The impeachment of President Bill Clinton intervened. On October

8, 1998, the House of Representatives voted to conduct an impeachment inquiry, and on December 19, 1998, the House filed articles of impeachment against President Clinton and ended the legislative session. The impeachment trial occurred in the Senate in January 1999, at the beginning of the next session of Congress. Although President Clinton was ultimately acquitted of all charges against him, the impeachment inquiry and trial consumed all of Congress's attention.

In February 1999, the conference report on the bankruptcy bill from the last session of Congress was introduced in the new session of Congress. Once again, Congress held extensive hearings on bankruptcy reform, including joint hearings with the House and the Senate. Dueling experts debated how many consumer debtors could repay creditors through Chapter 13 plans. The House and the Senate passed different bills but reached a compromise in October 2000. The compromise bill passed the House on October 12, 2000, and the Senate on December 19, 2000. President Clinton vetoed the bill.

Republicans regained the presidency and held both houses of Congress in the 2000 election. In January 2001, both houses of Congress introduced the conference report on the bankruptcy bill from the last session. Then Senator James M. Jeffords of Vermont changed party affiliation from Republican to Independent and caucused with the Democrats. Before the change, the Senate had been evenly divided 50-50, but it was controlled by the Republicans because of Republican vice president Dick Cheney's tie-breaking vote. After the change, control of the Senate passed to the Democrats, and the chair of the judiciary committee changed. The bankruptcy legislation was still pending in the Senate judiciary committee. After some parliamentary maneuvering, the Senate approved a bankruptcy bill and requested a conference with the House. The conferees left on August recess and scheduled the first meeting of the conference for September 12, 2001.

The terrorist attacks on September 11, 2001, intervened, and Congress indefinitely postponed the conference on the bankruptcy bill. The conference finally convened on November 14, 2001. Substantial differences existed between the two bills, and the scope of the legislation had grown significantly over the years. The sticking point turned out to be whether antiabortion protesters could discharge in bankruptcy fines imposed for blocking access to abortion clinics, and the bill died in conference. An attempt to pass the bill in the lame duck session after the 2002 election failed. Republicans regained the Senate and retained the House in the 2002 election, but an attempt to pass the bill in that session of Congress also failed.

In the 2004 election, the Republicans retained the Senate, the House, and the presidency. Republican senator Chuck Grassley of Iowa introduced the Bankruptcy Abuse Prevention and Consumer Protection Act into the Senate in February 2005. The Senate passed an amended bill by an overwhelming margin on March 10, 2005. The House passed the bill on April 14, 2005, and President George W. Bush signed the bill on April 20, 2005. The legislation has been highly controversial.

Bankruptcy was a partisan issue in the nineteenth century, as southern and rural Democrats opposed encroachment by a national state and a national economy championed by Republican commercial interests. After a long period of nonpartisan dominance by an expert policy community, bankruptcy became a partisan issue again. The interests represented by the political actors have changed, and we live in a different economy than before 1898. But the political conflict still represents widely divergent ideas about what America is and ought to be.

Bankruptcy Judges

While bankruptcy policy making became increasingly partisan after the enactment of the Bankruptcy Code of 1978, the appointment of bankruptcy judges became less partisan. This occurred as a result of the decision to remove the appointment power from the district court judges. All federal judicial appointments are partisan appointments, but district court judges seemed to retain a particularly close identification with local partisan organizations. When district court judges appointed bankruptcy judges, most of the candidates had deep roots in local political organizations or a powerful political patron. In the Northern District of Ohio, district court judges selected bankruptcy judges and other court appointees according to a rotation that varied primarily in allowing judges from certain geographic regions to choose appointees for those regions.

The Bankruptcy Amendments and Federal Judgeship Act of 1984 changed the way bankruptcy judges were appointed and profoundly diminished the influence of partisan politics in the selection of bankruptcy judges. The bankruptcy amendments of 1984 required the circuit court for the district where the bankruptcy judge would serve to appoint the bankruptcy judge from a slate distilled from an open application pool after review by a merit selection panel and the judicial council. District court judges did not lose all influence in the process of appointing bankruptcy judges; they sometimes sat on the merit panel or the judicial council, and they knew the circuit court judges. Similarly, politicians did not lose all influence in the process either. Politicians often had close relationships with the judges whose appointments they had secured. Both judges and politicians sometimes lobbied for their favorite candidates. However, the procedure after 1984 interposed layers of reviewers who had to justify their decisions in writing. Consequently, although most winning candidates had mentors pulling for their appointment, the direct influence of partisan politics greatly diminished.

The circuit court selection process has continued since 1984 with very minor modification. When the chief judge of the circuit learns of a vacancy, he or she publishes a notice of vacancy and appoints a merit selection panel of three to seven persons. Chaired by the circuit executive, the merit selection panel may include a district court judge from the district where the bankruptcy judge will serve and local law school professors. The panel always includes respected local lawyers, including elite bankruptcy practitioners and other prestigious big-firm lawyers as well as leaders in the state and local bar associations. Usually, bar association leaders are also big-firm lawyers. Applicants submit lengthy written applications and sample briefs. The merit selection panel reviews the applications and interviews those it finds most qualified. The panel then submits a list of the five to ten best qualified applicants to the circuit judicial council together with all supporting documentation.

The circuit judicial council ranks the top candidates and submits its list to the circuit court for decision. The applicants make financial disclosure to the judicial council and submit additional references, and the council may make any additional inquiries it wishes. Currently, to rank the candidates, the circuit judicial council uses a committee consisting of three court of appeals judges, the chief judge of the district where the bankruptcy judge will be appointed, and the bankruptcy judge representative to the judicial council. Preferably one of the court of appeals judges on the judicial council committee will be from the judicial district where the bankruptcy judge will be appointed. Also, the judicial council committee is directed to consult with the chief bankruptcy judge for the district where the applicant will serve. The names of the top three candidates are released to the public for comments.

In the final step in the selection process, the committee interviews the top three candidates and prepares a report. Any active circuit court judge may attend the interview. The judicial council then votes on the committee's report. The judicial council can reject the first list and direct the merit selection panel to start all over again, accept the committee's report, or make another recommendation as it deems appropriate. If the judicial council accepts the committee's report, all of the active judges on the circuit court select the appointee by majority vote from among the top three candidates submitted by the judicial council. The circuit court's appointment is conditioned on security clearance by the Federal Bureau of Investigation.

After these selection procedures were implemented, the bankruptcy judges appointed in the Northern District of Ohio had no obvious partisan political connections of any importance. Instead, most of the newly appointed bankruptcy judges were assistant US attorneys, big-firm lawyers, or bar association leaders. Many bankruptcy judges fall into more than one of those categories. Only the newspaper coverage of the first two bankruptcy judges appointed by the Sixth Circuit under the new system even reported the partisan affiliations of the candidates, and in those two cases, evidence of partisan influence was weak and ambiguous.

The district court expected to appoint a Republican to the bankruptcy bench in Youngstown in 1984, but it encountered opposition and ran out of time before the new procedures were to take effect. The three top candidates submitted to the circuit court by the judicial council were all Republicans, but the candidate supported by the Mahoning County Republican party was not on the list. The circuit court's appointee, William T. Bodoh, had the least partisan political résumé of the three top candidates. Bodoh self-identified as a strong Republican but had held no prior political office except Ohio assistant attorney general. The other top candidate from Youngstown was on the Mahoning County Republican Executive Committee. The third top candidate was from Akron, not Mahoning County. He had been an assistant county prosecutor and unsuccessful candidate for Akron City Council and mayor.[20] Bodoh was appointed in June 1985 and served as bankruptcy judge in Youngstown until his retirement on January 1, 2004. He was chief bankruptcy judge for the district from July 1, 2001, to December 31, 2003.

The newspaper article announcing the top three candidates for the second bankruptcy judge to be appointed under the new procedures did not disclose the partisan affiliation of the candidates, but the article announcing the Sixth Circuit's selection of Randolph Baxter revealed his political affiliation as a Republican. There is no indication that partisan affiliation played any role in Judge Baxter's appointment. Judge Baxter had received appointments and promotions from both Republican and Democratic political appointees during the course of his career, and his candidacy rested on his position as an experienced assistant US attorney. One of the other top three candidates was also an assistant US attorney, and the third candidate was a local litigator. Judge Baxter was also African American, and the circuit court was embarrassed by the lack of diversity on the bankruptcy court in northern Ohio. Judge Baxter was appointed in December 1985 and served as bankruptcy judge until his retirement in August 2011. He was chief bankruptcy judge from January 3, 2004, to January 2, 2008.

The next two bankruptcy judges appointed both worked in commercial litigation at the large, nationally prominent Cleveland corporate law firm Jones, Day, Reavis & Pogue. Boston native David P. Snow graduated from Dartmouth College in 1954 and Harvard Law School in 1960. He came to Cleveland right out of law school to work at Jones Day. Snow became a partner and chairman of the commercial litigation practice. Jones Day had some involvement with insolvency in California in the 1970s but White Motor was the first bankruptcy case that Jones Day's Cleveland office handled, and Snow worked on the case. Snow found bankruptcy practice intellectually stimulating, so when the circuit announced an opening for a bankruptcy judge in Cleveland in 1988, he applied. He was appointed in July 1988 and served until his retirement in July 2000.

Marilyn Shea-Stonum also worked in commercial litigation at Jones Day, and she also worked on the White Motor case. A native of southern California, Shea-Stonum worked as a reporter for the Riverside Press-Enterprise while an undergraduate. She began law studies as a night student while working as a research assistant at the Johns Hopkins Center for Urban Affairs. In 1973, Shea-Stonum transferred to the Case Western Reserve University School of Law when her husband, Gary Stonum, received a teaching appointment in Case Western Reserve's English department. She graduated in 1975 and clerked for Chief Judge Frank J. Battisti before joining Jones Day.

Shea-Stonum had considerable bankruptcy experience before applying for appointment as bankruptcy judge in Akron. She was a founding member of the bankruptcy practice at Jones Day in Cleveland in 1982, where she represented numerous creditors before the bankruptcy courts. She represented Lubrizol before the Fourth Circuit Court of Appeals in *Lubrizol Enterprises v. Richmond Metal Finishers, Inc.*, which held that a license of intellectual property constituted an executory contract that the debtor could reject or assume. In 1988, Congress passed legislation reversing the decision.[21] In September 1994, the circuit court appointed Shea-Stonum to replace retiring bankruptcy judge Harold F. White. Shea-Stonum served as chief bankruptcy judge from January 3, 2008, to January 2, 2012. She retired from the bench on May 1, 2014.

Judge White continued to serve on a recall basis for seven years after his retirement, until February 1, 2001. Sixth Circuit procedures instruct the chief judge to inquire in the last year of a judge's term whether he or she wishes to be reappointed. If the judge desires reappointment, the circuit judges make an initial determination whether to retain the judge at the next meeting of the court, and reappointment will not be denied unless the "incumbent has failed to perform the duties of a bankruptcy judge according to the high standards of performance regularly met by United States bankruptcy judges."[22] Alternatively, a bankruptcy judge could decide not to seek reappointment but to continue to serve instead on "recall." The judicial council decides whether to accept a recall appointment and, if so, the duration of the appointment. The circuit court briefly recalled Judge White again in August 2007. Judge White served as a bankruptcy judge for more than forty years and heard more than fifty thousand bankruptcy cases.

Pat E. Morgenstern-Clarren came to the bankruptcy court from a large corporate law firm, but her most compelling accomplishment was her leadership in the Ohio State Bar Association's effort to reduce barriers against women in the legal profession. In December 1995, the circuit court appointed Morgenstern-Clarren bankruptcy judge to replace retiring bankruptcy judge William J. O'Neill. Appointed referee in bankruptcy in 1961, Judge O'Neill retired on October 1, 1994, and continued on recall until October 1, 1995. He died on January 12, 2000.

Morgenstern-Clarren was a litigation partner with limited bankruptcy experience at the Cleveland law firm Hahn, Loeser & Parks. She graduated from the Case Western Reserve University School of Law in 1977 and went on to receive an advanced degree from the London School of Economics and Political Science. She clerked for Ohio Court of Appeals judge

Jack Grant Day before joining Hahn Loeser in 1979. Morgenstern-Clarren worked under Hahn Loeser's bankruptcy specialist, Forrest Weinberg, in the White Motor case; Weinberg represented the creditors' committee in that case. Morgenstern-Clarren's practice concentrated on commercial litigation, and her bankruptcy experience before her appointment consisted primarily of representation in adversary proceedings.

Morgenstern-Clarren achieved distinction as a leader of the Ohio State Bar Association. In November 1991, the Ohio Supreme Court and the Ohio State Bar Association established a Joint Task Force on Gender Fairness. Morgenstern-Clarren was appointed to the steering committee of the task force and chaired its Lawyer and Workplace Lifestyle Committee. In 1993, she was appointed chair of the Ohio State Bar Association Section on Women in the Profession. Morgenstern-Clarren served on the Ohio State Bar Association Board of Governors of the Section on Women from 1993 to 1998. In 1994, she was elected to the Ohio State Bar Association's Council of Delegates. Judge Morgenstern-Clarren began her term as chief bankruptcy judge on January 3, 2012.

The next bankruptcy judge appointments occurred in Canton and Toledo, regional urban centers of moderate size. In both cases, the circuit court chose lawyers with deep local roots who practiced in the best local law firms. Both Russ Kendig and Mary Ann Whipple had excellent academic credentials, stellar professional reputations, and bankruptcy experience. The circuit court appointed Russ Kendig to fill Judge James H. Williams's seat in Canton on February 28, 2001. Judge Williams's term ended in February 1999 and he served on recall until August 31, 1999. Judge Williams served as chief bankruptcy judge from November 6, 1987 to June 30, 1997, and was the longest-serving chief judge in the history of the Bankruptcy Court for the Northern District of Ohio. The circuit court appointed Mary Ann Whipple to Judge Walter J. Krasniewski's seat in Toledo in May 2001. Appointed referee in bankruptcy in 1965, Judge Krasniewiski retired on August 1, 1994, and served on recall until June 27, 1997. Because bankruptcy judge Richard Speer also sat in Toledo, the circuit did not immediately seek to fill Judge Krasniewski's seat.

Russ Kendig's family had lived in Canton, Ohio, since at least the early 1900s. Kendig received his undergraduate degree from Northwestern University in 1980 and his law degree from the Ohio State University in 1984. After graduation, Kendig began practice at Canton's largest law firm, Krugliak, Wilkins, Griffiths & Dougherty, where he received his introduction to bankruptcy law in the Mansfield Tire case, the first Chapter 11 reorganization filed under the new Bankruptcy Code in 1978. The Krugliak firm served as trustee in the liquidation of Mansfield Tire. Kendig's law practice primarily consisted of representing banks in insolvency situations, and Canton's small size limited his professional advancement. In 1995, Kendig joined the newly established Chicago office of the London law firm Lovells where he practiced international reinsurance law. Kendig returned to Canton in 1997 for family reasons. He briefly practiced in a small firm before joining Canton's second-largest law firm, Day, Ketterer, Raley, Wright & Rybolt. Kendig became a Chapter 7 trustee in Canton before his appointment as bankruptcy judge.

Mary Ann Whipple was born in Ann Arbor, Michigan, but grew up in Toledo, Ohio. She received her undergraduate degree from the University of Michigan in 1977 and her law degree from Stanford Law School in 1981. After graduation, Whipple practiced commercial law at the venerable Toledo law firm of Fuller & Henry, where she rose to managing partner. Founded in 1890, Fuller & Henry was Toledo's third-largest law firm. Whipple had an extensive bankruptcy practice at Fuller & Henry and has taught creditors' remedies as an adjunct professor at the University of Toledo College of Law from 1981 to the present.

Judge Whipple's most notorious case in private practice was the failure of the brokerage firm Bell & Beckwith. In February 1983, the Securities and Exchange Commission uncovered massive fraud at the firm and the Securities Investor Protection Corporation sought a protective order from the district court under the Securities Investor Protection Act of 1970. The district court granted the petition, appointed a trustee to liquidate the firm, and removed the case to bankruptcy court.[23] The managing partner, Edward P. Wolfram, pled guilty to embezzling $47 million, and served ten years in federal prison. Although not the largest brokerage to fail, Bell & Beckwith caused the Securities Investor Protection Corporation to make its largest payment by far up to that time: more than $30 million to the firm's defrauded investors.[24]

Whipple represented the trustee responsible for liquidating the firm and recovering assets for the benefit of creditors. The task involved thousands of legal actions over fourteen years. Wolfram's vast empire included cattle farms in Arkansas and Missouri, an oil-exploration company in Louisiana, a horse farm in Florida, and the Landmark Hotel & Casino in Las Vegas. Bell & Beckwith became the longest running bankruptcy case in Toledo history.[25]

Assistant US attorney Arthur I. Harris applied for a position as a bankruptcy judge in Cleveland when Judge O'Neill retired in 1994. Harris was one of the three finalists submitted to the circuit court when Judge Morgenstern-Clarren received the appointment. Harris applied again after Judge David Snow retired in July 2000. LTV general counsel Kay Woods also applied for the position and was one of the three finalists submitted to the circuit court. Harris received the appointment and was sworn in on October 7, 2002.

Harris grew up in Pepper Pike, Ohio, the grandchild of Russian immigrants. He received his undergraduate degree from Cornell University in 1979 and his law degree from the University of Michigan Law School in 1982. After law school, Harris clerked for Cleveland US District Court judge John M. Manos. Harris was appointed assistant US attorney in Cleveland after the conclusion of his clerkship. Harris tried civil cases of all kinds in the Office of the United States Attorney, and bankruptcy cases constituted approximately 20 percent of his total workload. He was coordinator of the bankruptcy unit in the civil division at the time of his appointment as bankruptcy judge.

Harris developed an expertise in environmental law, which often overlapped with bankruptcy cases, especially when old, dirty steel mills closed. For example, in March 1987, Harris represented the Environmental Protection Agency in litigation against Sharon Steel over its discharge of untreated wastewater into the Mahoning River watershed at its Warren, Ohio, steel mill. In April 1987, Sharon Steel filed the first of two bankruptcy petitions in the Western District of Pennsylvania.[26] Settlement of the environmental lawsuit had to be approved by the district court in the Northern District of Ohio and the bankruptcy court in the Western District of Pennsylvania. Harris also represented the United States in long-standing litigation with LTV over violations of the Clean Air Act when LTV filed its second petition for reorganization in bankruptcy in December 2000. The environmental litigation settled as part of the bankruptcy case.

When Harris was appointed bankruptcy judge in 2002, the bankruptcy court was located in leased space in the Society Center (now known as the Key Tower). The bankruptcy court moved into the newly renovated Howard M. Metzenbaum US Courthouse in June 2005. Harris had a very personal connection with the building: his maternal grandfather, Abraham Goler, was a foreman for the City Iron Works, Inc., and worked on the renovation of the courthouse after the post office vacated the building in 1934. In 1940, a half-ton steel beam fell on Goler while he was working on the construction of a concrete roof in the building's basement. Goler suffered a fractured skull and died ten days later from his injuries. Judge Harris was born in 1957 and never knew his grandfather.[27]

When Youngstown bankruptcy judge William T. Bodoh retired on January 2, 2004, LTV's associate general counsel, Kay Woods, applied for the position. The circuit court selected her, and Woods was sworn in on July 7, 2004. Woods was born in Van Wert, Ohio, and moved to Lima, Ohio, as a teenager. She received her undergraduate degree from Bowling Green State University in 1973 and her law degree from the Ohio State University College of Law in 1981. After law school she worked as a litigation associate at the Cleveland law firm Jones, Day, Reavis & Pogue.

In January 1986, Woods accepted a position as in-house counsel at LTV. Her principal duties involved litigation. Six months later, LTV filed its first petition for reorganization under Chapter 11 of the Bankruptcy Code in the Southern District of New York, and Woods began her bankruptcy career. LTV emerged from its first Chapter 11 reorganization in June 1993. LTV promoted Woods to associate general counsel, and her law practice expanded to include intellectual property and contract law as well as litigation. In December 2000, LTV filed another petition for reorganization under Chapter 11, this time in the Northern District of Ohio.

Woods believed it was inevitable that LTV would eventually liquidate when it filed its second petition for reorganization in 2000; the corporation was administratively insolvent. So when the circuit court announced the vacancy to replace Judge Snow in Cleveland, Woods decided to apply. Judge Harris received that appointment. When a bankruptcy judge position opened in Youngstown a few years later, Woods applied again. This time, she received the appointment. Because Woods had represented LTV as corporate counsel, the LTV bankruptcy case, which was still pending on the Youngstown docket, was reassigned to Judge Baxter in Cleveland. The case closed in 2012.

The next bankruptcy judge to be appointed in the Northern District of Ohio, Jessica E. Price Smith, represents a new generation on the Bankruptcy Court. On November 18, 2011, Price Smith assumed the bankruptcy judge position formerly occupied by Randolph Baxter. Price Smith is the first former law clerk to a bankruptcy judge in the Northern District of Ohio to receive an appointment to the bankruptcy court bench; she served as Judge Baxter's law clerk immediately after graduation from law school. In addition, she is the second African American bankruptcy judge to be appointed in the Northern District of Ohio.

Judge Price Smith's appointment as bankruptcy judge followed a distinguished academic and professional career. A Cleveland native, Price Smith graduated from Miami University in Oxford, Ohio, in 1994, where she was among the first group of students awarded the prestigious Harrison Scholarship. Price Smith received her law degree from the Ohio Northern University Claude W. Pettit College of Law in 1997, where she was a member of the Law Review and Moot Court Board of Advocates, served on the Law Review Judicial Review Board, and was inducted into the Willis Society, the highest academic honor society at the College of

Bankruptcy Judges in the Northern Judicial District of Ohio, 2011; front row, left to right: Judge Richard L. Speer, Judge Pat E. Morgenstern-Clarren, Judge Jessica E. Price Smith, Chief Judge Marilyn Shea-Stonum; back row, left to right: Judge Kay Woods, Judge Russ Kendig, Judge Mary Ann Whipple, Judge Arthur I. Harris. Photo by Rob Wetzler, Wetzler Studios, used with permission

Law. Price Smith spent two years as a bankruptcy associate with the law firm of Taft Stettinius & Hollister LLP before joining the regional corporate law firm, Brouse McDowell. She was the first African American to make partner in the law firm's ninety-year history. At Brouse McDowell, Price Smith represented corporate debtors, creditor committees, and trade creditors in all aspects of commercial bankruptcy cases and out-of-court debt restructuring. In addition, she taught legal studies at Ursuline College in the adult accelerated education program. Price Smith became a leader in the Cleveland Metropolitan Bar Association Commercial and Bankruptcy Law Section, serving as the section's treasurer in 2006, secretary in 2007, vice chair in 2008, and chair in 2009.

On April 3, 2013, Judge Speer died, leaving an open seat on the bankruptcy court in Toledo. One year later, on April 8, 2014, John P. Gustafson replaced him on that seat. Like Judge Price Smith, Judge Gustafson represents a new generation on the bankruptcy court; he was Judge Speer's law clerk from 1986 to 1990. Gustafson received his undergraduate degree from Miami University in Ohio and his law degree from the Wayne State University School of Law in Detroit. After practicing bankruptcy law in the Toledo, Ohio, law firm of Nathan and Roberts from 1990 to 2000, and in solo practice from 2000 to 2003, he served as staff attorney to the standing Chapter 13 trustee in Toledo from October 2003 to September 2007. He was appointed standing Chapter 13 trustee on September 30, 2007, and served in that position until his appointment as bankruptcy judge.

Judge Shea-Stonum retired as bankruptcy judge in Akron, Ohio, on May 1, 2014, and her replacement, Alan M. Koschik, was sworn in on May 2, 2014. He received his undergraduate and law degrees from the University of Michigan. After law school he clerked with the Ninth Circuit Court of Appeals in San Francisco and practiced bankruptcy law at several prestigious law firms before settling at the Akron law firm Brouse McDowell, where he was partner when he accepted appointment to the bankruptcy court.

The Bankruptcy Court

The 1984 bankruptcy amendments changed the way bankruptcy judges were selected and appointed, and in its wake a more professional bankruptcy court emerged that was more independent of the district court. Meanwhile, the old tensions between district court judges, higher court judges, and Congress over the status of bankruptcy judges and the scope of their authority have continued unresolved. Furthermore, the 2011 Supreme Court decision in *Stern v. Marshall* and the 2014 decision in *Executive Benefits Insurance Agency v. Arkinson* reopened bankruptcy court jurisdictional questions that the bankruptcy community presumed Bankruptcy Amendments and Federal Judgeship Act of 1984 had settled.[28]

Initially, the extent to which bankruptcy judges were considered real judges became an issue in the context of this question: Who should hear appeals from bankruptcy court decisions? Under the 1978 Bankruptcy Code, final orders from bankruptcy judges could be appealed to the district court; to a bankruptcy appellate panel consisting of sitting bankruptcy judges—if the circuit court authorized the panel; or directly to the circuit court of appeals if the parties consented. Only two circuits initially established bankruptcy appellate panels, and one of those dissolved after *Marathon*. The Sixth Circuit did not establish a bankruptcy appellate panel at that time.

Congress became very sympathetic to bankruptcy judges during the hearings leading up to the enactment of the Bankruptcy Reform Act of 1978 and was disappointed that more circuit courts did not establish bankruptcy appellate panels. Consequently, the Bankruptcy Reform Act of 1994 amended the judicial code to require that circuit courts establish bankruptcy appellate panels unless the circuit court found that judicial resources were insufficient or that the creation of a panel would cause undue delay or increase costs to bankruptcy litigants.[29] Fewer than half of the circuit courts established bankruptcy appellate panels in response to this act. Congress gave recalcitrant district court judges a chance to deny bankruptcy judges appellate authority: if a circuit established a bankruptcy appellate panel, the panel could not hear bankruptcy appeals from a judicial district unless the district court authorized it by majority vote of the judges. Where the bankruptcy appellate panel heard an appeal, litigants appealed the bankruptcy appellate panel's decisions directly to the circuit court of appeals bypassing district courts altogether.

The Sixth Circuit was among the first circuit courts to establish a bankruptcy appellate panel. President Clinton signed the Bankruptcy Reform Act of 1994 on October 22, 1994, and on November 30, 1994, the Sixth Circuit Judicial Council authorized an ad hoc committee to study and make recommendations with regard to establishing a bankruptcy appellate panel. In October 1995, the judicial council accepted the recommendation of the ad hoc committee that a bankruptcy appellate panel be established and created a subcommittee to draft rules and operating procedures for one. The judicial council appointed the first bankruptcy appellate panel in November 1996. The panel consisted of five bankruptcy judges, with at least one judge from each state in the circuit. Bankruptcy appellate panel judges serve staggered four-year terms. Cleveland bankruptcy judge Randolph Baxter served on the first bankruptcy appellate panel. Even though only the Northern and Southern districts of Ohio had voted to use the Sixth Circuit's bankruptcy appellate panel, the panel's first term began on January 1, 1997.

The Sixth Circuit's bankruptcy appellate panel proved to be efficient and effective. By the third year, litigants in more than 60 percent of bankruptcy appeals in Ohio elected for those appeals to be heard by the panel. A third district court voted to allow bankruptcy appeals to the bankruptcy appellate panel that year. Bankruptcy judges from the Northern District of Ohio have served continuously on the panel. Judge Morgenstern-Clarren replaced Judge Baxter on the panel in January 1999 and served through December 2002. Judge Bodoh served on the panel during calendar year 2003. Judge Whipple served from January 2004 through December 2007. The circuit court appointed Judge Shea-Stonum to a four-year term beginning January 2008. Judge Harris served from January 1, 2009, to December 31, 2012. By 2008, six districts in the Sixth Circuit had voted to allow bankruptcy appeals to the bankruptcy appellate panel.[30]

The enhanced status of the bankruptcy court brought with it improved facilities and greater control over resources. The bankruptcy court in Youngstown moved into a new federal courthouse in 2002, and the bankruptcy court in Canton moved into a new federal courthouse in 2010. The most visually striking illustration of the importance of the bankruptcy court in the Northern District of Ohio was the magnificent renovation of the Howard M. Metzenbaum U.S. Courthouse in Cleveland, with the bankruptcy court as the principal tenant.

The old Cleveland federal courthouse on Public Square was built between 1902 and 1910. In 1974, the courthouse was placed on the National

Howard M. Metzenbaum US Courthouse, Cleveland, Ohio. *Courtesy of Ken Hirz*

Register of Historic Places. Originally, the building housed the post office, customs house, and courthouse. In 1934, the post office moved into Terminal Tower and the old Cleveland federal courthouse underwent substantial renovation. Cleveland referees and their staff moved into the building in 1957. The number of authorized US district court judgeships increased in the 1960s, and the number of judges taking senior status also increased. When a judge took senior status, a replacement judge was appointed and new chambers were needed. Eventually, the district court expanded to fill the entire federal building. The US attorney moved out of the courthouse in 1982. In 1993, the bankruptcy court and the senior judges moved into the newly built Society Center.

Planning for the historic restoration of the old federal courthouse began in 1984. In 1990, studies began on federal court space needs, and plans for a new federal courthouse in Cleveland contemplated restoration of the old federal courthouse. The plan provided that the bankruptcy court and senior district court judges would return to the old federal courthouse after restoration. In 1997, Congress named the new federal courthouse after former Cleveland mayor Carl B. Stokes. In 1998, Congress renamed the old federal courthouse after former US senator from Ohio, Howard M. Metzenbaum. Construction of the new federal courthouse began in 1997 and was completed in 2002. Renovation of the old federal courthouse began as soon as the old tenants moved into the new Stokes US Courthouse. The restoration earned numerous awards, and the bankruptcy court in Cleveland moved back into the Metzenbaum Courthouse in June 2005.

The Bankruptcy Reform Act of 1978 made the clerk of bankruptcy court independent of the clerk of district court. However, the independence of the first clerk of bankruptcy court, Joseph Benik, was open to question. Benik had deep roots in the office of the clerk of district court. He began to work there in 1952 and was chief deputy clerk of district court immediately before his appointment to clerk of bankruptcy court. Moreover, he was a protégé of chief district court judge Frank J. Battisti, who had consolidated the bankruptcy clerks into the clerk of district court in the 1970s.

Benik retired on December 8, 1986, and chief bankruptcy judge John F. Ray Jr. appointed the first home-grown clerk of bankruptcy court, Beth A. Dick. Dick began her career as a secretary to bankruptcy judge James H. Williams in Canton, Ohio, in 1973. She served as president of the National Conference of Bankruptcy Clerks from 1992 to 1993. Dick retired on February 27, 1998, and the bankruptcy court appointed chief deputy clerk Ken Hirz to be the new clerk of bankruptcy court. In 1992, Dick recruited Hirz from Cuyahoga County Juvenile Court to become chief deputy clerk of the bankruptcy court. Hirz received his undergraduate degree from Oberlin College in 1974. He received an MS degree in social science administration from Case Western Reserve University in 1979 and an MBA from Cleveland State University in 1990. Hirz served as president of the National Conference of Bankruptcy Clerks from 2010 to 2012, member and chair of the Federal Judicial Center's Advisory

Figure 8.5. Total Bankruptcy Cases Filed, Northern District of Ohio, 1980–2004

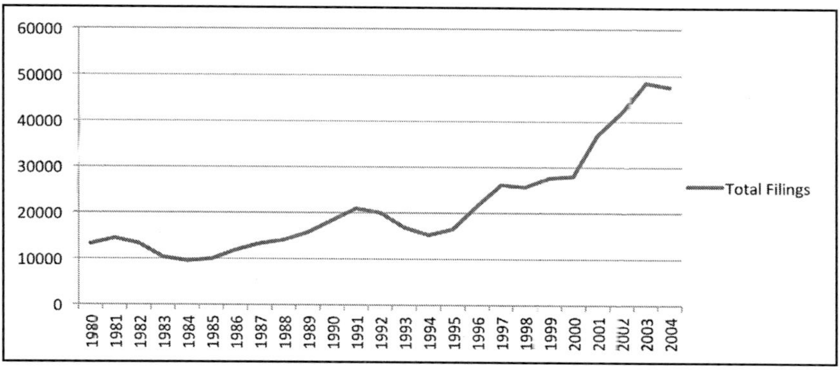

Note: The chart is prepared from data furnished by the Administrative Office of the United States Courts to the American Bankruptcy Institute and published at "Bankruptcy Filing Statistics—Filings by District," http://www.abiworld.org/AM/Template.cfm?Section=Filings_by_District1&Template=/TaggedPage/TaggedPageDisplay.cfm&TPLID=56&ContentID=36298.

Committee on Bankruptcy Education, and member of the Bankruptcy Clerk's Advisory Group.

In 1987, the clerk managed approximately eighty employees serving eight full-time bankruptcy judges and their staff. Over the next twenty years, the clerk's staff increased unevenly, leveling off at approximately one hundred full-time deputy clerks. During that same period, total bankruptcy cases filed per year increased more than 300 percent, from approximately 13,000 cases to more than 40,000 cases. (See Figure 8.5.) The bankruptcy court clerk maintained effective docket control over the increased volume of cases without significantly increasing staff through the aggressive use of automation. The implementation of decentralized budgeting by the Administrative Office in 1990, including decentralized personnel budgeting, allowed the clerk to prioritize personnel hiring in computer systems and automation. Automated systems extended to an automated personnel system and an automated financial program. All systems have been continuously updated and improved.

The clerk of bankruptcy court in the Northern District of Ohio was an early adapter of computer technology. The bankruptcy court employed electronic court reporters from the earliest days and adopted video conferencing systems as they became technologically feasible.

The clerk adopted automated noticing in 1985 and hired its first full-time systems administrator in 1987. Decentralized personnel management allowed the clerk to hire more systems administrators and technical staff. By 1990, the clerk's office adopted an automated case management system, and in 1991, the Administrative Office provided the bankruptcy clerk with a public access automated case retrieval system, known as PACER.[31] Eventually, PACER included an automated billing system and an automated system to track automated requests. In 1995, the clerk installed a computerized case assignment system and an automated docketing system. In 1996, the clerk installed a bar-code case-tracking system. By 2001, the clerk went to an Internet-based case management and automated docketing system. The Northern District of Ohio tested an Internet-based electronic case filing system for the Administrative Office in 1999 and implemented in it 2002. By 2004, all attorneys were required to file electronically.

Judicial administration became more bureaucratic as the twentieth century progressed. Judicial committees under the circuit judicial councils and the Judicial Conference assumed increasing authority for policy direction and lower court management. The Administrative Office and its subordinate divisions and offices assumed greater power to determine results through their mastery of information and the control of resources. As the bankruptcy courts became more independent of the district courts they became more deeply integrated into the organizational bureaucracy of the federal judiciary.

The establishment of an independent, autonomous bankruptcy court fully integrated into the organized judiciary fulfills one of the long-standing goals of the bankruptcy policy community. It is deeply ironic that this development occurred simultaneously with changes in domestic partisan politics that have marginalized the bankruptcy policy community from influencing substantive bankruptcy law and practice.

Epilogue

Bankruptcy is a kind of Rorschach test. People view bankruptcy in accordance with their idea of what America is or ought to be. Those people who imagine America as the homeland of independent, self-reliant entrepreneurs tend to view consumer bankruptcy as enabling the unworthy to escape responsibility for their bad decisions. Others view consumer bankruptcy as a necessary safety valve in an unequal, class-ridden society. Some economic conservatives consider corporate reorganization a sellout to management that enriches bankruptcy lawyers at the expense of shareholders and secured creditors. Some economic liberals view corporate reorganization as a devious plot to break unionized labor and shift environmental costs to the public sector. The close association between an ideological conception of America and attitudes toward bankruptcy was an important thread in nineteenth-century American politics. At the end of the twentieth century, the association became important again.

Bankruptcy attempts to balance debtors' desire for relief from the crushing burden of indebtedness and creditors' desire for cost-effective procedures for coercing the payment of debts. The balance has shifted from time to time, sometimes favoring debtors and sometimes favoring creditors. At first creditors held the upper hand; bankruptcy originated as a means for creditors to coerce debtors to disclose and turn over assets for the payment of debts. The idea of a bankruptcy discharge—that debtors would be discharged from their debts if they honestly disclosed and turned over all of their assets to their creditors—entered English law in 1705 with the Statute of 4 Anne. At that time, creditors controlled all the important bankruptcy decisions. Bankruptcy was an involuntary proceeding brought by creditors against traders and merchants who owed substantial debts, and creditors had to agree to the discharge. The first American bankruptcy statute in 1800 closely resembled the Statute of 4 Anne.[1]

Bankruptcy became more debtor friendly in the nineteenth century, especially in the United States. The short-lived Bankruptcy Act of 1841 (1841 to 1843) allowed private individuals as well as merchants and traders to seek bankruptcy protection on their own behalf, but a majority of creditors could block a discharge. The longer-lasting Bankruptcy Act of 1867 (1857–1878) contained similar provisions. The Bankruptcy Act of 1898 allowed all debtors except railroads, banks, insurance companies, and corporations to file for voluntary bankruptcy. Corporations would soon obtain the right to file for voluntary bankruptcy, but railroads would not be covered by the Bankruptcy Act until the 1930s; banks and insurance companies still have a different statutory regime for resolution. At first, only the commission of a bankruptcy crime, fraudulent concealment of a debtor's true financial condition, or destruction of financial records justified the denial of a discharge in bankruptcy. Creditors started pushing back almost immediately. Grounds for denying a discharge were expanded in 1903, but a debtor could still obtain a discharge unless he obtained credit by fraud, fraudulently conveyed assets within four months of filing bankruptcy, disobeyed the bankruptcy court's orders, or had received an earlier discharge in bankruptcy within six years.[2] The grounds for denying a discharge did not change materially until the 1980s.

Creditors have consistently complained that they received too little return on their debts under all of the bankruptcy acts. Sometimes creditors complained that the bankruptcy process was too expensive and cumbersome and consumed all of the debtors' assets. Sometimes creditors complained that it was too easy for debtors to discharge debts, and creditors would receive more if debtors were unable to discharge certain kinds of debts, were not allowed to retain as much property after bankruptcy, or were forced to repay some portion of their debts in order to obtain a discharge. Although consumer creditors and corporate creditors operate in very different legal and economic environments, deep dissatisfaction with current bankruptcy practice exists in both communities.

Creditors complained of low returns from bankruptcy estates under the bankruptcy acts of 1841 and 1867. Although there is no good comparative data, it is unlikely that bankruptcy was less efficient than state court creditor's remedies. In drafting the 1867 act, Congress responded to creditor complaints about the sources of inefficiency under the 1841 act, but creditors still complained that they received meager dividends. The 1867 bankruptcy act was unpopular with both creditors and debtors, and Congress repealed it in 1878. It is probable that creditors preferred bankruptcy to state court creditors' remedies, because creditors' organizations agitated incessantly for a uniform national bankruptcy act from repeal of the 1867 act until Congress enacted the Bankruptcy Act of 1898.

Creditors believed malfeasance by bankruptcy lawyers and other bankruptcy professionals contributed to the low dividends from bankruptcy estates under the bankruptcy acts of 1841 and 1867. Creditors complained that so-called "bankruptcy rings" consisting of lawyers and other bankruptcy professionals loitered around courthouses in order to secure lucrative bankruptcy appointments through fraud, bribery, or fortuitous happenstance, which they shared among themselves and their friends with the result that most of a bankruptcy estate was consumed in fees and expenses to the detriment of creditors. Creditors believed bankruptcy registers and district courts failed to adequately supervise bankruptcy appointments—and sometimes even shared in looting estates. In 1874, Congress amended the 1867 bankruptcy act in response to creditor complaints. The amendments halved the fees due registers, assignees, and other professionals appointed in bankruptcy cases and prohibited any clerk of court, register, or their law partner from taking any bankruptcy clients or having a financial interest of any kind in a bankruptcy case other than in their official capacity. The amendments did not end creditors' complaints, and Congress repealed the 1867 bankruptcy act in 1878.

Congress wrote the Bankruptcy Act of 1898 with creditors' complaints about the costs of administration in mind. Under the Bankruptcy Act, referees were paid by fees out of the bankruptcy estates and a percentage of the dividends that were paid to creditors, and they did not receive payment of their fees until the case was closed in order to encourage efficient administration. Even though referees were attorneys in private law practice, not salaried employees, they were prohibited from receiving any compensation, directly or indirectly through relatives or law partners, in connection with a bankruptcy case that had not been referred to them. General orders also prohibited referees from receiving additional compensation for "necessary acts required under the bankruptcy act" in cases referred to them, but the rule was strictly interpreted and referees received additional compensation for auxiliary services, such as presiding at depositions. Referees also assessed bankruptcy estates additional fees for administrative costs and expenses under local court rules. Accounting standards were lax, and referees often retained as income surplus expense payments. Consequently, many referees received substantial incomes from their bankruptcy practices, and many lawyers desired an appointment as referee in bankruptcy.

In the early 1920s, creditors' organizations complained again that bankruptcy rings looted bankruptcy estates, especially in big cities. A series of investigations were initiated beginning with a special conference in 1924 involving the National Association of Credit Men, the Commercial Law League, the American Bar Association, and a committee of the newly established Conference of Senior Circuit Judges and continuing through the 1929 joint investigation of numerous New York City bar associations into bankruptcy fraud in the Southern District of New York under the auspices of Judge Thomas D. Thacher of the Southern District of New York. Several egregious bankruptcy frauds were unearthed in the course of these investigations, and courts introduced numerous rule changes intended to reign in bankruptcy rings. This reform cycle culminated with enactment of the Chandler Act of 1938 and the Referees Salary Act in 1946. Ironically, the reforms intended to discourage bankruptcy rings produced conditions that encouraged a specialized, concentrated bankruptcy bar consisting primarily of low-status solo and small-firm practitioners, in other words, a bankruptcy ring.

In 1925, the Supreme Court promulgated General Orders prohibiting attorneys from soliciting powers of attorney to represent claims on behalf of creditors. These rules had the perverse effect of limiting the field of attorneys actively practicing in the bankruptcy courts to those with preexisting attorney-client relationships with organizations that delivered large numbers of potential claims, such as trade associations, consumer loan companies, or debt collection agencies. Furthermore, courts closely scrutinized claims for attorney compensation in bankruptcy cases. Invoking an overriding principle of economy in order to conserve estate assets for distribution to creditors, courts awarded attorney's fees in bankruptcy at considerably lower rates than similar work could command in other kinds of cases.[3] Consequently, few lawyers wanted to practice in bankruptcy court, and many of those who did could not get hired by established law firms because of social class or religious prejudice. Bankruptcy work was highly technical, and the bankruptcy bar was small, cohesive, and cooperative. The Cleveland bankruptcy bar of the 1960s was highly representative. To elite reformers and bar association leaders the bankruptcy bar looked like a bankruptcy ring. Many referees, including Carl Friebolin in Cleveland and Asa Herzog in the Southern District of New York, defended the reputation of the bankruptcy bar as attorneys who performed valuable services despite poor pay through specialization and professionalization.

Bankruptcy reformers in the 1930s believed bankruptcy lawyers were able to loot estates because referees in bankruptcy were not disinterested and independent of the bankruptcy bar. Furthermore, regardless of good intentions, they believed the volume of consumer bankruptcy cases was so pressing that referees could not adequately supervise the appointment of receivers, trustees, and their attorneys. Reformers unsuccessfully sought the creation of an administrative agency to process consumer bankruptcies outside of bankruptcy court. The bankruptcy policy community organized itself into the National Bankruptcy Conference and rallied to the defense of referees. The Chandler Act of 1938 retained consumer bankruptcy as a judicial proceeding. However, the Salary Act of 1946 also increased the institutional status and job security of referees in the hope that referees would better manage the cases and attorneys under their supervision. The federal courts finally developed internal administrative capacity in 1939 with the creation of the Administrative Office of the United States Courts, and the Bankruptcy Division of the Administrative Office furnished central direction and standardization, training, supervision, auditing, and other administrative services to referees. The involvement of the Administrative Office in the operation of the bankruptcy courts has increased steadily over time.

In the 1960s, when creditors complained again that bankruptcy rings looted estates to the detriment of creditors, the process repeated itself. Once again, bankruptcy reformers sought to move consumer bankruptcy out of bankruptcy courts into an administrative agency for processing. And once again, the bankruptcy policy community rallied to the defense of referees, with the result that bankruptcy courts and bankruptcy judges achieved even greater status and job security. In the 1970s, judicial reformers had written new, accessible bankruptcy rules integrating bankruptcy practice and general federal civil practice, and the Bankruptcy Code of 1978 replaced the Bankruptcy Act of 1898. By 1984, bankruptcy courts had become independent federal courts staffed by judges with almost permanent tenure. However, Congress also created a new administrative office in the Department of Justice—the Office of the United States Trustee—to take responsibility for the appointment and supervision of trustees in bankruptcy. No social scientist systematically surveyed the bankruptcy bar before 1980 so comparison is anecdotal, but complaints about bankruptcy rings ceased. Even though the bankruptcy bar remains more specialized than most areas of law practice, most commentators believe a higher proportion of nonspecialist lawyers appeared in bankruptcy courts after 1990 than before 1980.[4]

Traditionally, bankruptcy had been financed entirely by the parties to a bankruptcy proceeding. All of the personnel directly involved were private professionals compensated with fees from the parties or paid out of the bankruptcy estate. The only public funds used to support bankruptcy involved the cost of maintaining a federal court system. After 1946, bankruptcy court expenses were appropriated and paid as part of the federal judicial budget, but the Bankruptcy Division of the Administrative Office was tasked with setting fees in bankruptcy cases at a level such that bankruptcy would be self-supporting. The costs of maintaining the bankruptcy courts eventually became disassociated from the bankruptcy fees, but the fees continued to contribute materially to the costs of the system. Bankruptcy courts also have the authority to contract for additional facilities and services if necessary and to bill the costs directly to the bankruptcy estates using the services. The United States Trustee Program returns a profit to the US Treasury. In 1992, the fees paid to the US trustees exceeded the cost of running the trustee program by more than twenty percent.[5]

Although bankruptcy's cost to taxpayers was low, its cost to parties was high. Beginning in the 1990s, creditors demanded more administrative assurances that consumer debtors deserved bankruptcy relief, which resulted in higher costs to debtors seeking discharges. In the context of consumer bankruptcy, there is no evidence that imposing these costs on debtors increased returns to creditors, but it undoubtedly reduced consumer debtors' access to discharges of debt. Some critics argued that the unconditional debt discharge in consumer bankruptcy should be abolished altogether, and that all consumer debtors should be required to pay debts over time as is common in other countries.[6]

At the very least, creditors believed consumer debtors could pay more of their debts if they only wanted to, and creditors' attempts to push consumers into wage-earner plans began in the 1920s. Wage-earner plans allowed small consumer debtors to make partial payments to their creditors over time under the protection of the bankruptcy court. Creditors succeeded in establishing wage-earner plans with the Chandler Act of 1938, but few debtors preferred wage-earner plans over a simple debt discharge. Creditors continued to pressure for reforms that would force debtors into wage-earner plans, but many in the bankruptcy policy community strongly disapproved. The bankruptcy policy community considered the fresh start an individual obtained from the liberal discharge of debts to be the essence of bankruptcy; the fresh start embodied one vision of America as a land of opportunity where every person is entitled to a second chance in life. The Bankruptcy Code of 1978 compromised by encouraging straight Chapter 7 debtors to enter into Chapter 13 wage-earner plans with the promise of a superdischarge that discharged normally non-dischargeable debts upon successful completion of the plan.

The political climate changed in the 1980s, and creditors began to achieve greater success in limiting the dischargeability of certain kinds of debt. In 1984, amendments to the Bankruptcy Code gave bankruptcy judges the discretion to find a Chapter 7 bankruptcy abusive if a debtor had the means to pay down debts over time. The amendments authorized the bankruptcy court to dismiss a Chapter 7 proceeding or convert it to a Chapter 13 wage-earner plan, but bankruptcy judges almost never did so. After intense lobbying, creditors achieved most of their desired reforms with passage of the Bankruptcy Abuse Prevention and Consumer Protection Act of 2005. The legislation made it more difficult for consumer debtors to file bankruptcy and less beneficial to those debtors who succeeded in doing so. It lengthened the intervals allowed between bankruptcy filings and made more kinds of debt non-dischargeable. It created a presumption that a Chapter 7 bankruptcy filed by a debtor with above-average income was abusive and must be dismissed or converted to Chapter 13. It also extended the duration of Chapter 13 plans to five years and abolished the reward of a superdischarge upon successful completion of the plan.[7]

The 2005 legislation dramatically increased the cost of consumer bankruptcy to debtors. It created additional procedural requirements with strict time limits and severe consequences to debtors for noncompliance.

Most consumer bankruptcies were still filed under Chapter 7, and most Chapter 13 plans failed and were dismissed without a discharge of debts. Debtors had to go through credit counseling as part of the bankruptcy, and US trustees had to develop the curriculum and test its effectiveness. Debtors and their attorneys incurred substantial additional record-keeping obligations, especially those involving calculating and documenting the debtor's income in order to prove eligibility for Chapter 7 bankruptcy. Debtors were obligated to document information contained in their bankruptcy schedules, their attorneys were required to certify the accuracy of the schedules, and US trustees were required to audit a random sample. The Office of the United States Trustee received higher fees under the act, but the case trustees did not receive higher compensation.[8] Debtors had no right to file bankruptcy *in forma pauperis;* if a debtor could not afford a bankruptcy attorney, he was too poor to go bankrupt.

Bankruptcy's cost-benefit analysis was different in corporate bankruptcy than in consumer bankruptcy. There is no residual debtor to worry about in corporate bankruptcy; the corporation is a legal fiction, and the corporate shareholders have limited liability. State law corporation codes have procedures for dissolving insolvent corporations. Corporations secured the right to file voluntary bankruptcy petitions in 1910 primarily because they already did so as a matter of course through the legal fiction of having friendly creditors file involuntary petitions against them. Corporations did not reorganize in bankruptcy until the 1930s. Before that, they reorganized through federal court receivership—a nineteenth-century creditor-initiated legal innovation. Corporate reorganization in bankruptcy brought procedural efficiencies to receivership, and reformers believed the changes to corporate reorganization in the 1978 Bankruptcy Code would bring even greater efficiencies.

The number of corporate reorganizations increased dramatically after enactment of the Bankruptcy Code of 1978. Critics of corporate reorganization in bankruptcy alleged that the increase revealed a fatal defect in the bankruptcy law, while the bankruptcy policy community argued that the increase resulted from deterioration of the real economy coupled with increased corporate leverage and the growth of junk bond financing. With abolition of the "principle of economy" with regard to the payment of lawyers' fees, corporate reorganization became a highly lucrative area of practice in elite law firms. Critics claimed that excessive attorney's fees depleted bankruptcy estates to the detriment of creditors. Corporate reorganization in bankruptcy was an expensive, time-consuming process, and critics argued that it was economically inefficient compared with market-based alternatives. Some critics advocated abolishing corporate bankruptcy altogether in favor of creditor enforcement of their legal rights in civil courts.[9]

Critics of Chapter 11 complained that stockholders and bondholders lost disproportionately in corporate reorganizations because the reorganizations took too long and were dominated by management and well-paid hired professionals. The Bankruptcy Code of 1978 established a policy preference in favor of rehabilitation over liquidation of distressed corporations, and the code privileged management over creditors to achieve that goal. Most critics of Chapter 11 identified with the law and economics school of legal scholarship, and they argued that the neutral application of contract terms would waste less value. Judge Frank H. Easterbrook of the Seventh Circuit, a noted law and economics theorist, disagreed with the critics. He observed that corporate reorganization in bankruptcy had endured for a long time, and the only reasonable explanation was that bankruptcy was more efficient than market-based procedures in most cases.[10] In the Bankruptcy Abuse Prevention and Consumer Protection Act of 2005, critics of Chapter 11 convinced Congress to streamline corporate reorganizations by shortening deadlines and strengthening creditors' rights.

Critics of Chapter 11 decided that corporate reorganization wasted value before any serious empirical work had been done. Eventually, an extensive longitudinal study of business bankruptcies filed in 1994, supplemented by more limited analysis of business bankruptcies filed in 2002, established that corporate reorganization in Chapter 11 had been far more efficient than anybody had realized. Chapter 11 quickly sorted out those cases doomed to failure, and a substantial proportion of the remaining cases achieved a confirmed plan of reorganization reasonably expeditiously.[11] But the disagreement was not really about data; it was about ideology. People with profoundly different ideological orientations viewed the role of bankruptcy in a market economy in profoundly different ways.[12]

Defenders of Chapter 11 tend to be members of the traditional bankruptcy policy community: bankruptcy lawyers, bankruptcy judges, and bankruptcy scholars. They were instrumental in the creation of Chapter 11 in the Bankruptcy Code of 1978 and have strenuously defended its goals and priorities since then. They believe rehabilitating businesses maximizes value for the benefit of all stakeholders through collective action that reduces costs and limits destructive strategic behavior by creditors. They define stakeholder broadly to include communities, past and present employees, and unsecured creditors as well as senior secured creditors and shareholders.

Defenders of Chapter 11 believe going concern value is greater than liquidation value in most distressed corporations, but even where liquidation is inevitable, they believe an orderly liquidation will produce greater value for stakeholders. Furthermore, whether a distressed corporation is rehabilitated or liquidated, decisions about the allocation of assets and losses have consequences, and Chapter 11 strives to ensure the fair allocation of value by bringing all interested parties together into one forum. Ultimately, defenders of Chapter 11 recognize that business failures inevitably have redistributive consequences and believe that even parties without legal rights are entitled to be heard during the bankruptcy process. They believe the opportunity for all stakeholders to negotiate in one forum for the purpose of reaching agreement on a plan for reorganization enhances social solidarity in a democratic society.[13]

Critics of Chapter 11 tend to be academics without practical experience in bankruptcy. They believe market solutions to problems are generally more efficient than legal or administrative solutions, and they do not believe bankruptcy is an exception to the general rule. They think the bias toward rehabilitating distressed firms in Chapter 11 distorts the market and wastes value because it prevents the parties from achieving the most efficient allocation of assets. They argue that it is impossible to know a priori whether rehabilitation of a distressed firm is good or bad for workers and their community; they may benefit greatly from the sale of the assets of an incompetently managed firm to a gifted entrepreneur.

Critics of Chapter 11 generally believe it is a system designed for a world that no longer exists. Assets are fungible, and going concern value is nonexistent as a practical matter in a service economy. Furthermore, to the extent going concern value matters, it consists primarily of human relationships that can be reassigned by contract regardless of business structure or ownership. Critics of Chapter 11 also point to statistics that indicate that distressed corporations no longer use corporate reorganization for rehabilitation but to sell assets free and clear of inconvenient liabilities.

Critics of Chapter 11 see corporate bankruptcy from the point of view of creditors; fundamentally, they envision corporate bankruptcy as a competition between different kinds of creditors for control of the assets of the distressed corporation. They see no role for stakeholders who have no legal rights in the assets of the failing firm. These critics think it is a bad idea to create legal rights that are applicable only in one area of law, like bankruptcy. If certain interests deserve protection, they believe the law should create rights applicable in all situations. Critics of Chapter 11 believe the purpose of the law is to enforce legal rights, and market participants should be trusted to make informed choices in their contracts.

Businesses will continue to fail, and complex industrial societies will devise legal regimes for allocating the assets and losses. The United States has done this through bankruptcy for more than a century, and it is likely to continue to do so. In the nineteenth century, creditors demanded a national uniform system of bankruptcy in order to increase their return on bad debts, and all subsequent bankruptcy reforms were initiated with the purpose of increasing creditors' returns from bankruptcy estates. Sometimes the reforms aimed to increase returns by increasing the efficiency of administration or reducing costs from lawyers' fees and fraud; sometimes the reforms aimed to increase returns by capturing additional value from the debtor in the form of going concern value or future earnings. Ironically, the reforms inevitably resulted in greater procedural complexity and a larger administrative bureaucracy. Creditors still complain that bankruptcy costs too much to administer and wastes value.

A similar ideological divide separates the proponents of exempting derivatives and other financial products from the normal rules of bankruptcy from skeptical members of the traditional bankruptcy policy community. Derivatives and other financial products are contracts, and they contain provisions designed to protect the interests of a party in the event of increased risk or noncompliance by the counterparty, including rights to terminate the contract, seize assets, and net positions. Bankruptcy interferes with the strict enforcement of contractual rights by imposing an automatic stay that precludes a party from invoking contract remedies. Bankruptcy also enforces a look-back period before the filing of a petition in bankruptcy during which transactions may be voided as preferences or fraudulent conveyances. These bankruptcy provisions are designed to benefit both debtors and creditors. Debtors benefit from breathing room in which to rehabilitate. Creditors benefit by eliminating runs against failing debtors and ensuring that all creditors can expect to share equitably in the distribution of a debtor's assets.

As originally enacted, the Bankruptcy Code of 1978 provided a limited exemption from the automatic stay for non-debtor brokers and forward merchants with respect to deposits or transactions on margin in commodities contracts and forward transactions. Forward transactions are similar to futures contracts, but they do not trade on an exchange and are not regulated by the Commodities Futures Trading Commission. In 1982, Congress added an exemption to the look-back provisions for these transactions and expanded the kinds of transactions affected to include securities contracts. Proponents justified the special treatment on the grounds that these transactions were not like ordinary business transactions; thus, special treatment was necessary to ensure stability in the financial markets. In patchwork fashion, Congress expanded the exemptions to repurchase agreements in 1984, and swaps in 1990. With each act, Congress broadened the definition of the parties and the kinds of transactions entitled to exemption in order to eliminate inconsistencies and confusion regarding the treatment of financial products. In each case, the stated necessity for special treatment was the threat of systemic risk and market collapse if financial instruments were bound by the ordinary rules of bankruptcy.[14]

In September 1998, systemic risk threatened when the giant hedge fund Long Term Capital Management (LTCM) failed. Many feared that if the firm filed a bankruptcy petition, its counterparties would close contracts and seize assets as allowed by the special exemptions, thereby triggering a disorderly liquidation. Federal Reserve Board chairman Alan Greenspan arranged a bailout to avoid massive losses and potential failures in other financial firms because of ripple effects from LTCM's failure and possibly devastating consequences for the world economy.

Many studies of LCTM's collapse ensued, including the President's Working Group on Financial Markets, which consisted of treasury secretary Robert E. Rubin, Federal Reserve Board chairman Alan Greenspan, Securities and Exchange Commission chairman Arthur E. Levitt, and the Commodities Futures Trading Commission chairperson Brooksley Born. The President's Working Group issued a report in April 1999 finding that excessive leverage created the greatest systemic danger—LTCM's leverage at the end of 1997 was twenty-eight to one—and recommending reliance primarily on private market discipline to limit leverage. However, because of inconsistencies and confusion regarding the ability of parties to close and net positions in the event of an LCTM bankruptcy, the report also recommended bankruptcy amendments clarifying and expanding the rights of counterparties, especially with respect to master netting agreements. The report also recommended bankruptcy amendments to ensure that US law governed with respect to financial contracts in the bankruptcy of entities incorporated abroad—LTCM was incorporated in the Cayman Islands.[15]

Congress introduced the legislation recommended by the President's Working Group and incorporated it into pending bankruptcy reform legislation that ultimately became the Bankruptcy Abuse Prevention and Consumer Protection Act of 2005. The legislation greatly expanded the definition of parties and transactions entitled to special treatment and added the new category of master netting agreements.[16] Lobby groups for the derivatives industry strongly supported the proposed legislation, and Federal Reserve chairman Alan Greenspan and Treasury secretary Lawrence Summers testified before Congress in favor of it. Representatives of the National Bankruptcy Conference testified against expansion of the exemptions, questioning in particular the necessity of broad powers for netting across different financial products, but the reservations of the bankruptcy professionals were disregarded. Relying on the theories of economists with no bankruptcy experience, the legislation carved out a bankruptcy-free zone in bankruptcy cases for derivatives and other financial products.[17]

One proposed bankruptcy amendment that did not get enacted was extension of the special treatment for financial products to asset backed securities, such as the special-purpose entities used by Abbey National Treasury Services, PLC, and Chase National Bank in the LTV bankruptcy. The President's Working Group had not proposed that amendment in its report, and the National Bankruptcy Conference and the Commercial Law League of America strongly opposed it.[18] Many believe the widespread use of collateralized debt obligations, a kind of asset-backed security, precipitated the 2008 financial crisis.[19]

The proponents of special rules in bankruptcy for derivatives and other financial products share ideological ground with the conservative critics of Chapter 11. In general, they are market-oriented economists and financial services industry insiders who believe parties should be allowed to enforce their contracts, and they distrust government intervention in markets. For many years, they have promoted special treatment in bankruptcy products as necessary to ensure continued financial innovation and market stability. In general, they do not express concern over the success or failure of a debtor's reorganization, except to the extent it might affect the broader financial markets.

At first, the traditional bankruptcy policy community did not perceive the challenge to traditional bankruptcy posed by special exemptions for derivatives. In 1990, a representative of the National Bankruptcy Conference confessed to having no expertise on the appropriate treatment for derivatives in bankruptcy and deferred to the opinions of the Federal Reserve Board and industry lobbyists. When, in 1999, representatives of the National Bankruptcy Conference expressed reservations about further expansion of the special exemptions, their opinions carried no weight.[20]

Many in the traditional bankruptcy policy community believe shielding financial markets from the automatic stay and preference rules undermines the essential purpose of bankruptcy—debtor rehabilitation—by depriving debtors of resources necessary for reorganization. They argue that the creation of a bankruptcy-free market has weakened market discipline and produced an explosion in financial products specifically designed to replace traditional financial products that are subject to bankruptcy rules, such as secured loans, with financial products that are exempt from bankruptcy rules.[21]

An unintended natural experiment occurred with regard to the relationship between the exemption of derivatives and other financial products from bankruptcy rules and subsequent market volatility, but different people have drawn different conclusions from it depending on their ideological orientation. In 1999, the report of the President's Working Group opined that the situation could have been worse if LCTM had filed bankruptcy and counterparties had not been able to immediately terminate contracts and net positions; thus, the working group recommended further exemptions as a result. Subsequently, industry lobbyists and their regulators resisted all attempts to restrain the exemptions for derivatives in bankruptcy in the aftermath of the 2008 financial crisis. Conversely, when the 2008 financial crisis occurred despite the 2005 bankruptcy amendments, many in the traditional bankruptcy policy community questioned whether the bankruptcy amendments materially contributed to the financial crisis.[22]

The contemporary disagreement on bankruptcy policy is indicative of deeper divisions in American society that cannot be resolved empirically. There is no way to measure whether the administrative costs imposed by Chapter 11 are greater or less than the costs that would be incurred by the parties in the absence of Chapter 11 or whether the value that might be gained by superior allocation of the resources of distressed firms would be greater or less than the value lost through creditors' strategic action. Similarly, there is no way to measure whether periodic collapse in the financial markets is more or less likely or severe with special treatment for derivatives than without it.

Facts do matter, however. Understanding the evolution of institutions, and the costs and consequences of previous policy choices, can inform the values that will guide future policy decisions. This history of the Bankruptcy Court for the Northern District of Ohio seeks to facilitate that understanding by providing a case study of the institution as it copes with the social consequences of bankruptcy in a changing economy.

Appendix

Commissioners in Bankruptcy under the 1841 Act for the Counties in Northern Ohio That Became the Northern Judicial District of Ohio

Ashtabula County
N. C. Chaffee

Carroll County
Robert McLane

Columbiana County
Anson S. Brewer

Crawford County
Zalmon Rowse

Cuyahoga County
James K. Hitchcock
Royal Stewart

Erie County
Pitt Cooke

Geauga County
Alfred Phelps

Hardin County
H. B. Strother

Holmes County
W. S. Taneyhill

Huron County
Jarius Kennon

Lake County
Salmon L. Osborn

Lorain County
Herman Birch

Lucas County
Daniel Chase
Henry Reed Jr.

Marion County
B. R. Durfee

Medina County
William H. Canfield

Mercer County
Oliver C. Rood

Paulding County
Henry Reed (of Lucas County)

Portage County
Ebenezer Spalding

Richland County
L. C. Coffinberry

Sandusky County
Lucien B. Otis

Seneca County
Richard Williams

Stark County
Hinman B. Hurlbert

Summit County
Henry W. Krieg

Trumbull County
J. M. Edwards

Tuscarawas County
B. M. Atherton

Wayne
George W. Mason

Williams County
Henry Reed (of Lucas County)

Wood County
Hezekiah L. Hosmer

There were no known commissioners for Allen, Hancock, Henry, Ottawa, Putnam, and Van Wert counties

Registers in Bankruptcy under the 1867 Act in the Northern Judicial District of Ohio

Appointed May 27, 1867

R. P. Kennedy of Bellfontain, Logan County:
For the county of Logan in the 4th Congressional District (Champaign, Darke, Logan, Miami, and Shelby counties).

Moses B. Walker of Findlay, Hancock County:
For the 5th Congressional District (Allen, Auglaize, Hancock, Hardin, Mercer, Van Wert, and Wyandot counties). Replaced by James Irvin on January 25, 1869.

Henry C. Hedges of Mansfield, Richland County:
For the 8th Congressional District (Delaware, Marion, Morrow, Richland, and Union counties).

Franklin Sawyer of Norwalk, Huron County:
For the 9th Congressional District (Crawford, Erie, Huron, Ottawa, Sandusky, and Seneca counties).

J. R. Swigart of Napoleon, Henry County:
For the 10th Congressional District (Defiance, Fulton, Henry, Lucas, Paulding, Putnam, Williams, and Wood counties). Resigned on July 2, 1868, and replaced by J. R. Osborn.

Joseph C. Devin of Mount Vernon, Knox County:
For the counties of Knox and Coshocton in the 13th Congressional District (Coshocton, Knox, Licking, and Muskingham counties).

W. W. Boynton of Elyria, Lorain County:
For the 14th Congressional District (Ashland, Holmes, Lorain, Medina, and Wayne counties). Declined to serve. John C. Hale of Elyria, Lorain County was appointed register in his place on June 15, 1867.

Myron R. Keith of Cleveland, Cuyahoga County:
For the 18th Congressional District (Cuyahoga, Lake, Mahoning, and Summit counties).

Lucien C. Jones of Warren, Trumbull County:
For the 19th Congressional District (Ashtabula, Geauga, Portage, and Trumbull counties).

Appointed May 31, 1867
Cornelius Curry of Salem, Columbiana County:
For the 17th Congressional District (Carroll, Columbiana, Jefferson, and Stark Counties). Reassigned to Joseph J. Parker on November 20, 1867. Reassigned to J. D. Lewis in June 1877.

Appointed October 1867
Eli Sheppard
For Tuscarawas County in the 16th Congressional District (Belmont, Guernsey, Harrison, Noble, and Tuscarawas counties).

Referees in Bankruptcy under the 1898 Act in the Northern Judicial District of Oho from July 1898 through June 1947

Cleveland

Cuyahoga County
Richard Chappel Parsons (July 29, 1898, to January 9, 1899)
Harold Remmington (appointed referee for the 19th Ward of the city of Cleveland on July 30, 1898; jurisdiction was expanded to the whole county on January 12, 1899–1909)
A. F. Ingersoll (1909–1916)
Carl D. Friebolin (1916–1967)
William B. Woods (second judge, 1930–1963)

Lorain and Medina counties (Elyria)
Merged into Cleveland in 1931.
H. L. Fay (1899–1901)
Louis B. Fauver (1901–1907)
P. H. Boynton (1907–1911)
James H. Leonard (1911–1915)
Thomas A. Conway (1915–1931)

Akron

Summit County
Portage County merged into Summit County in 1916.
Dayton A. Doyle (1898–1906)
Harry L. Snyder (1906–1939)
Everette L. Foote (1939–1947)

Canton

Stark and Carroll counties
A. M. McCarty (1898–1915)
Celsus Pomerene (1915–1926)
Harvey F. Ake (1926–1928)
Paul D. Roach (1928–1947)

Tuscarawas County
Merged into Stark and Carroll counties in 1929.
T. H. Loller (Dennison) (1898–1915)
H. H. Hostetler (Canal Dover) (1915–1929)

Ashland County (Ashland)
Merged into Stark and Carroll counties in 1932.
George B. Smith (1898–?)
Frank N. Patterson (1912–1914)
Maurice V. Semple (1914–1925)
A. D. Metz (Wooster, Wayne County) (1925–1932)

Wayne and Holmes counties (Wooster)
Merged into Ashland County in 1923.
William F. Kean (1898–1914)
John McSweeney (1914–1918)
Joseph O. Fritz (1918–1923)

Bucyrus
Crawford County
Merged into Stark and Carroll counties in 1945.
W. L. Monnett (1898–1912)
William G. Beer (1912–1945)

Richland County (Mansfield)
Merged into Crawford County in 1925.
Charles H. Keating (1898–1906)
Harry L. Beam (1906–1914)
B. Franklin Long (1914–1915?)
R. E. Hutchinson (1915?–1921)
Van C. Cook (1921–1925)

Ashtabula
Ashtabula County (Ashtabula)
A. P. Laughlin (1898?; resigned January 11, 1900)
J. H. McGiffert (1900–1915)
J. F. Munsell (1915–1927)
A. T. Ullman (1927–1943)
Charles J. Starkey (1943–1947)

Border Counties
Geauga, Lake, Portage, and Ashtabula counties

Geauga County
Harold Remmington (Geauga County from July 30, 1898 to January 12, 1899; Portage County from December 27, 1898, to January 12, 1899)

Geauga, Lake, and Portage counties (Painesville)
Geauga and Lake counties merged into Ashtabula County in 1916. Portage County merged into Summit County in 1916.
Louis J. Wood (1899–1907)
Bartlett J. Shepherd (1907–1915)

Youngstown

Mahoning County (Youngstown)
Charles D. Dickenson (1898–?)
W. C. McKain (1903–?)
Samuel E. Joshua (1908–?)
Paul J. Jones (1912–1916)
Paul E. Carson (1916–1933)
William. J. Williams (1933–1943)
Ross E. Diser (1943–1947)

Trumbull County (Warren)
Merged into Mahoning County in 1918.
L. F. Hunter (1898–1918)

Columbiana County
Merged into Mahoning and Trumbull counties in the 1920s.
Charles D. Dickenson of Leetonia (1898–1908)
Charles C. Connell (Lisbon) (1908–1914)
C. F. Smith (Salem) (1914–1920)
W. W. Warren (Leetonia) (1920–1924)

Toledo

Lucas County (Toledo)
Fordyce Belford (1898–1929)
Fred H. Kruse (1927–1947)
Frank C. Kniffen (second Toledo referee, 1939–1965)

Fulton and Williams Counties
Merged into Lucas County in 1901.
Fred. S. Ham (1898–1901)

Erie County (Sandusky)
Jurisdiction enlarged to include Ottawa County in May 1901. Ottawa County had no previous referee. Erie and Ottawa Counties merged into Lucas County in 1914.
R. B. Fisher (1898–1900)
E. S. Stephens (1900–1906)
Claude B. DeWitt (1906–1914)

Wood and Henry Counties (Bowling Green)
Merged into Lucas County in 1914.
Edward M. Fries (1898–1903)
William G. Elliot (1903–1908)
J. E. Shatzell (1908–1914)

Huron County (Norwalk)
Merged into Lucas County in 1914.
H. L. Fay (1898–1899)
L. W. Wickham (1899–1904?)
Ben C. Wickham (1907?–1914)

Sandusky County (Fremont)
Merged into Lucas County in 1914.
Frank E. Seager (1898–1914)

Lima

Allen, Auglaize, and Putnam Counties
Merged into Lucas County in 1943.
S. S. Wheeler (Lima) (1898–1905)
J. W. Mowen (Lima) (1905–1908)
Harvey. D. Grindle (Lima) (1908–1930)
Herbert P. Eastman (Ottawa, Putnam County) (1930–1932)
Walter S. Jackson (Lima) (1931–1943)

Mercer County (Celina)
Merged into Allen, Auglaize, and Putnam counties in 1914.
S. S. Wheeler (1898–1899)

Chas. S. Younger (1899–1906)
E. J. Brookhart (1906–1914)

Van Wert County (Van Wert)
Merged into Allen, Auglaize, and Putnam counties in 1914.
H. G. Richie (1898–1914)

Paulding and Defiance Counties (Paulding)
Merged into Allen, Auglaize, and Putnam counties in 1914
John S. Snook (1898–1901)
W. B. Brattain (1901–?)
George H. Bayliss for Paulding County (Paulding) (1910–1914)
Kidder V. Haymaker for Defiance County (Defiance) (1910–1914)

Kenton
Hardin County (Kenton)
George E. Crane (1898–1916)
Hardin County merged into Lucas County in 1916.

Hancock County (Findlay)
Merged into Hardin County in 1914.
John W. Grimm (1898–1906)
Nimrod W. Bright (1906–1914)

Seneca County (Tiffin)
Merged into Hardin County in 1914.
George E. Schroth (1898–1903)
Charles E. Derr (1903–1914

Wyandot and Marion Counties
Robert Carey (Upper Sandusky) (1898–1914?)
Merged into Hardin County in 1914.
Hoke Donithen appointed for Marion County (Marion) (1910–1914)
Merged into Lucas County in 1914.

Referees in Bankruptcy and Bankruptcy Judges in the Northern Judicial District of Ohio from July 1947 to 2014

Cleveland

Includes Cuyahoga, Lorain, Lake, and Geauga counties. Until 1958, the area now included in the Akron and Canton districts was also included in the Cleveland district.

First Judge:
Carl D. Friebolin (1916–1967)
Donald C. Miller (1965–1977)
Mark Schlachet (1977–1982)
Alice Batchelder (1983–1985)
Randolph Baxter (1985–2011)
Jessica E. Price Smith (2011–present)

Second Judge:
William B. Woods (1930–1963)
Paul J. Gnau (1963–1969)
Joseph Patchan (1969–1975)
John Francis Ray Jr. (1975–1987)
David P. Snow (1988–2000)
Arthur I. Harris (2001–present)

Third Judge:
William J. O'Neill (1961–1994)
Pat E. Morgenstern-Clarren (1994–present)

Akron

Includes Medina, Portage, and Summit counties. There was no referee in bankruptcy in Akron from 1947 to 1958.

Harold F. White (1958–1994)
Marilyn Shea-Stonum (1994–2014)
Alan M. Koschik (2014–present)

Canton

Includes Ashland, Carroll, Crawford, Holmes, Richland, Stark, Tuscarawas, and Wayne counties. There was no bankruptcy referee in Canton from 1947 until 1961.

James H. Emsley (1961–1972)
James H. Williams (1972–1999)
Russ Kendig (2001–present)

Youngstown

Includes Ashtabula, Columbiana, Mahoning, and Trumbull counties.

Ross E. Diser (1951–1959)
Harold B. Doyle (1959–1965)
Joseph T. Molitoris (1965–1983)
William J. Bodoh (1985–2004)
Kay Woods (2004–present)

Toledo

Includes Allen, Auglaize, Defiance, Erie, Fulton, Hancock, Hardin, Henry, Huron, Lucas, Marion, Mercer, Ottawa, Paulding, Putnam, Sandusky, Seneca, Van Wert, Williams, Wood, and Wyandot counties.

First Judge:
Frank C. Kniffen (1939–1965)
Walter J. Krasniewski (1965–1994)
Mary Ann Whipple (2001–present)

Second Judge:
T. Kenneth Mattimoe (1961–1975)
Richard L. Speer (1975–2013)
John P. Gustafson (2014–present)

Notes

Preface

1. Noel F. Regis, *A History of the Bankruptcy Law* (1919; repr., New York: William S. Hein, 2002); Charles Warren, *Bankruptcy in United States History* (1935; repr., Buffalo, NY: William S. Hein, 2004); David A. Skeel, *Debt's Dominion: A History of Bankruptcy Law in America* (Princeton, NJ: Princeton University Press, 2001). For article-length treatments see also Charles Jordan Tabb, "The History of the Bankruptcy Laws in the United States," *American Bankruptcy Institute Law Review* 3 (1995): 5–51; David S. Kennedy and R. Spenser Cliff III, "An Historical Analysis of Insolvency Laws and Their Impact on the Role, Power, and Jurisdiction of Today's United States Bankruptcy Court and Its Judicial Officers," *Journal of Bankruptcy Law and Practice* 9 (2000): 165–200.

2. For example, Edward J. Balleisen, *Navigating Failure: Bankruptcy and Commercial Society in Antebellum America* (Chapel Hill: University of North Carolina Press, 2001); Bruce H. Mann, *Republic of Debtors: Bankruptcy in the Age of American Independence* (Cambridge, MA: Harvard University Press, 2002); Elizabeth Thompson, *The Reconstruction of Southern Debtors: Bankruptcy after the Civil War* (Athens: University of Georgia Press, 2004).

3. United States Courts for the Second Circuit, Committee on History and Commemorative Events, *The Development of Bankruptcy and Reorganization Law in the Courts of the Second Circuit of the United States* (New York: Matthew Bender, 1995).

Chapter 1

1. Stephen Skowronek, *Building a New American State: The Expansion of National Administrative Capacities, 1877–1920* (New York: Cambridge University Press, 1982); Ballard C. Campbell, *The Growth of American Government* (Bloomington: Indiana University Press, 1995).

2. The classic discussion comparing these two approaches to law and society is found in Robert W. Gordon, "Critical Legal Histories," *Stanford Law Review* 36 (1984): 57–125.

3. Jeremy Atack and Peter Passell, *A New Economic View of American History from Colonial Times to 1940*, 2nd ed. (New York: W. W. Norton, 1994), 484–87; Naomi R. Lamoreaux, *The Great Merger Movement in American Business, 1895–1904* (New York: Cambridge University Press, 1985).

4. U.S. Const. art. 1, §10; Sturges v. Crowninshield, 17 U.S. 122 (1819); Ogden v. Saunders, 25 U.S. 213 (1827).

5. Thomas Clifford Billig, *Equity Receiverships in the Common Pleas Court of Franklin County* (Baltimore: Johns Hopkins University Press, 1932).

6. Richard C. Sauer, "Bankruptcy Law and the Maturing of American Capitalism," *Ohio State Law Journal* 55 (1994): 291–339.

7. Bradley Hansen, "The People's Welfare and the Origins of Corporate Reorganization: The Wabash Receivership Reconsidered," *Business History Review* 71 (2000): 377–405.

8. For an overview of the early American ideology of republicanism, see Robert E. Shalhope, "Republicanism and Early American Historiography," *William and Mary Quarterly, 3rd Series* 39 (1982): 334–56.

9. Atack and Passell, *A New Economic View of American History*, 457–81.

10. Ibid., 523.

11. For an overview, see Harvey R. Miller and Shai Y. Waisman, "Is Chapter 11 Bankrupt?" *Boston College Law Review* 47 (2005): 129–81.

12. Bruce G. Carruthers and Terence C. Halliday, *Rescuing Business: The Making of Corporate Bankruptcy Law in England and the United States* (Oxford, UK: Clarendon Press, 1998), 254–66.

13. As Victor Posner learned, management did not always do well in corporate reorganization. "Sharon Steel Pact Reached," *New York Times*, July 30, 1990.

14. Miller, "Is Chapter 11 Bankrupt?" 145; Barry T. Hirsch and David A. Macpherson, *Union Membership and Coverage Database from the CPS*, Union Membership, Coverage, Density, and Employment Among Private Sector Manufacturing Workers, 1973–2011, http://www.unionstats.com.

15. Richard Levin and Alesia Marinelli, "The Creeping Repeal of Chapter 11: The Significant Business Provisions of the Bankruptcy Abuse and Consumer Protection Act of 2005," *American Bankruptcy Law Journal* 79 (2005): 603–44.

16. Miller, "Is Chapter 11 Bankrupt?" 130.

17. Ibid., 146–60.

18. "Is Chapter 11 Bankrupt?" 131; The data set is Lynn M. LoPucki's Bankruptcy Research Database, the significance of which is debated in Douglas G. Baird and Robert K. Rasmussen, "Chapter 11 at Twilight," *Stanford Law Review* 56 (2003): 673–99, and Lynn M. LoPucki, "The Nature of the Bankruptcy Firm: A Response to Baird and Rasmussen's *The End of Bankruptcy*," *Stanford Law Review* 56 (2003): 645–71.

19. For example, Douglas G. Baird and Robert K. Rasmussen, "The End of Bankruptcy," *Stanford Law Review* 55 (2002): 751–89.

20. Skowronek, *Building a New American State,* 5.

21. Robert H. Wiebe, *The Search for Order, 1877–1920* (New York: Hill & Wang, 1967); Wiebe coined the phrase "island community" to describe nineteenth-century social structure.

22. Wolf Heydebrand and Carroll Seron, *Rationalizing Justice: The Political Economy of Federal District Courts* (Albany: State University of New York Press, 1990), 30–43.

23. Royal E. Jackson, "Bankruptcy Administration: Then and Now," *American Bankruptcy Law Journal* 45 (1971): 249–80.

24. An Act: To Amend Title 28 of the United States Code Regarding Jurisdiction of Bankruptcy Proceedings, to Establish New Federal Judicial Positions, to Amend Title 11 of the United States Code, and for Other Purposes, Stat. 98 (1984): 333–992.

25. *Stern v. Marshall,* 564 U.S._, 131 S. Ct. 2594 (2011); *Executive Benefits Insurance Agency v. Arkinson,* 573 U.S._ (2014).

26. Heydebrand and Seron, *Rationalizing Justice,* 13–14.

27. Heydebrand and Seron, 100. Bankruptcy statistics are from the Bankruptcy Division of the Administrative Office of the United States Courts. Bankruptcy statistics after 1980 may be found at the American Bankruptcy Institute: http://www.abiworld.org/AM/AMTemplate.cfm?Section=Home&TEMPLATE=/CM/ContentDisplay.cfm&CONTENTID=65139.

28. For the "moral economy of debt," see Bruce Mann, *Republic of Debtors: Bankruptcy in the Age of American Independence* (Cambridge, MA: Harvard University Press, 2002). The next chapter discusses this concept more deeply.

Chapter 2

1. U.S. Const. art 1, §8. On the early history of bankruptcy see Charles Jordan Tabb, "The History of the Bankruptcy Laws in the United States," *American Bankruptcy Law Review* 3 (1965): 6–14; idem, "The Historical Evolution of the Bankruptcy Discharge," *American Bankruptcy Law Journal* 65 (1991): 325–71.

2. U.S. Const. art. 1, §10 prohibited the states from passing laws impairing the obligations of contracts. In Sturges v. Crowninshield, 17 U.S. 122 (1819), the United States Supreme Court held that state insolvency laws could not discharge the debts incurred before enactment of the law, and in Ogden v. Saunders, 25 U.S. 213 (1827), the court held that state insolvency laws could not discharge the debts of a nonresident creditor. These holdings severely impaired the effectiveness of any state bankruptcy statutes, although some states passed bankruptcy statutes during the nineteenth century. Ohio did not.

3. Andrew R. L. Clayton, "Law and Authority in the Northwest Territory," in *The History of Ohio Law,* eds. Michael Les Benedict and John F. Winkler (Athens: Ohio University Press, 2004). Primogeniture existed under Virginia law until 1786, and it became traditional for second sons to seek their own estates in the Ohio country on Virginia's western border.

4. Timothy J. Shannon, "The Ohio Company and the Meaning of Opportunity in the American West, 1786–1795," *New England Quarterly* 64 (1991): 393–413.

5. For more information on the Scioto Company, see Robert F. Jones, "William Duer and the Business of Government in the War of the American Revolution," *William and Mary Quarterly, 3rd Series* 32 (July 1975): 393–414; Archer Butler Hulbert, "The Methods and Operations of the Scioto Group of Speculators," *Mississippi Valley Historical Review* 1 (1915): 505–15; Archer Butler Hulbert, "The Methods and Operations of the Scioto Group of Speculators, continued," *Mississippi Valley Historical Review* 2 (1915): 56–73. On Platt, see Shannon, "The Ohio Company," 411.

6. On the panic of 1797, see Richard S. Chew, "Certain Victims of an International Contagion: The Panic of 1797 and the Hard Times of the Late 1790s in Baltimore," *Journal of the Early Republic* 25 (2005): 565–613. For a more sanguine view of the economy of the 1790s, see Douglas North, *The Economic Growth of the United States, 1790–1860* (Englewood Cliffs, NJ: Prentice-Hall, 1961), 24–55.

7. Bruce H. Mann, *Republic of Debtors: Bankruptcy in the Age of American Independence* (Cambridge, MA: Harvard University Press, 2002), 194–203. Indeed, much of the discussion on the 1800 Bankruptcy Act is informed by Mann.

8. An Act: To Establish a Uniform System of Bankruptcy Throughout the United States (1800), *Statutes at Large of the United States of America*, vol. 2 (Boston: Charles C Little and James Brown, 1845), 19–36.

9. Tabb, "The Historical Evolution of the Bankruptcy Discharge," 345–48.

10. Mann, *Republic of Debtors*, 55–76.

11. I am indebted to Bruce Mann's *Republic of Debtors* for the concept of a "moral economy of debt." On the development of a market economy in middle eighteenth-century New England, see Winifred Barr Rothenberg, *From Market-places to a Market Economy: The Transformation of Rural Massachusetts* (Chicago: University of Chicago Press, 1992). For a different view of the early development of a market economy, see Christopher Clark, *The Roots of Rural Capitalism: Western Massachusetts, 1780–1860* (Ithaca, NY: Cornell University Press, 1990).

12. Clayton, 18, quoting the Northwest Ordinance of 1787.

13. A Law Limiting Imprisonment for Debt, and Subjecting Certain Debtors and Delinquents to Servitude (August 15, 1795) found in Salmon P. Chase, ed., *The Statutes of Ohio and the Northwestern Territory* (Cincinnati: Corey and Fairbank, 1833), 1: 203–204. On the Pennsylvania law of insolvency, see Laurence Shaiman, "The History of Imprisonment for Debt and Insolvency Laws in Pennsylvania as They Evolved from the Common Law," *American Journal of Legal History* 4 (1960): 205–25.

14. An Act for the Relief of Poor Persons Imprisoned for Debt (1799), found in Chase, *The Statutes of Ohio*, 1: 258–60.

15. An Act for the Relief of Insolvent Persons (1805), found in Chase, *The Statutes of Ohio*, 1: 510–11.

16. See *Page's Ohio Revised Code Annotated* (Charlottesville, VA: Mathew Bender, 2006) §§ 1313.01 through 1313.59 (2011 supplement).

17. Wadsworth v. Wetmore, 6 Ohio 438 (1834).

18. An Act Regulating Prison Bounds (1805), found in Chase, *The Statutes of Ohio*, 1: 489–90; An Act Defining the Prison Bounds of the Several Counties of the State (1832), found in Chase, *The Statutes of Ohio*, 3: 1935.

19. Lucky v. Brandon, 1 Ohio 49 (1823).

20. Buttles v. Carlton, 1 Ohio 33 (1822).

21. An Act to Abolish Imprisonment for Debt, *Ohio Laws* 36 (1838): 75.

22. Ohio Constitution of 1851 art. 1, § 15. Imprisonment for Debt. Found at *Laws of Ohio* 50 (1952): 5.

23. *Page's Ohio Revised Code*, §§ 2331.02; 2713.02 (2011 supplement).

24. 7 *Ohio Jurisprudence*, 971–77. (Henry P. Farnham, ed., 1928).

25. Kenneth Nichols, *Yesterday's Akron: The First 150 Years* (Miami, FL: E. A. Seeman Publishing, 1975), 7–9.

26. See Harry N. Scheiber, "The Commercial Bank of Lake Erie, 1831–1843," *Business History Review* 40 (1966): 49–50.

27. Scheiber, "The Commercial Bank of Lake Erie," 58–61; "To the Public," Daily Herald and Gazette (Cleveland, Ohio), May 19, 1937; "Commercial Bank of Lake Erie," Cleveland Daily Herald, March 3, 1842, Issue 137, found in 19th Century U.S. Newspapers (Gale Digital Collections).

28. Peter L. Rousseau, "Jacksonian Monetary Policy, Specie Flows, and the Panic of 1837," *Journal of Economic History* 62 (2002): 480–83.

29. Ernest Ludlow Bogart, *Financial History of Ohio* (Urbana-Champaign: University of Illinois Press, 1912), 39–44.

30. David C. Hammack, "Economy," in *Encyclopedia of Cleveland History*, 2nd ed. (Bloomington: Indiana University Press, 1996), 371–76, available at ech.cwru.edu.

31. Charles Warren, *Bankruptcy in United States History* , (1935; repr. Buffalo, NY: William S. Hein, 1994), 69–79.

32. David A. Skeel, *Debt's Dominion: A History of Bankruptcy Law in America* (Princeton, NJ: Princeton University Press, 2001), 32, fn. 23.

33. An Act: To Establish a Uniform System of Bankruptcy Throughout the United States (1841), *Statutes at Large of the United States of America*, vol. 5 (Boston: Charles C. Little and James Brown, 1846), 440–49. See Tabb, "The Historical Evolution of Bankruptcy Discharge," 349–53.

34. An Act Regulating Judgments and Executions, *Laws of Ohio* 29 (1831) 101 et seq., §§ 10, 12 at 103–104; An Act to Amend an Act Entitled "An Act for the Relief of Insolvent Debtors," *Laws of Ohio* 32 (1834): 23.

35. Letter from the Secretary of State Transmitting Statements Showing Proceedings under the Bankrupt Act, February 23, 1847, 29th Cong., 2d Sess., H.R. Doc. 99.

36. An Act for the Relief of Insolvent Debtors (1824), found at Chase, *Statutes of Ohio*, 2: 1403–1406.

37. A list of commissioners in northern Ohio is included in the appendix.

38. Edward J. Balleisen, *Navigating Failure: Bankruptcy and Commercial Society in Antebellum America* (Chapel Hill: University of North Carolina Press, 2001).

39. Ron Chernow, *Titan: The Life of John D. Rockefeller, Sr.* (New York: Random House, 1998; Second Vintage Books Edition, 2004), 45.

40. Charles W. Calomiris and Larry Schweikart, "The Panic of 1857: Origins, Transmission, and Containment," *Journal of Economic History* 51 (1991): 807–34.

41. An Act: To Establish a Uniform System of Bankruptcy throughout the United States (1867), *Statutes at Large of the United States of America*, vol. 14 (Boston: Little, Brown & Co., 1868), 517–41; Warren, *Bankruptcy in United States History*, 103–110. See also Edwin James, *The Bankruptcy Law of the United States, 1867. With Notes and a Collection of American and English Decisions upon the Principles and Practice of Bankruptcy Adapted to the Use of the Lawyer and Merchant* (New York: Harper & Brothers, 1867); Tabb, "The Historical Evolution of the Bankruptcy Discharge," 353–62; Elizabeth Thompson, *The Reconstruction of Southern Debtors: Bankruptcy after the Civil War* (Athens: University of Georgia Press, 2004).

42. The National Bureau of Economic Research (NBER) dates the peak of the business cycle in October 1873 and the trough in March 1879, a sixty-five month period of economic contraction, NBER, *U.S. Business Cycle Expansions and Contractions*, http://www.nber.org/cycles.html.

43. An Act: To Amend and Supplement an Act Entitled "An Act to Establish a Uniform System of Bankruptcy throughout the United States," Approved March Second, Eighteen Hundred and Sixty-seven, and for Other Purposes, Stat. 18 (1874): 178–86.

44. Vern Countryman, "A History of American Bankruptcy Law," *Commercial Law Journal* 81(1976): 230, interpreting the bankruptcy statistics reported in the attorney general's report for 1879.

45. A list of registers is included in the appendix.

46. See, generally, Felice A. Bonadio, *North of Reconstruction: Ohio Politics, 1865–1870* (New York: New York University Press, 1970).

47. Ironically, Chase also unsuccessfully sought the Democratic presidential nomination in 1868. In 1872 he helped found the Liberal Republican Party and unsuccessfully sought its presidential nomination. He died on May 7, 1873.

48. The application files are found at NARA, Washington, DC, RG 267, U.S. Supreme Court, Entry 73: Applications and Endorsements, 1867–1909; Registers in Bankruptcy, Ohio, Boxes 39–42, hereinafter Entry 73, RG 267, NARA DC. Special thanks to NARA Washington, DC, archivist Robert Ellis who alerted me to the existence of the application file.

49. Applications and Endorsements for Register in Bankruptcy, Ohio, 19th District Candidates, File Unit Edward D. Horton and File Unit Alexander McConnell, Entry 73, RG 267, NARA DC.

50. Letter from Earl Bill to John Sherman, Applications and Endorsements for Register in Bankruptcy, Ohio, 18th District Candidates, File Unit Keith, Myron, both in Entry 73, RG 267, NARA DC.

51. James Harrison Kennedy, *The Bench and Bar of Cleveland* (Cleveland: Cleveland Printing and Publishing, 1889), 2, 53, 261–62.

52. Chernow, *Titan,* 224–25; Kenneth W. Rose, associate director, Research and Education, Rockefeller Archive Center, Sleepy Hollow, New York, confirmed the general dates and nature of the correspondence located in their files.

53. Letter from Jacob Heaton to Chief Justice Salmon P. Chase, March 24 1867, Applications and Endorsements for Register in Bankruptcy, Ohio, 17th District Candidates, File Unit Curry, Cornelius, Entry 73, RG 267, NARA DC.

54. Applications and Endorsements for Register in Bankruptcy, Ohio, 17th District Candidates, File Unit Parker, Joseph J., Entry 73, RG 267, NARA DC.

55. Applications and Endorsements for Register in Bankruptcy, Ohio, Applications and Endorsements, 1868–69, 5th District, File Unit Appointments Etc., Irvine, James, Entry 73, RG 267, NARA DC.

56. Population comes from the US Census. The number of cases filed in the Northern District of Ohio under the 1867 Bankruptcy Act was determined by the bankruptcy docket books at the National Archives in Chicago, Record Group 21, USDC Cleveland and Toledo. Assuming half of Ohio's population of 2,665,260 in 1870 lived in the northern district, the annual filing rate would be approximately 1/10,000 or 0.0001. Countryman, "A History of American Bankruptcy Law" at page 230 estimates the filing rate in the United States as a whole at 0.0002 of the population.

57. Jeremy Atack and Peter Passell, *A New Economic View of American History from Colonial Times to 1940*, 2nd ed. (New York: W. W. Norton, 1994), 457.

58. Michael S. Fogarty, Gasper S. Garofalo, and David Hammack, "Cleveland from Startup to the Present: Innovation and Entrepreneurship" (a report of the Center for Regional Economic Issues, Weatherhead School of Management, Case Western Reserve University, 2003), available at: http://www.generationfoundation.org/pubs/ClevelandFromStartupToPresent.pdf , 23–24.

59. NBER, *U.S. Business Cycle Expansions and Contractions.*

60. Robert P. Rogers, *An Economic History of the American Steel Industry* (New York: Routledge, 2009), 17–20.

61. City Planning Associates, *Preliminary Report 1 for Youngstown, Ohio Community Renewal Program R-108 (CR): Historical Development of Youngstown and the Mahoning Valley* (Youngstown, Ohio: City Planning Associates, 1968), 2–18.

62. Darwin Stapleton, "Automotive Industry" in *Encyclopedia of Cleveland History.*

63. Bradley Hansen, "Commercial Associations and the Creation of a National Economy: The Demand for a Federal Bankruptcy Law," *Business History Review* 72 (1998): 86–113.

64. For an overview, see Warren, *Bankruptcy in United States History,* 128–40. See also Charles Jordan Tabb, "A Century of Regress or Progress? A Political History

of Bankruptcy Legislation in 1898 and 1998," *Bankruptcy Developments Journal* 15 (1999): 362–78.

65. Minutes, March 15, 1898, Greater Cleveland Growth Assoc. Records, 1881–1971, Manuscript collection 3471, Western Reserve Historical Society.

66. Skeel, *Debt's Dominion*, 40–45.

Chapter 3

1. An Act: To Establish a Uniform System of Bankruptcy throughout the United States, Stat. 30 (1898): 544–66, hereinafter Bankruptcy Act of 1898.

2. Barney Warf and Brian Holly, "The Rise and Fall and Rise of Cleveland," *Annals of the American Academy of Political and Social Science* 551 (1997): 210.

3. *Annual Report of the Attorney General of the United States for the Year 1900* (Washington, DC: Government Printing Office, 1900), 79–80, 390–94; *Annual Report of the Attorney General of the United States for the Year 1910* (Washington, DC: Government Printing Office, 1910), 96, 154, 184–88.

4. Bankruptcy Act of 1898, § 1(15).

5. Ibid., §§ 1(16), 34.

6. Ibid., §§ 35, 39(b), 40.

7. Ibid., §§ 38, 39.

8. Ibid., § 34.

9. *Administration of the Bankruptcy Act: Report of the Attorney General's Committee on Bankruptcy Administration* (Washington, DC: Government Printing Office, 1941), ix.

10. *Administration of the Bankruptcy Act*, 58.

11. It is also possible that Fordyce Belford was a Republican. *The Bench and Bar of Northern Ohio*, Hon. William B. Neff, ed. (Cleveland: Historical Publishing, 1921) 285–86, lists Belford's party affiliation as Republican. Another possible exception is H. G. Ritchie of Van Wert County. Although the Ohio roster of state, federal, and county officials lists Ritchie as a Republican, his 1919 obituary claims that he had been an active Democrat for many years and a leader of the Democratic Party. Ritchie had practiced law in Van Wert since 1875 and had represented the Cincinnati Northern Railroad.

12. Please consult the list of referees included as an appendix to this book.

13. On Monnett, see *A Centennial Biographical History of Crawford County Ohio* (Chicago: Lewis Publishing, 1902), 271–73. On Scroggs, see Joseph Patterson Smith, ed., *History of the Republican Party in Ohio*, vol. 2 (Chicago: Lewis Publishing, 1898), 919–20.

14. James Henderson, ed., *A Treatise on the Bankruptcy Law of the United States by Harold Remington of the Bar of the City of New York*, 5th ed. (Rochester, NY: Lawyers Co-operative Publishing, 1950), v.

15. Harold Remington, *A Treatise on the Bankruptcy Law of the United States* (Charlottesville, VA: Michie Company, 1908).

16. Harold Remington, *A Treatise on the Elements of Bankruptcy Law, for the Use of Law Students* (Charlottesville, VA: Michie Company, 1911); idem, *Case Book on the Elements of Bankruptcy Law for the Use of Students* (Charlottesville, VA: Michie Company, 1926); idem, *Remington's Business Men's Manual of Bankruptcy Law: A Treatise in Plain Language for Business Men Who Have to Do with Bankruptcy Law and Bankruptcy Courts, to Aid Them in Understanding the Law and its Practice* (New York: Bankruptcy Book Concern, 1911).

17. Letter from Harold Remington to Carl D. Friebolin, March 7, 1933; letter from Remington to Friebolin, March 8, 1933, Correspondence, Carl D. Friebolin Papers, Manuscript collection 3309, Western Reserve Historical Society, hereinafter Friebolin Papers, WRHS.

18. Harold Remington, "The Preference Feature of the Ray Amendment," *Bulletin of the Commercial Law League of America* 7 (1903): 10–11.

19. Remington to Friebolin, March 7, 1933, Correspondence, Friebolin Papers, WRHS.

20. Letter from James M. Cox to Hugh Wells, January 17, 1956, Correspondence, Friebolin Papers, WRHS.

21. Letter from Referee Washabaugh to Friebolin, January 17, 1961, Correspondence, Friebolin Papers, WRHS.

22. Friebolin's personal papers and correspondence reside at the WRHS, and this study has been enriched immeasurably by access to the archive.

23. Bankruptcy Act of 1898, §§ 1(8), 23.

24. Erwin C. Surrency, *History of the Federal Courts*, 2nd ed. (Dobbs Ferry, NY: Oceana Publications, 2002), 55–65. For example, the terms of circuit and district courts in Ohio, then in the seventh circuit, were made concurrent by An Act to Change the Times of Holding the Circuit and District Courts of the United States in the Several Districts in the Seventh Circuit (1863), *Statutes at Large of the United States*, vol. 12 (Boston: Little, Brown, 1863), 657.

25. An Act: To Amend the Judicial System of the United States (1869), *Statutes at Large of the United States of America*, vol. 16 (Boston: Little, Brown, 1871), 44–45.

26. An Act: To Establish Courts of Appeals and to Define and Regulate in Certain Cases the Jurisdiction of the Courts of the United States and for Other Purposes, Stat. 26 (1891): 826–30.

27. An Act: To Codify, Revise, and Amend the Laws Relating to the Judiciary, Stat. 36 (1911): 1087–1169; Surrency, *History of the Federal Courts*, 96.

28. An Act: To Revise, Codify, and Enact into Law Title 28 of the United States Code entitled "Judicial Code and Judiciary," Stat. 62 (1948): 869–1009; Surrency, *History of the Federal Courts*, 108–11.

29. An Act: For Regulating Processes in the Courts of the United States, and Providing Compensations for the Officers of the said Courts, and for Jurors and Witnesses (1792), *Statutes at Large of the United Stated of America*, vol.1 (Boston: Charles C.

Little and James Brown, 1845), 276; An Act: To Regulate Processes in the Courts of the United States (1789), *Statutes at Large of the United Stated of America*, vol. 1 (Boston: Charles C. Little and James Brown, 1845), 93–94; An Act: To Further the Administration of Justice (1872), *Statutes at Large of the United Stated of America,* vol. 17 (Boston: Charles C. Little and James Brown, 1873), 197.

30. An Act: To Give the Supreme Court of the United States Authority to Make and Publish Rules in Actions at Law, Stat. 48 (1934): 1064.

31. US Supreme Court, *General Orders and Forms in Bankruptcy: Adopted and Established by the Supreme Court of the United States, November 28, 1898* (Washington, DC: Government Printing Office, 1898).

32. For a list of citations to Supreme Court modifications of the general orders, see Kenneth N. Klee, *Bankruptcy and the Supreme Court* (Newark, NJ: LexisNexis, 2008), 49 n. 220.

33. An Act: An Addition to the Act Entitled "An Act to Establish the Judicial Courts of the United States" (1793), *Statutes at Large of the United States of America*, vol. 1 (Boston: Charles C. Little and James Brown, 1845), 334; Surrency, *History of the Federal Courts,* 204; Minute Book In Bankruptcy: Act of 1898, No. 1, Bankruptcy Adjudication and Reference Journals, Bankruptcy Records 1898 Act, USDC Cleveland, Eastern Division, RG 21, NARA Chicago, hereinafter NARA Chicago.

34. "Bankruptcy Rules of the District Court of the United States for the Northern District of Ohio," 51–77, Law Journal No. 50, U.S. District Court for the Northern District of Ohio, NARA Chicago.

35. Local Rules 20, 21; "Bankruptcy Rules of the District Court of the United States for the Northern District of Ohio," 51–77, NARA Chicago.

36. Surrency, *History of the Federal Courts*, 116–117; Klee, *Bankruptcy and the Supreme Court*, 48; Felix Frankfurter and James M. Landis, "The Business of the Supreme Court of the United States—A Study in the Federal Judicial System," *Harvard Law Review* 40 (1927): 460–61; General Orders in Bankruptcy Promulgated April 13, 1925, 267 U.S. 613 (1925).

37. Jeremy Atack and Peter Passell, *A New View of Economic History*, 2nd ed. (New York: W. W Norton, 1994), 484–87. See also Naomi R. Lamoreaux, *The Great Merger Movement in American Business, 1895–1904* (New York: Cambridge University Press, 1985).

38. Bureau of the Census, *Historical Statistics of the United States, Colonial Times to 1970* (Washington, DC: Government Printing Office, 1976) Part I, p. 236, Series F 186–91.

39. Report to Accompany H.R. 20575, 61st Cong., 2d sess. (February 22, 1910), H.R. Rep. 511; An Act: To Amend an Act Entitled "An Act to Establish a Uniform System of Bankruptcy throughout the United States," Stat. 36 (1910): 838–42.

40. Annual reports of the attorney general to Congress from 1899 to 1933 included statistical reports on bankruptcy proceedings collected from the clerks of the district courts and referees.

41. Paul D. Cravath, "The Reorganization of Corporations; Bondholders; and Stockholders Protective Committees; Reorganization Committees; and the Voluntary Recapitalization of Corporations. A Lecture Delivered before the Association of the Bar of the City of New York by Paul D. Cravath, March 1, 1916," found in *Some Legal Phases of Corporate Financing, Reorganization and Regulation* (New York: Macmillan, 1917) 160–61.

42. This summarizes Cravath's description of corporate reorganization through equity receiverships in "The Reorganization of Corporations." On the development of railroad receiverships, see David A. Skeel, *Debt's Dominion: A History of Bankruptcy Law* (Princeton, NJ: Princeton University Press, 2001), 56–60; Bradley Hansen, "The People's Welfare and the Origins of Corporate Reorganization: The Wabash Receivership Reconsidered," *Business History Review* 71 (2000): 377–405.

43. Thomas Clifford Billig, *Equity Receiverships in the Common Pleas Court of Franklin County* (Baltimore: Johns Hopkins University Press, 1932). Billig documents the phenomenon in the southern district of Ohio. There is no comparable study for the northern district of Ohio.

44. 10 *Ohio Jurisprudence*, 1073–74 (Henry P. Farnham, ed., 1928).

45. Ibid., 1062–63.

46. Sturges v. Crowninshield, 17 U.S. 122, 196 (1819). See, generally, Klee, *Bankruptcy and the Supreme Court*, 168–74.

47. Stellwagen v. Clum, 218 F. 730 (6th Cir. 1914), decided 245 U.S. 605 (1918).

48. I am unable to determine from the published record whether the company or a creditor removed the case to the bankruptcy court. Corporations could file voluntary petitions in bankruptcy after July 1910, but it appears that this transaction anticipated that a friendly creditor would file an involuntary petition. Mrs. Zengerle could have been just such a friendly creditor.

49. Bureau of the Census, *Historical Statistics of the United States, Bicentennial Edition, Part I* (Washington, DC: Government Printing Office, 1975), 165, Series D 735–738, Average Annual and Daily Earnings of Nonfarm Employees: 1860 to 1900.

50. Douglas Steeples and David O. Whitten, *Democracy in Desperation: The Depression of 1893* (Westport, CT: Greenwood Press, 1998), 32–37.

51. David O. Whitten, "The Depression of 1893," EH.Net Encyclopedia, edited by Robert Whaples. August 14, 2001, http://eh.net/encyclopedia/article/whitten.panic.1893.

52. Steeples and Whitten, *Democracy in Desperation*, 50–51.

53. 11 *Ohio Jurisprudence* 855–60. Unfortunately, the insolvency court records at the Cuyahoga County Archives are very fragmentary.

54. National Bureau of Economic Research, "Business Cycle Expansions and Contractions," http://www.nber.org/cycles.html, hereinafter NBER.

55. The authors find evidence suggestive of local legal culture in Teresa A Sullivan, Elizabeth Warren, and Jay Lawrence Westbrook, "The Persistence of Local Legal

Culture: Twenty Years of Evidence From the Federal Bankruptcy Courts," *Harvard Journal of Law and Public Policy* 17 (1994): 801–65.

56. *Annual Report of the Attorney General of the United States for the Year 1905* (Washington, DC: Government Printing Office, 1905), 94–95.

57. Ibid., 96.

58. Gene Smiley, "US Economy in the 1920s," EH.Net Encyclopedia, edited by Robert Whaples, March 26, 2008, http://eh.net/encyclopedia/the-u-s-economy-in-the-1920s/.

59. NBER, "Business Cycle Expansions and Contractions." Recessions also occurred between May 1923 and July 1924, and October 1926 and November 1927. NBER dates the Great Depression from August 1929 to March 1933.

60. Smiley, "US Economy in the 1920s."

61. David A Moss and Gibbs A. Johnson, "The Rise of Consumer Bankruptcy: Evolution, Revolution, or Both?" *American Bankruptcy Law Journal* 73 (1999): 313–16.

Chapter 4

1. Friebolin to J. H. Donany, December 13, 1938, Correspondence, Carl D. Friebolin Papers, Manuscript collection 3309, Western Reserve Historical Society, hereinafter Friebolin Papers, WRHS.

2. Charles Jordan Tabb, "The History of the Bankruptcy Laws in the United States," *American Bankruptcy Institute Law Review* 3 (1995): 27; "An Old As Well As A New," *Journal of the National Association of Referees in Bankruptcy* (hereinafter *JNARB*) 1 (1927): 69.

3. Herbert M. Bierce, "Our Association in Retrospect and in Prospect," *JNARB* 11 (1936): 9–11.

4. On the history of the NARB, see Russell L. Hiller, "A Conference Anniversary—Fifty Years in Retrospect," *American Bankruptcy Law Journal* 51 (1977): 31–61.

5. "Proceedings of the Chicago Conference (Relative to Uniformity of Practice)," *JNARB* 3 (1929): 76–97.

6. "Returns on Questionnaire on Bankruptcy Practice," *JNARB* 2 (1928): 112.

7. *Annual Report of the Attorney General of the United States for the Fiscal Year Ending 1914* (Washington, DC: Government Printing Office, 1914), 9; *Annual Report of the Attorney General of the United States for the Fiscal Year Ending 1915* (Washington, DC: Government Printing Office, 1915), 45, 50.

8. Henry P. Chandler, "The Beginning of a New Era in Bankruptcy Administration: 1939–1947," *JNARB* 34 (1960): 5.

9. *Annual Report of the Attorney General of the United States for the Fiscal Year 1916* (Washington, DC: Government Printing Office, 1916), 58, 63–66.

10. Ibid.; *Annual Report of the Attorney General of the United States for the Fiscal Year 1917* (Washington, DC: Government Printing Office, 1917), 87; *Annual Report*

of the Attorney General of the United States for the Fiscal Year 1918 (Washington, DC: Government Printing Office, 1918), 107–108.

11. Handwritten summary, Bankruptcy Administration, Friebolin Papers, WRHS.

12. Typewritten worksheets for the years 1919 through 1931, "Referee's Report of Statutory Fees and Commissions, Allowances for sending notices, Clerical Aid, etc., and for expenses (actual or estimated) incurred for office accommodations, clerical aid, etc., for calendar years 1930 and 1931," Bankruptcy Administration, Friebolin Papers, WRHS; "Proceedings of the Chicago Conference," *JNARB* 3 at 82.

13. Harold Remington, appearing before the Senate Judiciary Committee in March 1910, reported in Attorney General William D. Mitchell, *Report to the President on the Bankruptcy Act and its administration in the Courts of the United States Dated December 5, 1931* (Washington, DC: Government Printing Office, 1931), 178.

14. Grenville Clark, "Reform in Bankruptcy Administration," *Harvard Law Review* 43 (1930): 1191–92.

15. This description of bankruptcy procedure is derived from William J. Donovan, *Administration of Bankrupt Estates: Report Submitted by Counsel to the Petitioners in the Matter of an Inquiry into the Administration of Bankruptcy Estates conducted before the Hon. Thomas D. Thacher, Judge of the United States District Court of the Southern District of New York*, House Judiciary Committee, 71st Cong., 3d Sess., Committee Print (Washington, DC: Government Printing Office, 1931).

16. Carl D. Friebolin, typewritten response to "Attorney General's Committee on Bankruptcy Administration; Questionnaire for Referees in Bankruptcy," Bankruptcy Administration, Friebolin Papers, WRHS; Donovan, *Administration of Bankrupt Estates*, 58–59.

17. Carl D. Friebolin, typewritten response to "Attorney General's Committee on Bankruptcy Administration; Questionnaire for Referees in Bankruptcy," Bankruptcy Administration, Friebolin Papers, WRHS.

18. Letter from Walter S. Jackson to Carl D. Friebolin dated February 27, 1936, Correspondence, Friebolin Papers, WRHS.

19. Ibid.

20. Ibid.

21. "Proceedings of the Chicago Conference," *JNARB* 3 (1929): 96. See Edward H. Smith, "Profit in Loss," *Saturday Evening Post*, February 5, 1921, 14, for an example of popular press coverage of bankruptcy rings.

22. Kenneth N. Klee, *Bankruptcy and the Supreme Court* (Newark, NJ: LexisNexis 2009) 48; US Supreme Court, *General Orders in Bankruptcy Promulgated April 13, 1925*, 267 U.S. 613 (1925).

23. Donovan, *Administration of Bankrupt Estates;* "The New York Bankruptcy Investigation Report," *JNARB* 4 (1930): 87–90.

24. Lloyd K. Garrison led a remarkable life. He was the great-grandson of abolitionist William Lloyd Garrison and grandson of Wendell Phillips Garrison of *The Nation*, and service on the Donovan commission was but the first of his many

notable achievements in public service. Garrison was dean of the University of Wisconsin Law School from 1932 to 1945. In 1935, he served as the first chairman of the National Labor Relations Board and was appointed to the National War Labor Board in 1944. Garrison joined the National Urban League in 1924 and served as its president from 1947 to 1952. A partner in the law firm of Paul, Weiss, Wharton & Garrison, Garrison represented Langston Hughes and Arthur Miller before the House Committee on Un-American Activities, and he represented J. Robert Oppenheimer before the Atomic Energy Commission.

25. "Proceedings of the Fourth Annual Conference of the National Association of Referees in Bankruptcy," *JNARB* 4 (1930): 47.

26. "A Bankruptcy Clinic," *JNARB* 4 (1930): 37; William O. Douglas, "Some Functional Aspects of Bankruptcy," *Yale Law Review* 41 (1932): 329–64; William O. Douglas and J. Howard Marshall, "A Factual Study of Bankruptcy Administration and Some Suggestions," *Columbia Law Review* 32 (1932): 25–59.

27. US Department of Commerce, *Causes of Business Failure and Bankruptcies of Individuals in New Jersey: A study made in cooperation with the Institute of Human Relations and the Law School of Yale University: Domestic Commerce Series—No. 54* (Washington, DC: Government Printing Office, 1931).

28. US Department of Commerce, Victor Sadd and Robert T. Williams, *Causes of Bankruptcies Among Consumers: A Study Made in Boston with the Cooperation of the Institute of Human Relations and the Law School of Yale University: Domestic Commerce Series—No. 82* (Washington, DC: Government Printing Office, 1933).

29. For an interest-group perspective, see David A. Skeel Jr., *Debt's Dominion: A History of Bankruptcy Law in America* (Princeton, NJ: Princeton University Press, 2001), 89–98.

30. Paul H. King, "Experimenting with Our Bankruptcy Act: Recent Changes and Prospects for Further Amendment," *JNARB* 7 (1933): 98–100; Watson Adair, "Report of the Conference Committee," *JNARB* 7 (1933): 68–69. For an overview of the national bankruptcy conference and its role in the passage of the Chandler Act, see Paul H. King, "The Chandler Amendatory Bill is Enacted," *JNARB* 12 (1938): 124–32. Much of the discussion that follows is pieced together from committee reports and conference discussions reported in the *JNARB* but not conveniently cited individually.

31. Paul H. King, "Strengthening Our Bankruptcy Law: A Sequel (or, a Serial)," *JNARB* 7 (1933) 157–58, cont. 161.

32. An Act: To Amend an Act Entitled "An Act to Establish a Uniform System of Bankruptcy throughout the United States," Approved July 1, 1898, and Acts Amendatory Thereof and Supplementary Thereto, Stat. 47 (1933): 1467–82. For a summary of the act see "Relief Without Adjudication—The New Bankruptcy Law," *Georgetown Law Journal* 21 (1933): 483–89. For an example of New Deal enthusiasm, see Thomas Clifford Billig, "The New Deal in Bankruptcy Legislation," *JNARB*. 9 (1934): 32–35, cont. 48.

33. An Act: To Amend an Act Entitled "An Act to Establish a Uniform System of Bankruptcy throughout the United States," Approved July 1, 1898, and Acts Amendatory Thereof and Supplementary Thereto, Stat. 48 (1934): 911–25, § 2 at 922.

34. An Act: To Amend an Act Entitled "An Act to Establish a Uniform System of Bankruptcy throughout the United States," Approved July 1, 1898, and Acts Amendatory Thereof and Supplementary Thereto, Stat. 48 (1934): 1289–91.

35. Louisville Joint Stock Land Bank v. Radford, 295 U.S. 555 (1935); An Act to Amend an Act Entitled "An Act to Establish a Uniform System of Bankruptcy throughout the United States," Approved July 1, 1898, and Acts Amendatory Thereof and Supplementary Thereto, Stat. 49 (1935): 942–45. For more discussion of the Frazier-Lemke Acts, see Z. N. Diamond and Alfred Letzler, "The New Frazier-Lemke Act: A Study," *Columbia Law Review* 37 (1937): 1092–1135.

36. Wright v. Vinton Branch of the Mountain Trust Bank, 300 U.S. 440 (1937).

37. Stat. 47 at 1474–82; Lloyd K. Garrison, "Reorganization of Railroads under the Bankruptcy Act," *University of Chicago Law Review* 1 (1933): 71–81; Churchill Rogers and Littleton Groom, "Reorganization of Railroad Corporations under Section 77 of the Bankruptcy Act," *Columbia Law Review* 33 (1933): 571–616; Robert T. Swaine, "A Decade of Rail Reorganization under Section 77 of the Federal Bankruptcy Act," *Harvard Law Review* 56 (1943): 1037–58.

38. An Act: To Amend an Act Entitled "An Act to Establish a Uniform System of Bankruptcy throughout the United States," Approved July 1, 1898, and Acts Amendatory Thereof and Supplementary Thereto, Stat. 49 (1935): 911–26 (1935), § 77(e) at 918.

39. Ian S. Haberman, *The Van Sweringens of Cleveland: The Biography of an Empire* (Cleveland: Western Reserve Historical Society, 1979), 143.

40. H. Roger Grant, *Erie Lackawanna: Death of An American Railroad, 1938–1992* (Stanford, CA: Stanford University Press, 1994), 20, 24.

41. An Act: To Amend an Act Entitled "An Act to Establish a Uniform System of Bankruptcy throughout the United States," Approved July 1, 1898, and Acts Amendatory Thereof and Supplementary Thereto, Stat. 48 (1934): 911–25.

42. John Gerdes, "Corporate Reorganizations Under Section 77B," *JNARB* 10 (1936): 75.

43. "Proceedings of the Tenth Annual Conference of the National Association of Referees in Bankruptcy," *JNARB* 10 (1935): 11.

44. Ibid. For a more detailed discussion of procedure under 77B see Carl Friebolin, "Section 77B—Sword or Shield," *JNARB* 10 (1935): 79–87.

45. "SEC Turns Eyes on Vans' Setup," *Cleveland Plain Dealer*, January 24, 1940.

46. "Referee William J. Woods concludes reorganization proceedings after 17 years," *JNARB* 27 (1953): 114.

47. U.S. Supreme Court General Order in Bankruptcy XLVI, 280 U.S. 617 (1930).

48. An Act: To Amend an Act entitled "An Act to Establish a Uniform System of Bankruptcy throughout the United States. . . ," Stat. 48, § 3 at 923; "The Corporate Receiver and Trustee Viewed by Bar and Creditors," *JNARB* 7 (1933): 88–90.

49. An Act: To Amend an Act Entitled "An Act to Establish a Uniform System of Bankruptcy throughout the United States," Approved July 1, 1898, and Acts Amendatory Thereof and Supplementary Thereto, Stat. 48 (1934): 798–803.

50. Henry W. Lehman, "The Federal Municipal Bankruptcy Act," *Journal of Finance* 5 (1950): 241–56.

51. Ashton v. Cameron County Water Improvement District No. 1, 298 U.S. 513 (1936).

52. An Act: To Amend an Act Entitled "An Act to Establish a Uniform System of Bankruptcy throughout the United States," Approved July 1, 1898, and Acts Amendatory Thereof and Supplementary Thereto, Stat. 50 (1937): 653–58. Confusingly, the statute added a new Chapter X to the 1898 Bankruptcy Act consisting of new sections 81 through 84. The Chandler Act, An Act: To Amend an Act Entitled "An Act to Establish a Uniform System of Bankruptcy throughout the United States", approved July 1, 1898, and Acts Amendatory Thereof and Supplementary Thereto, Stat. 52 (1938): 840–940 at 839, moved those sections to Chapter IX and created a new Chapter X.

53. United States v. Bekins et. al., 304 U.S. 27 (1938).

54. Lehman, "The Federal Municipal Bankruptcy Act," 248.

55. For an overview of the activities of the NBC and its involvement in the legislative history of the Chandler Act, see "Chandler Amendatory Bill Is Enacted," *JNARB* 12 (1938): 124–32.

56. "Proceedings of the 10th Annual Conference," 14–15; "Congressional Action," *JNARB* 10 (1936): 134.

57. An Act: To Amend an Act Entitled "An Act to Establish a Uniform System of Bankruptcy throughout the United States," Approved July 1, 1898, and Acts Amendatory Thereof and Supplementary Thereto, Stat. 52 (1938): 840–940, hereinafter Chandler Act.

58. "National Bankruptcy Conference Continues," *JNARB* 13 (1939): 82.

59. For an overview, see Carl Wilde, "The Chandler Act," *Indiana Law Journal* 14 (1938): 93–148.

60. An Act: To Amend an Act Entitled "An Act to Establish a Uniform System of Bankruptcy throughout the United States," Approved July 1, 1898, and Acts Amendatory Thereof and Supplementary Thereto, Stat. 53 (1939): 1134–41.

61. Chapter XIV provided for the appointment of the Maritime Commission as sole trustee for a corporation operating ships registered in the United States on which the United States held mortgages.

62. Chandler Act § 306.

63. Walter Chandler, "The Revised Bankruptcy Act of 1938,"*American Bar Association Journal* 24 (1938): 884.

64. Chandler Act §§ 1(9), 34.

65. *Administration of the Bankruptcy Act: Report of the Attorney General's Committee on Bankruptcy Administration* (Washington, DC: Government Printing Office, 1941). For an overview of the events leading to the enactment of the referees salary act, see Henry P. Chandler, "The Beginning of a New Era in Bankruptcy Administration: 1939–1947," *JNARB* 34 (1940): 3–6, cont. 25–26; idem, "The Beginning of a New Era in Bankruptcy Administration: 1939–1947 (second and concluded installment)," *JNARB* 34 (1960): 44–53. Henry P. Chandler served as the first director of the Administrative Office of the United States Courts.

66. Chandler, "The Beginning of a New Era in Bankruptcy Administration," 4.

67. An Act: To Provide for the Administration of the United States Courts, and for Other Purposes, Stat. 53 (1939): 1223–26.

68. Ibid., § 306, at 1224.

69. The Conference of Senior Circuit Judges would formally become the Judicial Conference of the United States under the Judicial Code of 1948, An Act: To Revise, Codify, and Enact into Law Title 28 of the United States Code entitled "Judicial Code and Judiciary," Stat. 62 (1948): 869–1009 at 902, but the term was already in use by 1940.

70. An Act: To Amend an Act Entitled "An Act to Establish a Uniform System of Bankruptcy throughout the United States," Approved July 1, 1898, and Acts Amendatory Thereof and Supplementary Thereto, Stat. 60 (1945): 323–32, hereinafter Salary Act; Chandler, "The Beginning of a New Era in Bankruptcy Administration (second installment)," 50.

71. Salary Act § 2.

72. Salary Act §§ 4, 7.

73. Salary Act § 6.

74. Chandler, "The Beginning of a New Era in Bankruptcy Aministration," 52.

Chapter 5

1. "Great Depression," *Ohio History Central*, August 15, 2010, http://www.ohiohistorycentral.org/entry.php?rec=500&nm=Great-Depression; "Toledo," *Ohio History Central*, August 15, 2010, http://www.ohiohistorycentral.org/entry.php?rec=808. On the Willys-Overland Motor Company, see Toledo History Scrapbook—Industries—JEEP—before 1959, Local History Department, Toledo-Lucas County Public Library.

2. Barney Warf and Brian Holly, "The Rise and Fall and Rise of Cleveland," *Annals of the American Academy of Political and Social Science* 551 (1997): 210–11; Michael S. Fogarty, Gasper S. Garolfalo, and David C. Hammack, *Cleveland from Startup to the Present: Innovation and Entrepreneurship in the 19th and Early 20th Centuries*, A report of the Center for Regional Economic Issues, Weatherhead School of Management (Cleveland: Case Western Reserve University, 2003), 10–11; David C. Hammack, "Economy," *Encyclopedia of Cleveland History*, 2nd ed., eds. David D.

Van Tassel and John Grabowski (Bloomington: Indiana University Press, 1996) 371–76; available at ech.cwru.edu.

3. Fogarty, Garolfalo, and Hammack, *Cleveland from Startup to the Present*, 11.

4. David A. Moss and Gibbs A. Johnson, "The Rise of Consumer Bankruptcy: Evolution, Revolution, or Both?" *American Bankruptcy Law Journal* 73 (1999): 322–25. Indeed, the consumer bankruptcy multiplier remained remarkably constant from 1920 to 1985.

5. "Questionnaire—in part: Consolidated Office: C. D. Friebolin and William B. Woods"; "Claim of C. D. Friebolin, Referee, for reimbursement for rent of referees joint quarters from July 1, 1947, to October 18, 1947, $1,783.39", Bankruptcy Administration; letter from Edwin Covey to William B. Woods and Carl D. Friebolin, July 5, 1947, letter from Carl Friebolin to Edwin Covey, July 7, 1947, Correspondence, Carl D. Friebolin Papers, Manuscript Collection 3309, Western Reserve Historical Society, hereinafter Friebolin Papers, WRHS. The collection has been processed since I began my research, and particular documents may have been moved as a result.

6. Morris G. Shanker. "Remembering Carl D. Friebolin (1878–1967)," *Cuyahoga County Law & Fact*, May/June 1993, 6.

7. The National Association of Credit Men changed its name to the National Association of Credit Management in 1931, although many people continued to refer to it as Credit Men into the 1980s.

8. In 1974, while Congress debated the new bankruptcy code, Mathew Bender began publishing bankruptcy judge opinions as Collier's Bankruptcy Cases, and Corporate Reorganization Reporter included them in its looseleaf Bankruptcy Court Reporter. In 1978, the Bankruptcy Code made bankruptcy a court of record, and Mathew Bender (sub nom Collier's), Commerce Clearing House, and West Publishing started comprehensive bankruptcy case reporting services.

9. Letter from Carl D. Friebolin to Edwin L. Covey, December 11, 1947; Letter from Edwin L. Covey to Carl D. Friebolin, December 19, 1947; letter from Covey to Friebolin, January 6, 1948; letter from Friebolin to Covey, January 19, 1948; letter from Friebolin to Covey, February 16, 1948; letter from Covey to Friebolin, February 20, 1948, Correspondence, Friebolin Papers, WRHS.

10. David T. Stanley and Marjorie Girth, *Bankruptcy: Problem, Process, Reform* (Washington, DC: Brookings Institution, 1971), 24–34.

11. Consumer Credit Protection Act, Stat. 82 (1968): 162–64, codified at Title III, Restrictions on Garnishment, 15 USC § 1671 et. seq.; William D. Hawkland, "Federal Restrictions on Garnishments of Earnings: Herein of Title III of the Consumer Credit Protection Act," *Commercial Law Journal* 75 (1970): 213–17 cont. 223.

12. National Bureau of Economic Research Business Cycles are dated from peak to trough, see http://www.nber.org/cycles/cyclesmain.html.

13. Letter from Covey to Friebolin, December 19, 1947, Correspondence, Friebolin Papers, WRHS.

14. "Bankruptcy Chief Named in Mahoning," *Cleveland Plain Dealer*, September 18, 1951.

15. Harold F. White, Interview October 18, 1996, 17, Randall J. Newsome Oral History Collection, National Bankruptcy Archives, Biddle Library, University of Pennsylvania, Philadelphia, Pennsylvania.

16. Ibid., 23.

17. "Referee Doyle has New Quarters," *Journal of the National Association of Referees in Bankruptcy* (hereinafter *JNARB)* 34 (1960): 2, quoting the Youngstown *Vindicator* of September 12, 1959.

18. Before the Federal Magistrates Act of 1968, Stat. 82 (1968): 1107–19, district courts had discretion to appoint inferior judicial officers called commissioners to four-year renewable terms. Commissioners could sign warrants, set bail, and try petty offenses. Magistrates assumed the duties of commissioners. See Frank P. Sanders, "The Organization and Function of the Commissioner System," *Western Political Quarterly* 21 (1968): 420–35.

19. Letter from Emsley to Friebolin dated June 8, 1961; letter from Friebolin to Emsley dated June 16, 1961, Correspondence, Friebolin Papers, WRHS.

20. Timothy W. Dixon and David G. Epstein, "Where Did Chapter 13 Come From and Where Should It Go?" *American Bankruptcy Institute Law Review* 10 (2002): 741–63. The filing statistics are based on published bankruptcy statistics from the Bankruptcy Division of the Administrative Office of the United States Courts.

21. Edwin Covey, Memorandum for the Bankruptcy Committee—Item XI of the Proposed Agenda—Report on the enlargement of the use of Chapter XIII, including attached Appendix 5 by Carl D. Friebolin, AOUSC Bankruptcy Committee Meetings, File Unit JCUS Sept. 1958, Entry 70, RG 116, National Archives and Records Administration, Washington, DC, hereinafter NARA DC.

22. Correspondence on this matter is found in Friebolin Papers, WRHS and in Central Subject Correspondence File, 1958–1975, Bankruptcy, vol. 2, Jan. 1962 through Dec. 1964, Entry 70, RG 116, NARA DC.

23. Report of Examiner Luck dated December 3, 1960, Central Subject Correspondence File, 1958–1975, File Unit Organization and Management, Inspections—Surveys Ohio (Northern) vol. 1. 1961, Entry 70, RG 116, NARA DC.

24. Letter by William O'Neill dated April 24, 1972, Bankruptcy Survey Reports 1961 to 1983, File Unit Northern District of Ohio, Entry 69, RG 116; William O'Neill to Edwin Covey, November 15, 1961, Central Subject Correspondence File, 1958–73, File Unit Bankruptcy, vol. 1, Sept. 1958 through Dec. 1961, Entry 70, RG 116; Edwin Covey, Memorandum for the Committee on Bankruptcy Administration of the Judicial Conference of the United States Re: Report on the use of Chapter XIII, July 11, 1962, Bankruptcy Committee Meetings, Records of Committee Meetings 1958–62, File Unit JCUS Sept. 1962, Entry 68, RG 116, NARA DC. See generally, Central Subject Correspondence File, 1958–74, File Unit Bankruptcy, Ohio, Vol. 1, Aug. 62 through Mar. 1971, Entry 70, RG 116, NARA DC.

25. National Bankruptcy Conference, Report of the Committee on Wage Earners' Plans (Chapter XIII), National Bankruptcy Conference, Friebolin Papers, WRHS; Friebolin to Asa Herzog May 19 1964; Herzog to Friebolin, May 4, 1964, Correspondence, Friebolin Papers, WRHS.

26. Stanley and Girth, *Bankruptcy: Problem, Process, Reform*, 3

27. Friebolin to Frank Lausche, July 29, 1957, Correspondence, Friebolin Papers, WRHS.

28. Carl D. Friebolin, Appendix No. 5 to Memorandum for the Bankruptcy Committee—Item XI of the Proposed Agenda—Report on the enlargement of the use of Chapter XIII, by Covey, File Unit JCUS Sept., 1958, Entry 68, RG 116, NARA DC.

29. General Orders and Forms in Bankruptcy Amended and Established by the Supreme Court of the United States, January 16, 1939, 305 U.S. 681 (1939).

30. Charles Elihu Nadler, *The Law of Bankruptcy* (Chicago: Callaghan, 1948); idem, *The Law of Debtor Relief; Bankruptcy and Non-Bankruptcy Devices* (Atlanta: Harrison, 1954).

31. Asa S. Herzog, "Referee in Bankruptcy: A Judge In Search Of A Name," *Journal of the National Conference of Referees in Bankruptcy* (hereinafter JNCRB) 44 (1970): 39–40. In 1965, the National Association of Referees in Bankruptcy changed its name to the National Conference of Referees in Bankruptcy.

32. Glenn W. Ferguson, "To Robe or Not to Robe?—A Judicial Dilemma," *Journal of the American Judicature Society* 39 (1955–56): 166–71.

33. *Cleveland Bar Association Journal* 11 (August 1940): 176; *Cleveland Bar Association Journal* 12 (February 1941): 74.

34. Royal E. Jackson, "Bankruptcy Administration: Then and Now," *American Bankruptcy Law Journal* 45 (1971): 271; "Referees Don Robes," *JNARB* 28 (July 1954): 87; "Judicial Robes," *JNCRB* 40 (October 1966): 125.

35. Thanks to attorney Marvin Sicherman of the law firm Dettelbach, Sicherman & Baumgart in Cleveland, Ohio, for information on the practice of bankruptcy law in the 1960s and thereafter.

36. The Sixth Circuit ended this practice in In re Cle-Ware Industries, Inc. v. Sokolsky, 493 F. 2d 863 (6th 1974).

37. Friebolin to Professor Frank R. Kennedy, October 17, 1963, Correspondence, Friebolin Papers, WRHS.

38. "Questionnaire Re: Appointment of Trustees in no-asset cases, conduct of first meetings of creditors and examination of bankrupts (to be returned to the Administrative Office, US Courts, on or before October 16, 1961)," Administration, Friebolin Papers, WRHS; Friebolin to Warren Olney, III, March 22, 1963, Correspondence, Friebolin Papers, WRHS. Cleveland practice was singled out for criticism in the Brookings Institution study of bankruptcy, Stanley and Girth, *Bankruptcy: Problem, Process, Reform*.

39. Harold F. White, Interview, 31, Randal J. Newsome Oral History Collection. I am also indebted to Judge White, Judge James H. Williams, Judge Richard L. Speer, and Professor Timothy O'Neill for information provided.

40. Robert L. Roper, vice president and secretary of the National Association of Credit Management to Hon. Warren Olney II, director, AOUSC, February 3, 1964, AOUSC Bankruptcy Committee Meetings, Committee Meetings 1962–64, File

Unit Bankruptcy Committee Meeting July 27–28, 1964 Agenda Items, Entry 68, RG 116, NARA DC

41. The so-called antimonopoly statute, Title 11 U.S.C. § 76(a), was repealed with the Bankruptcy Code of 1978. Royal E. Jackson, "Bankruptcy Administration: Then and Now," 260–61; "Memorandum No. 120: Judicial Policy re Administration of Bankruptcy Proceedings," October 21, 1959, Correspondence, Friebolin Papers, WRHS; Edwin L. Covey, January 29, 1960, Memorandum for the Committee on Bankruptcy Administration of the Judicial Conference of the United States Re: Report of study of appointments of receivers and trustees and audit of statistical reports, AOUSC Bankruptcy Committee Meetings, Records of Committee Meetings 1958–62, File Unit JCUS September 1959, Entry 68, RG 116, NARA DC.

42. An Act: To Amend the Bankruptcy Act in Regard to the Closing Fee of the Trustee and in Regard to the Fee for the Filing of a Petition, Stat. 74 (1960): 198.

43. "Draft 9-9-64-CDF, to Honorable James C. Connell," Administration, Friebolin Papers, WRHS.

44. Friebolin to J. Harry McGregor, September 18, 1958; Friebolin to Joe Newman, May 16, 1956, Correspondence, Friebolin Papers, WRHS.

45. "Report In Some Detail Pursuant to Your Memorandum No. 72, dated April 9, 1959," Correspondence, Friebolin Papers, WRHS.

46. J. C. Daschbach, "Bankruptcy Case Lawyers Probed," *Cleveland Plain Dealer*, November 9, 1963; "Portly Blane Has Served Some Shady Personages," ibid., November 9, 1963; J. C. Daschbach, "Prisoner to Testify in Blane Probe," ibid., November 12, 1963; Robert J. Holmes, "Blane Finally Sent to Jail," ibid., December 20, 1967.

47. "Jury Hears Testimony at Baird Trial," *Cleveland Plain Dealer*, May 17, 1960; "Executive Guilty in False Audit," ibid., May 27, 1960; "Lawyer's Ring Probed in Bankruptcy Court," *Cleveland Press*, November 11, 1963.

48. "Bankruptcy Rules of the United States District Court, Northern District of Ohio," Bankruptcy Administration, Friebolin Papers, WRHS; "Report of Bankruptcy Committee of Cleveland Bar Association," WRHS, Bankruptcy Court Committee, File 215, Manuscript Collection 3572, Cleveland Bar Association Records, Western Reserve Historical Society, hereinafter Cleveland Bar Association Records, WRHS.

49. Friebolin to Harold White, August 27, 1963; Friebolin to Frank Kennedy, August 12, 1963, Correspondence, Friebolin Papers, WRHS.

50. J. C. Daschbach, "Bankruptcy Case Lawyers Probed," *Cleveland Plain Dealer*, November 9, 1963; "Text of Statement Issued by Ex-Referee Woods," ibid., November 9, 1963.

51. Covey to Friebolin, December 8, 1955, Correspondence, Friebolin Papers, WRHS.

52. Jackson, "Bankruptcy Then and Now," 268–70.

53. "Introducing Newly Appointed Referees," *JNCRB* 40 (1966): 32; "Don Miller, Notre Dame Grid Legend, Dies Here," *Cleveland Plain Dealer*, July 30, 1979.

54. There is an earlier reference to "negative equity capital" in computing the excess profits tax under the Korean War–era statute, but it is an isolated instance

in a significantly different context, Mid-Southern Corporation v. Commissioner, 28 TC 918 (1957) *aff'd* 262 F2d 134 (6th Cir. 1958).

55. In re Dewie Sloan, 285 F.Supp. 1 (N.D. Ohio 1968).

56. Memorandum to Mr. Sweeny from Mr. Jackson, May 1, 1969, Subject: Expiration of term of referee Paul Gnau at Cleveland, Ohio, Committee on Bankruptcy, Bankruptcy survey reports 1961–1983, File Unit ND Ohio, folder 2, Entry 69, RG 116, NARA DC.

57. Ann Hellmuth, "U.S. Judges in Minor Struggle Over Bankruptcy Referee's Job," *Cleveland Plain Dealer*, November 21, 1969; Ann Hellmuth, "Bankruptcy Post Goes to Patchan," ibid., December 2, 1969.

58. Covey, Memorandum for the Committee on Bankruptcy Administration of the Judicial Conference of the United States Re: Report on the use of Ch. XIII, July 11, 1962, File Unit JCUS 1962, Entry 68, RG 116, NARA DC; Report of Examiner Raymond F. Burqhardt, January 18, 1968, Central Subject Correspondence, 1958–74, File Unit Organization – Management, Inspections – Surveys, Ohio (northern) 1968, Entry 70, RG 116, NARA DC; Jackson, "Bankruptcy Administration Then and Now," 263–66.

59. Lawrence P. King, "The History and Development of the Bankruptcy Rules," *American Bankruptcy Law Journal* 70 (1996): 217–43.

60. Morris G. Shanker to Carl D. Friebolin, June 4, 1965, Correspondence, Friebolin Papers, WRHS.

61. Postal Revenue and Federal Salary Act of 1967, Stat. 81 (1967): 642–45.

62. "Referees in Bankruptcy May Anticipate a Pay Raise in Early 1970," *JNCRB* 42 (1968): 35; Russell L. Hiller, "A Conference Anniversary, Fifty Years in Retrospect," *American Bankruptcy Law Journal* 51 (1977): 52. In 1971, the National Conference of Referees in Bankruptcy adopted standard law review format and continued its journal as the *American Bankruptcy Law Journal.*

63. In re National Mortgage Fund, Bankr. N. D. Ohio 76-1150; Rich Jaroslovsky, "Biting the Dust: Troubled REITs Face Added Uncertainties As Notes Come Due," *Wall Street Journal*, August 27, 1976; "National Mortgage Gets Court Approval On Plan To Pay Debts," ibid., December 15, 1976. I am grateful to attorney Marvin Sicherman for the lead. Sicherman represented National Mortgage Fund in the bankruptcy case.

Chapter 6

1. Northern Pipeline Construction Co. v. Marathon Pipe Line Co., 458 U.S. 50 (1982).

2. Erica L. Groshen and Laura Robertson, "Are the Great Lakes Cities Becoming Service Centers?" *Economic Commentary* (Federal Reserve Bank of Cleveland), June 1, 1993; Edward W. Hill and Thomas Bier, "Economic Restructuring: Earnings, Occupations, and Housing Values in Cleveland," *Economic Development Quarterly* 3, no. 2 (1989): 123–44; Barney Warf and Brian Holly, "The Rise and Fall and Rise of Cleveland," *Annals of the American Academy of Political and Social Science* 551 (1997): 208–221.

3. Standard Oil Co. of New Jersey v. United States, 221 U.S. 1 (1911).

4. *The Encyclopedia of Cleveland History,* sub nom. "BP America."

5. See, generally, Steve Love and David Giffels, *Wheels of Fortune: The Story of Rubber in Akron* (Akron, OH: University of Akron Press, 1999).

6. William Scheuerman, *The Steel Crisis: The Economics and Politics of a Declining Industry,* (New York: Praeger, 1986), 45–46, 64–94.

7. Ibid., 151, 164–72.

8. Kenneth Warren, *Big Steel: The First Century of the United States Steel Corporation, 1901–2001* (Pittsburgh: University of Pittsburgh Press, 2001) 310, 312–13.

9. For a list of steel plant closings, see Table 7.1 "Steel plant closings, 197882," at Scheuerman, *The Steel Crisis,* 165–169; Staughton Lynd, "The Genesis of the Idea of a Community Right to Industrial Property in Youngstown and Pittsburgh, 1977–1987," *Journal of American History* 74 (1987): 931.

10. Gordon L. Clark, "Regulating the Restructuring of the US Steel Industry: Chapter 11 of the Bankruptcy Code and Pension Obligations," *Regional Studies* 25 (1991); 138–41; Staunton Lynd, "The Genesis of the Idea of a Community Right to Industrial Property in Youngstown and Pittsburgh, 1977–1987," 953.

11. Thomas W. Gerdel, "Suppliers Here Face Ripple Effect," *Cleveland Plain Dealer,* July 18, 1986.

12. Christoph Scherrer, "Mini-Mills: A New Growth Path for the U.S. Steel Industry?" *Journal of Economic Issues* 22 (1988): 1180–86, 1190; Patricia Beesom and Frank Giarratani, "Spatial Aspects of Capacity Change by U.S. Integrated Steel Producers," *Journal of Regional Science* 38 (1998): 425–44; Lydia Chavez, "The Rise of Mini-Steel Mills," *New York Times,* September 23, 1981.

13. Vindu P. Goel, "New Life For Old Sites: Youngstown's Efforts Are Drawing Attention From Across the State," *Cleveland Plain Dealer,* August 13, 1995.

14. Ronald Randall, "Growth, Movement, and Decline of Central-city and Suburban Manufacturing Firms," Paper prepared for presentation at the Annual Conference of the Urban Affairs Association, in Toronto, April 16–19, 1997, http://uac.utoledo.edu/Publications/1997/growth-movement-decline.pdf, 3.

15. "Time in a Bottle: A History of Owens-Illinois, Inc.," University of Toledo Libraries, Canaday Center Digital Exhibit, December 2007, http://www.utoledo.edu/library/canaday/exhibit.html .

16. Sarah Bartlett, "Wall Street's Treacherous Side," *New York Times,* November 6, 1989.

17. Walker F. Todd, "Aggressive Uses of Chapter 11 of the Federal Bankruptcy Code," *Economic Trends* (Federal Reserve Bank of Cleveland), July 1986, 20–26, http://www.clevelandfed.org/research/review/1986/86-q3-todd.pdf.

18. David T. Stanley and Marjorie Girth, *Bankruptcy: Problem, Process, Reform* (Washington, DC: Brookings Institution, 1971). William J. Donovan, *Administration of Bankrupt Estates: Report Submitted by Counsel to the Petitioners,* House

Judiciary Committee, 71st Cong., 3d Sess., (Washington, DC: Government Printing Office, 1931); *Strengthening of Procedure in the Judicial System: Message from the President of the United States Recommending the Strengthening of Procedure in the Judicial System Together with the Report of the Attorney General on Bankruptcy Law and Practice*, Senate Judiciary Committee, 72nd Cong., 1st Sess., Sen. Doc. 65 (Washington, DC: Government Printing Office, 1932).

19. Geraldine Mund, "Appointed or Anointed: Judges, Congress, and the Passage of the Bankruptcy Act of 1978. Part One: Outside Looking In," *American Bankruptcy Law Journal* 81 (2007): 8–11; idem, "Appointed or Anointed: Judges, Congress, and the Passage of the Bankruptcy Act of 1978: Part Four: The Separate Clerk's Office," *American Bankruptcy Law Journal* 81 (2007): 515–40. Mund wrote a series of five articles on the history of the 1978 code as it pertained to the changes in structure and the role of bankruptcy judges.

20. *The Conference Newsletter*, editions for May 1971, November 1971, and February 1972, University of Pennsylvania, Biddle Law Library, National Bankruptcy Archives, NCBJ, Publications, hereinafter NCBJ Publications, National Bankruptcy Archives.

21. David Skeel, *Debt's Dominion: A History of Bankruptcy in America* (Princeton, NJ: Princeton University Press, 2001), 141–49; Geraldine Mund, "Appointed or Anointed . . . Part One: Outside Looking In," 17.

22. David Skeel, *Debt's Dominion: A History of Bankruptcy Law in America* (Princeton, NJ: Princeton University Press, 2001), 140; Geraldine Mund, "Appointed or Anointed . . . Part One: Outside Looking In," 29–30.

23. Geraldine Mund, "Appointed or Anointed: Judges, Congress, and the Passage of the Bankruptcy Act of 1978: Part Two: The Third Branch Reacts," *American Bankruptcy Law Journal* 81 (2007): 175.

24. On the legislative history of the bill, see Geraldine Mund, "Appointed or Anointed: Judges, Congress, and the Passage of the Bankruptcy Act of 1978: Part Three: On The Hill," *American Bankruptcy Law Journal* 81 (2007): 341–73.

25. An Act: To Establish a Uniform Law on the Subject of Bankruptcies, Stat. 92 (1978): 2549–2688. For a summary of the act see Martin I. Klein, "The Bankruptcy Reform Act of 1978," *American Bankruptcy Law Journal* 53 (1979): 1–33.

26. "Judges Treated Pursuant to Law," *Newsletter*, vol. 1984, no. 1 (January 1984); NCBJ Publications, National Bankruptcy Archives.

27. Northern Pipeline Construction Co. v. Marathon Pipe Line Co., 458 U.S. 50 (1982).

28. Harold F. White, interview with M. Susan Murnane, January 26, 2009.

29. Vern Countryman, "Scrambling to Define Bankruptcy Jurisdiction: The Chief Justice, the Judicial Conference, and the Legislative Process," *Harvard Journal on Legislation* 22 (1985): 19–25.

30. "Justice Department Reports on the Bankruptcy System," Newsletter, vol. 1984, no. 1 (January 1984), NCBJ Publications, National Bankruptcy Archives.

31. Joel Kaplan, "Judges' Actions Fuel Tenure Battle: Bankruptcy Cases Create Cozy Relationships Between Lawyers, Judges," in *Bankruptcy Courts: Judges in Conflict:*

A Special Report from the Tennessean (Nashville: Tennessean, August 1, 1983) found in the Harold F. White Papers, University of Akron School of Law Archives; NLRB v. Bildisco & Bildisco, 465 U.S. 513 (1984).

32. An Act: To Amend Title 28 of the United States Code Regarding Jurisdiction of Bankruptcy Proceedings, to Establish New Federal Judicial Positions, to Amend Title 11 of the United States Code, and for Other Purposes, Stat. 98 (1984): 333–992; §§ 105(a) and 106(a) at Stat. 98 at 336–42, codified as Title 28 United States Code §§ 151 through 158. See also Vern Countryman, "Scrambling to Define Bankruptcy Jurisdiction," 29–39.

33. Federal Magistrate Act, Stat. 82 (1968): 1107–1119; Mund, "Appointed or Anointed . . . Part Two: The Third Branch Reacts," 185–88.

34. Information on the personnel at the Administrative Office is reported in the NCBJ Newsletters at the National Bankruptcy Archives.

35. David Skeel, *Debt's Dominion*, 158; Vern Countryman, "Scrambling to Define Bankruptcy Jurisdiction," 43; Stern v. Marshall, 564 U.S._, 131 S. Ct. 2594 (2011); Executive Benefits Insurance Agency v. Arkinson, 573 U.S._ (2014).

36. Geraldine Mund, "Appointed or Anointed . . . Part Four: The Separate Clerk's Office," 515–40.

37. United States District Court for the Northern District of Ohio, Western Division, General Order No. 11, January 17 1974; idem, General Order No. 14, October 7, 1974.

38. Greg Stricharchuk, "The Back-Room Brotherhood," *Cleveland*, May 1962, 62, 69; Peter Almond, "Family, Friends, Law Profession Link Schlachet, Zipkin, Battisti," *Cleveland Press*, April 18, 1982.

39. Reed v. Rhodes, 422 F. Supp. 408 (N.D. Ohio 1976); Reed v. Rhodes, 455 F. Supp. 546 (N.D. Ohio 1978).

40. Gail Appleson, "Cleveland Judge Under Siege," *National Law Journal*, June 20, 1983; Stephanie Seal, "Judicial Report Slaps Schlachet," *Cleveland Plain Dealer*, October 21, 1982; Peter Almond, "Feds Investigate Judge's Deals," *Cleveland Press*, April 18, 1982; John Funk, "A Setback for Battisti in Court Row," *Akron Beacon Journal*, February 19, 1986.

41. An Act: To Amend the Bankruptcy Act to Provide for Uniform Supervision and Control of Employees of Referees in Bankruptcy, Stat. 92 (1978): 729; Frank R. Kennedy, "The Bankruptcy Court under the New Bankruptcy Law: Its Structure, Jurisdiction, Venue, and Procedure," *St. Mary's Law Journal* 11(1979): 254–69.

42. United States District Court, Northern District of Ohio, Eastern Division, General Order No. 27, Sept. 27, 1978.

43. "Benik to be U.S. Bankruptcy Clerk," *Cleveland Plain Dealer*, June 9, 1979; Ann Helmuth, "Battisti Hit on Clerk's Stand In," *Cleveland Plain Dealer*, February 11, 1970; idem, "Jurists Shun Appointment Dispute Here," *Cleveland Plain Dealer*, May 12, 1970.

44. Harold F. White, Interview, October 18, 1996, 29, Randall J. Newsome Oral History Collection, National Bankruptcy Archives; H. F. White to Chief Judge Pierce

Lively, August 22, 1984; United States Bankruptcy Court Northern District of Ohio In re: Certification and Appointment of Clerk, August 22, 1984, copy furnished by the clerk of Bankruptcy Court.

45. *Newsletter,* vol. 1985, no. 3 (August 1985), Conference Newsletters, NCBJ, Publications, National Bankruptcy Archives; GAO Decision B-217236.2, May 22, 1985.

46. In re Rini, 782 F. 2d 603 (6th Cir. 1986); *Newsletter*, vol. 1986, no. 1 (April), NCBJ Publications, Bankruptcy Archives.

47. Lloyd D. George, "From Orphan to Maturity: The Development of the Bankruptcy System During L. Ralph Mecham's Tenure as Director of the Administrative Office of the United States Courts," *American University Law Review* 44 (1995): 1491–1501; Richard S. Arnold, "L. Ralph Mecham: A Tribute," *American University Law Review* 44 (1995): 1479–82.

48. Harold F. White, Interview, October 18, 1996, 48–49, Randall J. Newsome Oral History Collection, National Bankruptcy Archives.

49. "Black Woman Nominated for Bankruptcy Position," *Cleveland Plain Dealer*, January 14, 1983.

50. Stephanie Saul, "Woman Fails to Get Nod as a Judge," *Cleveland Plain Dealer*, July 30, 1983.

51. Harry Stainer, "Groups That Barred Judge Called Racist," *Cleveland Plain Dealer*, July 31, 1983; Bertram de Souza, "Will Push Area Judge for Post," (Youngstown) *Vindicator*, January 29, 1984.

52. John Griffith, "Judges Shun Bankruptcy Nomination," *Cleveland Plain Dealer*, March 1, 1984; "Judges Give Up Pick for Bankruptcy Post," *Cleveland Plain Dealer*, March 8, 1984.

53. Jennifer Scott Cimperman, "Straight Shooter," *Cleveland Plain Dealer*, January 14, 2001.

54. Barbranda Lumpkins, "Ex-Akron Official Seeks Judgeship," *Akron Beacon Journal*, September 30, 1985, clipping found in the Harold F. White papers at the University of Akron School of Law Archives.

55. *Newsletter,* vol. 1990, no. 2 (May 1990), NCBJ Publications, National Bankruptcy Archives.

56. Diane Ellis, "The Effect of Consumer Interest Rate Deregulation on Credit Card Volumes, Charge-Offs, and the Personal Bankruptcy Rate," *Bank Trends* No. 98-5 (March 1998), http://www.fdic.gov/bank/analytical/bank/bt_9805.html; David A. Moss and Gibbs A. Johnson, "The Rise of Consumer Bankruptcy: Evolution, Revolution, or Both?" *American Bankruptcy Law Journal* 73 (1999): 311–51.

57. Marquette National Bank of Minneapolis v. First of Omaha Service Corporation, 439 U.S. 299 (1979).

58. Bankruptcy Judges, Bankruptcy Trustees, and Family Farmer Bankruptcy Act of 1986, Stat. 100 (1986): 3088–3128.

59. David Skeel, *Debt's Dominion*, 159.

60. The extent to which the bankruptcy bar changed after the bankruptcy reforms of 1978 is unknown because no systematic survey of the bankruptcy bar was made before 1985. In 1985, the University of Wisconsin conducted an extensive survey of the bankruptcy bar and found that, contrary to the popular conception of bankruptcy rings, most bankruptcy lawyers practiced in full-service law firms and represented clients in other areas of law, especially commercial law, litigation, general corporate practice, and real estate. Bankruptcy remains one of the most concentrated areas of law, however, especially in large cities. Fifty percent of bankruptcy lawyers spend between ninety and one hundred percent of their time on bankruptcy matters. Lynn M. LoPucki, "The Demographics of Bankruptcy Practice," *American Bankruptcy Law Journal* 63 (1989): 309–11, 318.

61. Conrad J. Morgenstern is no relation to bankruptcy judge Pat E. Morgenstern-Clarren.

62. Interview with Saul Eisen on June 30, 2011.

Chapter 7

1. John P. Butenas, "Establishing Attorney's Fees Under the New Bankruptcy Code," *Commercial Law Journal* 87 (1982): 237–43.

2. Eugene V. Rostow and Lloyd N. Cutler, "Competing Systems of Corporate Reorganization: Chapters X and XI of the Bankruptcy Act," *Yale Law Journal* 48 (1939): 1334–44.

3. For a summary of the provisions, see Martin I. Klein, "The Bankruptcy Reform Act of 1978," *American Bankruptcy Law Journal* 53 (1979): 7–17.

4. David A. Skeel, *Debt's Dominion: A History of Bankruptcy Law in America* (Princeton, NJ: Princeton University Press, 2001), 162–66.

5. Bruce G. Carruthers and Terence C. Halliday, *Rescuing Business: The Making of Corporate Bankruptcy Law in England and the United States* (Oxford, UK: Clarendon Press, 1998), 442–47; Skeel, *Debt's Dominion*, 222.

6. Theodore Eisenberg and Lynn M. LoPucki, "Shopping for Judges: An Empirical Analysis of Venue Choice in Large Chapter 11 Reorganizations," *Cornell Law Review* 84 (1999): 967–1003.

7. In re The Mansfield Tire and Rubber Co., 660 F.2d 1108 (6th Cir. 1981); In re The Mansfield Tire and Rubber Co., 39 B.R. 974 (Bankr. N.D. Ohio 1983); In re The Mansfield Tire and Rubber Co., 942 F.2d 1055 (6th Cir. 1991).

8. Conversation with G. Christopher Meyer, November 9, 2010.

9. Unless otherwise noted, the following narrative is based on records of the White Motor bankruptcy in the possession of G. Christopher Meyer and his very helpful explanations and clarifications. Squire, Sanders & Dempsey has since donated materials from their White Motor bankruptcy records to the Western Reserve Historical Society. I am deeply grateful to Mr. Meyer for his assistance and his insight.

10. In re White Motor Credit Corp., 50 B.R. 885, 886 (Bankr. N.D. Ohio 1985).

11. Sherry R. Sontag, "Amid Bust, a Boom," *National Law Journal*, April 2, 1990.

12. Diane Solov, "Law Firms Finding New Green Pastures in Bankruptcy Cases," *Cleveland Plain Dealer*, July 16, 1991.

13. Edward P. Whalen, "A Scandal in Ethics," *Cleveland*, June 1983, 70, 72, 128–29; Gail Appleson, "Cleveland Judge Under Siege," *National Law Journal*, June 28, 1983.

14. In re White Motor Credit Corp., 50 B.R. at 901–902.

15. In re White Motor Credit Corp., 18 B.R. 720 (Bankr. N.D. Ohio 1980).

16. In re White Motor Credit Corp., 27 B.R .554 (Bankr. N.D. Ohio 1982); Winston Williams, "Holders get Bankruptcy Voice," *New York Times*, June 28, 1982.

17. For analysis of the absolute priority rule before and after bankruptcy reform in 1978, see Lynn M. LoPucki and William C. Whitford, "Bargaining over Equity's Share in the Bankruptcy Reorganization of Large, Publicly Held Corporations," *University of Pennsylvania Law Review* 139 (November1990): 125–96.

18. In re White Motor Credit Corp., 50 B.R. at 887.

19. In re White Motor Credit Corp., 14 B.R. 584 (Bankr. N.D. Ohio 1981).

20. In re White Motor Corp., 42 B.R. 693 (Bankr. N.D. Ohio 1984).

21. Employee Retirement Income Security Act of 1974, Stat. 88 (1974): 829–1035.

22. In re White Farm Equipment Co., 788 F.2d 1186 (6th Cir. 1986).

23. Retiree Benefits Bankruptcy Protection Act of 1988, Stat. 102 (1988): 610–15.

24. Daniel Keating, "Bankruptcy Code § 1114: Congress' Empty Response to the Retiree Plight," *American Bankruptcy Law Journal* 67 (1993): 24–32.

25. David S. Dunkel, "Final Regulations Stimulate Use of Section 501(c)(9) Trusts," *Taxes* 99 (April 1981): 226–30; Segal Group, "Study of Retiree Health VEBAs," *Survey* (Winter 2008), http://www.sibson.com/uploads/65896ec7d78c973e-6a5e5666d448da26.pdf.

26. David Kauffman, "Procedures for Estimating Contingent or Unliquidated Claims in Bankruptcy," *Stanford Law Review* 35 (November 1982): 153–58.

27. In re White Farm Equipment Co., 38 B.R. 718 (Bankr. N.D. Ohio 1984).

28. Northern Pipeline Construction Co. v. Marathon Pipe Line Co., 458 U.S. 50 (1982).

29. In re White Motor Credit Corp., 23 B.R. 276 (Bankr. N.D. Ohio 1982).

30. White Motor Corp. v. Citibank, N.A, 704 F.2d 254 (6th Cir. 1983).

31. In re White Motor Credit Corp., 37 B.R. 631 (Bankr. N.D. Ohio 1984).

32. In re White Farm Equipment Co., 38 B.R. at 723.

33. Mark L. Goldstein, "Lou Gussetti Hammers Together A New Old Company . . . and the Pieces Keep Getting Bigger," *Industry Week*, February 15, 1988, 47–48.

34. "History of Euclid," Hudson, OH: Hudson Library and Historical Society.

35. Folder 1, Hudson Planning Committee, Series 1, Terex Papers, SP T620, Hudson Library and Historical Society, Hudson, Ohio, hereinafter Terex Papers, Hudson Historical Society.

36. Folder 2 Texextra Oct. 1972, Series 2A, Texextra, Terex Papers, Hudson Historical Society.

37. Roger Thurow and George Anders, "Germany's IBH Seeks Protection From Creditors: Its Bold Leader Turns to GM and Saudis for Help," *Wall Street Journal*, November 7, 1983; Terence Roth, "Aristocrat's Fraud Trial Intrigues Germans," *Wall Street Journal*, January 22, 1986.

38. Folder 6, IBH Reorganization, Series 4, Terex Papers, Hudson Historical Society.

39. Folder 5, Union problems, Series 4, Terex Papers, Hudson Historical Society.

40. NLRB v. Bildisco & Bildisco, 465 U.S. 513 (1984).

41. "Solicitation of All Acceptances of Chapter 11 Plan of Reorganization," filed June 24, 1986, from the files of Squire, Sanders & Dempsey, Cleveland, Ohio.

42. Folder 7, Plant Closings 198–89, Series 4, Terex Papers, Hudson Historical Society.

43. Bill Karaly, "Enterprise Zone Detailed," *Hudson Hub-Times*, March 30, 1988. For more information on Ohio's enterprise zones, see William Henderson, "In the Zone: How Enterprise Zones Have Promoted Urban Sprawl in Northeast Ohio," in *Moving to Cornfields: A Reader on Urban Sprawl and the Regional Future of Northeast Ohio* (Cleveland Heights, OH: Ecocity Cleveland, 1996), 18–23, http://www.gcbl.org/files/resources/movingtocornfields.pdf.

44. W. Braddock Hickman, *The Volume of Corporate Bond Financing since 1900* (Princeton, NJ: Princeton University Press, 1953); idem, *Corporate Bond Quality and Investor Experience* (Princeton, NJ: Princeton University Press, 1958); Thomas R. Atkinson, *Trends in Corporate Bond Quality* (New York: Columbia University/NBER, 1967).

45. Connie Bruck, *The Predators' Ball* (New York: American Lawyer/Simon and Schuster, 1988), 28; Roy C. Smith, "After the Ball," *Wilson Quarterly* 16 (Autumn 1992): 40. *The Predators' Ball* provides much general information on the rise and fall of Michael Milken and the junk bond industry of the 1980s.

46. The early history of Revco may be found in *International Directory of Company Histories* (Chicago: St. James Press, 1988–2003). The later history may be found in the Preliminary Report of Examiner Professor Barry Lewis Zaretsky, Appendix to In re Revco D.S., Inc., 118 B.R. 468 (Bankr. N.D. Ohio 1990). The final report of the examiner, Professor Barry Lewis Zaretsky, may be found in the papers of Judge Harold F. White at the University of Akron School of Law Archives.

47. Karen Wruck, "What Really Went Wrong at Revco?" *Journal of Applied Corporate Finance* 4 (Summer 1991): 79–92. This article clearly summarizes the financial aspects of the Revco leveraged buyout.

48. A list of fees distributed at closing is found in the preliminary report of the examiner, at 118 B.R. at 493.

49. Thomas E. Ricks and Gregory Stricharchuk, "Insider Trading Linked to Buy-Out of Revco Alleged," *Wall Street Journal*, May 2, 1989; Thomas E. Ricks, "Dangerous Game: How 4 Pals Who Mixed Golf and Stock Tips Landed in the Rough—Middle Class Memphis Lives Are Jolted When the SEC Charges Insider Trading," *Wall*

Street Journal, July 21, 1989; Paul Duke Jr., "Eight More Cited in SEC Inquiry Into Revco Trades," *Wall Street Journal*, July 25, 1989.

50. Greg Gardner, "Revco Filing Means a Heavy Load for Court," *Akron Beacon Journal*, July 30, 1988; *United States Bankruptcy Court for the Northern District of Ohio, Annual Report, Fiscal Years 1989 and 1990*; *United States Bankruptcy Court for the Northern District of Ohio, Annual Report, Fiscal Year 1991.*

51. Conrad J. Morgenstern is no relation to bankruptcy judge Pat E. Morgenstern-Clarren.

52. In re Revco, D.S., Inc., 898 F.2d 498, 500 (6th Cir. 1990).

53. In re Revco, D.S., Inc., 118 B.R. 468 (Bankr. N.D. Ohio 1990).

54. Robert F. Bruner and Kenneth M. Eades, "The Crash of the Revco Leveraged Buyout: The Hypothesis of Inadequate Capital," *Financial Management* 21 (Spring 1992): 35–49.

55. Sherry R. Sontag, "Revco's Collapse a Symbol: After Two Years, the Bankruptcy Is Stalled," *National Law Journal*, September 3, 1990.

56. George Anders, "Revco Saga: Or How Buy-Out Bonanza Became a Frenzy of Fees in Chapter 11," *Wall Street Journal*, May 16, 1991.

57. United States v. Tabor Court Realty Corp., 803 F.2d 1288 (3d Cir. 1986) *cert. denied*, 483 U.S. 1005 (1987); Kupetz v. Wolf, 845 F.2d 842 (9th Cir. 1988).

58. Margaret Howard, "Vern Countryman and Barry Zaretsky: A Legacy of Ideas," *American Bankruptcy Law Journal* 75 (2001): 287, quoting Douglas G. Baird and Thomas H. Jackson, "Fraudulent Conveyance Law and Its Proper Domain," *Vanderbilt Law Review* 38 (1985): 852.

59. Nancy M. Funk and Delinda Karle, "Judge Puts Heat on Revco for Settlement," *Cleveland Plain Dealer*, October 24, 1990; Delinda Karle, "Suppliers to Revco Bide Time with Suit," *Cleveland Plain Dealer*, November 6, 1990.

60. Sam Zell earned the nickname "grave dancer" by becoming very wealthy from successfully investing in distressed properties and companies.

61. Stephen Philips, "Revco Finally Holding the Cards; Chain to Emerge from Bankruptcy as an Independent Company," *Cleveland Plain Dealer*, February 23, 1992.

62. Viral V. Acharya, Julian Franks, and Henri Servaes, "Private Equity: Boom and Bust?" *Journal of Applied Corporate Finance* 4 (Fall 2007): 1–4; Steven N. Kaplan and Per Strömberg, "Leveraged Buyouts and Private Equity," *Journal of Economic Perspectives* 23 (Winter 2009): 121–46.

63. "Founder Regains Helm at HBJ Publications," *New York Times*, November 19, 1987.

64. Lori Ashyk, "Edgell Pinching Pennies, Working Itself Out of Debt," *Crain's Cleveland Business*, July 31, 1989.

65. Many thanks to G. Christopher Meyer at Squire, Sanders & Dempsey for sharing the November 20, 1991, "Confidential Restructuring and Disclosure Statement." See also Barbara Mooney and Chris Thompson, "Goldman Sachs Stands to Gain

Reins at Edgell," *Crain's Cleveland Business*, January 13, 1992; Floyd Norris, "Edgell May Show the Way to Heal Buyout Casualties," *New York Times*, January 24, 1992.

66. Jennifer Scott Cimperman and Thomas W. Gerdel, "This Time is Different for LTV," *Cleveland Plain Dealer*, December 31, 2000.

67. Gary Clyde Hufbauer and Ben Goodrich, "Steel: Big Problems, Better Solutions," *International Economics Policy Briefs*, Policy Brief No. 01-9 (Washington, DC: Petersen Institute for International Economics, July 2001), Table 1, http://www.iie.com/publications/pb/pb.cfm?ResearchID=77.

68. Thomas W. Gerdel, "Enduro Owner Convicted of Fraud," *Cleveland Plain Dealer*, December 21, 1989; Jennifer Scott Cimperman, "Nearing the End of the Roll Massillon Stainless' Third Closing Could Be Its Last," *Cleveland Plain Dealer*, October 22, 2002.

69. Thomas M. Buynak, "Is the U.S. Pension-Insurance System Going Broke?" *Economic Commentary*, January 15, 1987 http://www.clevelandfed.org/research/commentary/1987/econcomm19870115.pdf; Mark A. Casciari and John T. Murray, "*PBGC v. LTV Corp.*: The Supreme Court Endorses Broad Agency Discretion," *Employee Relations Law Journal* 16 (1991): 481–92.

70. PBGC v. LTV, 496 U.S. 633 (1990); "LTV to Reassume Funding of Terminated Plans," *Employee Benefit Plan Review*, February 1991, 6–70.

71. Republic Technologies, the successor corporation to Republic Engineered Steel, would file for Chapter 11 protection in April 2001. WCI would file in September 2003.

72. Staughton Lynd, "Why We Opposed the Buyout at Weirton Steel," *Labor Research Review* 6 (1985): 41–53.

73. Peter T. Kilborn, "Scrapping 'Us Versus Them,' Industry Is Giving Workers a Say and a Stake," *New York Times*, November 22, 1991; John H. Sheridan, "Counting on Cash," *Industry Week*, September 2, 1996, 10.

74. Jennifer Scott Cimperman, "Big Steel Waging Last-Ditch Fight for Survival; Higher Energy Costs, Worldwide Glut Cripple Industry," *Cleveland Plain Dealer*, May 27, 2001; Thomas W. Gerdel, "Steel Mills Fall to 64% capacity," *Cleveland Plain Dealer*, January 2, 2001.

75. Thomas W. Gerdel, "Too Many Steel Bars Chasing too Few Buyers; Rapid Industry Decline Threatens Thousands of Jobs," *Cleveland Plain Dealer*, June 3, 2001.

76. Jennifer Scott Cimperman, "Straight Shooter," *Cleveland Plain Dealer*, January 14, 2001.

77. Gabriella Stern and Clare Ansberry, "Fouling Out: A Founder Embezzled Millions for Basketball, Phar-Mor Chain Says," *Wall Street Journal*, August 5, 1992; Gabriella Stern, "Phar-Mor Seeks Chapter 11 Protection from Creditors," *Wall Street Journal*, August 18, 1992.

78. Gregg Johnson, "Bankrupt Wheeling-Pitt Still Kicking," *The Daily Deal*, March 28, 2003, ProQuest document ID: 318979571.

79. Jennifer Scott Cimperman, "'A Cry of Desperation,' LTV Chief's Letter Raises Eyebrows on Wall Street," *Cleveland Plain Dealer,* December 29, 2000; Thomas W. Gerdel, "LTV Begs for Life," *Cleveland Plain Dealer,* December 29, 2000.

80. For more information on the treatment of derivative securities under the Bankruptcy Code, see Jonathan Keath Hance, "Derivatives at Bankruptcy: Lifesaving Knowledge for the Small Firm," *Washington & Lee Law Review* 65 (2008): 711–66.

81. In re LTV Steel, 274 B.R. 278, 285–86 (Bankr. N.D. Ohio 2001).

82. Robert Stark, "Viewing the LTV Steel ABS Opinion in its Proper Context," *Journal of Corporation Law* 27 (Winter 2002): 211–29.

83. Kenneth C. Kettering, "True Sale of Receivables: A Purposive Analysis," *American Bankruptcy Institute Law Review* 16 (2008): 511–62; John A. Pearce II and Ilya A. Lipin, "Special Purpose Vehicles in Bankruptcy Litigation, *Hofstra Law Review* 40 (2011): 180–81.

84. On the demise of Bethlehem Steel, see Carol J. Loomis, Patricia Neering, and Christopher Tkacyk, "The Sinking of Bethlehem Steel," *Fortune*, April 5, 2004, 174.

85. Jennifer Scott Cimperman, "LTV Shutdown Begins," *Cleveland Plain Dealer,* December 8, 2001.

86. Alison Grant, "Steel Suffers 41st Setback; Fairlawn-based Republic Files for Bankruptcy Protection," *Cleveland Plain Dealer,* October 7, 2003.

87. Jennifer Scott Cimperman, "The State of Steel," *Cleveland Plain Dealer,* December 30, 2001; Peter Krouse, "Steel Officials: Consolidation Led the Revival," *Cleveland Plain Dealer,* May 3, 2006.

Chapter 8

1. An Act: To Amend Title 28 of the United States Code Regarding Jurisdiction of Bankruptcy Proceedings, to Establish New Federal Judicial Positions, to Amend Title 11 of the United States Code, and for Other Purposes, Stat. 98 (1984): 333–992; Northern Pipeline Construction Co. v. Marathon Pipe Line Co., 458 U.S. 50 (1982).

2. Stern v. Marshall, 564 US_, 131 S. Ct. 2594 (2011); Executive Benefits Insurance Agency v. Arkinson, 573 U.S._ (2014). I am indebted to attorney Andrew Turscak Jr. who provided concise analysis of this important issue on very short notice.

3. Bankruptcy Abuse Prevention and Consumer Protection Act, Stat. 119 (2005): 23–217.

4. David A. Moss and Gibbs A. Johnson, "The Rise of Consumer Bankruptcy: Evolution, Revolution, or Both?" *American Bankruptcy Law Journal* 73 (1999): 322–23.

5. Ibid., 332–46.

6. Robert J. Landry III, "An Empirical Analysis of the Causes of Consumer Bankruptcy: Will Bankruptcy Reform Really Change Anything?" *Rutgers Business Law Journal* 3 (2006): 2–49.

7. The Northern District of Ohio consumer bankruptcy filings for the years 2007 through 2010 may be found at http://www.ohnb.uscourts.gov/. National consumer bankruptcy filings for those years may be found at http://www.abiworld.org/.

8. American Bankruptcy Institute, "Households per Consumer Filing, Rank: During the 12-Month Period Ending December 31, 2005," http://www.abiworld.org/statcharts/householdStat2005.pdf.

9. Kyle Fee and Bob Sadowski, "Regional Activity: The Cleveland Metropolitan Statistical Area," *Economic Trends* (Federal Reserve Bank of Cleveland), August 6, 2007, http://www.clevelandfed.org/research/trends/2007/0807/02regact_080607.cfm. The payroll employment chart is published in the article.

10. Roger Mezger, "As the Decade Dawned, Signs of the Financial Crisis to Come Were Plentiful Here," *Cleveland Plain Dealer*, September 28, 2008, http://blog.cleveland.com/business/2008/09/as_decade_dawned_signs_of_cris.html (accessed June 2011).

11. Northern Pipeline Construction Co. v. Marathon Pipe Line Co., 458 U.S. 50 (1982).

12. NLRB v. Bildisco & Bildisco, 465 U.S. 513 (1984).

13. David A. Skeel, *Debt's Dominion: A History of Bankruptcy Law in America* (Princeton, NJ: Princeton University Press, 2001), 194–96.

14. Charles Jordan Tabb, "A Century of Regress or Progress? A Political History of Bankruptcy Legislation in 1898 and 1998," *Bankruptcy Developments Journal* 15 (1999): 345–50.

15. Bankruptcy Reform Act of 1994, Stat. 108 (1994): 4106–4151.

16. Ibid., 4147.

17. *U.S. House, The Bankruptcy Reform Act of 1994*, 103rd Cong., 2d sess., 1994, H.R. Rep. 103-835, 59 (1994), quoted in *Bankruptcy: The Next Twenty Years, National Bankruptcy Review Commission Final Report*, (Washington, DC: Commission, 1997), 50–51.

18. Tabb, "A Century of Regress or Progress?" 347–53; Elizabeth Warren, "The Changing Politics of American Bankruptcy Reform," *Osgoode Hall Law Journal* 37 (1999): 189–204.

19. Moss and Johnson, "The Rise of Consumer Bankruptcy," 312–22; Susan Jensen, "A Legislative History of the Bankruptcy Abuse Prevention and Consumer Protection Act of 2005," *American Bankruptcy Law Journal* 79 (2005): 490–91. The narrative that follows relies heavily on Jensen.

20. "3 Lawyers Recommended for Bankruptcy Judgeship," *Cleveland Plain Dealer*, January 22, 1985.

21. Lubrizol Enterprises v. Richmond Metal Finishers, Inc., 756 F.2d 1043 (4th Cir. 1985), *cert. denied*, 457 U.S. 1057 (1986); Patrick Law, "Intellectual Property Licenses and Bankruptcy—Has the IPLBA thawed the "chilling effects" of Lubrizol v. Richmond Metal Finishers?" *Commercial Law Journal* 99 (1994): 261–75.

22. "Sixth Circuit Judicial Council, Procedures for the Selection of Bankruptcy Judges and Procedures for the Reappointment of Bankruptcy Judges," (June 26, 2005,

as corrected February 4, 2011), http://www.ca6.uscourts.gov/internet/circuit_executive/documents/bkproce.pdf.

23. SIPC v. Bell & Beckwith, 28 B.R. 285 (Bankr. N.D. Ohio 1983); Title 15, U.S.C. §§ 78aaa et seq.; § 78eee.

24. N. R. Kleinfield, "Beckwith Partner Gets 25-Year Jail Term," *New York Times*, September 7, 1983.

25. Homer Brickley, "After 14 Years, Bell & Beckwith Bankruptcy Ends," *Toledo Blade*, January 16, 1997.

26. Karen E. Henderson, "Sharon Steel Settles Pollution Case," *Cleveland Plain Dealer*, February 6, 1980.

27. "Injured by Beam at Federal Building," *Cleveland Plain Dealer*, April 14, 1940; "Abraham Goler," *Cleveland Plain Dealer*, April 14, 1940.

28. 564 U.S._, 131 S. Ct. 2594 (2011); 573 U.S._ (2014).

29. § 104 (c), at Stat. 108, 4109–4110.

30. For more information on the Sixth Circuit bankruptcy appellate panel, see Irene M. Milan, "The Bankruptcy Appellate Panel of the U.S. Court of Appeals for the Sixth Circuit" (2009), History of the Sixth Circuit, available through the Library for the U.S. Court of Appeals for the Sixth Circuit.

31. PACER is the acronym for Public Access to Court Electronic Records. It provides access to federal district court and circuit court records as well as bankruptcy court records.

Epilogue

1. For a more complete discussion, see Charles J. Tabb, "The Top Twenty Issues in the History of Consumer Bankruptcy," *University of Illinois Law Review* 2007 (2007): 9–29.

2. Ibid., 22.

3. For an informative discussion of fees in bankruptcy cases, see In re Cle-Ware Industries, Inc., v. Sokolsky, 493 F. 2d 863 (6th 1974).

4. Lynn M. LoPucki, "The Demographics of Bankruptcy Practice," *American Bankruptcy Law Journal* 63 (1989): 289–319.

5. Elizabeth Warren, "Bankruptcy Policymaking in an Imperfect World," *Michigan Law Review* 92 (1993): 364–65.

6. Douglas G. Baird, "A World Without Bankruptcy," *Law and Contemporary Problems* 50 (1987): 175–81; Jason J. Kilborn, "Mercy, Rehabilitation, and Quid Pro Quo: A Radical Reassessment of Individual Bankruptcy," *Ohio State Law Journal* 64 (2003): 855–96.

7. Eugene R. Wedoff, "Major Consumer Bankruptcy Effects of BAPCPA," *University of Illinois Law Review* 2007 (2007): 31–65.

8. For a bankruptcy judge's interpretation, see Keith M. Lundin, "Ten Principles of BAPCPA: Not What Was Advertised," *American Bankruptcy Institute Journal* 24, no. 7 (2005): 1.

9. There is a vast literature on the effectiveness of Chapter 11. For example, Michael Bradley and Michael Rosenzweig, "The Untenable Case for Chapter 11," *Yale Law Journal* 101 (1992): 1043–96; contra Elizabeth Warren, "The Untenable Case for Repeal of Chapter 11," *Yale Law Journal* 102 (1992): 437–79 and Jagdeep S. Bhandari and Lawrence A. Weiss, "The Untenable Case for Chapter 11: A Review of the Evidence," *American Bankruptcy Law Journal* 57 (1993): 131–50. See also Douglas G. Baird and Robert K. Rasmussen, "The End of Bankruptcy," *Stanford Law Review* 55 (2002): 752–89, contra Lynn M. LoPucki, "The Nature of the Bankruptcy Firm: A Response to Baird and Rasmussen's *The End of Bankruptcy*," *Stanford Law Review* 56 (2003): 646–71.

10. Frank H. Easterbrook, "Is Corporate Bankruptcy Efficient?" *Journal of Financial Economics* 27 (1990): 411–17.

11. Elizabeth Warren and Jay Lawrence Westbrook, "The Success of Chapter 11: A Challenge to the Critics," *Michigan Law Review* 107 (2009): 503–41.

12. Compare Douglas G. Baird, "Bankruptcy's Uncontested Axioms," *Yale Law Journal* 108 (1998): 573–99; Elizabeth Warren, "Bankruptcy Policymaking in an Imperfect World," *Michigan Law Review* 92 (1993): 336–87.

13. Warren, "Bankruptcy Policymaking in an Imperfect World," 344–56; Harvey R. Miller and Shai Y. Waisman, "Is Chapter 11 Corrupt?" *Boston College Law Review* 47 (2005): 169–74.

14. Jonathan Keath Hance, "Derivatives at Bankruptcy: Lifesaving Knowledge for the Small Firm," *Washington & Lee Law Review* 65 (2008): 720–22, 737–48; David A. Skeel, "Bankruptcy Boundary Games," *Brooklyn Journal of Corporate Finance & Commercial Law* 4 (2009): 6–7.

15. Franklin R. Edwards and Edward R. Morrison, "Derivatives and the Bankruptcy Code: Why the Special Treatment?" *Yale Journal on Regulation* 22 (2005): 92–93; Hance, "Derivatives at Bankruptcy," 748–53; Rhett G. Campbell, "Financial Markets Contracts and BAPCPA," *American Bankruptcy Law Journal* 79 (2005): 698–701; President's Working Group on Financial Markets, *Hedge Funds, Leverage, and the Lessons of Long-Term Capital Finance* (1999), http://www.treasury.gov/resource-center/fin-mkts/Documents/hedgfund.pdf., 26–29, 40.

16. For an explanation of the 2005 provisions, see Edward R. Morrison and Jeorg Riegel, "Financial Contracts and the New Bankruptcy Code: Insulating Markets from Bankruptcy Debtors and Bankruptcy Judges," *American Bankruptcy Institute Law Review* 13 (2005): 641–64.

17. Skeel, "Bankruptcy Boundary Games, 10–11.

18. Campbell, "Financial Markets and BAPCPA," 710–11.

19. Michael Simkovich, "Secret Liens and the Financial Crisis of 2008," *American Bankruptcy Law Journal* 83 (2009): 253–95.

20. Skeel, "Bankruptcy Boundary Games," 11.

21. Simkovich, "Secret Liens," 259, 282. There are many ways to convert secured debt to protected financial products, Edwards and Morrison, "Derivatives and the Bankruptcy Code," 119–121.

22. For example, Mark J. Roe, "The Derivatives Market's Payment Priorities as Financial Risk Accelerator," *Stanford Law Review* 63 (2011): 539–90.

Selected Bibliography

Archives Visited

Cuyahoga County Archives, Cleveland, Ohio.

Hudson Library and Historical Society, Hudson, Ohio. Terex Papers.

National Archives and Records Administration, Chicago. US District Court Records, Record Group 21.

National Archives and Records Administration, Washington, DC Administrative Office of the US Courts, Record Group 116. US. Supreme Court Applications and Endorsements, 1867–1909. Record Group 267, Entry 73.

National Bankruptcy Archives, Biddle Library, University of Pennsylvania, Philadelphia, Pennsylvania. National Conference of Bankruptcy Judges Publications. Randall J. Newsome Oral History Collection.

Toledo-Lucas County Public Library, Local History Department, Toledo, Ohio. Toledo History Scrapbook—Industries—JEEP—before 1959.

Western Reserve Historical Society, Cleveland, Ohio. Cleveland Bar Association, Manuscript Collection 4332. Cuyahoga County Bar Association, Manuscript Collection 3600. Carl D. Friebolin Papers, Manuscript Collection 3309. Greater Cleveland Growth Association, Manuscript Collection 3471. LTV Steel Co. Records, Manuscript Collection 4950. Republic Steel Co, Manuscript Collection 4949. Local Government Records. Federal Court Records (correspondence).

Articles, Books, and Periodicals

"A Bankruptcy Clinic." *Journal of the National Association of Referees in Bankruptcy* 4 (1930): 37.

Acharya, Viral V., Julian Franks, and Henri Servaes. "Private Equity: Boom and Bust?" *Journal of Applied Corporate Finance* 4 (Fall 2007): 1–10.

Adair, Watson. "Report of the Conference Committee." *Journal of the National Association of Referees in Bankruptcy* 7 (1933): 68–69.

American Bankruptcy Institute. *Bankruptcy Filing Statistics—Filings by District.* http://www.abiworld.org/AM/Template.cfm?Section=Filings_by_District1&Template=/TaggedPage/TaggedPageDisplay.cfm&TPLID=56&ContentID=36298. Accessed June 2011.

American Bankruptcy Institute. *Households per Consumer Filing, Rank: During the 12-Month Period Ending December 31, 2005.* http://www.abiworld.org/statcharts/householdStat2005.pdf. Accessed June 2011.
Appleson, Gail. "Cleveland Judge Under Siege." *National Law Journal,* June 20, 1983.
Arnold, Richard S. "L. Ralph Mecham: A Tribute." *American University Law Review* 44 (1995): 1479–82.
Ashyk, Lori. "Edgell Pinching Pennies, Working Itself Out of Debt." *Crain's Cleveland Business,* July 31, 1989.
Atack, Jeremy, and Peter Passell. *A New Economic View of American History from Colonial Times to 1940.* 2nd ed. New York: W. W. Norton, 1994.
Atkinson, Thomas R. *Trends in Corporate Bond Quality.* New York: Columbia University/NBER, 1967.
Baird, Douglas G. "A World Without Bankruptcy." *Law and Contemporary Problems* 50 (1987): 173–93.
———. "Bankruptcy's Uncontested Axioms." *Yale Law Journal* 108 (1998): 573–99.
Baird, Douglas G., and Thomas H. Jackson. "Fraudulent Conveyance Law and Its Proper Domaine." *Vanderbilt Law Review* 38 (1985): 829–55.
Baird, Douglas G., and Robert K. Rasmussen. "The End of Bankruptcy." *Stanford Law Review* 55 (2002): 751–89.
———. "Chapter 11 at Twilight." *Stanford Law Review* 56 (2003): 673–99.
Balleisen, Edward J. *Navigating Failure: Bankruptcy and Commercial Society in Antebellum America.* Chapel Hill: University of North Carolina Press, 2001.
Beesom, Patricia, and Frank Giarratani. "Spatial Aspects of Capacity Change by U.S. Integrated Steel Producers." *Journal of Regional Science* 38 (1998): 425–44.
Benedict, Michael Les, and John F. Winkler, eds. *The History of Ohio Law.* Athens: Ohio University Press, 2004.
Bhandari, Jagdeep S., and Lawrence A. Weiss. "The Untenable Case for Chapter 11: A Review of the Evidence." *American Bankruptcy Law Journal* 57 (1993): 131–50.
Bierce, Herbert M. "Our Association in Retrospect and in Prospect." *Journal of the National Association of Referees in Bankruptcy* 11 (1936): 9–11.
Billig, Thomas Clifford. *Equity Receiverships in the Common Pleas Court of Franklin County.* Baltimore: Johns Hopkins University Press, 1932.
———. "The New Deal in Bankruptcy Legislation." *Journal of the National Association of Referees in Bankruptcy* 9 (1934): 32–35, 48.
Bogart, Ernest Ludlow. *Financial History of Ohio.* Urbana-Champaign: University of Illinois Press, 1912.
Bonadio, Felice A. *North of Reconstruction: Ohio Politics, 1865–1870.* New York: New York University Press, 1970.
Bradley, Michael, and Michael Rosenzweig. "The Untenable Case for Chapter 11." *Yale Law Journal* 101 (1992): 1043–96.
Bruck, Connie. *The Predators' Ball.* New York: American Lawyer/Simon and Schuster, 1988.
Bruner, Robert F., and Kenneth M. Eades. "The Crash of the Revco Leveraged Buyout: The Hypothesis of Inadequate Capital." *Financial Management* 21 (Spring1992): 35–49.

Butenas, John P. "Establishing Attorney's Fees under the New Bankruptcy Code." *Commercial Law Journal* 87 (1982): 237–43.

Buynak, Thomas M. "Is the U.S. Pension-Insurance System Going Broke?" *Economic Commentary*, January 15, 1987. http://www.clevelandfed.org/research/commentary/1987/econcomm19870115.pdf.

Calomiris, Charles W., and Larry Schweikart. "The Panic of 1857: Origins, Transmission, and Containment." *Journal of Economic History* 51 (1991): 807–34.

Campbell, Ballard C. *The Growth of American Government*. Bloomington: Indiana University Press, 1995.

Campbell, Rhett G. "Financial Markets Contracts and BAPCPA." *American Bankruptcy Law Journal* 79 (2005): 697–712.

Carruthers, Bruce G., and Terence C. Halliday. *Rescuing Business: The Making of Corporate Bankruptcy Law in England and the United States*. Oxford, UK: Clarendon Press, 1998.

Casciari, Mark A., and John T. Murray. "*PBGC v. LTV Corp.*: The Supreme Court Endorses Broad Agency Discretion." *Employee Relations Law Journal* 16 (1991): 481–92.

A Centennial Biographical History of Crawford County Ohio. Chicago: Lewis Publishing, 1902.

Chandler, Henry P. "The Beginning of a New Era in Bankruptcy Administration: 1939–1947." *Journal of the National Association of Referees in Bankruptcy* 34 (1960): 3–6, 25–26.

———. "The Beginning of a New Era in Bankruptcy: 1939–1947 [second and concluding installment]." *Journal of the National Association of Referees in Bankruptcy* 34 (1960): 44–53.

Chandler, Walter. "The Revised Bankruptcy Act of 1938." American Bar Association Journal 24 (1938): 880–84.

Chase, Salmon P., ed. *The Statutes of Ohio and the Northwestern Territory*. 3 vols., Cincinnati: Corey and Fairbank, 1833.

Chernow, Ron. *Titan: The Life of John D. Rockefeller, Sr.* New York: Random House, 1998; 2nd ed., Vintage Books, 2004.

Chew, Richard S. "Certain Victims of an International Contagion: The Panic of 1797 and the Hard Times of the Late 1790s in Baltimore." *Journal of the Early Republic* 25 (2005): 565–613.

City Planning Associates. *Preliminary Report 1 for Youngstown, Ohio Community Renewal Program R-108 (CR): Historical Development of Youngstown and the Mahoning Valley*. Youngstown, Ohio: City Planning Associates, 1968.

Clark, Christopher. *The Roots of Rural Capitalism: Western Massachusetts, 1780–1860*. Ithaca, NY: Cornell University Press, 1990.

Clark, Gordon L. "Regulating the Restructuring of the US Steel Industry: Chapter 11 of the Bankruptcy Code and Pension Obligations." *Regional Studies* 25 (1991); 135–53.

Clark, Grenville. "Reform in Bankruptcy Administration." *Harvard Law Review* 43 (1930): 1189–1216.

Clayton, Andrew R. L. "Law and Authority in the Northwest Territory." In *The History of Ohio Law*, edited by Michael Les Benedict and John F. Winkler, 13–39. Athens: Ohio University Press, 2004.

Clerk of Bankruptcy Court for the Northern District of Ohio. *Annual Reports of the United States Bankruptcy Court for the Northern District of Ohio.* Cleveland: Court for the Northern District of Ohio, 1989–2008.

Cleveland Bar Journal, 1968–2000.

Cleveland Plain Dealer, 1845–2010.

"Congressional Action." *Journal of the National Association of Referees in Bankruptcy* 10 (1936): 134.

"The Corporate Receiver and Trustee Viewed by Bar and Creditors." *Journal of the National Association of Referees in Bankruptcy* 7 (1933): 88–90.

Countryman, Vern. "A History of American Bankruptcy Law." *Commercial Law Journal* 81 (1976): 226–33.

———. "Scrambling to Define Bankruptcy Jurisdiction: The Chief Justice, the Judicial Conference, and the Legislative Process." *Harvard Journal on Legislation* 22 (1985): 1–45.

Cravath, Paul D. "The Reorganization of Corporations; Bondholders; and Stockholders Protective Committees; Reorganization Committees; and the Voluntary Recapitalization of Corporations. A Lecture Delivered before the Association of the Bar of the City of New York by Paul D. Cravath, March 1, 1916." In *Some Legal Phases of Corporate Financing, Reorganization and Regulation.* New York: Macmillan, 1917.

Diamond, Z. N., and Alfred Letzler. "The New Frazier-Lemke Act: A Study." *Columbia Law Review* 37 (1937): 1092–1135.

Dixon, Timothy W., and David G. Epstein. "Where Did Chapter 13 Come From and Where Should It Go?" *American Bankruptcy Institute Law Review* 10 (2002): 741–63.

Douglas, William O. "Some Functional Aspects of Bankruptcy." *Yale Law Review* 41 (1932): 329–64.

Douglas, William O., and J. Howard Marshall. "A Factual Study of Bankruptcy Administration and Some Suggestions." *Columbia Law Review* 32 (1932): 25–59.

Downes, Randolph C. *Lake Port: Lucas County Historical Series.* Toledo, OH: Toledo Printing Co., 1951.

Dunkel, David S. "Final Regulations Stimulate Use of Section 501(c)(9) Trusts." *Taxes* 99 (April 1981): 226–30.

Easterbrook, Frank H. "Is Corporate Bankruptcy Efficient?" *Journal of Financial Economics* 27 (1990): 411–17.

Edwards, Franklin R., and Edward R. Morrison. "Derivatives and the Bankruptcy Code: Why the Special Treatment?" *Yale Journal on Regulation* 22 (2005): 91–122.

Eisenberg, Theodore, and Lynn M. LoPucki. "Shopping for Judges: An Empirical Analysis of Venue Choice in Large Chapter 11 Reorganizations." *Cornell Law Review* 84 (1999): 967–1003.

Ellis, Diane. "The Effect of Consumer Interest Rate Deregulation on Credit Card Volumes, Charge-Offs, and the Personal Bankruptcy Rate." *Bank Trends* No. 98-5. Division of Insurance, FDIC, March 1998. http://www.fdic.gov/bank/analytical/bank/bt_9805.html.

Farnham, Henry P., ed. *Ohio Jurisprudence.* Rochester, NY: Lawyers' Cooperative Publishing House, 1928–1938.

Fee, Kyle, and Bob Sadowski. "Regional Activity: The Cleveland Metropolitan Statistical Area." *Economic Trends.* Federal Reserve Bank of Cleveland, August 6, 2007. http://www.clevelandfed.org/research/trends/2007/0807/02reg act_080607.cfm.

Ferguson, Glenn W. "To Robe or Not to Robe?—A Judicial Dilemma." *Journal of the American Judicature Society* 39 (1955–1956): 166–171.

Fogarty, Michael S., Gasper S. Garofalo, and David Hammack. "Cleveland from Startup to the Present: Innovation and Entrepreneurship." A report of the Center for Regional Economic Issues, Weatherhead School of Management, Case Western Reserve University, 2003. http://www.generationfoundation.org/pubs/ClevelandFromStartupToPresent.pdf.

Frankfurter, Felix, and James M. Landis. "The Business of the Supreme Court of the United States—Study in the Federal Judicial System." *Harvard Law Review* 40 (1927): 431–68.

Friebolin, Carl. "Section 77B—Sword or Shield." *Journal of the National Association of Referees in Bankruptcy* 10 (1935): 79–87.

Garrison, Lloyd K. "Reorganization of Railroads under the Bankruptcy Act." *University of Chicago Law Review* 1 (1933):71–81.

George, Lloyd D. "From Orphan to Maturity: The Development of the Bankruptcy System During L. Ralph Mecham's Tenure as Director of the Administrative Office of the United States Courts." *American University Law Review* 44 (1995): 1491–1501.

Gerdes, John. "Corporate Reorganization Under Section 77B." *Journal of the National Association of Referees in Bankruptcy* 10 (1936): 75–78.

Goldstein, Mark L. "Lou Gussetti Hammers Together a New Old Company . . . and the Pieces Keep Getting Bigger." *Industry Week,* February 15, 1988, 47–48.

Gordon, Robert W. "Critical Legal Histories." *Stanford Law Review* 36 (1984): 57–125.

Grant, H. Roger. *Erie Lackawanna: Death of An American Railroad, 1938–1992.* Stanford, CA: Stanford University Press, 1994.

Groshen, Erica L., and Laura Robertson. "Are the Great Lakes Cities Becoming Service Centers?" *Economic Commentary.* Federal Reserve Bank of Cleveland, June 1, 1993.

Haberman, Ian S. *The Van Sweringens of Cleveland: The Biography of an Empire.* Cleveland: Western Reserve Historical Society, 1979.

Hance, Jonathan Keath. "Derivatives at Bankruptcy: Lifesaving Knowledge for the Small Firm." *Washington & Lee Law Review* 65 (2008): 711–66.

Hansen, Bradley. "Commercial Associations and the Creation of a National Economy: The Demand for a Federal Bankruptcy Law." *Business History Review* 72 (1998): 86–113.

———. "The People's Welfare and the Origins of Corporate Reorganization: The Wabash Receivership Reconsidered." *Business History Review* 71 (2000): 377–405.

Hawkland, William D. "Federal Restrictions on Garnishments of Earnings: Herein of Title III of the Consumer Credit Protection Act." *Commercial Law Journal* 75 (1970): 213–17, 223.

Henderson, James, ed., *A Treatise on the Bankruptcy Law of the United States by Harold Remington of the Bar of the City of New York,* 5th ed. Rochester, NY: Lawyers Co-operative Publishing, 1950.

Henderson, William. "In the Zone: How Enterprise Zones Have Promoted Urban Sprawl in Northeast Ohio." In *Moving to Cornfields: A Reader on Urban Sprawl and the Regional Future of Northeast Ohio.* Cleveland Heights, OH: Ecocity Cleveland, 1996. http://www.gcbl.org/files/resources/movingtocornfields.pdf.

Herzog, Asa S. "Referee in Bankruptcy: A Judge In Search Of A Name," *Journal of the National Conference of Referees in Bankruptcy* 44 (1970): 39–40.

Heydebrand, Wolf, and Carroll Seron. *Rationalizing Justice: The Political Economy of Federal District Courts.* Albany: State University of New York Press, 1990.

Hickman, W. Braddock. *The Volume of Corporate Bond Financing since 1900.* Princeton, NJ: Princeton University Press, 1953.

———. *Corporate Bond Quality and Investor Experience.* Princeton, NJ: Princeton University Press, 1958.

Hill, Edward W., and Thomas Bier. "Economic Restructuring: Earnings, Occupations, and Housing Values in Cleveland." *Economic Development Quarterly* 3, no. 2 (May 1989): 123–44.

Hiller, Russell L. "A Conference Anniversary—Fifty Years in Retrospect." *American Bankruptcy Law Journal* 51 (1977): 31–61.

Hirsch, Barry T., and David A. Macpherson. *Union Membership and Coverage Database from the CPS,* http://www.unionstats.com.

"History of Euclid." Hudson, OH: Hudson Library and Historical Society.

Howard, Margaret. "Vern Countryman and Barry Zaretsky: A Legacy of Ideas." *American Bankruptcy Law Journal* 75 (2001): 283–305.

Hufbauer, Gary Clyde, and Ben Goodrich. "Steel: Big Problems, Better Solutions." *International Economics Policy Briefs,* No. 01-9. Petersen Institute for International Economics, July 2001. http://www.iie.com/publications/pb/pb.cfm?ResearchID=77.

Hulbert, Archer Butler. "The Methods and Operations of the Scioto Group of Speculators." *Mississippi Valley Historical Review* 1 (1915): 505–15.

———. "The Methods and Operations of the Scioto Group of Speculators, continued." *Mississippi Valley Historical Review* 2 (1915): 56–73.

International Directory of Company Histories. Chicago: St. James Press, 1988–2003.

Jackson, Royal E. "Bankruptcy Administration: Then and Now." *American Bankruptcy Law Journal* 45 (1971): 249–280.

James, Edwin. *The Bankruptcy Law of the United States, 1867, With Notes and a collection of American and English decisions upon the principles and practice of bankruptcy adapted to the use of the lawyer and merchant.* New York: Harper & Brothers, 1867.

Jensen, Susan. "A Legislative History of the Bankruptcy Abuse Prevention and Consumer Protection Act of 2005." *American Bankruptcy Law Journal* 79 (2005): 485–569.

Johnson, Gregg. "Bankrupt Wheeling-Pitt Still Kicking." *The Daily Deal,* March 28, 2003. ProQuest document ID: 318979571.

Jones, Robert F. "William Duer and the Business of Government in the War of the American Revolution." *William and Mary Quarterly, 3rd series.* 32 (July 1975): 393–414.

Journal of the National Association of Referees in Bankruptcy. 1926–1970.

Kaplan, Joel. *Bankruptcy Courts: Judges in Conflict: A Special Report from the Tennessean.* [Nashville] *Tennessean*, August 1, 1983.

Kaplan, Steven N., and Per Strömberg. "Leveraged Buyouts and Private Equity." *Journal of Economic Perspectives* 23 (Winter 2009): 121–46.

Kauffman, David. "Procedures for Estimating Contingent or Unliquidated Claims in Bankruptcy." *Stanford Law Review* 35 (November 1982): 153–74.

Keating, Daniel. "Bankruptcy Code § 1114: Congress' Empty Response to the Retiree Plight." *American Bankruptcy Law Journal* 67 (1993): 17–47.

Kennedy, David S., and R. Spenser Cliff III. "An Historical Analysis of Insolvency Laws and their Impact on the Role, Power, and Jurisdiction of Today's United States Bankruptcy Court and Its Judicial Officers." *Journal of Bankruptcy Law and Practice* 9 (2000): 165–200.

Kennedy, Frank R. "The Bankruptcy Court under the New Bankruptcy Law: Its Structure, Jurisdiction, Venue, and Procedure." *St. Mary's Law Journal* 11(1979): 251–309.

Kennedy, James Harrison. *The Bench and Bar of Cleveland.* Cleveland: Cleveland Printing and Publishing, 1889.

Kettering, Kenneth C. "Article: True Sale of Receivables: A Purposive Analysis." *American Bankruptcy Institute Law Review* 16 (2008): 511–62.

Kilborn, Jason J. "Mercy, Rehabilitation, and Quid Pro Quo: A Radical Reassessment of Individual Bankruptcy." *Ohio State Law Journal* 64 (2003): 855–96.

King, Lawrence P. "The History and Development of the Bankruptcy Rules." *American Bankruptcy Law Journal*, 70 (1996): 217–43.

King, Paul H. "Experimenting With Our Bankruptcy Act: Recent Changes and Prospects for Further Amendment." *Journal of the National Association of Referees in Bankruptcy* 7 (1933): 98–100.

———. "Strengthening Our Bankruptcy Law: A Sequel (or, a serial)." *Journal of the National Association of Referees in Bankruptcy* 7 (1933): 157–58, 161.

———. "The Chandler Amendatory Bill Is Enacted." *Journal of the National Association of Referees in Bankruptcy* 12 (1938): 124–132.

Klee, Kenneth N. *Bankruptcy and the Supreme Court.* Newark, NJ: LexisNexis, 2009.

Klein, Martin I. "The Bankruptcy Reform Act of 1978." *American Bankruptcy Law Journal* 53 (1979): 1–33.

Lamoreaux, Naomi R. *The Great Merger Movement in American Business, 1895–1904.* New York: Cambridge University Press, 1985.

Landry, Robert J., III. "An Empirical Analysis of the Causes of Consumer Bankruptcy: Will Bankruptcy Reform Really Change Anything?" *Rutgers Business Law Journal* 3 (2006): 2–49.

Law, Patrick. "Intellectual Property Licenses and Bankruptcy—Has the IPLBA thawed the "chilling effects" of Lubrizol v. Richmond Metal Finishers?" *Commercial Law Journal* 99 (1994): 261–75.

Lehman, Henry W. "The Federal Municipal Bankruptcy Act." *Journal of Finance* 5 (1950): 241–56.

Levin, Richard, and Alesia Marinelli, "The Creeping Repeal of Chapter 11: The Significant Business Provisions of the Bankruptcy Abuse and Consumer Protection Act of 2005." *American Bankruptcy Law Journal* 79 (2005): 603–44.

Loomis, Carol J., Patricia Neering, and Christopher Tkacyk, "The Sinking of Bethlehem Steel." *Fortune,* April 5, 2004, 174.

LoPucki, Lynn M. "The Demographics of Bankruptcy Practice." *American Bankruptcy Law Journal* 63 (1989): 289–319

———. "The Nature of the Bankruptcy Firm: A Response to Baird and Rasmussen's *The End of Bankruptcy." Stanford Law Review* 56 (2003): 645–71.

LoPucki, Lynn M., and William C. Whitford. "Bargaining over Equity's Share in the Bankruptcy Reorganization of Large, Publicly Held Corporations." *University of Pennsylvania Law Review* 139 (November 1990): 125–96.

Love, Steve, and David Giffels. *Wheels of Fortune: The Story of Rubber in Akron.* Akron, OH: University of Akron Press, 1999.

"LTV to Reassume Funding of Terminated Plans." *Employee Benefit Plan Review,* February 1991, 69–70.

Lundin, Keith M. "Ten Principles of BAPCPA: Not What Was Advertised." *American Bankruptcy Institute Journal* 24, no. 7 (2005): 1.

Lynd, Staughton. "Why We Opposed the Buyout at Weirton Steel." *Labor Research Review* 6 (1985): 41–53.

———. "The Genesis of the Idea of a Community Right to Industrial Property in Youngstown and Pittsburgh, 1977–1987." *Journal of American History* 74 (December 1987): 926–58.

Mann, Bruce H. *Republic of Debtors: Bankruptcy in the Age of American Independence.* Cambridge, MA: Harvard University Press, 2002.

Mezger, Roger. "As the Decade Dawned, Signs of the Financial Crisis to Come Were Plentiful Here." *Cleveland Plain Dealer,* September 28, 2008. http://blog.cleveland.com/business/2008/09/as_decade_dawned_signs_of_cris.html. Accessed June 2011.

Milan, Irene M. "The Bankruptcy Appellate Panel of the U.S. Court of Appeals for the Sixth Circuit." 2009. History of the Sixth Circuit. Library for the U.S. Court of Appeals for the Sixth Circuit.

Miller, Harvey R., and Shai Y. Waisman. "Is Chapter 11 Bankrupt?" *Boston College Law Review* 47 (2005): 129–81.

Mooney, Barbara, and Chris Thompson, "Goldman Sachs Stands to Gain Reins at Edgell." *Crain's Cleveland Business,* January 13, 1992, 1.

Morrison, Edward R., and Jeorg Riegel. "Financial Contracts and the New Bankruptcy Code: Insulating Markets from Bankruptcy Debtors and Ban Bankruptcy Judges." *American Bankruptcy Institute Law Review* 13 (2005): 641–64.

Moss, David A., and Gibbs A. Johnson, "The Rise of Consumer Bankruptcy: Evolution, Revolution, or Both?" *American Bankruptcy Law Journal* 73 (1999): 311–51.

Moving to Cornfields: A Reader on Urban Sprawl and the Regional Future of Northeast Ohio Cleveland Heights, OH: Ecocity Cleveland, 1996.

Mund, Geraldine. "Appointed or Anointed: Judges, Congress, and the Passage of the Bankruptcy Act of 1978: Part Four: The Separate Clerk's Office." *American Bankruptcy Law Journal* 81 (2007): 515–40.

———. "Appointed or Anointed: Judges, Congress, and the Passage of the Bankruptcy Act of 1978. Part One: Outside Looking In." *American Bankruptcy Law Journal* 81 (2007): 1–30.

———. "Appointed or Anointed: Judges, Congress, and the Passage of the Bankruptcy Act of 1978: Part Three: On The Hill." *American Bankruptcy Law Journal* 81 (2007): 341–73.

———. "Appointed or Anointed: Judges, Congress, and the Passage of the Bankruptcy Act of 1978: Part Two: The Third Branch Reacts." *American Bankruptcy Law Journal* 81 (2007): 165–93.

Nadler, Charles Elihu. *The Law of Bankruptcy.* Chicago: Callaghan, 1948.

———. *The Law of Debtor Relief; Bankruptcy and Non-Bankruptcy Devices.* Atlanta, GA: Harrison Co., 1954.

"National Bankruptcy Conference Continues." *Journal of the National Association of Referees in Bankruptcy* 13 (1939): 82.

National Bureau of Economic Research. *U.S. Business Cycle Expansions and Contractions.* http://www.nber.org/cycles.html.

Neff, William B., ed. *The Bench and Bar of Northern Ohio.* Cleveland: Historical Publishing, 1921.

"The New York Bankruptcy Investigation Report." *Journal of the National Association of Referees in Bankruptcy* 4 (1930): 87–90.

New York Times. 1980–2010.

Nichols, Kenneth. *Yesterday's Akron: The First 150 Years.* Miami, FL: E. A. Seeman Publishing, 1975.

North, Douglas. *The Economic Growth of the United States, 1790–1860.* Englewood Cliffs, NJ: Prentice-Hall, 1961.

Pearce, John A., II, and Ilya A. Lipin, "Special Purpose Vehicles in Bankruptcy Litigation, *Hofstra Law Review* 40 (2011):177–233.

"Proceedings of the Chicago Conference (Relative to Uniformity of Practice)." *Journal of the National Association of Referees in Bankruptcy* 3 (1929): 76–97.

"Proceedings of the Fourth Annual Conference of the National Association of Referees in Bankruptcy." *Journal of the National Association of Referees in Bankruptcy* 4 (1930): 39–78.

"Proceedings of the Tenth Annual Conference of the National Association of Referees in Bankruptcy." *Journal of the National Association of Referees in Bankruptcy* 10 (1935): 3–32.

Randall, Ronald. "Growth, Movement, and Decline of Central-city and Suburban Manufacturing Firms." Paper presented at the Annual Conference of the Urban Affairs Association, in Toronto, Canada, April 16–19, 1997. http://uac.utoledo.edu/Publications/1997/growth-movement-decline.pdf. Accessed April 2011.

"Referee William B. Woods Concludes Reorganization Proceedings after 17 Years." *Journal of the National Association of Referees in Bankruptcy* 27 (1953): 114.

Regis, Noel F. *A History of the Bankruptcy Law.* 1919. Reprinted New York: William S. Hein, 2002.

"Relief Without Adjudication—The New Bankruptcy Law." *Georgetown Law Journal* 21 (1933): 483–89.

Remington, Harold. "The Preference Feature of the Ray Amendment." *Bulletin of the Commercial Law League of America* 7 (1903): 10–11.

———. *A Treatise on the Bankruptcy Law of the United States*. Charlottesville, VA: Michie Company, 1908.

Roe, Mark J. "The Derivatives Market's Payment Priorities as Financial Risk Accelerator." *Stanford Law Review* 63 (2011): 539–90.

Rogers, Churchill, and Littleton Groom. "Reorganization of Railroad Corporations under Section 77 of the Bankruptcy Act." *Columbia Law Review* 33 (1933): 571–616.

Rogers, Robert P. *An Economic History of the American Steel Industry.* New York: Routledge, 2009.

Rostow, Eugene V., and Lloyd N. Cutler. "Competing Systems of Corporate Reorganization: Chapters X and XI of the Bankruptcy Act." *Yale Law Journal* 48 (1939): 1334–76.

Rothenberg, Winifred Barr. *From Market-Places to a Market Economy: The Transformation of Rural Massachusetts.* Chicago: University of Chicago Press, 1992.

Rousseau, Peter L. "Jacksonian Monetary Policy, Specie Flows, and the Panic of 1837." *Journal of Economic History,* 62 (2002): 457–88.

Sanders, Frank P. "The Organization and Function of the Commissioner System," *Western Political Quarterly* 21 (1968): 420–35.

Sauer, Richard C. "Bankruptcy Law and the Maturing of American Capitalism." *Ohio State Law Journal* 55 (1994): 291–339.

Scheiber, Harry N. "The Commercial Bank of Lake Erie, 1831–1843." *Business History Review* 40 (1966): 47–65.

Scherrer, Christoph. "Mini-Mills: A New Growth Path for the U.S. Steel Industry?" *Journal of Economic Issues* 22 (December 1988): 1179–1200.

Scheuerman, William. *The Steel Crisis: The Economics and Politics of a Declining Industry.* New York: Praeger, 1986.

Segal Group. "Study of Retiree Health VEBAs." *Survey* (Winter 2008). http://www.sibson.com/uploads/65896ec7d78c973e6a5e5666d448da26.pdf. Accessed September 2011.

Shaiman, Laurence. "The History of Imprisonment for Debt and Insolvency Laws in Pennsylvania as They Evolved from the Common Law." *American Journal of Legal History* 4 (1960): 205–25.

Shalhope, Robert E. "Republicanism and Early American Historiography." *William and Mary Quarterly, 3rd Series* 39 (1982): 334–56.

Shanker, Morris G. "Remembering Carl D. Friebolin (1878–1967)." *Cuyahoga County Law & Fact,* May/June 1993.

Shannon, Timothy J. "The Ohio Company and the Meaning of Opportunity in the American West, 1786–1795." *New England Quarterly* 64 (1991): 393–413.

Sheridan, John H. "Counting on Cash." *Industry Week*. September 2, 1996, 10.

Simkovich, Michael. "Secret Liens and the Financial Crisis of 2008." *American Bankruptcy Law Journal* 83 (2009): 253–95.

Skeel, David A. "Bankruptcy Boundary Games" *Brooklyn Journal of Corporate Finance & Commercial Law* 4 (2009): 1–21
———. *Debt's Dominion: A History of Bankruptcy Law in America*. Princeton, NJ: Princeton University Press, 2001.
Skowronek, Stephen. *Building a New American State: The Expansion of National Administrative Capacities, 1877–1920*. New York: Cambridge University Press, 1982.
Smith, Edward H. "Profit in Loss." *Saturday Evening Post,* February 5, 1921, 14.
Smith, Joseph Patterson, ed. *History of the Republican Party in Ohio,* vol. 2. Chicago: Lewis Publishing, 1898.
Smith, Roy C. "After the Ball." *Wilson Quarterly* 16 (Autumn 1992): 31–43.
Sontag, Sherry R. "Amid Bust, a Boom." *National Law Journal,* April 2, 1990, 1.
———. "Revco's Collapse a Symbol: After Two Years, the Bankruptcy is Stalled." *National Law Journal,* September 3, 1990, 1.
Stanley, David T., and Marjorie Girth. *Bankruptcy: Problem, Process, Reform*. Washington, DC: Brookings Institution, 1971.
Stark, Robert. "Viewing the LTV Steel ABS Opinion in its Proper Context." *Journal of Corporation Law* 27 (Winter 2002): 211–29.
Steeples, Douglas, and David O. Whitten. *Democracy in Desperation: The Depression of 1893*. Westport, CT: Greenwood Press, 1998.
Stricharchuk, Greg. "The Back-Room Brotherhood." *Cleveland*, May 1962, 62.
Sullivan, Teresa A., Ellizabeth Warren, and Jay Lawrence Westbrook. "The Persistence of Local Legal Culture: Twenty Years of Evidence From the Federal Bankruptcy Courts." *Harvard Journal of Law and Public Policy* 17 (1994): 801–65.
Surrency, Erwin C. *History of the Federal Courts*. 2nd ed. Dobbs Ferry, NY: Oceana Publications, 2002.
Swaine, Robert T. "A Decade of Rail Reorganization under Section 77 of the Federal Bankruptcy Act." *Harvard Law Review* 56 (1943): 1037–1058.
Tabb, Charles Jordan . "A Century of Regress or Progress? A Political History of Bankruptcy Legislation in 1898 and 1998." *Bankruptcy Developments Journal* 15 (1999): 343–81
———. "The Historical Evolution of the Bankruptcy Discharge." *American Bankruptcy Law Journal* 65 (1991): 325–71.
———. "The History of the Bankruptcy Laws in the United States." *American Bankruptcy Institute Law Review* 3 (1995): 5–51.
———. "The Top Twenty Issues in the History of Consumer Bankruptcy," *University of Illinois Law Review* 2007 (2007): 9–29.
Thompson, Elizabeth. *The Reconstruction of Southern Debtors: Bankruptcy after the Civil War.* Athens: University of Georgia Press, 2004.
"Time in a Bottle: A History of Owens-Illinois, Inc." University of Toledo Libraries, Canaday Center Digital Exhibit, December 2007. http://www.utoledo.edu/library/canaday/exhibit.html. Accessed April, 2011.
Todd, Walker F. "Aggressive Uses of Chapter 11 of the Federal Bankruptcy Code." *Economic Trends.* Federal Reserve Bank of Cleveland, July 1986, 20–26. http://www.clevelandfed.org/research/review/1986/86-q3-todd.pdf.

United States Courts for the Second Circuit, Committee on History and Commemorative Events. *The Development of Bankruptcy and Reorganization Law in the Courts of the Second Circuit of the United States.* New York: Mathew Bender, 1995.

Warf, Barney, and Brian Holly. "The Rise and Fall and Rise of Cleveland." *Annals of the American Academy of Political and Social Science* 551 (1997): 208–21.

Warren, Charles. *Bankruptcy in United States History.* Buffalo: William S. Hein & Co., Inc., 1994; Cambridge: Harvard University Press, 1935.

Warren, Elizabeth. "Bankruptcy Policymaking in an Imperfect World." *Michigan Law Review* 92 (1993): 336–87.

———."The Changing Politics of American Bankruptcy Reform." *Osgoode Hall Law Journal* 37 (1999): 189–204.

———. "The Untenable Case for Repeal of Chapter 11." *Yale Law Journal* 102 (1992): 437–79.

Warren, Elizabeth, and Jay Lawrence Westbrook. "The Success of Chapter 11: A Challenge to the Critics." *Michigan Law Review* 107 (2009): 603–41.

Warren, Kenneth. *Big Steel: The First Century of the United States Steel Corporation, 1901–2001.* Pittsburgh: University of Pittsburgh Press, 2001.

Wedoff, Eugene R. "Major Consumer Bankruptcy Effects of BAPCPA." *University of Illinois Law Review* 2007 (2007): 31–65

Whalen, Edward P. "A Scandal in Ethics." *Cleveland,* June 1983, 70.

Wiebe, Robert H. *The Search for Order, 1877–1920.* New York: Hill & Wang, 1967.

Wilde, Carl. "The Chandler Act." *Indiana Law Journal,* 14 (1938):93–148.

Wruck, Karen. "What Really Went Wrong at Revco?" *Journal of Applied Corporate Finance* 4 (Summer 1991): 79–92.

Public Documents

An Act: For Regulating Processes in the Courts of the United States, and Providing Compensations for the Officers of the said Courts, and for Jurors and Witnesses (1792). *Statutes at Large of the United Stated of America,* vol.1 (Boston: Charles C. Little and James Brown, 1845): 275–79.

An Act: An addition to the Act Entitled "An Act to Establish the Judicial Courts of the United States" (1793). *Statutes at Large of the United States of America,* vol.1 (Boston: Charles C. Little and James Brown, 1845): 333–35.

An Act: To Amend an Act Entitled "An Act to Establish a Uniform System of Bankruptcy throughout the United States," Stat. 36 (1910): 838–42.

An Act: To Amend an Act Entitled "An Act to Establish a Uniform System of Bankruptcy throughout the United States," Approved July 1, 1898, and Acts Amendatory Thereof and Supplementary Thereto. Stat. 47 (1933): 1467–82.

An Act: To amend an Act entitled "An Act to Establish a Uniform System of Bankruptcy throughout the United States," Approved July 1, 1898, and Acts Amendatory Thereof and Supplementary Thereto. Stat. 48 (1934): 798–803.

An Act: To Amend an Act Entitled "An Act to Establish a Uniform System of Bankruptcy throughout the United States," Approved July 1, 1898, and Acts Amendatory Thereof and Supplementary Thereto. Stat. 48 (1934): 911–25.

An Act: To Amend an Act Entitled "An Act to Establish a Uniform system of Bankruptcy throughout the United States," Approved July 1, 1898, and Acts Amendatory Thereof and Supplementary Thereto. Stat. 48 (1934): 1289–91.

An Act: To Amend an Act Entitled "An Act to Establish a Uniform System of Bankruptcy throughout the United States," Approved July 1, 1898, and Acts Amendatory Thereof and Supplementary Thereto. Stat. 49 (1935): 911–26.

An Act to Amend an Act Entitled "An Act to Establish a Uniform System of Bankruptcy throughout the United States," approved July 1, 1898, and Acts Amendatory Thereof and Supplementary Thereto. Stat. 49 (1935): 942–45.

An Act: To amend an Act Entitled "An Act to Establish a Uniform System of Bankruptcy throughout the United States," Approved July 1, 1898, and Acts Amendatory Thereof and Supplementary Thereto. Stat. 50 (1937): 653–58.

An Act: To Amend an Act Entitled "An Act to Establish a Uniform System of Bankruptcy throughout the United States," Approved July 1, 1898, and Acts Amendatory Thereof and Supplementary Thereto. Stat. 52 (1938): 840–940.

An Act: To Amend an Act Entitled "An Act to Establish a Uniform System of Bankruptcy throughout the United States," Approved July 1, 1898, and Acts Amendatory Thereof and Supplementary Thereto. Stat. 53 (1939): 1134–41.

An Act: To Amend an Act Entitled "An Act to Establish a Uniform System of Bankruptcy throughout the United States," Approved July 1, 1898, and Acts amendatory Thereof and Supplementary Thereto. Stat. 60 (1946): 323–32.

An Act: To Amend and Supplement an Act Entitled "An Act to Establish a Uniform System of Bankruptcy throughout the United States," Approved March Second, Eighteen Hundred and Sixty-seven, and for Other Purposes. Stat. 18 (1874): 178–86.

An Act: To Amend the Bankruptcy Act in Regard to the Closing Fee of the Trustee and in Regard to the Fee for the Filing of a Petition. Stat. 74 (1960): 198.

An Act: To Amend the Bankruptcy Act to Provide for Uniform Supervision and Control of Employees of Referees in Bankruptcy. Stat. 92 (1978): 729.

An Act: To Amend the Judicial System of the United States (1869). *Statutes at Large of the United States of America*, vol. 16 (Boston: Little, Brown, 1871): 44–45.

An Act: To Amend Title 28 of the United States Code Regarding Jurisdiction of Bankruptcy Proceedings, to Establish New Federal Judicial Positions, to Amend Title 11 of the United States Code, and for Other Purposes. Stat. 98 (1984): 333–992.

An Act to Change the Times of Holding the Circuit and District Courts of the United States in the Several Districts in the Seventh Circuit (1863). *Statutes at Large of the United States of America*, vol. 12 (Boston: Little, Brown, 1863): 657.

An Act: To codify, Revise, and Amend the Laws Relating to the Judiciary. Stat. 36 (1911): 1087–1169.

An Act: To Establish a Uniform Law on the Subject of Bankruptcies. Stat. 92 (1978): 2549–688.

An Act: To Establish a Uniform System of Bankruptcy throughout the United *States* (1800), *Statutes at Large of the United States of America*, vol. 2 (Boston: Charles C. Little & James Brown, 1845), 19–36.

An Act: To Establish a Uniform System of Bankruptcy throughout the United States (1841). *Statutes at Large of the United States of America*, vol. 5 (Boston: Charles C. Little and James Brown, 1846), 440–49.

An Act: To Establish a Uniform System of bankruptcy throughout the United States (1867). *Statutes at Large of the United States of America*, vol. 14 (Boston: Little, Brown, 1868), 517–41.

An Act: To Establish a Uniform System of Bankruptcy throughout the United States. Stat. 30 (1898): 544–66.

An Act: To Establish Courts of Appeals and to Define and Regulate in Certain Cases the Jurisdiction of the Courts of the United States and for Other Purposes. Stat. 26 (1891): 826–30.

An Act: To Further the Administration of Justice (1872). *Statutes at Large of the United States of America*, vol. 17 (Boston: Little, Brown, 1873): 196–99.

An Act: To Give the Supreme Court of the United States Authority to Make and Publish Rules in Actions at Law. Stat. 48 (1934): 1064.

An Act: To Provide for the Administration of the United States Courts, and for Other Purposes. Stat. 53 (1939): 1223–26.

An Act: To Regulate Processes in the Courts of the United States (1789). *Statutes at Large of the United Stated of America*, vol.1 (Boston: Charles C. Little and James Brown, 1845): 93–94.

An Act: To Revise, Codify, and Enact into Law Title 28 of the United States Code Entitled "Judicial Code and Judiciary." Stat. 62 (1948): 869–1009.

Bankruptcy Abuse Prevention and Consumer Protection Act. Stat. 119 (2005): 23–217.

Bankruptcy Judges, Bankruptcy Trustees, and Family Farmer Bankruptcy Act of 1986. Stat. 100 (1986): 3088–128.

Bankruptcy Reform Act of 1994. Stat. 108 (1994): 4106–4151.

Bureau of the Census. *Historical Statistics of the United States, Colonial Times to 1970*. Washington DC: Government Printing Office, 1976.

Consumer Credit Protection Act. Stat. 82 (1968): 146–67.

Donovan, William J. Administration of Bankrupt Estates: Report Submitted by Counsel to the Petitioners in the Matter of an Inquiry into the Administration of Bankruptcy Estates conducted before the Hon. Thomas D. Thacher, Judge of the United States District Court of the Southern District of New York, House Judiciary Committee, 71st Cong., 3rd Sess., Committee Print. Washington, DC: Government Printing Office, 1931.

Employee Retirement Income Security Act of 1974. Stat. 88 (1974): 829–1035.

Federal Magistrates Act of 1968. Stat. 82 (1968): 1107–19.

Federal, State, County, Township and Municipal Officers. Columbus, OH: Fred J. Heer, State Printer, 1899, 1904, 1907–1908, 1910.

National Bankruptcy Review Commission. *Bankruptcy: The Next Twenty Years, National Bankruptcy Review Commission Final Report*. Washington, DC: Bankruptcy Commission, 1997.

Ohio Revised Code Annotated. Cleveland, OH: Banks-Baldwin Publishing, West Publishing, 1994- .

Ohio Secretary of State. *Official Roster, Federal, State, County Officers and Departmental Information*. Columbus, OH: Secretary of State, 1911, 1914–23, 1925, 1935, 1939–46, 1949-54.

Page's Ohio Revised Code Annotated. Charlottesville, VA: Mathew Bender, 2006.
Postal Revenue and Federal Salary Act of 1967. Stat. 81 (1967): 613–48.
President's Working Group on Financial Markets. *Hedge Funds, Leverage, and the Lessons of Long-Term Capital Finance*. 1999. http://www.treasury.gov/resource-center/fin-mkts/Documents/hedgfund.pdf.
Retiree Benefits Bankruptcy Protection Act of 1988. Stat. 102 (1988): 610–15.
Sixth Circuit Judicial Council. *Procedures for the Selection of Bankruptcy Judges and Procedures for the Reappointment of Bankruptcy Judges*. June 26, 2005, as corrected February 4, 2011. http://www.ca6.uscourts.gov/internet/circuit_executive/documents/bkproce.pdf.
US Attorney General William D. Mitchell. *Report to the President on the Bankruptcy Act and its Administration in the Courts of the United States Dated December 5, 1931*. Washington, DC: Government Printing Office, 1931.
US Attorney General's Committee on Bankruptcy Administration. *Administration of the Bankruptcy Act: Report of the Attorney General's Committee on Bankruptcy Administration*. Washington, DC: Government Printing Office, 1941.
US Congress. *Annals of Congress of the United States: Abridgment of the Debates of Congress from 1789 to 1856*, New York: D. Appleton, 1857.
US Congress. *Congressional Globe: containing sketches of the debates and proceedings of the Congress*. Washington, DC: Blair & Rives, 1834–73.
US Congress. *Congressional Record: proceedings and debates of the Congress*. Washington, DC, Government Printing Office, 1873–1913.
US Constitution.
US Department of Commerce. *Causes of Business Failure and Bankruptcies of Individuals in New Jersey: A Study Made in Cooperation with the Institute of Human Relations and the Law School of Yale University: Domestic Commerce Series—No. 54*. Washington, DC: Government Printing Office, 1931.
US Department of Commerce, Victor Sadd and Robert T. Williams. *Causes of Bankruptcies Among Consumers: A Study Made in Boston with the Cooperation of the Institute of Human Relations and the Law School of Yale University: Domestic Commerce Series—No. 82*. Washington, DC: Government Printing Office, 1933.
US Department of Justice. *Annual Reports of the Attorney General of the United States*. Washington, DC: Government Printing Office, 1871–1880; 1899–1939.
US House. *The Bankruptcy Reform Act of 1994*. 103rd Cong., 2d sess., 1994. H.R. Rep. 103-835.
US House. Letter from the Secretary of State Transmitting Statements showing proceedings under the Bankrupt Act, February 23, 1847. 29th Cong,, 2d sess., 1947. House Doc. No. 99.
US House. Report to Accompany H.R. 20575. 61st Cong., 2d sess. February 22, 1910. H. Report 511.
US Senate Judiciary Committee, Strengthening of Procedure in the Judicial System: Message from the President of the United States Recommending the Strengthening of Procedure in the Judicial System Together with the Report of the Attorney General on Bankruptcy Law and Practice, 72d Cong., 1st sess., Sen. Doc. 65. Washington, DC: Government Printing Office. 1932.

US Supreme Court. *General Orders and Forms in Bankruptcy: Adopted and Established by the Supreme Court of the United States, November 28, 1898.* Washington, DC: Government Printing Office, 1898.

US Supreme Court. General Orders and Forms in Bankruptcy Amended and Established by the Supreme Court of the United States, January 16, 1939, 305 US 681 (1939).

US Supreme Court. General Orders in Bankruptcy Promulgated April 13, 1925, 267 US 613 (1925).

Index